UNHOMELY STATES
THEORIZING ENGLISH-CANADIAN POSTCOLONIALISM

Unhomely States
Theorizing English-Canadian Postcolonialism

edited by
Cynthia Sugars

broadview press

National Library of Canada Cataloguing in Publication

Unhomely states : theorizing English-Canadian postcolonialism / edited by Cynthia Sugars.

Includes bibliographical references.
ISBN 1-55111-437-2

1. Postcolonialism in literature. 2. Postcolonialism—Canada. 3. Canadian literature (English)—20th century—History and criticism. I. Sugars, Cynthia Conchita, 1963–   .

PS8101.P68U55 2004   C810.9′358   C2003-906289-9

Broadview Press Ltd. is an independent, international publishing house, incorporated in 1985. Broadview believes in shared ownership, both with its employees and with the general public; since the year 2000 Broadview shares have traded publicly on the Toronto Venture Exchange under the symbol BDP.

We welcome comments and suggestions regarding any aspect of our publications – please feel free to contact us at the addresses below or at broadview@broadviewpress.com.

North America
Post Office Box 1243, Peterborough, Ontario, Canada K9J 7H5
3576 California Road, Orchard Park, NY, USA 14127
Tel: (705) 743-8990; Fax: (705) 743-8353;
e-mail: customerservice@broadviewpress.com

UK, Ireland, and continental Europe
NBN Plymbridge, Eastover Road, Plymouth PL6 7PY UK
Tel: 44 (0) 1752 202301   Fax: 44 (0) 1752 202331
Fax Order Line: 44 (0) 1752 202333
Customer Service: cserv@plymbridge.com Orders: orders@nbnplymbridge.com

Australia and New Zealand
UNIREPS, University of New South Wales
Sydney, NSW, 2052
Tel: 61 2 9664 0999; Fax: 61 2 9664 5420
email: info.press@unsw.edu.au

www.broadviewpress.com

Advisory editor for this volume: Michel W. Pharand

Broadview Press Ltd. gratefully acknowledges the financial support of the Government of Canada through the Book Publishing Industry Development Program for our publishing activities.

Typesetting and assembly: True to Type Inc., Mississauga, Canada.

PRINTED IN CANADA

Contents

Part VIII: Postcolonial Pedagogies

ACKNOWLEDGEMENTS

I would like to acknowledge the Faculty of Arts of the University of Ottawa for a Research and Publications grant to aid in the preparation of this manuscript. I am also indebted to the fine and detailed work of my research assistant, Amanda Mullen, who worked on the manuscript in its early stages, as well as to Josephene Grabetz and Lia Marie Talia. Thanks are also due to Neil Besner, Diana Brydon, Paul Keen, and Stephen Slemon for their input and suggestions at various stages along the way. Most importantly, I am grateful to the authors and copyright holders of the books and essays; they are acknowledged below:

Grant, George. *Lament for a Nation: The Defeat of Canadian Nationalism.*
Toronto: McClelland, 1965; rpt. Montreal: McGill-Queen's UP, 1997.
Reprinted by permission of McGill-Queen's University Press.

Frye, Northrop. "Conclusion to a *Literary History of Canada*" from *The Bush Garden: Essays on the Canadian Imagination* by Northrop Frye. © copyright 1971. Reprinted with permission of House of Anansi Press.

Atwood, Margaret. *Survival: A Thematic Guide to Canadian Literature.* Used by permission, McClelland & Stewart Ltd. *The Canadian Publishers.*

Robertson, R.T. "Another Preface to an Uncollected Anthology: Canadian Criticism in a Commonwealth Context." *ARIEL* 4.3 (1973): 70-81.
Reprinted by permission of *ARIEL* and the Board of Governors, University of Calgary, Calgary, Alberta.

Moss, John. Editorial. *Journal of Canadian Fiction* 3.4 (1975): 1-2. Reprinted by permission of the author.

Lee, Dennis. "Cadence, Country, Silence: Writing in Colonial Space." *Open Letter* 2.6 (1973): 34-53; *Boundary 2* 3.1 (1974): 151-68. © copyright *Boundary 2.* Used with permission of the publisher and the author.

Kroetsch, Robert. "Disunity as Unity: A Canadian Strategy." *The Lovely Treachery of Words: Essays Selected and New.* Toronto: Oxford UP, 1989. 21-33. © copyright 1989 Robert Kroetsch. Reprinted with permission of the author.

Hutcheon, Linda. "'Circling the Downspout of Empire': Post-Colonialism and Postmodernism." *ARIEL* 20.4 (1989): 149-75. Reprinted by permission of *ARIEL* and the Board of Governors, University of Calgary, Calgary, Alberta.

Brydon, Diana. "The White Inuit Speaks: Contamination as Literary Strategy." *Past the Last Post.* Ed. Ian Adam and Helen Tiffin. Calgary: U of Calgary P, 1990. 191-203. Reprinted by permission of the University of Calgary Press.

Bennett, Donna. "English Canada's Postcolonial Complexities." *Essays on Canadian Writing* 51/52 (1993/94): 164-210. Reprinted with the kind permission of *Essays on Canadian Writing*.

Slemon, Stephen. "Unsettling the Empire: Resistance Theory for the Second World." *World Literature Written in English* 30.2 (1990): 30-41. Reprinted by permission of the author.

Lawson, Alan. "Postcolonial Theory and the 'Settler' Subject." *Essays on Canadian Writing* 56 (1995): 20-36. Reprinted with the kind permission of *Essays on Canadian Writing*.

Brydon, Diana. "Introduction: Reading Postcoloniality, Reading Canada." *Essays on Canadian Writing* 56 (1995): 1-19. Reprinted with the kind permission of *Essays on Canadian Writing*.

King, Thomas. "Godzilla vs. Post-Colonial." *World Literature Written in English* 30.2 (1990): 10-16. Reprinted by permission of the author.

Goldie, Terry. "Semiotic Control: Native Peoples in Canadian Literatures in English." *Studies on Canadian Literature: Introductory and Critical Essays*. New York: MLA, 1990. 110-23. Reprinted by permission of the Modern Language Association of America.

Maracle, Lee. "The 'Post-Colonial' Imagination." *Fuse Magazine* 16.1 (1992): 12-15. Reprinted by permission of the author.

Battiste, Marie. "Introduction: Unfolding the Lessons of Colonization." Reprinted with the permission of the publisher from *Reclaiming Indigenous Voice and Vision* edited by Marie Battiste. © copyright The University of British Columbia Press 2000. All rights reserved by the Publisher.

Boire, Gary. "Canadian (Tw)ink: Surviving the White-Outs." *Essays on Canadian Writing* 35 (1987): 1-16. Reprinted with the kind permission of *Essays on Canadian Writing*.

Padolsky, Enoch. "'Olga in Wonderland': Canadian Ethnic Minority Writing and Post-Colonial Theory." *Canadian Ethnic Studies* 28.3 (1996): 16-28. Reprinted by permission of *CES*.

Mukherjee, Arun. "How Shall We Read South Asian Canadian Texts?" Reprinted from *Postcolonialism: My Living* by Arun Mukherjee with permission from TSAR Publications.

Fee, Margery. "What Use is Ethnicity to Aboriginal Peoples in Canada?" *Canadian Review of Comparative Literature* 22.3-4 (1995): 683-91. Reprinted by permission of *CRCL*.

Walcott, Rinaldo. "'A Tough Geography': Towards a Poetics of Black Space(s) in Canada." *Black Like Who?: Writing Black Canada*. Toronto: Insomniac Press, 1997. 35-51. Reprinted by permission of the author and Insomniac Press.

Bannerji, Himani. "Geography Lessons: On Being an Insider/Outsider to the Canadian Nation." © copyright 1997 from *Dangerous Territories: Struggles for Difference and Equality in Education* by Leslie G. Roman and Linda

Eyre, eds. Reproduced by permission of Routledge, Inc., part of The Taylor & Francis Group.

Miki, Roy. "Sliding the Scale of Elision: 'Race' Constructs/Cultural Praxis." *Broken Entries: Race, Subjectivity, Writing*. Toronto: Mercury Press, 1998. 125-59. Reprinted by permission of The Mercury Press and the author.

Razack, Sherene. "To Essentialize or Not To Essentialize: Is This the Question?" *Looking White People in the Eye: Gender, Race, and Culture in Courtrooms and Classrooms*. Toronto: U of Toronto P, 1998. 157-70. Reprinted by permission of the University of Toronto Press.

Cavell, Richard. "Transvestic Sites: Postcolonialism, Pedagogy, and Politics." © copyright 1997 from *Dangerous Territories: Struggles for Difference and Equality in Education* by Leslie G. Roman and Linda Eyre, eds. Reproduced by permission of Routledge, Inc., part of The Taylor & Francis Group.

Kamboureli, Smaro. "Critical Correspondences: The Diasporic Critic's (Self-) Location." From *Scandalous Bodies: Diasporic Literature in English Canada* by Smaro Kamboureli. © copyright Oxford University Press 2000. Reprinted by permission of Oxford University Press Canada.

Findlay, Len. "Always Indigenize!: The Radical Humanities in the Postcolonial Canadian University." *ARIEL* 31.1-2 (2000): 307-26. Reprinted by permission of *ARIEL* and the Board of Governors, University of Calgary, Calgary, Alberta.

INTRODUCTION: UNHOMELY STATES

> For if you are Canadian, home is a place that is not home to you. . . .
> Dennis Lee, "Cadence, Country, Silence" (54)*

Written in 1973, Dennis Lee's diagnosis of a Canadian dis-ease is perhaps as applicable now as it was then. The difference in the ways this dis-ease is articulated today, however, is in its multiple locations *intra*-nationally. No longer understood as a singular conceptualization of *the* Canadian psyche (as, for example, in Margaret Atwood's assessment of the colonial mentality in *Survival* or of a constitutive Canadian "paranoid-schizophrenia" in *The Journals of Susanna Moodie*), one might instead say that this dis-ease within the real and/or textual space of the Canadian nation-state can take numerous forms. If "there is more than one Canadian post-colonial voice" (97), as Diana Brydon states in "The White Inuit Speaks," there are more ways than one of experiencing the unhomeliness of the Canadian locale: from early anti-colonial, yet nevertheless anglo-white, statements of the inherent paradox of Canadian cultural and social space, to settler-invader figurations of the settler's ambivalent location in the New World, to aboriginal accounts of the dis-ease/disease that was forced upon indigenous peoples as a result of European colonization, to diasporic accounts of various kinds of "in-betweenness," to immigrant experiences of disjunction and alienation, to articulations of the racist elements of the Canadian state and national imaginary.

This collection of essays attempts to show these various conceptualizations of "Canadian" postcolonial experience, and the impossibility, therefore, of settling on any one definition of postcolonialism in a Canadian context. Does "postcolonial" mean that we have securely superceded the legacy of various processes of colonization? No. Is "postcolonialism" a methodological approach one takes to a text or is it a matter of content? It can be both (see Slemon and Cavell in this volume). The essays in this collection assume, at the very least, that it involves the former. Does the postcolonial refer to particular segments of the world to the exclusion of others, and if so, what place does Canada have in this global mapping of the postcolonial? This last is a question that has been hotly debated by postcolonial theorists inside Canada and beyond.

---

*Throughout this volume, page references to the selections collected here are keyed to those articles in this volume. For reasons of space, some selections had to be abridged; these include the selections by Grant, Frye, Atwood, Kroetsch, Bennett, Bannerji, Miki, Razack, and Kamboureli. All editorial deletions or additions are noted in square brackets.

A collection of this kind clearly assumes that postcolonialism is a useful and valid approach when applied in a Canadian context. What is not as easily assumed, however, is what precisely it is that makes the Canadian locale postcolonial. Is Canada postcolonial in different ways, depending on the perspective of the writer/critic? Commonwealth critics of the 1970s saw Canadian postcolonialism to reside in the similarity of its cultural expression with other previously colonized segments of the British empire. Canadian cultural nationalists regarded the anti-colonial current of Canadian expression, voiced contra Britain or the United States, as indicative of a "post" colonial experience, or at least as a move in that direction. Theorists of Canadian settler-invader identity have looked at the compromised position of the settler-invader's articulation of belonging in Canada. Aboriginal critics have either rejected the First-World and nationalist origins of postcolonial theory, or they have strategically turned to postcolonial theory as a way of expressing the continued legacy of colonialism for Native peoples in Canada. Other critics have assessed the ways the national metanarrative excludes various racial and/or ethnic groups from the Canadian imaginary. If Benedict Anderson is right in defining the nation as an "imagined community," Himani Bannerji is also correct in asking, "*whose* imagination is advanced as the national imaginary" (290).

One thing that Canadian postcolonial theory does address, as Brydon puts it in "Reading Postcoloniality, Reading Canada," is "how Canadians see themselves and their world" (165). However, the necessary plurality of this experience makes the task of choosing a representative selection of essays on Canadian postcolonialism a daunting one. The heterogeneity of the field of postcolonial studies is part of the problem, for it extends into various related realms which are also complex fields in themselves, fields such as race theory, ethnic studies, and aboriginal studies. Different notions of history and of public and private memory form part of this context, along with an enduring interest in the complex and often controversial relations between empire, nation, and culture. The energy of these debates makes this an important classroom subject, yet paradoxically, the sheer richness of the field also makes it difficult to teach when course titles, reading lists, and assessment procedures seem to demand a contained field for study. This anthology grows out of my own experience preparing a course reader for a graduate course in Canadian postcolonial theory at the University of Ottawa in 2001. While I wanted to give students a sense of the background of the field (and hence include some items written before what we might consider the "boom" in academic postcolonial debates in the 1980s), I also wanted to provide a sense of some of the central arguments that continue to mark the field of postcolonialism in Canada.

Processes of selection and omission put the editor of such a volume in a necessarily compromised position—sitting in judgement on the scene of

Canadian postcolonial expression. Inevitably, pragmatic concerns made it impossible to include everything that I would like to have included here. I have therefore consigned many important readings to a brief mention in this introduction (which are then referenced in the works cited, to be used as suggestions for further reading). Let me begin by outlining the selection criteria for this anthology—including some mention of those essays which, regrettably, I had to leave out—criteria that set this work apart from related collections of Canadian cultural theory.

First, essays were chosen according to whether they undertook a postcolonial approach to broad issues of Canadian culture and society, as opposed to a sustained postcolonial analysis of particular literary texts. I wanted to make this anthology of use for pedagogical purposes in a Canadian literature and/or postcolonial classroom. Hence, I tried to avoid limiting the use-value of the volume by collecting a series of essays focussed on specific texts. Instead, these essays can be used as a companion to a course in Canadian literature, with particular essays to be paired with a variable selection of literary texts, or they can provide the core content of a course specifically focussed on Canadian postcolonialism. Of course, many of these writers do turn to particular texts as a means of elucidating their approach, but generally all of these authors are attempting a more wide-ranging articulation of a Canadian postcolonial politics/poetics or a critique, using postcolonial theory, of delimiting and hierarchizing narratives of national and/or subaltern identities.

Second, I have chosen essays that focus on Canada, rather than those offering a general theorization of global postcolonial issues. Regrettably, this meant excluding such important essays as Arun Mukherjee's controversial and oft-cited "Whose Post-Colonialism and Whose Postmodernism?" (1990), Sneja Gunew's "Postcolonialism and Multiculturalism: Between Race and Ethnicity" (1997), and Alan Lawson's provocative study, "Proximities: From Asymptote to Zeugma" (2000). My selection from Terry Goldie was also influenced by the Canadian focus of this collection: I have included his essay that focusses on the representation of Native peoples in *Canadian* literature, rather than his more usually cited introduction to *Fear and Temptation* (1989) which explores these representations in Canadian, Australian, and New Zealand literatures. More specifically, the focus of this volume, as its subtitle indicates, is English-Canadian postcolonialism. This term is meant to denote works written in English, and not those written by authors of Anglo-Celtic descent. With a few exceptions (see Desroches; Vautier; Söderlind, *Margin/Alias*), comparable debates taking place in or about French Canada do not use postcolonial discourse in the same way, and because many of the articles gathered here make overt reference to one another, I decided to limit the scope to these debates as they have taken place in an English-language context.

Third, I wanted this collection to provide a sense of the history of postcolonial theorizing in Canada as well as a sense of the current directions this critical discourse has taken. Thus, I have tried to include some of the foundational essays of Canadian postcolonialism (even though they may not expressly use this term to describe their approach), beginning in 1965 with George Grant's *Lament for a Nation*, a text that persists as one of Canada's most memorable and prescient expressions of self-interpretation, even if Grant failed to foresee how his lament would in fact spark a renewed body of *post*-colonial discourse amongst Canadian cultural nationalists (see, for example, Lee's account of the epiphanic impact Grant had on him). Nevertheless, as Bennett states, "one could read an inchoate postcolonialism out of the whole history of the Canadian literary and cultural dialogue" (112). I could, therefore, have begun much before this, even into the nineteenth century, and included early anti-colonial pieces by Charles G.D. Roberts and Edward Hartley Dewart, and later essays by E.K. Brown, Earle Birney, and others. Two important articles, neither of which could be included here, have attempted to position some of these earlier writings within the context of contemporary postcolonial theory in Canada: Heather Murray's follow-up to Dennis Lee, "Reading for Contradiction in the Literature of Colonial Space" (1989), in which she analyzes the long-standing role of contradiction in Canadian cultural expression; and my "Can the Canadian Speak?: Lost in Postcolonial Space" (2001), which provides a discussion of the theoretical ramifications of the native vs. cosmopolitan debate in accounts of Canadian (post)coloniality.

However, for pragmatic reasons, I decided to begin more recently, with the period of avid cultural-nationalist revival in the late 1960s and after. Thus, I have included early pieces by Grant, Northrop Frye, Margaret Atwood, R.T. Robertson, John Moss, Dennis Lee, and Robert Kroetsch. While Frye's presence here may seem anomalous, much early anti-colonial cultural expression in Canada was in a sense a response to the kind of intellectualized colonialism articulated by Frye. In effect, Frye's account of the "strangled articulateness" (Conclusion 12) that characterizes Canadian expression is given a somewhat different twist by Atwood, Lee, and Kroetsch, who attempt to turn this predicament into a source of empowerment. In fact, a "strangled articulateness"—what Kroetsch describes as a suspicion of inherited and/or imposed "metanarratives"—may be what defines the discourse of many postcolonial cultures.

Even in this selection, I have had to exclude many important pieces: Atwood's interesting personal account of her coming into her "Canadianness" in "Nationalism, Limbo and the Canadian Club" (1971); Kroetsch's "Unhiding the Hidden" (1974) and Robin Mathews's "Literature and Colonialism" (1978), both of which overlap in many ways with Lee's account of a strategic Canadian "silence"; Malcolm Ross's informative "Canadian Culture and the Colonial Question" (1986), which provides a valuable consideration of Canadian cultural relations with Britain and the United States over the course of the twentieth century; and William H. New's "New Language, New World" (1978)—amongst numerous other important works by New, such as *Among Worlds* and *Dreams of Speech and Violence*—which is a seminal account of the importance of the strategic modification of English in various Commonwealth contexts.

One interesting point to note here is that while Donna Bennett proposes that Brydon was, in 1982, the first Canadian critic to use the term "postcolonial" (128), this contention is corrected by this collection, for John Moss makes use of the term as early as 1975 in his editorial to the Commonwealth issue of the *Journal of Canadian Fiction* (39). Brydon may therefore be right to fear that "The history of Canadian contributions to postcolonial studies is now being erased from both Canadian literary history and current accounts of postcolonialism" ("Reading" 165-66; see also her essay, "Canada and Postcolonialism"). I am hoping that this book will help to rectify this erasure.

A fourth criterion in the selection of essays for this anthology was their pedagogical value for graduate and undergraduate courses in Canadian literature, Canadian studies, and/or postcolonial theory. The early "foundational" essays are part of this goal, as are a number of articles that provide a history of the field of postcolonialism in Canada, such as Donna Bennett's "English Canada's Postcolonial Complexities" and Brydon's "Reading Postcoloniality, Reading Canada." Both of these essays provide an excellent survey of the field up to the time of the article's composition (see also Sugars, "National Posts"). In combination with these historical assessments, I have tried to include articles that cover a range of issues and periods—from early nationalist pieces in the 60s and 70s to more recent explorations (and critiques) of Canadian nationality in the late 1990s. I have also included a number of the most oft-cited meditations on Canadian postcolonialism, articles such as Linda Hutcheon's "'Circling the Downspout of Empire,'" Brydon's "The White Inuit Speaks," Stephen Slemon's "Unsettling the Empire," Thomas King's "Godzilla vs. Post-Colonial," and, more recently, Len Findlay's "Always Indigenize!"

Finally, I wanted this collection to give a sense of the energetic debate and dialogue that constitutes postcolonial discourse in Canada. This, it seems to me, is the most important contribution of this anthology. There are a number of articles, for instance, that are in explicit dialogue with one another. Brydon's "White Inuit" is a direct response to Hutcheon's "'Circling the Downspout,'" while Brydon's critique was subjected to Enoch Padolsky's subsequent interrogation in "'Olga in Wonderland.'" Together, these three articles offer a sense of some of the central concerns informing debates about Canadian postcoloniality, and provide a useful exploration of the various problematics of the field. The debate does not end here, however, for Padolsky's claim that postcolonial theory in Canada ignores the vector of the local and fails to engage with issues of nationalism and ethnicity is belied by many of the articles included in this collection. Indeed, many race theorists would not agree with the underlying nationalist impetus of Canadian ethnic studies discourse, as expressed by Padolsky, many of whom launch their anti-racist critiques by deploying postcolonial theoretical insights (eg. Bannerji, Miki, Mukherjee, and Walcott). Likewise, the question of authenticity, which is central to all three pieces, becomes an important theoretical issue in subsequent selections, not only those by aboriginal critics, but also in the essays by Roy Miki, Sherene Razack, Richard Cavell, and Smaro Kamboureli. Kamboureli, in particular, offers a potential response to Padolsky through her assessment of the ways the postcolonial critic is caught between a recognition that identity is a production and an awareness of the necessity of self-positioning (352). Similarly, Brydon's "Reading Postcoloniality" provides a corrective to Bennett's "English Canada's Postcolonial Complexities" regarding the latter's pinpointing of a "beginning" of postcolonial theorizing in Canada. Indeed, many of the essays included here make reference to other pieces in the volume, constituting an extended intertextual dialogue: Lee invokes the inspirational influence of Grant; Miki makes reference to Hutcheon; Lawson looks back to Lee and Slemon; and Fee's emphasis on critical self-positioning is echoed by Kamboureli and Razack.

With this context of active debate in mind, I have included a separate section entitled "Critiques of the (Canadian) Postcolonial." The three pieces included here critique the application of postcolonial theory to a Canadian context from different perspectives: Gary Boire examines the "whiting-out" of the indigenous presence in some central Canadian modernist texts, texts that are often celebrated for their postcolonial expression of Canadian identity; Padolsky critiques the omission of Canadian ethnic studies in much postcolonial discourse in Canada; Arun Mukherjee identifies the contradictory ways South-Asian Canadian writers are both made to be "essentially" postcolonial, and, by extension, not-quite-Canadian. King's "Godzilla vs. Post-Colonial" and Lee Maracle's "The 'Post-Colonial' Imagination" might also have been included in this section, for both launch an important critique of the application of postcolonial theory to a Canadian context which, for aboriginal peoples in this country, remains a colonizing one. Nevertheless, four important articles had to be omitted from this section: Amaryll Chanady's excellent summary of some of these debates in "Canadian Literature and the Postcolonial Paradigm" (1994); Sylvia Söderlind's astute critique, in "The Contest of Marginalities" (1995), of the dubious trope of "marginality" that is central to much postmodern and postcolonial theorizing in Canada; Di Brandt's "Putting the Mother Back in the Language" (1999), which explores postcolonialism's excision of women from debates about nationalism and globalization; and Mukherjee's "Whose Post-Colonialism and Whose Postmodernism?" (1990), which is not focussed on a Canadian context, but which does launch a critique of the conflating impetus of much postcolonial discourse, particularly when the label is used to include settler colonies such as Canada.

One also finds many overlaps in the central issues explored in these essays. Grant, Frye, and Atwood are linked by their articulation of the Canadian suspicion of an individualism associated with the United States. The defensive anti-Americanism of these early pieces goes hand-in-hand with their assessment of the central preoccupations of Canadian culture—it is a short step from Frye's identification of the "garrison mentality" to Atwood's exposé of Canada's colonial mentality and her survival thesis. Padolsky and Fee are interested in the relationship of ethnicity to postcolonial discourse in Canada: while Padolsky notes the separation of the two discourses, Fee wonders about the usefulness of "ethnicity" for the political struggles of Canada's aboriginal peoples. A related essay in this context is Tamara Palmer Seiler's "Multi-Vocality and National Literature." Seiler insists on the important and necessary overlaps between multicultural discourse and postcolonial theory, a link that she forges with reference to Charles Taylor's account of the imperative need for a notion of "deep diversity" to describe Canadian society. Nationalism is also a central concern for many of the critics gathered here, from Padolsky's claim that postcolonialism is not sufficiently concerned with nationalism, to Boire's critique of a mystifying nationalist agenda that is integral to the early postcolonial enterprise in Canada (clearly evident, for instance, in the selections from Grant, Atwood, and Lee), to Lawson's account of the ways the cultural nationalism of the settler-imperium dichotomy (through which the settler was figured as "colonized") was used as "a strategic disavowal of the colonizing act" (160), to Fee's exploration of the ways a nationalist discourse is of strategic value for aboriginal peoples, to King's rejection of the nationalist impetus of Canadian postcolonial theory in general. This grappling with the nationalist undercurrents of postcolonial theory is also central to many of the articles that engage with questions of race and the national imaginary. Bannerji, Miki, and Rinaldo Walcott each offers a critique of the ways the national narrative in Canada has erased the presence of non-white others in its midst. As Walcott notes of the ways Black people have been "written out" of the Canadian nation, "Canadian state institutions and official narratives attempt to render blackness outside of [the national] narratives" (278).

This returns us to the notion of the unhomeliness of the Canadian locale. Walcott describes this in terms of the "in-between-ness" experienced by Black writers in Canada (281). For Kamboureli, this is comparable to the diasporic writer/critic's dialogic location in Canadian space. For Bannerji, it is the (non-white) immigrant experience of being both "insider/outsider" at one and the same time. Maracle evokes this paradoxical emplacement through that space on the edge of the riverbank, a liminal place from which the Native writer is able to speak. Earlier essays express a similar sentiment, though in a different context. For Slemon and Lawson, this "in-betweenness" is characteristic of "that neither/nor territory of white settler-colonial writing" (Slemon 139), where "the *illusion* of a stable self/other, here/there binary division has *never* been available to Second-World writers" (148). For Kroetsch, this "in-betweenness" of the settler subject is evident in the constitutive "disunity" of Canadian expression (evident, according to Kroetsch, in much Canadian literature), while Lee uses the term "cadence" to conjure this "alien inauthenticity" (54). Together, these critics seek to give words to an inexpressible unhomeliness, an unhomeliness that carries both the familiar and defamiliarizing senses of the term as Freud uses it in "The 'Uncanny.'" If this disjunction is at times marked by an intangible sensation of unbelonging, at others it represents an all too material experience of prejudice and alienation.

* * *

And so, after surveying the field up to this point, what can one conclude? That the ostensibly unifying anti-colonial nationalism and (sometimes) colonial expression of the 60s and 70s has given way to a more complicated and heterogenous sense of the postcolonial as it applies to Canada? Yes, though nevertheless, I hesitate to be so complacent. From early on, Canadian postcolonial theorists recognized that what Frye characterized as Canada's "quest for the peaceable kingdom" (Conclusion 18) was a chimera. One won't get there by idealizing a Canadian society that does not exist, but by tugging at its edges. If there is one thing this collection does highlight it is that the Canadian locale is far from *post*-colonial (by which I mean a sense that the forces of colonization have been superceded in some idealized utopian postcolonial time/space). No-one who is versed in contemporary Canadian postcolonial theory can convincingly argue this. There may be some quibbling with the terminology itself, and much debate about how postcolonial theory is to be applied in a Canadian context (if at all), and, perhaps, little agreement on "whose postcolonialism" we are speaking of when we invoke such a label as "Canadian postcolonialism," but throughout, these essays clearly illustrate that the postcolonial is anything but "post." As Helen Tiffin so clearly puts it, "The term post-colonial . . . implies the *persistence* of colonial legacies in post-independence cultures, not their disappearance or erasure" (158).

However, one *can* see some shifts in emphasis. In an essay in the proceedings of the "Is Canada Postcolonial?" conference held at the University of Manitoba in 2000, Susan Gingell explores the shift that has taken place in Canadian postcolonial theory since the publication of Diana Brydon's seminal *Testing the Limits: Postcolonial Theories and Canadian Literature*, a special issue of *Essays on Canadian Writing* published in 1995 (the introduction to which is included here). Brydon's collection was ground-breaking for its extended attempt at bringing postcolonialism and Canada together (167), and it remains an important collection today. One shift that Gingell notes is the growing emphasis on aboriginal writings and politics in Canada, a concern that was not as evident in the 1995 *ECW* collection. The absence of Native peoples from earlier accounts of Canadian national identity is of course glaringly apparent, in retrospect, when reading Frye's famous "'Where is here?'" anecdote in his "Conclusion" (12). However, one sees it as well in various accounts of "native" or "indigenous" white Canadian experience, each instance of which, as Goldie notes, is a comment on the willed indigenization of the invader-settler (195). For example, George Grant speaks of creating an "indigenous society" in Canada (5), Moss writes of a "native or indigenous" vocabulary (38), Lee refers to "native space" (52, 54), while Robin Mathews refers to white settlers as "native inhabitants" (4). Indeed, Mathews's positing of two Canadian prototypes, settlers vs. entrepreneurs (5), omits aboriginal peoples altogether. This impetus to "indigenize" the settler-invader, as Goldie expresses it in his essay here (and as further explored by those theorists of settler-invader postcolonialism in this anthology), is given an innovative twist in Len Findlay's exhortation to "always indigenize!", a call to keep at the forefront the priority of aboriginal peoples in Canada (and elsewhere).

Gingell's observation about the increasing attention to aboriginal contexts in recent discussions of Canadian postcoloniality is important, for over the last decade or more the field of Canadian postcolonialism has seen the notable intervention of important aboriginal critics. Hutcheon claimed, in 1989, that "when Canadian culture is called post-colonial today the reference is very rarely to the Native culture" (76). This situation has changed radically in recent years. I have tried to give some sense of the development of this theory here, with selections from King, Maracle, and Marie Battiste. Battiste's articulation of "postcolonial Indigenous thought" (212) is an important development in aboriginal postcolonialism. Nonetheless, this selection entailed the exclusion of a number of significant accounts of Native cultural expression and colonialism/postcolonialism, such as Kateri Damm's important piece, "Says Who: Colonialism, Identity and Defining Indigenous Literature" (1993), in Jeannette Armstrong's *Looking at the Words of Our People*; Julia Emberley's fine study of Native women and the textuality of colonialism in *Thresholds of Difference* (1993); Armstrong's "The Disempowerment of First North American Native Peoples and Empowerment Through Their Writing" in *An Anthology of Native Literature in English* (1998); Armand Ruffo's well-known "Why Native Literature?" (1999) in Renée Hulan's collection, *Native North America*, as well as his recent edition of writings by aboriginal critics, *(Ad)dressing Our Words* (2001); any number of the essays in Marie Battiste's excellent collection, *Reclaiming Indigenous Voice and Vision* (2000); and Helen

Hoy's provocative account of the problematics of reading Native women's writing from a non-aboriginal perspective in *How Should I Read These?* (2001).

In addition to this shift in emphasis in accounts of Canadian postcolonialism, there has been increased attention to the politics of race (as opposed, perhaps, to ethnicity) in a Canadian context. Miki's assessment of the controversy surrounding the 1994 "Writing Thru Race" conference provides an insightful and illustrative account of the ways "race" continues to be a stumbling block for Canadian cultural theorists. The essays by Bannerji, Walcott, and Mukherjee take a similar approach, as does Razack's call for a "politics of accountability" (325) in "To Essentialize or Not To Essentialize." These interrogations of national Canadian metanarratives call into question the notion of a singular "postcolonial" identity for Canada. Indeed, such accounts mark a shift in understandings of the term "postcolonialism"— from a strict emphasis on the historical legacy of imperialism to a concern with hierarchical and hegemonic practices in contemporary postcolonial (often also global) contexts.

The connection between postcolonialism and pedagogy is another recent and compelling development in the field of postcolonial theory. While this is not limited to a Canadian context (see, for example, Gayatri Spivak's *Outside in the Teaching Machine* and "Teaching for the Times," Linda Smith's *Decolonizing Methodologies,* and the essays collected in Leslie Roman and Linda Eyre's *Dangerous Territories),* a number of Canadian critics have provided important interventions in this area (see the articles by Arun Mukherjee collected in *Postcolonialism: My Living,* Aruna Srivastava's "Anti-Racism Inside and Outside the Classroom," and Judith Leggatt's "Native Writing, Academic Theory"). I have included three selections here: Richard Cavell's account of his pedagogical approach in a postcolonial seminar at UBC in "Transvestic Sites: Postcolonialism, Pedagogy, and Politics"; Smaro Kamboureli's "The Diasporic Critic's (Self-)Location," which concludes with an exploration of "negative pedagogy" and what that might mean for a renewed postcolonial politics; and Len Findlay's increasingly cited "Always Indigenize!: The Radical Humanities in the Postcolonial Canadian University." The continued interest in the interrelations of postcolonialism and pedagogical concerns was evident in the recent "Postcolonialism and Pedagogy: Canadian Literatures in the Classroom" symposium, held at the University of Ottawa in 2002 (the proceedings of which are forthcoming with the University of Ottawa Press; see Sugars).

In the final section of this collection, "Postcolonial Pedagogies," Cavell, Kamboureli, and Findlay each address the disturbing divide between the academy and the "'real' world 'outside'" (Cavell 341)—a problematic dichotomy, as Cavell notes, but one which nevertheless holds sway in configurations of the ivory tower. Central to all three is a sense that the field of the humanities needs to become accountable to the imperialist practices that continue to inform Canadian society. A postcolonial approach can therefore constitute an enabling and potentially interventionist methodology, providing a much-needed link between the realms of aesthetics and social practice. Findlay's article highlights the persistent complicity of academia with colonialism (370). The continued emphasis on objectivity and standards, he maintains, is compromised: it is dangerous to pretend disinterestedness in the name of standards that "appeal to the best and the brightest in order to privilege the best-off and the whitest" (378). The goal of "always indigenizing" might be to keep Canada's "discursive, ethical, and social deficits" (Findlay 375) at the forefront of consciousness, what Miki and Walcott also intend when they speak of the ways race must continue to be made visible in Canadian cultural praxis (Miki 313). This might also include Kamboureli's notion, via Barbara Johnson, of a "negative pedagogy" (361), a way of learning to explore what we do not know. This collection, I hope, will take us that much closer to the "impossible necessity" (Goldie 194) of the foregoing of mastery, a way into what Gayatri Spivak refers to as "un-learning our privilege as our loss" (*Post-Colonial Critic* 9). With any luck, it might lead to an unsettling of assumptions about postcolonial discourse, and a more conscious habitation of the unhomely states of being in Canada.

WORKS CITED

Anderson, Benedict. *Imagined Communities: Reflections on the Origin and Spread of Nationalism.* London: Verso, 1991.

Armstrong, Jeannette. "The Disempowerment of First North American Native Peoples and Empowerment Through Their Writing." *An Anthology of Native Literature in English.* Ed. Daniel David Moses and Terry Goldie. 2nd ed. Toronto: Oxford UP, 1998. 239-42.

—, ed. *Looking at the Words of Our People: First Nations Analysis of Literature.* Penticton: Theytus, 1993.

Atwood, Margaret. *The Journals of Susanna Moodie.* Toronto: Oxford UP, 1970.

—. "Nationalism, Limbo and the Canadian Club." *Saturday Night* (January 1971): 75-77.

Battiste, Marie, ed. *Reclaiming Indigenous Voice and Vision.* Vancouver: UBC P, 2000.

Brandt, Di. "Putting the Mother Back in the Language: Maria Campbell's Revisionary Biogeographies & Margaret Laurence's *The Diviners.*" *West Coast Line* 29 (1999): 86-105.

Brydon, Diana. "Canada and Postcolonialism: Questions, Inventories, and Futures." Moss 49-77.

—, ed. *Testing the Limits: Postcolonial Theories and Canadian Literature.* Special issue of *Essays on Canadian Writing* 56 (1995).

Chanady, Amaryll. "Canadian Literature and the Postcolonial Paradigm." *Textual Studies in Canada* 5 (1994): 15-21.

Damm, Kateri. "Says Who: Colonialism, Identity and Defining Indigenous Literature." Armstrong, *Looking* 9-26.

Desroches, Vincent. *Is Quebec Postcolonial?* Special issue of *Quebec Studies* (2003): forthcoming.

Emberley, Julia V. *Thresholds of Difference: Feminist Critique, Native Women's Writings, Postcolonial Theory.* Toronto: U of Toronto P, 1993. 100-26.

Freud, Sigmund. "The 'Uncanny.'" 1919. *Art and Literature.* Ed. Albert Dickson. Trans. James Strachey. Vol. 14 of The Pelican Freud Library. Harmondsworth: Penguin, 1985. 339-76.

Gingell, Susan. "The Absence of Seaming, Or How I Almost Despair of Dancing: How Postcolonial Are Canada's Literary Institutions and Critical Practices?" Moss 97-110.

Goldie, Terry. *Fear and Temptation: The Image of the Indigene in Canadian, Australian, and New Zealand Literatures.* Montreal: McGill-Queen's UP, 1989.

Gunew, Sneja. "Postcolonialism and Multiculturalism: Between Race and Ethnicity." *Yearbook of English Studies* 27 (1997): 22-39.

Hoy, Helen. *How Should I Read These?: Native Women Writers in Canada.* Toronto: U of Toronto P, 2001.

Kroetsch, Robert. "Unhiding the Hidden: Recent Canadian Fiction." *Journal of Canadian Fiction* 3 (1974): 43-45. Rpt. in *The Lovely Treachery of Words: Essays Selected and New.* Toronto: Oxford UP, 1989. 58-63.

Lawson, Alan. "Proximities: From Asymptote to Zeugma." *Postcolonizing the Commonwealth: Studies in Literature and Culture.* Ed. Rowland Smith. Waterloo: Wilfrid Laurier UP, 2000. 19-37.

Leggatt, Judith. "Native Writing, Academic Theory: Post-Colonialism Across the Cultural Divide." Moss 111-26.

Mathews, Robin. "Literature and Colonialism." *Canadian Literature: Surrender or Revolution.* Toronto: Steel Rail, 1978. 1-9.

Moss, Laura, ed. *Is Canada Postcolonial?: Unsettling Canadian Literature.* Waterloo: Wilfrid Laurier UP, 2003.

Mukherjee, Arun. "Whose Post-Colonialism and Whose Postmodernism?" *World Literature Written in English* 30.2 (1990): 1-9. Rpt. in *Postcolonialism: My Living* 215-24.

—. *Postcolonialism: My Living.* Toronto: TSAR, 1998.

Murray, Heather. "Reading for Contradiction in the Literature of Colonial Space." *Future Indicative: Literary Theory and Canadian Literature.* Ed. John Moss. Ottawa: U of Ottawa P, 1987. 71-84.

New, William H. *Among Worlds: An Introduction to Modern Commonwealth and South African Fiction.* Erin, ON: Press Porcépic, 1975.

—. "New Language, New World." *Awakened Conscience: Studies in Commonwealth Literature.* Ed. C.D. Narashimhaiah. New Delhi: Sterling, 1978. 360-77.

—. *Dreams of Speech and Violence: The Art of the Short Story in Canada and New Zealand.* Toronto: U of Toronto P, 1987.

Roman, Leslie G., and Linda Eyre, eds. *Dangerous Territories: Struggles for Difference and Equality in Education.* New York: Routledge, 1997.

Ross, Malcolm. "Canadian Culture and the Colonial Question." *The Impossible Sum of*

Our Traditions: Reflections on Canadian Literature. Intro. David Staines. Toronto: McClelland, 1986. 163-83.

Ruffo, Armand Garnet, ed. *(Ad)dressing Our Words: Aboriginal Perspectives on Aboriginal Literatures.* Penticton: Theytus, 2001.

—. "Why Native Literature?" *Native North America: Critical and Cultural Perspectives.* Ed. Renée Hulan. Toronto: ECW, 1999. 109-21.

Seiler, Tamara Palmer. "Multi-Vocality and National Literature: Towards a Post-Colonial and Multicultural Aesthetic." *Literary Pluralities.* Ed. Christl Verduyn. Peterborough: Broadview, 1998. 47-63.

Smith, Linda Tuhiwai. *Decolonizing Methodologies: Research and Indigenous Peoples.* London: Zed Books, 1999.

Söderlind, Sylvia. "The Contest of Marginalities." *Essays on Canadian Writing* 56 (1995): 96-109.

—. *Margin/Alias: Language and Colonization in Canadian and Québécois Fiction.* Toronto: U of Toronto P, 1991.

Spivak, Gayatri Chakravorty. *Outside in the Teaching Machine.* New York: Routledge, 1993.

—. *The Post-Colonial Critic: Interviews, Strategies, Dialogues.* Ed. Sarah Harasym. New York: Routledge, 1990.

—. "Teaching for the Times." *Dangerous Liaisons: Gender, Nation, and Postcolonial Perspectives.* Ed. Anne McClintock, Aamir Mufti, and Ella Shohat. Minneapolis: U of Minnesota P, 1997. 468-90.

Srivastava, Aruna. "Anti-Racism Inside and Outside the Classroom." Roman and Eyre 113-26.

Sugars, Cynthia. "Can the Canadian Speak? Lost in Postcolonial Space." *ARIEL* 32.3 (2001): 115-52.

—. "National Posts: Theorizing Canadian Postcolonialism." *International Journal of Canadian Studies* 25 (2002): 15-41.

—, ed. *Home-Work: Postcolonialism, Pedagogy, and Canadian Literature.* Ottawa: U of Ottawa P, 2004.

Tiffin, Helen. "Plato's Cave: Educational and Critical Practices." *New National and Post-Colonial Literatures: An Introduction.* Ed. Bruce King. Oxford: Clarendon, 1996. 143-63.

Vautier, Marie. *New World Myth: Postmodernism and Postcolonialism in Canadian Fiction.* Montreal: McGill-Queen's UP, 1998.

PART I
⊷ ANTI-COLONIAL NATIONALISM ⊷

From *Lament for a Nation: The Defeat of Canadian Nationalism**

George Grant

[. . .] To lament is to cry out at the death or at the dying of something loved. This lament mourns the end of Canada as a sovereign state. Political laments are not usual in the age of progress, because most people think that society always moves forward to better things. Lamentation is not an indulgence in despair or cynicism. In a lament for a child's death, there is not only pain and regret, but also celebration of passed good.

> I cannot but remember such things were
> That were most precious to me.

In Mozart's great threnody, the Countess sings of *la memoria di quel bene.* One cannot argue the meaninglessness of the world from the facts of evil, because what could evil deprive us of, if we had not some prior knowledge of good? The situation of absolute despair does not allow a man to write. In the theatre of the absurd, dramatists like Ionesco and Beckett do not escape this dilemma. They pretend to absolute despair and yet pour out novels and plays. When a man truly despairs, he does not write; he commits suicide. At the other extreme, there are the saints who know that the destruction of good serves the supernatural end; therefore they cannot lament. Those who write laments may have heard the propositions of the saints, but they do not know that they are true. A lament arises from a condition that is common to the majority of men, for we are situated between despair and absolute certainty.

I have implied that the existence of a sovereign Canada served the good. But can the disappearance of an unimportant nation be worthy of serious grief? For some older Canadians it can. Our country is the only political entity to which we have been trained to pay allegiance. Growing up in Ontario, the generation of the 1920's took it for granted that they belonged to a nation. The character of the country was self-evident. To say it was British was not to deny it was North American. To be Canadian was to be a unique species of North American. Such alternatives as F.H. Underhill's—"Stop being British

---

* *Lament for a Nation: The Defeat of Canadian Nationalism* (Toronto: McClelland, 1965).

if you want to be a nationalist"—seemed obviously ridiculous. We were grounded in the wisdom of Sir John A. Macdonald, who saw plainly more than a hundred years ago that the only threat to nationalism was from the South, not from across the sea. To be a Canadian was to build, along with the French, a more ordered and stable society than the liberal experiment in the United States. Now that this hope has been extinguished, we are too old to be retrained by a new master. We find ourselves like fish left on the shores of a drying lake. The element necessary to our existence has passed away. As some form of political loyalty is part of the good life, and as we are not flexible enough to kneel to the rising sun, we must be allowed to lament the passing of what had claimed our allegiance. Even on a continent too dynamic to have memory, it may still be salutary to celebrate memory. [. . .]

This meditation is limited to lamenting. It makes no practical proposals for our survival as a nation. It argues that Canada's disappearance was a matter of necessity. But how can one lament necessity—or, if you will, fate? The noblest of men love it; the ordinary accept it; the narcissists rail against it. But I lament it as a celebration of memory; in this case, the memory of that tenuous hope that was the principle of my ancestors. The insignificance of that hope in the endless ebb and flow of nature does not prevent us from mourning. At least we can say with Richard Hooker: "Posterity may know we have not loosely through silence permitted things to pass away as in a dream." [. . .]

The confused strivings of politicians, businessmen, and civil servants cannot alone account for Canada's collapse. This stems from the very character of the modern era.[1] The aspirations of progress have made Canada redundant. The universal and homogenous state is the pinnacle of political striving. "Universal" implies a world-wide state, which would eliminate the curse of war among nations; "homogeneous" means that all men would be equal, and war among classes would be eliminated. The masses and the philosophers have both agreed that this universal and egalitarian society is the goal of historical striving. It gives content to the rhetoric of both Communists and capitalists. This state will be achieved by means of modern science—a science that leads to the conquest of nature. Today scientists master not only non-human nature, but human nature itself. Particularly in America, scientists concern themselves with the control of heredity, the human mind, and society. Their victories in biochemistry and psychology will give the politicians a prodigious power to universalize and homogenize. Since 1945, the world-wide and uniform society is no longer a distant dream but a close possibility. Man will conquer man and perfect himself.

Modern civilization makes all local cultures anachronistic. Where modern science has achieved its mastery, there is no place for local cultures. It has often been argued that geography and language caused Canada's defeat. But behind these there is a necessity that is incomparably more powerful. Our culture floundered on the aspirations of the age of progress. The argument that Canada, a local culture, must disappear can, therefore, be stated in three steps. First, men everywhere move ineluctably toward membership in the universal and homogenous state. Second, Canadians live next to a society that is the heart of modernity. Third, nearly all Canadians think that modernity is good, so nothing essential distinguishes Canadians from Americans. When they oblate themselves before "the American way of life," they offer themselves on the altar of the reigning Western goddess. [. . .]

The impossibility of conservatism in our era is the impossibility of Canada. As Canadians we attempted a ridiculous task in trying to build a conservative nation in the age of progress, on a continent we share with the most dynamic nation on earth. The current of modern history was against us.

A society only articulates itself as a nation through some common intention among its people. The constitutional arrangements of 1791, and the wider arrangements of the next century, were only possible because of a widespread determination not to become part of the great Republic. Among both the French and the British, this negative intention sprang from widely divergent traditions. What both peoples had in common was the fact they both recognized, that they could only be preserved outside the United States of America. The French were willing to co-operate with the English because they had no alternative but to go along with the endurable arrangements proposed by the ruling power. Both the French and the British had limited common ground in their sense of social order—belief that society required a high degree of law, and respect for a public conception of virtue. Both would grant the state much wider rights to control the individual than was recognized in the libertarian ideas of the American constitution. If their different conservatisms could have become a conscious bond, this nation might have preserved itself. An indigenous society might have continued to exist on the northern half of this continent.

To see why this intention failed in Canada, it is necessary to look more closely at the origins of [. . .] the British traditions to see what has happened to them. [. . .] [I]t would be foolish to over-emphasize the niceties of theory among those who came to the St. John Valley or Upper Canada in the late eighteenth and early nineteenth centuries. It is difficult to put into words the conservatism of the English-speaking peoples in the Atlantic colonies or Upper Canada. The manifold waves of differing settlers must not be simplified into any common pattern. Much of English-speaking conservatism was simply a loyalty based on the flow of trade, and therefore destined to change when that flow changed. [. . .]

This does not imply that the nationalism in English-speaking Canada was simply a front for interest. Many of its elements were shaped by that strange phenomenon, British conservatism, which led the settlers to try to build on the northern half of this continent an independent society. British conservatism is difficult to describe because it is less a clear view of existence than an appeal to an ill-defined past. The writings of Edmund Burke are evidence of this. Yet many of the British officials, many Loyalists, and later many immigrants felt this conservatism very strongly. It was an inchoate desire to build, in these cold and forbidding regions, a society with a greater sense of order and restraint than freedom-loving republicanism would allow. It was no better defined than a kind of suspicion that we in Canada could be less lawless and have a greater sense of propriety than the United States. The inherited determinism not to be Americans allowed these British people to come to a *modus vivendi* with the more defined desires of the French. English-speaking Canadians have been called a dull, stodgy, and indeed costive lot. In these dynamic days, such qualities are made particularly unattractive to the chic.[2] Yet our stodginess has made us a society of greater simplicity, formality, and perhaps even innocence than the people to the south. Whatever differences there were between the Anglicans and the Presbyterians, and however differently their theologians might interpret the doctrine of original sin, both communities believed that the good life made strict demands on self-restraint. Nothing was more alien to them than the "emancipation of the passions" desired in American liberalism. An ethic of self-restraint naturally looks with suspicion on utopian movements, which proceed from an ethic of freedom. The early leaders of British North America identified lack of public and personal restraint with the democratic Republic. Their conservatism was essentially the social doctrine that public order and tradition, in contrast to freedom and experiment, were central to the good life. The British Crown was a symbol of a continuing loyalty to the state—less equivocal than was expected from republicans. In our early expansions, this conservative nationalism expressed itself in the use of public control in the political and economic spheres. Our opening of the West differed from that of the United States, in that the law of the central government was used more extensively, and less reliance was placed on the free settler. Until recently, Canadians have been much more willing than Americans to use governmental control over economic life to protect the public good against private freedom. To repeat, Ontario Hydro, the CNR, and the CBC were all established by Conservative governments. The early establishment of Ontario Hydro succeeded because of the efforts of an administrator, a politician, and a journalist, all of whom wrapped themselves in the Union Jack in their efforts to keep the development of electric power out of the hands of individual freedom.[3]

English-speaking Canadians had never broken with their origins in Western Europe. Many of them had continuing connections with the British Isles, which in the nineteenth century still had ways of life from before the age of progress. That we never broke with Great Britain is often said to prove that we are not a nation but a colony. But the great politicians who believed in this connection—from Joseph Howe and Robert Baldwin to Sir John A. Macdonald and Sir Robert Borden, and indeed to John G. Diefenbaker himself—

make a long list. They did not see it this way, but rather as a relation to the font of constitutional government in the British Crown. Many Canadians saw it as a means of preserving at every level of our life—religious, educational, political, social—certain forms of existence that distinguish us from the United States. [. . .]

Many levels of argument have been used to say that it is good that Canada should disappear. In its simplest form, continentalism is the view of those who do not see what all the fuss is about. The purpose of life is consumption, and therefore the border is an anachronism. The forty-ninth parallel results in a lower standard of living for the majority to the north of it. Such continentalism has been an important force throughout Canadian history. Until recently it was limited by two factors. Emigration to the United States was not too difficult for Canadians, so that millions were able to seek their fuller future to the south. Moreover, those who believed in the primacy of private prosperity have generally been too concerned with individual pursuits to bother with political advocacy. Nevertheless, this spirit is bound to grow. One has only to live in the Niagara peninsula to understand it. In the mass era, most human beings are defined in terms of their capacity to consume. All other differences between them, like political traditions, begin to appear unreal and unprogressive. As consumption becomes primary, the border appears an anachronism, and a frustrating one at that. [. . .]

It has already been argued that, because of our modern assumptions about human good, Canada's disappearance is necessary.[4] In deciding whether continentalism is good, one is making a judgement about progressive political philosophy and its interpretation of history. Those who dislike continentalism are in some sense rejecting that progressive interpretation. It can only be with an enormous sense of hesitation that one dares to question modern political philosophy. If its assumptions are false, the age of progress has been a tragic aberration in the history of the species. To assert such a proposition lightly would be the height of irresponsibility. Has it not been in the age of progress that disease and overwork, hunger and poverty, have been drastically reduced? Those who criticize our age must at the same time contemplate pain, infant mortality, crop failures in isolated areas, and the sixteen-hour day. As soon as that is said, facts about our age must also be remembered: the increasing outbreaks of impersonal ferocity, the banality of existence in technological societies, the pursuit of expansion as an end in itself. Will it be good for men to control their genes? The possibility of nuclear destruction and mass starvation may be no more terrible than that of man tampering with the roots of his humanity. Interference with human nature seems to the moderns the hope of a higher species in the ascent of life; to others it may seem that man in his pride could corrupt his very being. The powers of manipulation now available may portend the most complete tyranny imaginable. At least, it is feasible to wonder whether modern assumptions may be basically inhuman. [. . .]

The discussion of issues such as these is impossible in a short writing about Canada. Also, the discussion would be inconclusive, because I do not know the truth about these ultimate matters. Therefore, the question as to whether it is good that Canada should disappear must be left unsettled. If the best social order is the universal and homogenous state, then the disappearance of Canada can be understood as a step toward that order. If the universal and homogenous state would be a tyranny, than the disappearance of even this indigenous culture can be seen as the removal of a minor barrier on the road to that tyranny. As the central issue is left undecided, the propriety of lamenting must also be left unsettled. [. . .]

Notes

1. In what follows I use "modern" to describe the civilization of the age of progress. This civilization arose in Western Europe and is now conquering the whole globe and perhaps other parts of the universe. "Modern" is applied to political philosophy to distinguish the thought of Western Europe from that of the antique world of Greece.
2. In his recent book *The Scotch* (New York and Toronto: Macmillan, 1964), Professor J.K. Galbraith has patronized his ancestors from western Ontario in this vein. A great human advance has been made from the Presbyterian farm to the sophistication of Harvard.
3. The three men were Sir Adam Beck, Sir Richard Whitney, and "Black Jack" Robinson.
4. In our day, necessity is often identified with some fate in the atoms or the "life force." But historical necessity is chiefly concerned with what the most influential souls have thought about human good. Political philosophy is not some pleasant cultural game reserved for those too impotent for practice. It is concerned with judgements about goodness. As these judgements are apprehended and acted upon by practical men, they become the unfolding of fate.

2

From "Conclusion to
A Literary History of Canada"*

Northrop Frye

Some years ago, a group of editors met to draw up the first tentative plans for a history of English Canadian literature. What we then dreamed of is substantially what we have got, changed very little in essentials. I expressed at the time the hope that such a book would help to broaden the inductive basis on which some writers on Canadian literature were making generalizations that bordered on guesswork. By "some writers" I meant primarily myself: I find, however, that more evidence has in fact tended to confirm most of my intuitions on the subject.

To study Canadian literature properly, one must outgrow the view that evaluation is the end of criticism, instead of its incidental by-product. If evaluation is one's guiding principle, criticism of Canadian literature would become only a debunking project, leaving it a poor naked *alouette* plucked of every feather of decency and dignity. True, what is really remarkable is not how little but how much good writing has been produced in Canada. But this would not affect the rigorous evaluator. The evaluative view is based on the conception of criticism as concerned mainly to define and canonize the genuine classics of literature. And Canada has produced no author who is a classic in the sense of possessing a vision greater in kind than that of his best readers (Canadians themselves might argue about one or two, but in the perspective of the world at large the statement is true). There is no Canadian writer of whom we can say what we can say of the world's major writers, that their readers can grow up inside their work without ever being aware of a circumference. Thus the metaphor of the critic as "judge" holds better for a critic who is never dealing with the kind of writer who judges him.

This fact about Canadian literature, so widely deplored by Canadians, has one advantage. It is much easier to see what literature is trying to do when we

---

* *Literary History of Canada: Canadian Literature in English*, ed. Carl F. Klinck (Toronto: U of Toronto P, 1965), 821-49; rev. and rpt. in *The Bush Garden: Essays on the Canadian Imagination* (Toronto: Anansi, 1971), 213-51. [Editor's note: I have chosen Frye's revised version of the Conclusion, published in *The Bush Garden*, as my copy text, in part because Frye's revisions make the text more readable as a self-standing essay.]

are studying a literature that has not quite done it. If no Canadian author pulls us away from the Canadian context toward the centre of literary experience itself, then at every point we remain aware of his social and historical setting. The conception of what is literary has to be greatly broadened for such a literature. The literary, in Canada, is often only an incidental quality of writings which, like those of many of the early explorers, are as innocent of literary intention as a mating loon. Even when it is literature in its orthodox genres of poetry and fiction, it is more significantly studied as a part of Canadian life than as a part of an autonomous world of literature. [. . .]

The question: why has there been no Canadian writer of classic proportions? may naturally be asked. At any rate it often has been. Our authors realize that it is better to deal with what is there than to raise speculations about why something else is not there. But it is clear that the question haunts their minds. And we know so little about cultural history that we not only cannot answer such a question, but we do not even know whether or not it is a real question. The notion, doubtless of romantic origin, that "genius" is a certain quantum that an individual is born with, as he might be born with red hair, is still around, but mainly as a folktale motif in fiction, like the story of Finch in the Jalna books. "Genius" is as much, and essentially, a matter of social context as it is of individual character. We do not know what the social conditions are that produce great literature, or even whether there is any causal relation at all. If there is, there is no reason to suppose that they are good conditions, or conditions that we should try to reproduce. The notion that the literature one admires must have been nourished by something admirable in the social environment is persistent, but has never been justified by evidence. One can still find books on Shakespeare that profess to make his achievement more plausible by talking about a "background" of social euphoria produced by the defeat of the Armada, the discovery of America a century before, and the conviction that Queen Elizabeth was a wonderful woman. There is a general sense of filler about such speculations, and when similar arguments are given in a negative form to explain the absence of a Shakespeare in Canada they are no more convincing. Puritan inhibitions, pioneer life, "an age too late, cold climate, or years"—these may be important as factors or conditions of Canadian culture, helping us to characterize its qualities. To suggest that any of them is a negative cause of its merit is to say much more than anyone knows. [. . .]

Canada began as an obstacle, blocking the way to the treasures of the East, to be explored only in the hope of finding a passage through it. English Canada continued to be that long after what is now the United States had become a defined part of the Western world. One reason for this is obvious from the map. American culture was, down to about 1900, mainly a culture of the Atlantic seaboard, with a western frontier that moved irregularly but steadily back until it reached the other coast. The Revolution did not essentially change the North Atlantic that had London and Edinburgh on one side of it and Boston and Philadelphia on the other. But Canada has, for all practical purposes, no Atlantic seaboard. The traveller from Europe edges into it like a tiny Jonah entering an inconceivably large whale, slipping past the Straits of Belle Isle into the Gulf of St. Lawrence, where five Canadian provinces surround him, for the most part invisible. Then he goes up the St. Lawrence and the inhabited country comes into view, mainly a French-speaking country, with its own cultural traditions. To enter the United States is a matter of crossing an ocean; to enter Canada is a matter of being silently swallowed by an alien continent.

It is an unforgettable and intimidating experience to enter Canada in this way. But the experience initiates one into that gigantic east-to-west thrust which historians regard as the axis of Canadian development, the "Laurentian" movement that makes the growth of Canada geographically credible. This drive to the west has attracted to itself nearly everything that is heroic and romantic in the Canadian tradition. The original impetus begins in Europe, for English Canada in the British Isles, hence though adventurous it is also a conservative force, and naturally tends to preserve its colonial link with its starting-point. Once the Canadian has settled down in the country, however, he then becomes aware of the longitudinal dimension, the southward pull toward the richer and more glamorous American cities, some of which, such as Boston for the Maritimes and Minneapolis for the eastern prairies, are almost Canadian capitals. This is the axis of another kind of Canadian mentality, more critical and analytic, more inclined to see Canada as an unnatural and politically quixotic aggregate of disparate northern extensions of American culture—"seven fishing-rods tied together by the ends," as Goldwin Smith put it.

The simultaneous influence of two larger nations speaking the same language has been practically beneficial to English Canada, but theoretically confusing. It is often suggested that Canada's identity is to be found in some *via media*, or *via mediocris*, between the other two. This has the disadvantage that the British and American cultures have to be defined as extremes. Haliburton seems to have believed that the ideal for Nova Scotia would be a combination of American energy and British social structure, but such a chimera, or synthetic monster, is hard to achieve in practice. It is simpler merely to notice the alternating current in the Canadian mind, as reflected in its writing, between two moods, one romantic, traditional and idealistic, the other shrewd, observant and humorous. Canada in its attitude to Britain tends to be more royalist than the Queen, in the sense that it is more attracted to it as a symbol of tradition than as a fellow-nation. The Canadian attitude to the United States is typically that of a smaller country to a much bigger neighbour, sharing in its material civilization but anxious to keep clear of the huge mass movements that drive a great imperial power. The United States, being founded on a revolution and a written constitution, has introduced a deductive or *a priori* pattern into its cultural life that tends to define an American way of life and mark it off from anti-American heresies. Canada, having a seat on the sidelines of the American Revolution, adheres more to the inductive and the expedient. The Canadian genius for compromise is reflected in the existence of Canada itself. [. . .]

Cultural history, we said, has its own rhythms. It is possible that one of these rhythms is very like an organic rhythm: that there must be a period, of a certain magnitude, as Aristotle would say, in which a social imagination can take root and establish a tradition. American literature had this period, in the north-eastern part of the country, between the Revolution and the Civil War. Canada has never had it. English Canada was first a part of the wilderness, then a part of North America and the British Empire, then a part of the world. But it has gone through these revolutions too quickly for a tradition of writing to be founded on any one of them. Canadian writers are, even now, still trying to assimilate a Canadian environment at a time when new techniques of communication, many of which, like television, constitute a verbal market, are annihilating the boundaries of that environment. This foreshortening of Canadian history, if it really does have any relevance to Canadian culture, would account for many features of it: its fixation on its own past, its penchant for old-fashioned literary techniques, its preoccupation with the theme of strangled articulateness. It seems to me that Canadian sensibility has been profoundly disturbed, not so much by our famous problem of identity, important as that is, as by a series of paradoxes in what confronts that identity. It is less perplexed by the question "Who am I?" than by some such riddle as "Where is here?"

We are obviously not to read the mystique of Canadianism back into the pre-Confederation period. Haliburton, for instance, was a Nova Scotian, a Bluenose: the word "Canadian" to him would have summoned up the figure of someone who spoke mainly French and whose enthusiasm for Haliburton's own political ideals would have been extremely tepid. The mystique of Canadianism was specifically the cultural accompaniment of Confederation and the imperialistic mood that followed it. But it came so suddenly after the pioneer period that it was still full of wilderness. To feel "Canadian" was to feel part of a no-man's land with huge rivers, lakes, and islands that very few Canadians had ever seen. "From sea to sea, and from the river unto the ends of the earth"—if Canada is not an island, the phrasing is still in the etymological sense isolating. One wonders if any other national consciousness has had so large an amount of the unknown, the unrealized, the humanly undigested, so built into it. Rupert Brooke speaks of the "unseizable virginity" of the Canadian landscape. What is important here, for our purposes, is the position of the frontier in the Canadian imagination. In the United States one could choose to move out to the frontier or to retreat from it back to the seaboard.

The tensions built up by such migrations have fascinated many American novelists and historians. In the Canadas, even in the Maritimes, the frontier was all around one, a part and a condition of one's whole imaginative being. The frontier was primarily what separated the Canadian, physically or mentally, from Great Britain, from the United States, and even more important, from other Canadian communities. Such a frontier was the immediate datum of his imagination, the thing that had to be dealt with first. [. . .]

Culture is born in leisure and an awareness of standards, and pioneer conditions tend to make energetic and uncritical work an end it itself, to preach a gospel of social unconsciousness, which lingers long after the pioneer conditions have disappeared. The impressive achievements of such a society are likely to be technological. It is in the inarticulate part of communication, railways and bridges and canals and highways, that Canada, one of whose symbols is the taciturn beaver, has shown its real strength. Again, Canadian culture, and literature in particular, has felt the force of what may be called Emerson's law. Emerson remarks in his journals that in a provincial society it is extremely easy to reach the highest level of cultivation, extremely difficult to take one step beyond that. In surveying Canadian poetry and fiction, we feel constantly that all the energy has been absorbed in meeting a standard, a self-defeating enterprise because real standards can only be established, not met. Such writing is academic in the pejorative sense of the term, an imitation of a prescribed model, second-rate in conception, not merely in execution. It is natural that academic writing of this kind should develop where literature is a social prestige symbol. However, it is not the handicaps of Canadian writers but the distinctive features that appear in spite of them which are our main concern at present. [. . .]

Civilization in Canada, as elsewhere, has advanced geometrically across the country, throwing down the long parallel lines of the railways, dividing up the farm lands into chessboards of square-mile sections and concession-line roads. There is little adaptation to nature: in both architecture and arrangement, Canadian cities and villages express rather an arrogant abstraction, the conquest of nature by an intelligence that does not love it. The word conquest suggests something military, as it should—one thinks of General Braddock, preferring to have his army annihilated rather than fight the natural man on his own asymmetrical ground. There are some features of this generally North American phenomenon that have a particular emphasis in Canada. It has often been remarked that Canadian expansion westward had a tight grip of authority over it that American expansion, with its outlaws and sheriffs and vigilantes and the like, did not have in the same measure. America moved from the back country to the wild west; Canada moved from a New France held down by British military occupation to a northwest patrolled by mounted police. Canada has not had, strictly speaking, an Indian war: there has been much less of the "another redskin bit the dust" feeling in our historical imagination, and only Riel remains to haunt the later period of it, though he is a formidable figure enough, rather like what a combination of John Brown and Vanzetti would be in the American conscience. Otherwise, the conquest, for the last two centuries, has been mainly of the unconscious forces of nature, personified by the dragon of the Lake Superior rocks in Pratt's *Towards the Last Spike*:

On the North Shore a reptile lay asleep—
A hybrid that the myths might have conceived,
But not delivered.

Yet the conquest of nature has its own perils for the imagination, in a country where the winters are so cold and where conditions of life have so often been bleak and comfortless, where even the mosquitoes have been described as "mementoes of the fall." I have long been impressed in Canadian poetry by a tone of deep terror in regard to nature, a theme to which we shall return. It is not terror of the dangers or discomforts or even the mysteries of nature, but a terror of the soul at something that these things manifest. The human mind has nothing but human and moral values to cling to if it is to preserve its integrity or even its sanity, yet the vast unconsciousness of nature in front of it seems an unanswerable denial of those values. A sharp-witted Methodist circuit rider speaks of the "shutting out of the whole moral creation" in the loneliness of the forests.

If we put together a few of these impressions, we may get some approach to characterizing the way in which the Canadian imagination has developed in its literature. Small and isolated communities surrounded with a physical or psychological "frontier," separated from one another and from their American and British cultural sources: communities that provide all that their members have in the way of distinctively human values, and that are compelled to feel a great respect for the law and order that holds them together, yet confronted with a huge, unthinking, menacing, and formidable physical setting—such communities are bound to develop what we may provisionally call a garrison mentality. In the earliest maps of the country the only inhabited centres are forts, and that remains true of the cultural maps for a much later time. Frances Brooke, in her eighteenth-century *Emily Montague*, wrote of what was literally a garrison; novelists of our day studying the impact of Montreal on Westmount write of a psychological one.

A garrison is a closely knit and beleaguered society, and its moral and social values are unquestionable. In a perilous enterprise one does not discuss causes or motives: one is either a fighter or a deserter. Here again we may turn to Pratt, with his infallible instinct for what is central in the Canadian imagination. The societies in Pratt's poems are always tense and tight groups engaged in war, rescue, martyrdom, or crisis, and the moral values expressed are simply those of that group. In such a society the terror is not for the common enemy, even when the enemy is or seems victorious, as in the extermination of the Jesuit missionaries or the crew of Franklin (a great Canadian theme that Pratt pondered but never completed). The real terror comes when the individual feels himself becoming an individual, pulling away from the group, losing the sense of driving power that the group gives him, aware of a conflict within himself far subtler than the struggle of morality against evil. It is much easier to multiply garrisons, and when that happens, something anti-cultural comes into Canadian life, a dominating herd-mind in which nothing original can grow. [. . .]

Canada, of course, or the place where Canada is, can supply distinctive settings and props to a writer who is looking for local colour. Tourist-writing has its own importance (*e.g., Maria Chapdelaine*), as has the use of Canadian history for purposes of romance, of which more later. But it would be an obvious fallacy to claim that the setting provided anything more than novelty. When Canadian writers are urged to use distinctively Canadian themes, the fallacy is less obvious, but still there. The forms of literature are autonomous: they exist within literature itself, and cannot be derived from any experience outside literature. What the Canadian writer finds in his experience and environment may be new, but it will be new only as content: the form of his expression of it can take shape only from what he has read, not from what he has experienced. The great technical experiments of Joyce and Proust in fiction, of Eliot and Hopkins in poetry, have resulted partly from profound literary scholarship, from seeing the formal possibilities inherent in the literature they have studied. A writer who is or who feels removed from his literary tradition tends rather to take over forms already in existence. We notice how often critics of Canadian fiction have occasion to remark that a novel contains a good deal of sincere feeling and accurate observation, but that it is spoiled by an unconvincing plot, usually one too violent or dependent on coincidence for such material. What has happened is that the author felt he could make a novel out of his knowledge and observation, but had no story in particular to tell. His material did not come to him in the form of a story, but as a consolidated chunk of experience, reflection, and sensibility. He had to invent a plot to put this material in causal shape (for writing, as Kafka says, is an art of causality), to pour the new wine of content into the old bottles of form. Even Grove works in this way, though Grove, by sheer dogged persistence, does get his action powerfully if ponderously moving.

Literature is conscious mythology: as society develops, its mythical stories become structural principles of storytelling, its mythical concepts, sun-gods and the like, become habits of metaphorical thought. In a fully mature literary tradition the writer enters into a structure of traditional stories and images. He often has the feeling, and says so, that he is not actively shaping his material at all, but is rather a place where a verbal structure is taking its own shape. If a novelist, he starts with a story-telling impetus; if a poet, with a metaphor-crystallizing impetus. Down to the beginning of the twentieth century at least, the Canadian who wanted to write started with a feeling of detachment from his literary tradition, which existed for him mainly in his school books. He had probably, as said above, been educated in a way that heavily stressed the conceptual and argumentative use of language. We have been shown how the Indians began with a mythology which included all the main elements of our own. It was, of course, impossible for Canadians to establish any real continuity with it: Indians, like the rest of the country, were seen as nineteenth-century literary conventions. Certain elements in Canadian culture, too, such as the Protestant revolutionary view of history, may have minimized the importance of the oral tradition in ballad and folk song, which seems to have survived best in Catholic communities. In Canada the mythical was simply the "prehistoric" (this word, we are told, is a Canadian coinage), and the writer had to attach himself to his literary tradition deliberately and voluntarily. And though this may be no longer true or necessary, attitudes surviving from an earlier period of isolation still have their influence.

The separation of subject and object is the primary fact of consciousness, for anyone so situated and so educated. Writing for him does not start with a rhythmical movement, or an impetus caught from or encouraged by a group of contemporaries: it starts with a reportage, a single mind reacting to what is set over against it. Such a writer does not naturally think metaphorically but descriptively; it seems obvious to him that writing is a form of self-expression dependent on the gathering of a certain amount of experience, granted some inborn sensitivity toward that experience. We note how many Canadian novelists have written only one novel, or only one good novel, how many Canadian poets have written only one good book of poems, generally their first. Even the dream of "the great Canadian novel," the feeling that somebody some day will write a Canadian fictional classic, assumes that whoever does it will do it only once. This is a characteristic of writers dominated by the conception of writing up experiences of observations: nobody has enough experience to keep on writing about it, unless his writing is an incidental commentary on a non-literary career. [. . .]

Reading through any good collection of modern Canadian poems or stories, we find every variety of tone, mood, attitude, technique, and setting. But there is a certain unity of impression one gets from it, an impression of gentleness and reasonableness, seldom difficult or greatly daring in its imaginative flights, the passion, whether of love or anger, held in check by something meditative. It is not easy to put the feeling in words, but if we turn to the issue of the *Tamarack Review* that was devoted to West Indian literature, or to the Hungarian poems translated by Canadians in the collection *The Plough and the Pen*, we can see by contrast something of both the strength and the limitations of the Canadian writers. They too have lived, if not in Arcadia, at any rate in a land where empty space and the pervasiveness of physical nature have impressed a pastoral quality on their minds. From the deer and fish in Isabella Crawford's "The Canoe" to the frogs and toads in Layton, from the white narcissus of Knister to the night-blooming cereus of Reaney, everything that is central in Canadian writing seems to be marked by the imminence of the natural world. The sense of this imminence organizes the mythology of Jay Macpherson; it is the sign in which Canadian soldiers conquer Italy in Douglas LePan's *The Net and the Sword*; it may be in the foreground, as in Alden Nowlan, or in the background, as in Birney; but it is always there.

To go on with this absorbing subject would take us into another book: *A Literary Criticism of Canada*, let us say. Here we can only sum up the present argument emblematically, with two famous primitive American paintings. One is "Historical Monument of the American Republic," by Erastus Salisbury Field. Painted in 1876 for the centennial of the Revolution, it is an encyclopaedic portrayal of events in American history, against a background of soaring towers, with clouds around their spires, and connected by railway bridges. It is a prophetic vision of the skyscraper cities of the future, of the tremendous technological will to power of our time and the civilization it has built, a civilization now gradually imposing a uniformity of culture and habits of life all over the globe. Because the United States is the most powerful centre of this civilization, we often say, when referring to its uniformity, that the world is becoming Americanized. But of course America itself is being Americanized in this sense, and the uniformity imposed on New Delhi or Singapore, or on Toronto and Vancouver, is no greater than that imposed on New Orleans or Baltimore. A nation so huge and so productive, however, is deeply committed to this growing technological uniformity, even though many tendencies may pull in other directions. Canada has participated to the full in the wars, economic expansions, technological achievements, and internal stresses of the modern world. Canadians seem well adjusted to the new world of technology and very efficient at handling it. Yet in the Canadian imagination there are deep reservations to this world as an end of life in itself, and the political separation of Canada has helped to emphasize these reservations in its literature.

English Canada began with the influx of defeated Tories after the American Revolution, and so, in its literature, with a strong anti-revolutionary bias. The Canadian radicalism that developed in opposition to Loyalism was not a revival of the American revolutionary spirit, but a quite different movement, which has something in common with the Toryism it opposed: one thinks of the Tory and radical elements in the social vision of William Cobbett, who also finds a place in the Canadian record. A revolutionary tradition is liable to two defects: to an undervaluing of history and an impatience with law, and we have seen how unusually strong the Canadian attachment to law and history has been. The attitude to things American represented by Haliburton is not, on the whole, hostile: it would be better described as non-committal, as when Sam Slick speaks of a Fourth of July as "a splendid spectacle; fifteen millions of freemen and three millions of slaves a-celebratin' the birthday of liberty." The strong romantic tradition in Canadian literature has much to do with its original conservatism. When more radical expressions begin to creep into Canadian writing, as in the poetry of Alexander McLachlan, there is still much less of the assumption that freedom and national independence are the same thing, or that the mercantilist Whiggery which won the American Revolution is necessarily the only emancipating force in the world. In some Canadian writers of our own time—I think particularly of Earle Birney's *Trial of a City* and the poetry of F.R. Scott—there is an opposition, not to the democratic but to the oligarchic tendencies in North American civilization, not to liberal but to laissez-faire political doctrine. Perhaps it is a little easier to see these distinctions from the vantage-point of a smaller country, even one which has, in its material culture, made the "American way of life" its own.

The other painting is the much earlier "The Peaceable Kingdom," by Edward Hicks, painted around 1830. Here, in the background, is a treaty between the Indians and the Quaker settlers under Penn. In the foreground is a group of animals, lions, tigers, bears, oxen, illustrating the prophecy of Isaiah about the recovery of innocence in nature. Like the animals of the Douanier Rousseau, they stare past us with a serenity that transcends consciousness. It is a pictorial emblem of what Grove's narrator was trying to find under the surface of America: the reconciliation of man with man and of man with nature: the mood of Thoreau's Walden retreat, of Emily Dickinson's garden, of Huckleberry Finn's raft, of the elegies of Whitman. This mood is closer to the haunting vision of a serenity that is both human and natural which we have been struggling to identify in the Canadian tradition. If we had to characterize a distinctive emphasis in that tradition, we might call it a quest for the peaceable kingdom.

The writers of the last decade, at least, have begun to write in a world which is post-Canadian, as it is post-American, post-British, and post everything except the world itself. There are no provinces in the empire of aeroplane and television, and no physical separation from the centres of culture, such as they are. Sensibility is no longer dependent on a specific environment or even on sense experience itself. A remark of one critic about Robert Finch illustrates a tendency which is affecting literature as well as painting: "the interplay of sense impressions is so complicated, and so exhilarating, that the reader receives no sense impression at all." Marshall McLuhan speaks of the world as reduced to a single gigantic primitive village, where everything has the same kind of immediacy. He speaks of the fears that so many intellectuals have of such a world, and remarks amiably: "Terror is the normal state of any oral society, for in it everything affects everything all the time." The Canadian spirit, to personify it as a single being dwelling in the country from the early voyages to the present, might well, reading this sentence, feel that this was where he came in. In other words, new conditions give the old ones a new importance, as what vanishes in one form reappears in another. The moment that the peaceable kingdom has been completely obliterated by its rival is the moment when it comes into the foreground again, as the eternal frontier, the first thing that the writer's imagination must deal with. Pratt's "The Truant," already referred to, foreshadows the poetry of the future, when physical nature has retreated to outer space and only individual and society are left as effective factors in the imagination. But the central conflict, and the moods in which it is fought out, are still unchanged.

One gets very tired, in old-fashioned biographies, of the dubious embryology that examines a poet's ancestry and wonders if a tendency to fantasy in him could be the result of an Irish great-grandmother. A reader may feel the same unreality in efforts to attach Canadian writers to a tradition made up of earlier writers whom they may not have read or greatly admired. I have felt this myself whenever I have written about Canadian literature. Yet I keep coming back to the feeling that there does seem to be such a thing as an imaginative continuum, and that writers are conditioned in their attitudes by their predecessors, or by the cultural climate of their predecessors, whether there is conscious influence or not. Again, nothing can give a writer's experience and sensitivity any form except the study of literature itself. In this study the great classics, "monuments of its own magnificence," and the best contemporaries have an obvious priority. The more such monuments or such contemporaries there are in a writer's particular cultural traditions, the more fortunate he is; but he needs those traditions in any case. He needs them most of all when what faces him seems so new as to threaten his identity. For present and future writers in Canada and their readers, what is important in Canadian literature, beyond the merits of the individual works in it, is the inheritance of the entire enterprise. The writers of Canada have identified the habits and attitudes of the country, as Fraser and Mackenzie have identified its rivers. They have also left an imaginative legacy of dignity and high courage.

3

FROM *Survival: A Thematic Guide to Canadian Literature**

Margaret Atwood

When I started to write this book I intended to produce a short, easy-to-use guide to Canadian literature, largely for the benefit of students and of those teachers in high schools, community colleges and universities who suddenly find themselves teaching a subject they have never studied: "Canlit." Through my own struggles with the same problem I knew there was a considerable amount of material already available, but it consisted primarily of all-inclusive historical surveys, individual biographies, or in-depth academic studies which discuss works often out of print. In Canada there are many authors and many books, but few obvious classics; as a result, those compiling sources or distributing information tend to fall back on long lists of writers and book-titles, among which the prospective reader or teacher must scrabble around and choose as best he may. But the inevitable question will be raised, sooner or later, in one or another of its forms: "Why are we studying *him* (instead of Faulkner)?" "Why do we have to read *this* (instead of Hermann Hesse)?" Or, in its true shape, "What's Canadian about Canadian literature, and why should we be bothered?" [. . .]

Until recently, reading Canadian literature has been for me and for everyone else who did it a personal interest, since it was not taught, required or even mentioned (except with derision) in the public sphere. Like many of those who encountered it before, say, 1965, my involvement has been as a writer, not as a student or teacher, and several though by no means all of the patterns I've found myself dealing with here were first brought to my attention by my own work. Also by my surprise at finding the concerns of that work shared by writers with whom—I found myself concluding—I seemed to participate in a cultural community that had never been defined for me. I don't talk much about my work in this book because I happen to believe that an author is always his own trickiest critic. However, I approach many of the patterns, and the problems connected with them, from the writer's point of view; which is perhaps the best one, since that's how the writers themselves approach them. The answer to the question, "What is there to read about in

---

* *Survival: A Thematic Guide to Canadian Literature* (Toronto: Anansi, 1972).

this country?" is really also an answer to the question, "What is there to write about in this country?"

Writing Canadian literature has been historically a very private act, one from which even an audience was excluded, since for a lot of the time there was no audience. Teaching it, however, is a political act. If done badly it can make people even more bored with their country than they already are; if done well, it may suggest to them *why* they have been taught to be bored with their country, and whose interests that boredom serves.

But back to my original question. The first part of that question, "What's Canadian about Canadian literature," is answered, I hope, by the rest of this book. The second part, "Why should we be bothered," shouldn't have to be answered at all because, in any self-respecting nation, it would never even be asked. But that's one of the problems: Canada *isn't* a self-respecting nation and the question does get asked. Therefore.

The answers you get from literature depend on the questions you pose. If you ask, "Why do writers write?" the answer will be psychological or biographical. If you ask, "*How* do they write?" you may get an answer something like "With a pencil" or "With pain," or you may get an answer that talks about how the books are put together, an answer that treats the book as a self-contained verbal pattern and talks about style or form. These are entirely legitimate questions; but the one I'm concerned with here is "What do writers write about?"

The character Stephen Dedalus in James Joyce's *Portrait of the Artist as a Young Man* looks at the flyleaf of his geography book and finds a list he has written there:

Stephen Dedalus
Class of Elements
Clongowes Wood College
Sallins
County Kildare
Ireland
Europe
The World
The Universe

That's a fairly inclusive list of everything it is possible for a human being to write about and therefore to read about. It begins with the personal, continues through the social or cultural or national and ends with "The Universe," the universal. Any piece of fiction or poetry may contain elements of all three areas, though the ratio may vary: a love lyric is more likely to be personal or universal than it is to be national, a novel may be about a family or about a man's life as a politician, and so forth. The tendency in Canada, at least in high school and university teaching, has been to emphasize the personal and the universal but to skip the national or cultural. This is like trying to teach human anatomy by looking only at the head and the feet. That's one reason for reading Canadian literature then; it gives you a more complete idea of how any literature is made: it's made by people living in a particular space at a particular time, and you can recognize that more easily if the space and the time are your own. If you read only the work of dead foreigners you will certainly reinforce the notion that literature can be written only by dead foreigners.

But there's another reason that has to do not with the reader as student of literature but with the reader as citizen. A piece of art, as well as being a creation to be enjoyed, can also be (as Germaine Warkentin suggests) a mirror. The reader looks at the mirror and sees not the writer but himself; and behind his own image in the foreground, a reflection of the world he lives in. If a country or a culture lacks such mirrors it has no way of knowing what it looks like; it must travel blind. If, as has long been the case in this country, the viewer is given a mirror that reflects not him but someone else, and told at the same time that the reflection he sees is himself, he will get a very distorted idea of what he is really like. He will also get a distorted idea of what other people are like: it's hard to find out who anyone else is until you have found out who *you* are. Self-knowledge, of course, can be painful, and the extent to which Canadian literature has been neglected in its home territory suggests, among other things, a fear on the part of Canadians of knowing who they are; while the large number of mirror and reflection images contained within that literature suggest a society engaged in a vain search for an image, a reflection that will answer it, like A.M. Klein's mad poet who "stares at a mirror all day long, as if / to recognize himself."

There are, of course, reflections of us to be found in places other than Canadian literature. There's the placid, jolly, woodcutting and woodchuck-eating "Canadian" in Thoreau's *Walden*; there's Edmund Wilson saying "In my youth, of the early nineteen-hundreds, we tended to imagine Canada as a kind of vast hunting preserve convenient to the United States." (Right on, Edmund.) In Malcolm Lowry's *Under the Volcano*, Canada is the protagonist's cool fantasy escape-land; if he can only make it there from steamy Mexico, everything will be all right. There's Shreve, the pinkish-grey Canadian roommate of Faulkner's Quentin in *Absalom, Absalom!* who is healthy, does exercises and plays Wedding Guest to Quentin's Ancient Mariner. And, for fun, there's the Canadian man who carries off the protagonist's girlfriend in Radclyffe Hall's *The Well of Loneliness*, the first Lesbian novel; he's muscular, competent, faceless and *heterosexual.* That's more or less the range of Canada as viewed by "international" literature: a place you escape to from "civilization," an unspoiled, uncorrupted place imagined as empty or thought of as populated by happy archaic peasants or YMCA instructors, quaint or dull or both. Watching made-in-Canada beer ads and tourist literature often gives you the uneasy feeling that the perpetrators are basing their images on these kinds of reflections because that's what everyone, inside and out, wants to believe. But Canadian literature itself tells a very different story.

To say that you must read your own literature to know who you are, to avoid being a sort of cultural moron, is not the same as saying that you should read nothing else, though the "internationalist" or Canada Last opponents of this notion sometimes think it is. A reader cannot live by Canlit alone, and it is a disservice to Canlit to try it. If a man from outer space were to be dropped on an island and supplied with all of Canadian literature and nothing else, he would be rendered completely incapable of deducing anything meaningful about Canadian literature because he would have nothing to compare it with; he would take it to be human literature *in toto.* The study of Canadian literature ought to be comparative, as should the study of any literature; it is by contrast that distinctive patterns show up most strongly. To know ourselves, we must know our own literature; to know ourselves accurately, we need to know it as part of literature as a whole.

But in Canada, as Frye suggests, the answer to the question "Who am I?" is at least partly the same as the answer to another question: "Where is here?" "Who am I?" is a question appropriate in countries where the environment, the "here," is already well-defined, so well-defined in fact that it may threaten to overwhelm the individual. In societies where everyone and everything has its place a person may have to struggle to separate himself from his social background, in order to keep from being just a function of the structure.

"Where is here?" is a different kind of question. It is what a man asks when he finds himself in unknown territory, and it implies several other questions. Where is this place in relation to other places? How do I find my way around in it? If the man is really lost he may also wonder how he got "here" to begin with, hoping he may be able to find the right path or possibly the way out by retracing his steps. If he is unable to do this he will have to take stock of what "here" has to offer in the way of support for human life and decide how he should go about remaining alive. Whether he survives or not will depend partly on what "here" really contains—whether it is too hot, too cold, too wet or too dry for him—and partly on his own desires and skills—whether he can utilize the resources available, adapt to what he can't change, and keep from going crazy. There may be other people "here" already, natives who are cooperative, indifferent or hostile. There may be animals, to be tamed, killed and eaten, or avoided. If, however, there is too large a gap between our hero's expectations and his environment he may develop culture shock or commit suicide.

There's a good moment in Carol Bolt's play *Buffalo Jump:* a high school teacher in the thirties makes his students recite the names of all the wives of Henry the Eighth while a protest march is going past the window. He tells them they aren't in school to watch parades, which just about sums up the approach to Canadian history and culture that prevailed for many decades: history and culture were things that took place elsewhere, and if you saw them just outside the window you weren't supposed to look.

The wives of Henry the Eighth may be taken as standing for the deluge of values and artefacts flowing in from outside, from "there"; America, England or France. The values and artefacts—and they could as easily be symbolized by comic books, portraits of the Queen, The Ed Sullivan Show or marches on Ottawa (!) to stop the war in Vietnam—imply that "there" is always more important than "here" or that "here" is just another, inferior, version of "there"; they render invisible the values and artefacts that actually exist "here," so that people can look at a thing without really seeing it, or look at it and mistake it for something else. A person who is "here" but would rather be somewhere else is an exile or a prisoner; a person who is "here" but *thinks* he is somewhere else is insane.

But when you are here and don't know where you are because you've misplaced your landmarks or bearings, then you need not be an exile or a madman: you are simply lost. Which returns us to our image of the man in an unknown territory. Canada is an unknown territory for the people who live in it, and I'm not talking about the fact that you may not have taken a trip to the Arctic or to Newfoundland, you may not have explored—as the travel folders have it—This Great Land of Ours. I'm talking about Canada as a state of mind, as the space you inhabit not just with your body but with your head. It's that kind of space in which we find ourselves lost.

What a lost person needs is a map of the territory, with his own position marked on it so he can see where he is in relation to everything else. Literature is not only a mirror; it is also a map, a geography of the mind. Our literature is one such map, if we can learn to read it as *our* literature, as the product of who and where we have been. We need such a map desperately, we need to know about here, because here is where we live. For the members of a country or a culture, shared knowledge of their place, their here, is not a luxury but a necessity. Without that knowledge we will not survive. [. . .]

* * *

I'd like to begin with a sweeping generalization and argue that every country or culture has a single unifying and informing symbol at its core. (Please don't take any of my oversimplifications as articles of dogma which allow of no exceptions; they are proposed simply to create vantage points from which the literature may be viewed.) The symbol, then—be it word, phrase, idea, image, or all of these—functions like a system of beliefs (it *is* a system of beliefs, though not always a formal one) which holds the country together and helps the people in it to co-operate for common ends. Possibly the symbol for America is The Frontier, a flexible idea that contains many elements dear to the American heart: it suggests a place that is *new*, where the old order can be discarded (as it was when America was instituted by a crop of disaffected Protestants, and later at the time of the Revolution); a line that is always expanding, taking in or "conquering" ever-fresh virgin territory (be it The West, the rest of the world, outer space, Poverty or The Regions of the Mind); it holds out a hope, never fulfilled but always promised, of Utopia, the perfect human society. Most twentieth century American literature is about the gap between the promise and the actuality, between the imagined ideal Golden West or City Upon a Hill, the model for all the world postulated by the Puritans, and the actual squalid materialism, dotty small town, nasty city, or redneck-filled outback. Some Americans have even confused the actuality with the promise: in that case Heaven is a Hilton hotel with a coke machine in it.

The corresponding symbol for England is perhaps The Island, convenient for obvious reasons. In the seventeenth century a poet called Phineas Fletcher wrote a long poem called *The Purple Island*, which is based on an extended body-as-island metaphor, and, dreadful though the poem is, that's the kind of island I mean: island-as-body, self-contained, a Body Politic, evolving organically, with a hierarchical structure in which the King is the Head, the statesmen the hands, the peasants or farmers or workers the feet, and so on. The Englishman's home as his castle is the popular form of this symbol, the feudal castle being not only an insular structure but a self-contained microcosm of the entire Body Politic.

The central symbol for Canada—and this is based on numerous instances of its occurrence in both English and French Canadian literature—is undoubtedly Survival, *La Survivance*. Like the Frontier and The Island, it is a multi-faceted and adaptable idea. For early explorers and settlers, it meant bare survival in the face of "hostile" elements and/or natives: carving out a place and a way of keeping alive. But the word can also suggest survival of a crisis or disaster, like a hurricane or a wreck, and many Canadian poems have this kind of survival as a theme; what you might call "grim" survival as opposed to "bare" survival. For French Canada after the English took over it became cultural survival, hanging on as a people, retaining a religion and a language under an alien government. And in English Canada now while the Americans are taking over it is acquiring a similar meaning. There is another use of the word as well: a survival can be a vestige of a vanished order which has managed to persist after its time is past, like a primitive reptile. This version crops up in Canadian thinking too, usually among those who believe that Canada is obsolete.

But the main idea is the first one: hanging on, staying alive. Canadians are forever taking the national pulse like doctors at a sickbed: the aim is not to see whether the patient will live well but simply whether he will live at all. Our central idea is one which generates, not the excitement and sense of adventure or danger which The Frontier holds out, not the smugness and/or sense of security, of everything in its place, which The Island can offer, but an almost intolerable anxiety. Our stories are likely to be tales not of those who made it but of those who made it back, from the awful experience—the North, the snowstorm, the sinking ship—that killed everyone else. The survivor has no triumph or victory but the fact of his survival; he has little after his ordeal that he did not have before, except gratitude for having escaped with his life.

A preoccupation with one's survival is necessarily also a preoccupation with the obstacles to that survival. In earlier writers these obstacles are external—the land, the climate, and so forth. In later writers the obstacles tend to become both harder to identify and more internal; they are no longer obstacles to physical survival but obstacles to what we may call spiritual survival, to life as anything more than a minimally human being. Sometimes fear of these obstacles becomes itself the obstacle, and a character is paralyzed by terror (either of what he thinks is threatening him from the outside, or of elements in his own nature that threaten him from within). It may even be life itself that he fears; and when life becomes a threat to life, you have a moderately vicious circle. If a man feels he can survive only by amputating himself, turning himself into a cripple or a eunuch, what price survival? [. . .]

* * *

Let us suppose, for the sake of argument, that Canada as a whole is a victim, or an "oppressed minority," or "exploited." Let us suppose in short that Canada is a colony. A partial definition of a colony is that it is a place from which a profit is made, but *not by the people who live there*: the major profit from a colony is made in the center of the empire. That's what colonies are for, to make money for the "mother country," and that's what—since the days of Rome and, more recently, of the Thirteen Colonies—they have always been for. Of course there are cultural side-effects which are often identified as "the colonial mentality," and it is these which are examined here. [. . .]

PART II
THE COMMONWEALTH CONTEXT

4

"ANOTHER PREFACE TO AN UNCOLLECTED ANTHOLOGY: CANADIAN CRITICISM IN A COMMONWEALTH CONTEXT"*

R. T. Robertson

Most Canadian literature studied at University appears in Canadian literature courses. But in about half of the thirty courses offered in Commonwealth literature there is a sprinkling of Canadian texts. Some of these are anthologies which, together with anthologies of Australian, African and Indian writing, make up a sort of multi-volume anthology of Commonwealth literature. There is no single anthology of that literature in existence, although there are anthologies such as Howard Sergeant's and W.H. New's of Commonwealth poetry and stories.

Responding to criticism of the use of anthologies in university courses (during the ACUTE programme at the Learned Societies meeting), R.E. Watters reminded younger teachers that when the *Canadian Anthology* first appeared in 1955 it was the only available source for much of its material. It seems that a discipline in the making needs a primitive tool like the anthology. How that tool assists the process is indeed a fascinating area of study, as Alec Lucas has recently remarked. Equally fascinating in Commonwealth literary studies is the way a development in one national literature will recur later in another, and in the general discipline now aborning in those thirty (or so) courses. The itch to anthologise is beginning to infect teachers of Commonwealth literature, and while we are not likely to break out in a rash of anthologies we are certainly casting round for a model we can imitate. At which point Klinck and Watters enters Commonwealth literary studies not as a text to be used in our courses but as a form more advanced than any available in other national literatures. Not only does it include poetry and prose; it is a prime teaching text because it adds a full bibliography and "Recent Selected Criticism." Its form tells us something about the shape an anthology of Commonwealth literature might assume.

Let our model be *Canadian Anthology*, and now let us turn to the question of which Canadian criticism would be selected for a Commonwealth anthology. Ignoring the business of which literature or bibliographical entries would be carried over from the *Canadian Anthology* (or any other Canadian anthology), let us see how we would go about selecting from the growing

---

*   *ARIEL* 4.3 (1973): 70-81.

mass of Canadian criticism in order to place that selection in the context of Commonwealth literature and literary studies—a context in which the criticism at least has not so far appeared.

The grounds for our selection would determine our choice of articles and extracts, and establishing our criteria is more interesting than following it. We appear to have two criteria. Most editors assure us in their prefaces that they follow one criterion only: they have chosen the best; then they cite the awkward realities that made their selection fall short of its noble goal. But since we are contemplating a hypothetical—perhaps even a mythical—anthology, we can ignore practical considerations. Indeed, given the mass of Canadian critical writing listed in Klinck and Watters and noted by Brandon Conron, our most practical first step would be to find a way through the forest to the tall timber.

Our first criterion appears to be that of all editors: we can select the best Canadian criticism of Canadian literature, the canonical pieces whose status is attested by the frequency of their reprinting in existing anthologies of Canadian criticism and their common citation in studies and theses. Lacking a history or survey or even a single competent study of Canadian criticism, we probably need a computer to discover those pieces; and we might end up with the critical equivalent of "In Flanders Fields" or "The Cremation of Sam McGee."

The second criterion would be to select that Canadian criticism of Canadian literature which illuminates at one and the same time the national literature and Commonwealth literature as a whole and which appears to be talking about Canadian literature but to the discerning eye is *applicable* to Commonwealth literature. Our two lines of choice, then, appear to be determined by a canonical or a comparative criterion. But that is an illusion: the best Canadian criticism—and this is why it is the best—is talking ostensibly about Canadian literature but really about Commonwealth literature.

Such an assumption is the first premise of Commonwealth literary studies—that there is a Commonwealth dimension to the better writing, creative and critical, in any national literature in English. It may even derive from early Canadian critics; certainly it has been occasionally entertained by them. From the industry of Commonwealth scholars in Canada today we can trace a direct line back to Claude Bissell's "A Common Ancestry: Literature in Australia and Canada" which was prompted by a visit Down Under but inherits (possibly unawares) W.D. Lighthall's tentative and gorgeous comparison of Australian and Canadian poetry: "Australian rhyme is a poetry of the *horse*, Canadian, of the *canoe*" (xxiii). At the recent ACUTE programme on "Canadian Literature in Commonwealth Anthologies" Clara Thomas pointed out that Sir John G. Bourinot felt a similar relationship between the two countries in the 1880's, a relationship expressed in Lighthall's terms, "daughter-nation" and "sister-dominion."

This intermittent consciousness of kinship has blossomed into the studies of Commonwealth literature by R.L. McDougall, R.E. Watters, John P. Matthews, Edgar Wright, D.G. Killam, Margaret Laurence, Bruce Nesbitt, Grant McGregor, Patricia Morley, Adrian Roscoe, Barry Argyle, W.H. New and others, all of which have been produced in Canada in the last fifteen years. Such industry springs from Lighthall's unprepossessing acorn; but the habit persists of referring occasionally to a Commonwealth parallel in order to make a point about Canadian literature. Northrop Frye in his Conclusion to the *Literary History* referred to an extract from George Lamming's *Pleasures of Exile* which appeared in the West Indian number of *Tamarack Review* in order to make a point about the rapid development of genres in Canadian literary history (16).

This habit (if we may call it that) is a matter of necessity. There is no other literature which shows the similarity the critic needs in order to support his contention about a particular aspect of Canadian literature. For Commonwealth literary scholars it is a reassuring habit: it suggests on the one hand that there is a latent awareness of the Commonwealth dimension of Canadian literature and literary studies waiting to be stimulated, and on the other that it may be just as valid in Commonwealth studies to find the support we need for our contentions in Canadian criticism, which is thus the prime reason for including it in our Commonwealth anthology. And if all this sounds as if the subtitle of this article should be "Canadian Cousins," even for that quaint term we have Frye's precedent in the "Preface to an Uncollected Anthology" when he suggested that Tom the Cat from Zanzibar is "the Canadian cousin of Roy Campbell's flaming terrapin" (523).

More important, however, for our immediate purpose of establishing the ground-rules for selecting Canadian criticism are not the publications of Commonwealth scholars in Canada or the teasing allusions by Canadian scholars but two other aspects of Canadian criticism which give it a paramount position in all Commonwealth literary studies. These are the formal and conceptual models which are applicable to those studies.

The title of this paper imitates that of Frye's "Preface" and thus alters its nature from that of a standard piece in Canadian criticism to that of a formal model in Commonwealth studies. Similarly the *Canadian Anthology* serves as a formal model to frame up our ideas about a Commonwealth anthology, and the fact that Frye's "Preface" appears in the *Anthology* suggests that both the form of and the ideas expressed in the critical selections in the *Anthology* may serve as two kinds of models for a Commonwealth anthology.

The reason for accepting our formal and conceptual models from Canadian and not from Australian or other criticism—that is, the justification for asserting the paramountcy of Canadian criticism in Commonwealth studies—lies deeper than the happy accident of Frye's "Preface" appearing in Klinck and Watters' anthology. That anthology is probably derived from models in the United States, and, as the *Literary History of Canada* imitates the form of the *Literary History of the United States*, the reason for the imitation lies in the absence of such models in British literary studies and practice. The American model and the Canadian imitation are New World responses to New World literature, and the imitation in turn of a Canadian model is appropriate for an anthology of New World literature in English, which is what our Commonwealth anthology would be in part.

It should be noted that the *Canadian Anthology* has also become a model in Canada. Its innovation in including critical material in the second revised edition of 1966 was a response to the "remarkable growth" in scholarly attention paid to Canadian literature since 1955 as the editors noted in their preface (as well as being, as I contend, an imitation of an American model.) And that innovation (and that growth) is reflected in two recent anthologies, *The Evolution of Canadian Literature in English* edited by Mary Jane Edwards, George Parker and Paul Denham, and the *Oxford Anthology of Canadian Literature* edited by Robert Weaver and William Toye.

Both of these anthologies offer different formal models. The first is in four volumes; the desperate Commonwealth anthologist, trying to cope with the geographical spread and diversity of his material, is tempted by a multi-volume solution. The second ignores chronology in favour of an alphabetical order of authors, and this too would solve some problems in a Commonwealth ordering. But the critical selections in each also touch on Commonwealth concerns and thus qualify as conceptual models we could possibly include in our anthology. The *Evolution* anthology includes (in the third volume) W.P. Wilgar's essay "Poetry and the Divided Mind in Canada" (1944) which is an early statement of the "divided mind" found elsewhere in the Commonwealth. It is, indeed, a Commonwealth phenomenon: the greater response of young students in Commonwealth countries to American than to British poetry, a change of taste that has affected the writing as well as the reading of poetry throughout the Commonwealth in the post-war years. The *Oxford Anthology*, the latest in a long list of services performed by that Press for the national literatures of the Commonwealth, contains Frye's preface to *The Bush Garden*, a title Frye says is taken from Margaret Atwood's *Journals of Susanna Moodie* and ultimately from Mrs. Moodie, a Canadian writer whose proper dimension is obviously the colonial period of Commonwealth literature where she joins Lady Barker, Lady Anne Barnard, Mary Fullerton and many others in delineating the frontier experience of the English-speaking people in the nineteenth century which is the historical basis for considering Commonwealth literature as a single body of writing. The term "bush," after all, is pure Commonwealth, not mere Canadian; the kinship in the use of the term gives us a sort of composite of Moodie, Frye and Tutuola that would read "Roughing it in the Bush Garden of Ghosts."

The conceptual models we are seeking in Canadian criticism may well be found in the formal models we propose to imitate, provided we can show the applicability of those concepts to Commonwealth literature. The 1966 edition of the *Canadian Anthology* contains twelve pieces in its "Recent Selected Criticism." At first sight the general rather than the particular essays seem more apt to our purpose, which decision would exclude those on Callaghan, Pratt, Leacock and others. And on Sarah Binks? Here we should be careful. The particular essays are useful to the Commonwealth reader in grappling with Pratt or Leacock but the reader would have to see their Commonwealth dimension for himself. Paul Hiebert, on the other hand, is describing a Commonwealth phenomenon, and the Commonwealth reader greets it with a shriek of recognition.

Sarah Binks is a fable in the form of a satire of the local poetess and the local literary historian, of F.R. Scott's Miss Crotchett and Hiebert's Miss Drool. Given its double Commonwealth dimension, it is the latter which is the more interesting since it is comic where the fate of the local poetess is tragic—witness Sarah's end. Hiebert satirizes the two prime assumptions of the local literary historian; the first is that Sarah lived in "the halcyon days . . . the golden days" of a perfect post-pioneer period, the curious moment of rest after the labour of settlement that is common to all national literatures in English and probably most finely used by Katherine Mansfield. In *Sarah Binks* it is a short period of thirty years which the local historian generally calls an "era"; this magnification is commonly recognised in Commonwealth studies as "the Mariposa syndrome." The second assumption reinforces the telescoped historicity of the first: that Sarah is "a product of her soil . . . an expression of her environment," which is the easiest and most obvious way of validating the magnification. We know the distant source of that validation—through Taine back to Buckle—and we feel there is something to it but we hesitate to assert it as confidently as Sarah's editor. Nevertheless, every assertion of national identity in all early national literary studies will be found to depend on this assumption. It is thus common in Commonwealth literary studies but it has another applicability; *Sarah Binks* is the Awful Example of the Double Standard in operation, about which graduate students ambitious of becoming, say, the Heavysege man in Amcan are still warned by their professors of Renaissance Studies.

Sarah Binks also illustrates the conditions of local literary studies. We have all had to deal with our Horace B. Marrowfat, B.A., Professor Emeritus of English and Swimming of St Midget's College, but nowhere else has he been so gloriously pilloried. And we have all worked in the local equivalent of the Binksian Collection of the Provincial Archives. What Sarah's editor says of his labours is both wildly funny and sadly true of Canadian and Commonwealth studies: "The papers which have appeared from time to time have been fragmentary . . . much inference has been published as fact. Many of the details of [the] life are still vague and have to be filled in" (xix). (Which sounds very like pre-Spettigue Grove.) In both its generous assumptions and its portrait of preposterous activity *Sarah Binks* is the ultimate and artistic portrait of all early Commonwealth studies. It is, indeed, the magma of our discipline and the Commonwealth editor ignores its message at his peril.

In another way Marshall McLuhan is just as magmatic to our discipline. Klinck and Watters reprint McLuhan's "Culture Without Literacy" (1953). Such a title in the hands of, say, A.D. Hope would immediately suggest an attack on the so-called culture, including the literature, of Australia, since both terms are heavily loaded in critical discussion in that country. The title would seem to describe the milieu of an Australian Sarah. McLuhan of course has a very different argument, so different as to be revolutionary in a Commonwealth context. Including both Hiebert's introduction and McLuhan's article would thus have different effects in a Commonwealth context: the first would demonstrate the affinity of Canadian critics with their Commonwealth cousins; the second would show the difference and support the argument for the paramountcy of Canadian critics in the family or tribe.

But neither applicability or relationship quite illustrates what I mean by a "conceptual model"—an idea which would stimulate critical thinking about Commonwealth literature if we simply substituted "Commonwealth" for "Canadian" wherever the latter term occurred in the model article. If we look deeper into McLuhan's "Culture Without Literacy" we can see two ways in which he is "magmatic" to our subject. His argument about the effect of imposing a literate book and print medium on an oral culture amounts to a thesis about the first two stages in the process of making national literatures: in the first they were imposed on and largely obliterated the native oral culture wherever they settled (although not always permanently); in the second stage their first intention and reason for existence was to rescue and preserve in literate form what was circulating in oral fashion—as I believe *Sarah Binks* first circulated. Again, McLuhan reminds us that the bothersome diversity of the literatures that make up Commonwealth literature is an aspect of the multilateral diversity that McLuhan insists is a consequence of an instantaneous communications medium.

It would be dangerous, of course, simply to borrow McLuhan directly in Commonwealth studies. Perhaps the best effect of including an extract from his work as a conceptual model in our anthology would be that through him we can meet the Canadian thinkers who made McLuhan possible—George Grant, for instance, who is represented in the *Evolution* anthology, Innis and Cochrane—and who in turn form the core of an exciting Commonwealth critical anthology, Eli Mandel's *Contexts of Canadian Criticism*.

We would have to include Mandel's introduction to his anthology because of its very innocence of a Commonwealth context to Canadian criticism; it outlines a formal model and summarizes the conceptual models inside that form, and in both respects demonstrates the applicability of the best Canadian criticism to Commonwealth literature. The most fruitful hypothesis about the making of *Commonwealth* criticism, as distinct from criticism of a national literature, is in the relationship of Mandel's three contexts to form a field or total context for a Commonwealth criticism.

Of Mandel's three contexts, the first ("Social and Historical") obviously offers a Canadian equivalent or model to Commonwealth literary study and the theory of Commonwealth literatures. It has given rise to a whole school of Australian critics who in turn are opposed by a formalist group who emphasize the literary nature of Australian literature as against the Binksian environmentalists. Mandel's second context ("Theoretical") shows how to escape this fruitless antagonism by rethinking the nature of literature. Thus the selection from Frye, McLuhan and Sparshott which constitutes Mandel's second context offers also certain conceptual models for rethinking the nature of Commonwealth literature, such as along mythopoeic lines. If we were to include Mandel's selection in a Commonwealth anthology it would afford a third dimension in addition to those of literature and of Canadian literature. From this stems the relevance of Frye and others to that middle ground of Commonwealth literature, the immediate family of literatures which is the context of Canadian literature.

Mandel's most interesting context is the third, "Patterns of Criticism." Until we can objectively study what affects or determines the response of the national literary critic to his subject matter (and see those responses as constituting both a national and general pattern), then the whole body of critical writing on individual writers as well as all the general commentary remains unexamined. It is mainly for this reason that the critical section of our Commonwealth anthology should contain not the best articles on White, Curnow, Achebe, Gordimer, Lamming or Narayan but those general papers whose ideas would stimulate thinking about Commonwealth literature and thus make the anthology a tool in the evolution of the discipline.

In reaching through the *Canadian Anthology* to the *Contexts of Canadian Criticism* we recognise that the former has performed one of the services an anthology offers, that of introducing us to the subject it represents. But it is more important to see that the form of the model is itself a theoretical statement, a conceptual model, and not just a convenient pattern to imitate. This is not to dismiss the value of studies of individual writers or general commentary on a whole national literature, such as the Frye "Preface." We can find conceptual models in both kinds of criticism but also in the critical act performed by the editor of an anthology. And we would thus expect our Commonwealth anthology also to make a statement about Commonwealth literature by virtue of the shape or form or order it eventually adopts.

Our Commonwealth anthology, then, would not be a slavish or knavish imitation of the *Canadian Anthology* but a reflection in Commonwealth studies of the achievement of Canadian scholars in using the anthology to shape statements or hypotheses about the nature of their literature. In return, it is possible that some benefit would flow to Canadian scholars from their inclusion in our anthology. The strategy Frye uses in the "Preface" (and elsewhere) is to begin with a general proposition about literature, demonstrate its value for the Canadian matter under consideration, and conclude with the reverse demonstration—the relationship of that matter to literature. In his deft moves from one pole to the other one senses the lack of a middle range or resting point, a body of literature larger than Canadian yet showing an affinity to or possessing a cousinship with it wherein Frye's ideas and conclusions could be tested. This, indeed, is a missing dimension in Canadian criticism as a whole and when found it could settle the whole business of identity. The discussion of identity is not dead nor will it die until identity can be defined within its true context, that of Commonwealth literature. And that move might correspond to the political reality of our time as Canada finds its world identity as a nation assuming the leading role in the Commonwealth of Nations.

Works Cited

Bissell, Claude. "A Common Ancestry: Literature in Australia and Canada." *University of Toronto Quarterly* 25.2 (1956): 131-42.

Conron, Brandon. "A Bountiful Choice of Critics in English Canadian Literature." *Literary Half-Yearly* 13.2 (1972): 44-55.

Edwards, Mary Jane, et al., eds. *The Evolution of Canadian Literature in English.* 4 vols. Toronto: Holt, Rinehart, 1973.

Frye, Northrop. Conclusion. *Literary History of Canada: Canadian Literature in English.* Ed. Carl F. Klinck. Toronto: U of Toronto P, 1965. 821-49.

—. "Preface to an Uncollected Anthology." Klinck and Watters 515-23.

Hiebert, Paul. Introduction. *Sarah Binks.* Toronto: McClelland, 1964. xv-xxi.

Klinck, C.F., and R.E. Watters, eds. *Canadian Anthology.* Toronto: Gage, 1955.

Lighthall, W.D., ed. Introduction. *Songs of the Great Dominion: Voices from the Forests and Waters, the Settlements and Cities of Canada.* London: W. Scott, 1889. xxi-xxxvii.

Lucas, Alec. "The Anthology: A Notable and Unacclaimed Achievement in Canadian Literature." *Literary Half-Yearly* 13.2 (1972): 111-19.

Mandel, Eli. *Contexts of Canadian Criticism.* Chicago: U of Chicago P, 1971.

Weaver, Robert, and William Toye, eds. *The Oxford Anthology of Canadian Literature.* Toronto: Oxford UP, 1973.

5

EDITORIAL TO THE *Journal of Canadian Fiction**

John Moss

The criticism in this issue is a departure from our usual fare. Occasionally we have focussed on a few writers or on a region or a particular period of Canadian literature, but this is the first time we have extended our scope beyond the borders of Canada. For many of our readers, this will be an introduction to the literatures of the British Commonwealth. For all, it will draw attention to a wider and more varied context within which to see ourselves. Other Commonwealth literatures are no more universal than our own but their specifics are quite different. For this reason, perhaps, they are particularly attractive to us. Presented here is an eclectic sampling, with the hope that it will stimulate interest in these other literatures and a renewed interest in our own from another perspective.

* * *

Countries of the British Commonwealth outside of the United Kingdom, to marvelously different degrees, share in the geographical dislocation of language and history. Whether colonial in the past—Canada, Australia and New Zealand—or colonized—the remainder, where incomers could not displace the indigenous peoples, so undertook to govern them instead—whether colonial or colonized in the past, each country in the Commonwealth struggles now to discover and rediscover an identity native to its own place. This does not mean a rejection of British heritage: it means coming to terms with it and with the illusions it has nurtured.

Language, like history, is a phenomenon of geography, born of human experience in a particular place through a period of time. The variables are human and temporal: location is constant. History and language both endure a sea-change when transported abroad. The history is no longer lived within, no longer a context of time. It becomes a linear sequence abstracting reality into an amorphous and alien past, and another history into which its facts are absorbed grows out of the new experience. Similarly, the language ceases to be mental environment and becomes only a means of communication, until conditions of the new place (new from the point of view

* *Journal of Canadian Fiction* 3.4 (1975): 1-2.

of the history and the language) permeate both vocabulary and linguistic structures.

It is an empirical distortion to consider language and history as the common factors amongst such a diverse group of nations as exist in the Commonwealth. Rather, their dislocation is what these countries have in common. It is not surprising, then, that Britain should be so often excluded from Commonwealth studies as somehow an outsider. And, of course, the United States is a case apart, for the dislocation is ancillary at best to the dramatic caesura of revolution. Nigeria and New Zealand, on the other hand, both belong to the Commonwealth and they have quite different histories, even where they appear to merge. The British past contributing to the existence of modern New Zealand is not the past that contributed to bringing about today's Nigeria. Present perspectives clearly alter the structure of history, altering the significance of various events and their interrelationships as they are seen to lead in one direction or another. Less obviously, the English language of Nigeria is not the English language of New Zealand. The differences are both subtle and profound. And the English language of Canada is quite different again. The fact that we are able to communicate with others within the Commonwealth should not mislead us into thinking we therefore understand them. We are not a community in common but a community of differences— though a community, nonetheless.

If the language variance were just a matter of simple vocabulary, it would be of little significance. Words are flexible but so is our capacity to learn. The word "snow," for instance, will evoke quite different responses in an Englishman and in a Canadian or a West Indian. Descriptive words like "autumnal," relative words like "cold," naming words like "garden" or "house," action words like "swim," all sorts of words by the thousands produce quite different image clusters from place to place throughout the Commonwealth. Although their dictionary definitions may remain the same. But from each of our Commonwealth perspectives we sort out appropriate meanings for ourselves and, as we learn and relearn to live within the transported language, the words become ours. Idiomatic expressions grow around us that belong to us alone. "Razzed," "rooted" and "shagged" are vulgarisms in the West Indies, Australia and Canada, respectively, but not outside these places. Across this idiom gap a complex vocabulary develops that is native or indigenous and only has meaning elsewhere through intellectual abstraction or through art.

In this respect, the language of the formerly colonized countries is infinitely rich and vital, refreshed by the words and syntax and ways of thinking and feeling of other languages, some of which evolved in these places while others, like the English they infiltrate, were brought from abroad. The implosive density of language that is Wilson Harris's genius speaks of his native Guyana the way no abstract study nor descriptive essay possibly could. The ingenuous dignity of Chinua Achebe's prose tells more of his ancestral heritage than all the histories of Nigeria. These and other writers infuse a language that is alien to their place with all that in their sensibilities is natural to that place, transmuting geography, mythology, collective memory into linguistic phenomena.

The case of the post-colonial countries is another thing. Indigenous cultures have exerted little influence except in stories of ignominy and through the appropriation of place names and the like. The language has been more affected by geography, by climatic conditions and the apparently untrammeled lay of the land. Not having had to submerge identities inimical to the British way, we have emerged from the past with fewer resources properly felt to be our own. As nations of immigrants, we—and Canada, in particular, with our more diverse ethnic make-up—have incorporated once alien words and ways of thinking into our vocabulary, even when we have most resisted the traditions they represent. More importantly, we have continuously exploited our histories in these places in search of better ways in which to express and understand what we are. In earlier times our writers romanticized the past because that was the current mode but also because romance was less threatening to the colonial connection. Now, and in the last few decades, they have tried to draw that past into the present in search of moral analogies which reflect our truer and otherwise hidden natures. Place imposes meaning on language and on literature, but the past, redeemed, shapes them both in our image.

Our writers in Canada respond to the felt dislocation of language and history as spokesmen for the common sensibility. We all live with the effects of the dislocation, but it is the artist, and the writer in particular, who rises to meet the challenge it generates, to resolve the anxiety it sustains. All art in Canada, as in these other countries, in some way struggles to answer or at least clarify the questions that are a part of our sense of identity. The best of our writers have been and continue to be intensely aware of place as they force a fusion between a language that is essentially alien and the surroundings within which they so consciously live. What Walt Whitman did with a vengeance for the United States as a primary purpose, our writers do reflexively as they pursue less rhetorical ends. As they define the nature of their world, they redefine the language they use, altering its structures and vocabulary to make it adequate to their artistic purpose.

The process of this response is what Canadian writers share with others in the Commonwealth. The dissociation engendered by variations of the English language spoken in common and by the various relationships to a British historical vortex is inseparable from the artist's essential experience of himself. As in the theory of an infinitely expanding universe, the farther these countries move away from one another, the more important their association with each other becomes. This association and the necessity of the mutual understanding it implies are maintained in good part by another, more select (or, at least, more self-selecting), community of artists, of writers, who can make of their own experience a vision of private and universal reality which, paradoxically, draws them together as it defines and separates. Each of our perspectives within the Commonwealth becomes clarified as we share in the experience of the others and in the illusions of language and history through which they experience themselves.

PART III
WHAT IS CANADIAN POSTCOLONIALISM?

6

"Cadence, Country, Silence: Writing in Colonial Space"*[1]

Dennis Lee

What am I doing when I write?

I don't know.

A hockey player may understand very little about the principles of anatomy. But he gets his body across the ice somehow.

What am I doing when I write? The question is too important to be discussing at a writers' conference, even this one. For myself, I write to find out—among other things—what it would be to write authentically. The question is posed by the writing to be done, and it is answered—sometimes—in terms of the writing *as* it is done. There is very little of me left over to analyse what is going on.

Hence I have little theory to offer, and not much analysis. But it is still possible to make friendly noises—in much the same spirit as when one is lifting a heavy load with someone else, or moving a piano or making love. My noises fall into three groups.

1. CADENCE

Most of my life as a writer is spent listening in to a cadence which is a kind of taut cascade, a luminous tumble. If I withdraw from immediate contact with things around me I can sense it churning, flickering, dancing, locating things in more shapely relation to one another without robbing them of themselves. I say it is present continuously, but certainly I spend days on end without noticing it. I hear it more clearly because I have recognised it in Hölderlin or Henry Moore, but I don't think it originates in their work. I think they heeded it too.

What I hear is initially without content; but when the poem does come, the content must accord with the cadence I have been overhearing or I cannot make it. (I speak of "hearing" cadence, but in fact I am baffled by how to

* *Open Letter* 2.6 (1973): 34-53; rpt. *Boundary 2* 3.1 (1974): 151-68. [Editor's note: I have used the *Boundary 2* essay as my copy-text for this reprinting. A substantially revised and updated version of this essay appears in Lee's essay collection *Body Music* (Toronto: Anansi, 1998), 3-25.]

describe it. There is no auditory sensation—I don't hallucinate; yet it is like sensing a continuous, changing tremour with one's ear and one's whole body at the same time. It seems very matter-of-fact, yet I do not know the name of the sense with which I perceive it.)

More and more I sense this cadence as presence—though it may take 50 or 100 revisions before a poem enacts it—I sense it as presence, both outside myself and inside my body opening out and trying to get into words. What is it? I can convey some portion of that by pointing to things I have already written, saying "Listen to the cadence here, and here—no, listen to the deeper cadence in which the poem is locally sustained." But the cadence of the poems I have written is such a small and often mangled fraction of what I hear, it tunes out so many wave-lengths of that massive, infinitely fragile polyphony, that I frequently despair. And often it feels perverse to ask what is cadence, when it is all I can manage to heed it.

Have I stressed enough that I am not making an ideal statement? This is not what I think poets *should* be confronted with; in fact I had seldom heard of it until it started up, almost out of my range of perception, 8 or 10 years ago—not through drugs, as it happens—and now it is what surrounds me. Nor do I think every writer needs to be haunted by cadence in order to write well; I speak only of my own experience. In the terms of this conference, the *errance* that is most immediate to me is hearing poems in my head, my forearms, my gut—hearing cadence with my body but not being able to write its poems.

I take my vocation to consist of listening in this cadence—for a time it was most like the fusion of a raunchy saxophone with a very vibrant cello, but now lately there have been organ and flute as well—I take my vocation to consist of listening into it with enough life concentration that it can become words through me if it chooses. I hear it more often in sculpture and music than in poetry, though it is strong for me in Hölderlin and Pindar. As in Henry Moore, the Brandenburg Concertos, Charlie Parker, John Coltrane, early Van Morrison.

What is the relation of cadence and poem?

Michaelangelo said he could sense the figure in the uncut stone; his job was to prune away marble till it emerged. Eskimo sculptors say the same thing. It makes sense to me. Cadence is the medium, the raw stone. Content is already there in the cadence. And writing a poem means cutting away everything in the cadence that isn't that poem. You can't "write" a poem, in fact: you can only help it stand free in the torrent of cadence. Most of my time with a pen is spent giving words, images, bright ideas that are borne along in cadence their permission to stay off the paper. The poem is what remains; it is local cadence minus whatever is extraneous to its shapely articulation.

A bad poem, on the other hand, is something a poet made up.

This is why a poem, at least in my sense of it, wants to exist in two ways at once: as a teeming process which overflows every prior canon of form (or is prepared to, and can when it chooses)—and simultaneously as a beautifully disciplined structure whose order flowers outward from the centre of its own necessity, and which does not miss a single checkpoint along the way. Cadence, which is the medium of existence for the content all along—cadence teems; content has the other task, of filling out the orderly space of its own more limited being.

So those two ways, the energy of infinite process and the shapeliness of that which lives outward to its own limits, have been coinciding all along; if the poem is any good they will simply go on coinciding in it. It will be intelligible out of courtesy, not timidity; its form is not to obey form but to include and carry beyond it.

In the presence of cadence—which is continuous, both as goad and as grace and as something I experience almost as mockery—the chance to turn a good phrase, write a deft poem, the chance to be a *poet*, leaves me cold. It seems like the cheapest evasion. For this jazzy, majestic, delicately cascading process I hear surging and thudding and pausing is largely without the witness I might be, if it chose to become incarnate in the words I set down.

I do not say any of this with false humility, for I am convinced that it does so choose. But it impresses me with the sheer silliness of most of what a writer is tempted to do, and it leaves me impatient that I can't organise my life so as to listen with greater concentration, and let my craft be more fully entered by it. For finally, I believe, cadence chooses to issue in the articulate gestures of being human.

2. COUNTRY

I have been writing of cadence as though one had merely to hear its words and set them down. But that is not true, at least not in my experience. There is a check on one's pen which seems to take hold at the very moment that cadence declares itself. Words arrive, but words have also gone dead.

To get at this complex experience we must begin from the hereness, the local nature of cadence. We never encounter cadence in the abstract; it is insistently here and now. Any man aspires to be at home where he lives, to celebrate communion with men on earth around him, under the sky where he actually lives. And to speak from his own dwelling—however light or strong the inflections of that place—will make his words intelligible to men elsewhere, because authentic. In my case, then, cadence seeks the gestures of being a Canadian human: *mutatis mutandi*, the same is true for anyone here—an Israeli, an American, a Quebecker.

But if we live in space which is radically in question for us, that makes our barest speaking a problem to itself. For voice does issue in part from civil space. And alienation in that space will enter and undercut our writing, make it recoil upon itself, become a problem to itself.

The act of writing "becomes a problem to itself" when it raises a vicious circle; when to write necessarily involves something that seems to make writing impossible. Contradictions in our civil space are one thing that make this happen, and I am struck by the subtle connections people here have drawn between words and their own problematic public space.

These take different forms in different nations. To compare them is not simply to compare degrees of political repression, of course. If one does wish to make such comparisons, the repressions borne by a Jew, a Pole, a Rumanian, or—on a lesser scale—a Quebecker have all been vastly more painful than a Canadian's. But it is with dislocation in our total civil space that I am concerned here; political repression is one crucial element in that, but it is still only one.

To explore the obstructions to cadence is, for a Canadian, to explore the nature of colonial space. Here I am particularly concerned with what it does to writing. One can also analyse it economically or politically, or try to act upon it; but at this point I want only to find words for our experience of it.

* * *

Abraham Yehoshuah spoke of writing in a divided language. In part modern Hebrew is charged with religious connotations which go back millenia, but with which some Israelis no longer feel at home; and in part it is brand new, without the grainy texture of a living language—new words, technical ones in particular, are regularly created ex nihilo to make modernity articulate in Israel. Thus contemporary Hebrew embodies the tensions of ancient and modern, sacred and profane, which tug at Israel itself; using it well already demands a provisional triumph of citizenship, a reconciliation of jostling civil currents at the level of words and phrases.

And Michèle Lalonde speaks of coming to verbal maturity in Quebec in a kind of linguistic no-man's-land, speaking a French one has been taught to despise and a rag-tag-and-bobtail American-Canadian English fit only for the Pepsi billboards which denote one's servitude. In such a situation, good writing must be achieved in a language that embodies the very experience—societal humiliation—which one must transcend in order to write well. In Quebec, as in Israel, writing is a problem to itself right at the level of diction.

For a Canadian, our form of civil alienation is not manifested that dramatically in language. The prime fact about my country as a public space is that in the last 25 years it has become an American colony. But we speak the same tongue as our new masters; we are the same colour, the same stock. We know their history better than our own. Thus while our civil inauthenticity has many tangible monuments, from *Time* to Imperial Esso, the way it undercuts

our writing is less easy to discern—precisely because there are so few symptomatic literary battlegrounds (comparable to the anglicized French of Quebec) in which the takeover is immediately visible. Nevertheless, many writers
here know how the act of writing calls itself radically into question.

I will take the external pressure for granted—the American tidal-wave that
inundates us, in the cultural sphere as much as in the economic and political. How maybe 2 per cent of the books on our paperback racks are Canadian, because the American-owned distributors refuse to carry them. How
Canadian film-makers have to go to the U.S. to seek distribution arrangements for Canada—where they are commonly turned down, which means the
film is usually not made. How almost all our prime TV time is filled with yan-
kee programs. How a number of Alberta schoolchildren were still being
taught, recently, that Abraham Lincoln was their country's greatest president.
But brushing past these things for now I want to explore how, in a colony, the
simple act of writing becomes a problem to itself.

* * *

I shall be speaking of "words," but not merely those you find in a dictionary.
I mean all the resources of the verbal imagination, from single words through
verse forms, conventions about levels of style, characteristic versions of the
hero, resonant structures of plot. And I use my own experience with words
because I know it best. It tallies with things other writers in their thirties have
said, but I don't know how many would accept it fully.

My sense when I began writing, about 1960—and this lasted five or six
years—was that I had access to a great many words: those of the British, the
American, and (so far as anyone took it seriously) the Canadian traditions.
Yet at the same time those words seemed to lie in a great random heap, which
glittered with promise so long as I considered it in the mass but within which
each individual word went stiff, inert, was somehow clogged with sludge, the
moment I tried to move it into place in a poem. I could stir words, prod at
them, cram them into position; but there was no way I could speak them
directly. They were completely external to me, though since I had never
known the words of poetry in any other way I assumed that was natural.

Writers everywhere don't have to begin with a resistant, external language;
there was more behind the experience than just getting the hang of the medium during apprenticeship. In any case, after I had published one book of
poems and finished another a bizarre thing happened: I stopped being able
to use words on paper at all.

All around me—in England, America, even in Canada—writers opened
their mouths and words spilled out like crazy. But increasingly when I opened
mine I simply gagged; finally, the words no longer came. For about four years
at the end of the decade I tore up everything I wrote— twenty words on a

page were enough to set me boggling at their palpable inauthenticity. And looking back at my previous writing, I felt as if I had been fishing pretty beads out of a vat of crank-case oil and stringing them together. The words weren't limber or alive or even mine.

To discover that you are mute in the midst of all the riches of a language is a weird experience. I had no explanation for it; by 1967 it had happened to me, but I didn't know why. Today, as I go back and try to stylize the flux to understand it, I am suspicious of the cause-and-effect categories that assert themselves; half the effects, it seems, came before their causes. But this is a recent scruple. At that time I could barely take in *what* had happened; I had just begun to write, and now I was stopped. I would still sit down in my study with a pen and paper from time to time, and every time I ended up ripping the paper to pieces and pitching it out. The stiffness and falsity of the words appalled me; the reaction was more in my body than my mind, but it was very strong.

* * *

Those of us who stumbled into this kind of problem in the nineteen-sixties—whatever form it took—were suffering the recoil from something Canadians had learned very profoundly in the fifties. To want to see one's life, we had been taught, to see one's own most banal impulses and deeper currents made articulate on paper, in a film, on records—that was ridiculous, uppity. Canadians were by definition people who looked over the fence and through the windows at America, un-self-consciously learning from its movies, comics, magazines and TV shows how to go about being alive. The disdainful amusement I and thousands like me felt for Canadian achievement in any field, especially those of the imagination, was a direct reflection of our self-hatred and sense of inferiority. And while we dismissed American mass culture, we could only separate ourselves from it by soaking up all the elite American culture we could get at. If anyone from another country was around we would outdo ourselves with our knowledge of Mailer and Fiedler and Baldwin, of the beatniks and the hipsters, of—if we were really showing our breadth of mind—the new plays from angry London. And we fell all over ourselves putting down the Canadians. This was between 1955 and 1965.

We were shaping up to be perfect little Toms and vendus. And like intellectual Toms in most places we were prepared to sell out, not for a cut of the action or a position of second-level power, but simply on condition that we not be humiliated by being treated like the rest of the natives. We were desperate to make that clear: we weren't like the rest. The fact that we would never meet the Americans we admired from one end of the year to the next did not cramp our style; we managed to feel inferior and put down anyway, and we compensated like mad. We kept up with *Paris Review* and *Partisan,* shook our heads over how Senator McCarthy had perverted the traditions of our country; in some cases we went down to Selma or Washington to confront our power structure, and in all cases we agreed that the greatest blot on our racial history was the way we had treated the Negroes. It boggles the imagination now, but that was really what we did—it was how we really *felt*. We weren't pretending, we were desperate. And the idea that these things confirmed our colonialism with a vengeance would have made us laugh our continentalized heads off. We weren't all that clear on colonialism to begin with, but if anybody had colonialism it was our poor countrymen, the Canadians, who in some unspecified way were still in fetters to England. But we weren't colonials; hell, *we* could have held our heads up in New York, if it had occurred to anyone to ask us down. Though it was a bit of a relief that no one ever did.

* * *

My awakening from this astonishing condition was private and extremely confusing. It was touched off by the radical critiques of America that originated in America, especially over Viet Nam; but it ended up going further. From that muddled process I remember one particularly disorienting couple of months in 1965, after a teach-in on Viet Nam held at the University of Toronto (in the fashion of American teach-ins) by a group of first-rate professors and students. It lasted a weekend, and as I read the background material and followed the long, dull speeches in the echoing cavern of Varsity Arena, two things dawned on me. The first was that the American government had been lying about Viet Nam. The second was that the Canadian media, from which I had learnt all I knew about the war, were helping to spread its lies.

I present these discoveries in all the crashing naivete with which they struck me then. Interestingly, while the first revelation shocked me more at the time, it was the second that gnawed at me during the ensuing months. I couldn't get my mind around it. I did not believe that our newspapers or radio and TV stations had been bought off directly by Washington, of course. But if it was not a case of paid corruption, the only reason for co-operating in such a colossal deception—consciously or unconsciously—was that they were colonial media, serving the interests of the imperial rulers.

This language made me bridle—it conjured up images of mindless five-hour harangues in Havana or Peking, foreign frenzies of auto-hypnosis, numb rhetoric. I'd read about *that* in the papers too. But no matter: it was the only language that made sense of what had been happening, and though I did not accept the terms for another five years I accepted their substance almost at once.

Worse than that, however, was the recognition that the sphere of imperial influence was not confined to the pages of newspapers. It also included my head. And that shook me to the core, because I could not even restrict the brainwashing I began to recognize to the case of Viet Nam. More and more of the ideas I had, my assumptions, even the instinctive path of my feelings well before they jelled into notions, seemed to have come north from the States unexamined. That had once been what I strove for (though I wouldn't have put it that way). But now the whole thing began to turn around, and I was jarred loose. After ten years of continentalizing my ass, what had I accomplished? . . . I was a colonial.

It was during the period when my system began to rebel against our spineless existence in this colonial space—by 1967, say—that I began to find literary words impossible. I read far less, I stopped going to Stratford, I squirmed in front of TV. And nothing I wrote felt real. I didn't know why. I couldn't even say what was the problem, for any words I might use to articulate it were already deadened, numb, inert in the same peculiar way. So none of this got said, except by the revulsion of my nervous system; otherwise I was mute. Writing had become a full-fledged problem to itself; it had grown into a search for authenticity, but all it could manage to be was a symptom of inauthenticity. I couldn't put my finger on what was inauthentic, but I could feel it with every nerve-end in my body. And I only wanted to write, I said, if I could also convey the muteness that established—like a key in music—the particular inauthenticity of this word, and of that word. (At the time I called it "silence," but most if it—I think now—was simple muteness.) I couldn't write that way. So for four years I shut up.

* * *

Though I hope not to over-dramatize this, it was when I read a series of essays by the philosopher George Grant that I started to comprehend what we had been living inside. Many people were turning to Marcuse for such clarification, and through him to Marx; others found perspective in Leary and Brown. I find that I want to know more now about Marx. But at the time I found a greater toughness and depth in Grant's thought. And it felt like home. That mattered to me, because I never wanted to spend time again chasing somebody else's standards of what was good.

Grant's analysis of "Canadian Fate and Imperialism," which I read in *Canadian Dimension*, was the first that made any contact whatsoever with my tenuous sense of living here— the first that seemed to be speaking the words of our civil condition. My whole system had been coiling in on itself for want of them. As subsequent pieces appeared (they eventually came out as *Technology and Empire*), I realised that somehow it had happened: a man who knew this paralysing condition first-hand was nevertheless using words authentically, from the very centre of everything that had tied my tongue. Grant's thought is still growing and changing, of course, so it could not be treated as a body of doctrine. Its subtlety, breadth and austerity can be conveyed only in a glancing way here.

One central perception was that, in refusing the American dream, our Loyalist forebears (the British Americans who came north after 1776) were groping to reaffirm a classical European tradition, one which embodies a very different sense of public space. By contrast with the liberal assumptions that gave birth to the United States, it taught that reverence for what is is more deeply human than conquest of what is. That men are subject to sterner civil necessities than liberty or the pursuit of happiness—that they must respond, as best they can, to the demands of the good. And that men's presence here is capable of an organic continuity which cannot be ruptured except at the risk of making their condition worse—that any such change should be undertaken in fear and trembling. (Grant would not claim that all Hellenic or Christian societies used to live by these ideals, only that they understood themselves to be acting well or badly in their light.) And while our ancestors were often mediocre or muddling, convictions like these demonstrably did underlie many of their attitudes to law, the land, indigenous peoples and Europe. Their refusal of America issued, in part, from disagreement with the early Americans about what it meant to be a human being.

What the Loyalists were refusing was the doctrine of essential human freedom, which in an argument of inspired simplicity Grant sees as the point of generation of technological civilization. That doctrine led to a view of everything but one's own will—the new continent, native peoples, other nations, outer space, one's own body—as raw material, to be manipulated and remade according to the hungers of one's nervous system and the demands of one's technology. But not only did this view of an unlimited human freedom seem arrogant and suicidal; it also seemed inaccurate, wrong, a piece of self-deception. For we are not radically free, in simple fact, and to act as if we were is to behave with lethal naivete. What is more, trying to force everything around us to conform to our own wills is just not the best use of what freedom we do have.

This overstates what Grant finds in the Loyalists, in order to clarify the deep novelty of his perspective. In fact, he declares that the typical Loyalist was "straight Locke with a dash of Anglicanism"; the British tradition he held to had already broken with the classical understanding of the good which Grant cherishes. Loyalism was a gesture in the right direction, perhaps, but it never succeeded in being radically un-American; it did not have the resources.

This undercutting of a past he would have liked to make exemplary is a characteristic moment in Grant's thought, and it reveals the central strength and contradiction of his work. He withdraws from the contemporary world, and judges it with passionate lucidity, by standing on a "fixed point" which he then reveals to be no longer there. To dismiss his thought for that reason is sheer self-indulgence, of course, for it is to shy back from the extremity of our impasse, to imply that we ourselves have access to more-than-liberal resources which stand up where Grant's crumble. Nevertheless, this strange way of proceeding makes Grant's thought difficult to live with—a fact which his own best work explores rigorously.

I found the account of being alive that Grant saw in the classic tradition far less self-indulgent than the liberal version that achieved its zenith in America—far closer to the way things are. And suddenly there were terms in which to recognize that, as we began to criticize our new masters during the sixties, we were not just wanting to be better Americans than the Americans, to dream their dream more humanely. Our dissent went as deep as it did because, obscurely, we did not want to be American at all. Their dream was wrong.

Before Grant, a person who grew up in as deeply colonized a Canadian decade as the fifties had no access to such a fundamental refusal of America, no matter how viscerally he felt it. Hence before Grant many of us had no way of entering our native space. Moreover our tiresome beginnings had always been a source of embarrassed amusement to us; they were hardly something we could have lapsed from or betrayed. As this was stood on its head, relatively at least, Grant gave us access to our past as well.

But Grant is scarcely an apostle of public joy. His next perception virtually cancels his reclamation of space to be in. By now, he says, we have replaced our forebears' tentative, dissenting North American space with a wholehearted and colonial American space. The sellout of Canada which has been consummated over the last few decades does not just involve real estate or corporate takeovers, nor who will put the marionettes in Ottawa through their dance. It replaces one human space with another.

For the political and military rule of the United States, and the economic rule of its corporations, are merely the surface expression of modernity in the West. That modernity is also inward. It shapes the expression of our bodies' impulses, the way we build cities, what we do in our spare time. Always we are totally free men, faced with a world which is raw material, a permanent incitement to technique. Any problem caused by our use of our freedom is merely accidental, and can be remedied by a greater application of the technology which expresses that freedom. There is simply no court of appeal outside that circuit. And even though we can observe the results of that world-view destroying the planet, the capacity for such gloomy perception does not give us access to another world-view.

Finally, Grant declares that to dissent from liberal modernity is necessarily to fall silent, for we now have no terms in which to speak that do not issue from the space we are trying to speak against. The conservative impulse, in which Grant sees the future we almost used to have, he judges finally to be mute as a contemplative stance and half impotent as a practical one. It can sense "intimations of deprival" to which liberal men are not open, but it can sense them only in waiting and silence.

What is most implacable about this modern despair, Grant holds, is that it cannot get outside itself. Any statement of ideals by which we might bring our plight into perspective turns out to be either a hollow appeal to things we no longer have access to, or (more commonly) a restatement of the very liberal ideals that got us into the fix in the first place. While this is not a problem that preoccupies most people in their day-to-day lives, it creates a Catch-22 situation at the levels from which any civilization draws its deepest resources. Grant explores that Catch-22 with a clarity which induces vertigo.

I recognise all the bleakness for which Grant is often criticised. But only with my head; for months after I read his essays I felt a surge of release and exhilaration. To find one's tongue-tied sense of civil loss and bafflement given words at last, to hear one's own most inarticulate hunches out loud, because most immediate in the bloodstream—and not prettied up, and in prose like a fastidious groundswell—was to stand erect at last in one's own space.

I do not expect to spend my life agreeing with George Grant. But, in my experience at least, the sombre Canadian has enabled us to say for the first time where we are, who we are—to become articulate. That first gift of speech is a staggering achievement. And in trying to comprehend the deeper ways in which writing is a problem to itself in Canada, I can start nowhere but with Grant.

* * *

Grant showed me that we have been colonized, not just by American corporations and governments, but by the assumptions and reflexes of the liberalism they embody. And this inward colonisation is a serious thing; it means that we are now ex-Canadians—or to put it at its most recklessly hopeful, that we are not-yet-Canadians. What does that do to a writer who wants to work from his roots?

In *Survival,* Margaret Atwood suggests an alarming answer: much of our literature, she says, is an involuntary symptom or projection of colonial experience. The dominant themes of Canadian writing have been death, failure of nerve, and the experience of being victimized by forces beyond our control. Heroes lose, personal relations go awry, animals, Indians and immigrants are mowed down with such knee-jerk regularity that we have clearly moved past candour to compulsiveness.

Why do Canadian writers return to the lot of the victim with such dreary zest? Atwood's explanation is tempting: the species "Canadian human" has felt itself to be powerless and threatened from the beginning, and as a result the collective author "Canada" projects itself time and again as a victim.

But I wonder whether there isn't more to it. The colonial writer does not have words of his own. Is it not possible that he projects his own condition of voicelessness into whatever he creates? that he articulates his own powerlessness, in the face of alien words, by seeking out fresh tales of victims? Over and above Atwood's account of it, perhaps the colonial imagination is driven to recreate, again and again, the experience of writing in colonial space.

We are getting close to the centre of the tangle. Why did I stop being interested in Shakespeare at Stratford, when I had gone assiduously for ten summers? Why did I fidget and squirm in front of TV, and read so much less? And why did I dry?

The words I knew said Britain, and they said America, but they did not say my home. They were always and only about someone else's life. All the rich structures of language were present, but the currents that animated them were not home to the people who used the language here.

But the civil self seeks nourishment as much as the biological self; it too fuels the imagination. And if everything it can find is alien, it may protect itself in a visceral spasm of refusal. To take an immediate example: the words I used above—"language," "home," "here"—have no native charge; they convey only meanings in whose face we have been unable to find ourselves since the eighteenth century. This is not a call for arbitrary new Canadian definitions, of course. It is simply to point out that the texture, weight and connotation of almost every word we use comes from abroad. For a person whose medium is words, who wants to use words to recreate our being human here—and where else do we live?—that fact creates an absolute problem.

Why did I dry for four years? The language was drenched with our non-belonging, and words—bizarre as it sounds, even to myself—words had become the enemy. To use them as a writer was to collaborate further in one's extinction as a rooted human being. And so, by a drastic and involuntary stratagem of self-preserval, words went dead.

The first necessity for the colonial writer—so runs the conventional wisdom—is to start writing of what he knows. His imagination must come home. But that first necessity is not enough. For if you are Canadian, home is a place that is not home to you—it is even less your home than the imperial centre you used to dream about. Or to say what I really know best, the *words* of home are silent. And to write a jolly ode to harvests in Saskatchewan, or set an American murder mystery in Newfoundland, is no answer at all. Try to speak the words of your home and you will discover—if you are a colonial—that you do not know them.

To speak unreflectingly in a colony, then, is to use words that speak only alien space. To reflect is to fall silent, discovering that your authentic space does not have words. And to reflect further is to recognise that you and your people do not in fact have a privileged authentic space just waiting for words; you are, among other things, the people who have made an alien inauthenticity their own. You are left chafing at the inarticulacy of a native space which may not exist. So you shut up.

* * *

But perhaps—and here was the breakthrough—perhaps our job was not to
fake a space of our own and write it up, but rather to find words for our space-
lessness. Perhaps that *was* home. This dawned on me gradually. Instead of
pushing against the grain of an external, uncharged language, perhaps we
should finally come to writing *with* that grain.

To do that was a homecoming—and a thoroughly edgy, uncertain homecoming it was. You began by giving up the idea of writing in the same continuum as Lowell, Roethke, Ginsberg, Olson, Plath. It was not a question of
accepting lower standards; finding your own standards would be much riski-
er, they could become just as exacting as other peoples' were for them. It was
a question of starting from your own necessities. And you began striving to
hear what happened in words—in "love," "inhabit," "fail," "earth," "house"—
as you let them surface in your own mute and native land. It was a funny, visceral process; there was nothing as explicit as starting to write in *joual*, though
the process was comparable. There was only the decision to let words be how
they actually are for us. But I am distorting the experience again by writing it
down. There was nothing conscious about this decision, initially at least—it
was a direction one's inner ear took up. I know I fought it.

The first mark of words, as you began to re-appropriate them in this space-
less civil space, was a kind of blur of unachieved meaning. That I had already
experienced, though only as something oppressing and negative. But then I
began to sense something more.

Where I lived, a whole swarm of inarticulate meanings lunged, clawed,
drifted, eddied, sprawled in half-grasped disarray beneath the tidy meaning
which the simplest word had brought with it from England and the States.
"City": once you learned to accept the blurry, featureless character of that
word—responding to it as a Canadian word, with its absence of native connotation—you were dimly savaged by the live, inchoate meanings trying to
surface through it. The whole tangle and sisyphean problematic of people's
existing here, from the time of the *coureurs de bois* to the present day, came
struggling to be included in the word "city." Cooped up beneath the familiar
surface of the word as we use it ("city" as London, as New York, as Los Angeles)—and cooped up further down still, beneath the blank and blur you
heard when you sought some received indigenous meaning for the word—listening all the way down, you began to overhear the strands and communal
lives of millions of people who went their particular ways here, whose roots
and lives and legacy come together in the cities we live in. Edmonton, Toronto, Montreal, Halifax: "city" meant something still unspoken, but rampant
with held-in energy. Hearing it was like watching the contours of an unex-
pected continent gradually declare themselves through the familiar lawns
and faces of your block.

Though that again is hindsight: all of it. You heard an energy, and those
lives were part of it. Under the surface alienation and the second-level blur of

our words there was a living barrage of meaning: private, civil, religious—unclassifiable finally, but there, and seamless, and pressing to be spoken. And I *felt* that press of meaning: I had no idea what it was, but I could feel it teeming towards words. I called it cadence.

And hearing that cadence, I started to write again.

* * *

I should say something at once: as a chronological account of things, this tale of writing, falling silent for four years, beginning to write again, may be misleading. It streamlines and dramatizes many things which were tangled, murky and banal as they happened. It may imply a ten-year coherence of purpose, for example, but what I have most often felt as a writer is a sense of beleaguered drifting. And while that has been punctuated with flashes of clarity, the content was seldom the same on two successive occasions.

Moreover the chronological account is false, in this case, if it appears as a series of causes and effects. A reader might get the impression of a causal sequence that went like this: poet writes artificial early work; in dissatisfaction, he stops writing; reading George Grant, he finds an explanation for his own impasse; as a result something called "cadence" happens to him, and he starts writing again.

That causal chain is easy to follow, but it has little to do with what actually happened. Even the sequence is over-simplified. As I recall, it went more like this: poet writes artificial early work, some of it being a log-jammed attempt to write in a cadence he has heard in Hölderlin and elsewhere; unexpectedly, he finds it possible to write in a rather stilted version of that cadence, and does a book-length poem (published as *Civil Elegies*); throughout this period, he is reading George Grant in dribs and snatches; for no reason he can see, he stops being able to write; after four years, again for no apparent reason, he starts writing in cadence again and revises the long poem.

That chronological sequence has so many loose ends that I've given up looking for a cause-and-effect pattern in it. The causes and effects just aren't in the right places. To write a thematic account of the decade is a different matter, I believe. But I hope the reader will be suspicious of any sequential "explanation" I may have resorted to; it is probably wrong-headed.

* * *

One thing I find now is that I can work only from the insistings of cadence; I can no more have some experience on a streetcar, come home and write it up than I can fly to Mars. And as a colonial writer, I discover that that cadence surfaces mainly through the silence that ensues when we try to hear words which say ourselves, and learn that we do not possess them.

It will not do to ignore our halting tongues and try to write of other things; nor to spend all our energy castigating the causes, as if the condition was purely external; nor to invert that tongue-tied estate and try to write from everything that is its opposite. In fact, I conclude, the impasse of writing that is problematic to itself is transcended only when the impasse becomes its own subject, when writing accepts and enters and names its own condition as it is naming the world. Any other course (except in minor work—although I do not put that down) leads to writing whose joints and musculature never work together, which remains constantly out of synch with itself. We have had a lot of both in Canada.

Putting it differently: to be authentic, the voice of being alive here and now must include the inauthenticity of our lives here and now. We can expect no lightning or thunder to come down from heaven, to transform our past or our present. Part of the truth about us is that we have betrayed our own truths, by letting ourselves be robbed of them. To say that for real, the betrayal must be incorporated faithfully—in both sorrow and anger—in the saying.

To name your colonial condition is not necessarily to assign conceptual terms to it. It may be, as in some of the poetry of bill bissett or Gaston Miron. But the weight of the silence can also be conveyed by the sheer pressure of the words that break it. Then to name one's own condition is to recreate the halt and stammer, the wry self-deprecation, the rush of celebratory elan and the vastness of the still unspoken surround, in which a colonial writer finally comes to know *his* house, *his* father, *his* city, *his* terrain—encounters them in their own unuttered terms and finds words being born to say them. I think of Al Purdy's poems. Or, in a different explosion, bill bissett's barbaric native tongue.

Beneath the words our absentee masters have given us, there is an undermining silence. It saps our nerve. And beneath that silence, there is a raw welter of cadence that tumbles and strains toward words and that makes the silence a blessing because it shushes easy speech. That cadence is home.

We do not own cadence. It is not in Canada—vice-versa—nor is it real only for colonials. But it has its own way of being-here for us, if we are willing to be struck dumb first. And through us it seeks to issue in the articulate gestures of being human. Here.

3. SILENCE

What are these gestures of being human?

In one session of the conference, Claude Vigée spoke of the silence and death one must continually re-enter before words can be spoken at all. The void underlies each syllable, and is its context. And many of the hallowed terms of the century were invoked around the table to echo that "silence": nothingness, the abyss, absence, nonbeing, meaninglessness.

Abraham Yehoshuah disagreed. No writer starts with an experience of nothingness: you begin with a character, a situation, a fragment of rhythm—some real thing you decide to write from or about. At once you have your project: to make the story, the poem or the novel, and make it as well as you can. And when you write it, it's written. What part does the void play in that? It is merely mumbo-jumbo, called in for its fashionable aura of spiritual extremis.

Notice that the disagreement is not between abstract theories of literature; it arose when two writers described the daily act of putting words on the page. Their workaday experience is diametrically opposed, or at least their descriptions of it are.

I find myself in complete agreement with both descriptions: a good piece of writing bespeaks encounter with emptiness as its first source; a good piece of writing bespeaks encounter with things, things most as they are, nothing but things alive with their own mode of thingness, as its first source. What is more, I am convinced that both descriptions must be true of any piece of writing—and simultaneously—or it will degenerate into portentousness or banality.

* * *

There is a moment in which I experience other people, or things, or situations, as standing forth with a clarity and a preciousness which makes me want to cry and to celebrate physically at the same time. I imagine many people have felt it.

It is the moment in which something becomes overwhelmingly real in two lights at once. An old man or woman whose will to live and whose mortality reach one at the same instant. A child who is coursed through with the lovely energies of its body, and yet who is totally fragile before the coming decades of its life. A social movement charged at the same time with passion for decent lives and with the pettiness, ego-tripping and lack of stamina that will debase it. A table, at once a well-worn companion and a disregarded adjunct.

Each stands forth as what it is most fully, and most preciously, because the emptiness in which it rests declares itself so overpoweringly. We realise that this thing or person, this phrase, this event, *need not be.* And at that moment, as if for the first time, it reveals its vivacious being as though it had just begun to be for the first time.

The recognition is "subjective," I suppose; it is we who change at that moment. But the real situation of the child, the social movement, the table, is neither subjective nor objective; the particular form of its life and the particular form of its death are simultaneous there for us whether we notice it or not. The fact that we can be open to it only rarely does not change this grounding of what is in its own nonbeing. But at those moments the table, the child, the grandparent stand fast and also come toward us in full clarity, saying "Write me."

Thus Claude Vigée is right. It is in meeting the nonbeing with which living
particulars are shot through—their mortality, their guilt, their incipient
meaninglessness; or here in Canada their wordlessness for us—that we cherish them most fully as what they are. Until that time, we may have cared for
them only as things we can own. But in that luminous, perishable aspect they
assume their own being for us.

And Abraham Yehoshuah is right. What we know is never a giant emptiness—unless we are merely playing with the idea of emptiness, which is a pursuit for dilettantes. We do not encounter Void, we encounter this void and
that. And in the particular ground of their own lapsed existence (which
haunts Abraham's own splendid stories, by the way), it is *this* friendship, *this*
orange-tree, *this* street-corner which take on resonance and demand to be
written.

But each is true only in the embrace of the other. Nonbeing and what is:
we cannot know either authentically by itself. Each is home to the other.
Hence to give homage to the world for itself is idolatry—but to give homage
to the void for itself is also idolatry. To accept nonbeing at home in what is,
to accept what-is at home in nonbeing, is perhaps the essential act of being
human. Certainly it is the beginning of art. And of much philosophy, and (if
very great scientists are to be believed) of much of science as well.

And what is—this tree, this enemy, this rooted housing bylaw—makes its
being known to us as cadence. That is what I started to hear. In cadence each
thing declares not only *what* it is, nor even *how* it is—but *that it is*. At all.

For some of us at least, the cadence of what is abounds only when we meet
it in its fullest grounding in nonbeing. Then each thing comes to resound in
its own silence. And the inauthenticity of our civil space is one such grounding. It is what I have written of here, but it is only one mode among many; I
am certain that the silence I go into is more than civil, and that men in many
countries enter it on *their* proper terms. But to write in colonial space is to
have that civil silence laid irrefutably upon you; whatever else overtakes you,
civil nonbeing cannot be evaded. The world you move around in and the
words you want to use are already cankered with it, and when they come alive
in cadence they come alive in it.

There is one more thing. Nobody sane can give thanks for what seems to
be evil; death, deprivation, corruptibility can hardly be slotted into place in
some higher scheme of things, explained away with relief as convenient aids
to ontological contemplation. We do well to see how relative and simplistic
our notions of evil usually are. But that can be no excuse for wriggling off the
hook which evil and suffering still compose.

That said, however, your first response to things that strike at life and goodness undergoes a change, when you discern that every thing that is is most
fully itself in the presence of its own emptiness. I cannot say more about that
change, however, as I do not understand it.

* * *

A poem enacts in words the presence of what we live among. It arises from the tough, delicate, heartbreaking rooting of what-is in its own nonbeing. Out of our participation in that rooting, there rises an elemental movement of being—of celebration, of desire, of grief, of anger, of play, of dying. That movement is always particular, speaking the things which are. It does not issue just from what is outside us, nor just from what is inside us. A poem enacts that moving cadence of being.

To be human is to live through such movements of being.

Quick in its own silence, cadence seeks to issue in the articulate gestures of being human here.

Notes

1. Expanded from a talk given at the *Rencontre québécoise internationale des Écrivains,* held in Montreal in the spring of 1972 under the sponsorship of the editors of *Liberté* magazine. The general subject was "*L'Écriture et l'errance.*"

7

"Disunity as Unity: A Canadian Strategy"*

Robert Kroetsch

The organizers of this conference,[1] by a narrative strategy that fills me with admiration, juxtapose the completion of the CPR tracks across Canada with the hanging of Louis Riel, in 1885. Two narratives, here, come into violent discord. In 1885 the completion of the railway seemed the dominant narrative, an expression of, as the journalists would have it, the national dream. The story of the Métis leader, Louis Riel, with his rebellion or uprising or resistance—the troubles in the northwest—seemed at best a sub-plot. In the Canadian imagination one hundred years later, the story of the railway has turned into a nasty economic scrap in the name of something called The Crow Rates, while the Riel story has become the stuff of our imaginative life, with fifty-some plays, for example, making use of Louis Riel's uncertain career.

My concern here is with narrative itself. The shared story—what I prefer to call the assumed story—has traditionally been basic to nationhood. As a writer I'm interested in these assumed stories—what I call meta-narratives. It may be that the writing of particular narratives, within a culture, is dependent on these meta-narratives.

An obvious example is the persistence of The American Dream, with its assumptions about individual freedom, the importance of the frontier, the immigrant experience, as it functions in the literature of the United States. Even the cowboy story and the American version of the detective story are dependent on that meta-narrative.

To make a long story disunited, let me assert here that I'm suggesting that Canadians cannot agree on what their meta-narrative is. I am also suggesting that, in some perverse way, this very falling-apart of our story is what holds our story together.

In the 1970s the Conseil des Universités of the Government of Quebec invited the French critic Jean-François Lyotard to write a report on the state of universities in the western world. Lyotard's reflections were published in English in 1984 under the title *The Postmodern Condition: A Report on Knowledge*. In that report Lyotard writes: "Simplifying to the extreme, I define *postmodern*

* *The Lovely Treachery of Words: Essays Selected and New* (Toronto: Oxford UP, 1989), 21-33.

as incredulity toward meta-narratives. . . . To the obsolescence of the meta-narrative apparatus of legitimation corresponds, most notably, the crisis of metaphysical philosophy and of the university institution which in the past relied on it. The narrative function is losing its functors, its great hero, its great dangers, its great voyages, its great goal. It is being dispersed in clouds of narrative language elements . . ." (xxiv).

I am suggesting that by Lyotard's definition, Canada is a postmodern country.

The high modern period is a period that ended at some time during or shortly after the Second World War. T.S. Eliot, living in London in the 1940s, was writing his great modernist text *Four Quartets* at the same time that William Carlos Williams, in New Jersey, was writing his great postmodernist text *Paterson*. In Eliot I hear still a longing for the unity of story or narrative. In Williams I hear an acceptance of, even a celebration of, multiplicity. The stories that gave centre and circumference to the modern world were losing their centripetal power. As Yeats observed, the centre does not hold.

It was this very decentring that gave a new energy to countries like Canada. Canada is supremely a country of margins, beginning from the literal way in which almost every city borders on a wilderness. The centredness of the high modern period—the first half of the twentieth century—made us almost irrelevant to history. I remember the shock, after the Second World War, of reading a popular history of that war and finding Canada mentioned only once—and that in connection with the Dieppe raid. Yet as a high-school student during the war years I, with my community, was obsessively concerned with the war. In a high modern world, with its privileged stories, Canada was invisible.

Lyotard attributes the decentring to developments in science. I feel that the movement away from the European-centred empires to the current domination by America and the USSR has had an equal impact. In fact, I suspect that those two empires, in attempting to assert or reassert their meta-narratives, turn all other societies into postmodern societies.

Timothy Findley in his novel *The Wars* gives an account of the particularly Canadian experience. His protagonist, Robert Ross, in the course of being destroyed by and in a marginal way surviving the First World War, acts out for the colonial society the destruction and the loss of its European centres, cultural, political, economic. For Findley, form and content speak each other's plight in *The Wars* as the traditional authority of the novel itself begins to falter. He resorts to an archival approach, using letters, photographs, interviews, family history, to recover the story, allowing the reader in turn to wonder how the fictional narrative centre relates to the writer writing. A doubt about our ability to know invades the narrative. What we witness is the collapse, for North American eyes, of the meta-narrative that once went by the name Europe. Europa. Findley's more recent novels, *Famous Last Words* and *Not*

Wanted on the Voyage, in their titles and in their stories remind us of Lyotard's observation that in postmodern writing there appears a scepticism or hesitation about the meta-narrative's great voyages, its great goal.

The centre does not hold. The margin, the periphery, the edge, now, is the exciting and dangerous boundary where silence and sound meet. It is where the action is. In our darker moments we feel we must resist the blind and consuming power of the new places with their new or old ideas that now want to become centres. In our happier moments we delight in the energy of the local, in the abundance that is diversity and difference, in the variety and life that exist on any coastline of the human experience.

This willingness to refuse privilege to a restricted or restrictive cluster of meta-narratives becomes a Canadian strategy for survival. We must, in Mikhail Bakhtin's terms, remain polyphonic, and the great Russian theorist was in his carnivalesque way a great master of survival. We are under pressure from many versions of the meta-narrative, ranging from *Star Wars* to programs like *Dynasty* and *Dallas*—and again we hear the shorthand of the meta-narrative in the naming. The trick is, I suppose, to resist the meta-narrative and still to avoid Riel's fate. Or did he, rather, by his very strategies, trick the privileged centre into allowing and even applauding his survival? *Sir* John A. Macdonald becomes a failure, even as villain. Louis Riel, the outcast, the halfbreed, the man from the periphery, becomes, as villain or hero, the stuff of myth.

Rudy Wiebe, in his novels *The Temptations of Big Bear* and *The Scorched-Wood People*, explores the process by which we reject the meta-narrative and assert the validity of our own stories. Rudy, as a Mennonite, the first Canadian-born child of exiles from Russia, living on a bush farm in Saskatchewan, then in a small town in southern Alberta, experienced the margin and its silence and its compulsion to speak its own validity. But what I want to do now is to look at some of the implications operating behind his and similar texts.

In this postmodern world, we trust a version of archaeology over the traditional versions of history. History, in its traditional forms, insisted too strongly on a coherent narrative. Timothy Findley speaks for many Canadians when he uses an archival method in *The Wars*, trusting to fragments of story, letting them speak their incompleteness. There is resistance to this mode, of course. A great Canadian architect like Arthur Erickson is at heart a modernist. A great Canadian critic like Northrop Frye is at heart a modernist, trying to assert the oneness, the unity, of all narrative. But the writers of stories and poems nowadays, in Canada, are not terribly sympathetic to Frye and his unifying sense of what a mythic vision is. Against this *over*riding view, we posit an archaeological sense that every unearthing is problematic, tentative, subject to a story-making act that is itself subject to further change as the "dig" goes on.

One of the functions of art, traditionally, is the location and elaboration of the meta-narratives. Canadian writing is obsessively about the artist who can't make art. That model is securely established by Sinclair Ross and Ernest Buckler.

Ross, in his novel of the Saskatchewan prairies during the Depression, *As For Me and My House,* has a minister's wife tell the story in the form of her diary. Her husband is a minister who doubts his ministry and who wants both to paint and to write and who succeeds at neither. The book is in effect a powerful novel about the inability to make art—it is a novel as a set of diary entries about an unwritten novel. The meta-narratives—religious, artistic, social, economic—do not hold. Even the great European meta-narrative about "nature" does not hold here, as nature turns into wind and moving dust and an unreachable horizon.

Ernest Buckler sets his novel *The Mountain and the Valley* in Nova Scotia. His protagonist, David Canaan, is a young man who wants to write great stories and who dies with his ambition unrealized. The meta-narratives of art, of family, of love, don't hold. The narrative itself turns into brilliant and static passages of description, speculation, repetition. The story quite simply cannot *move.*

Both these novels are set on geographical margins—the prairies, a rural area in Nova Scotia on the Bay of Fundy. Both deal with lives that the people themselves see as marginal—in both novels the ambition is obsessively to move into a bigger city. David Canaan gets into a car that will take him there, then gets out when he sees it's actually going to happen. Mrs. Bentley in Ross's novel—and we never know her first name or her family name—believes she and her husband are going to succeed by opening a secondhand bookstore in a city—and again, I hear Ross mocking this metaphoric (or is it metonymic?) representation of the meta-narratives.

In both it is a kind of archaeological act that succeeds, against the traditional narrative. Mrs. Bentley does keep a journal, and in that journal, without recognizing it, she makes her art. In *The Mountain and the Valley* it is David Canaan's grandmother, hooking a rug out of the scraps of clothing that represent traces of family history, who is the successful artist.

In this model of narrative, the generalizations are tentative. In traditional narrative, a new detail fits into the story. Here, a single new detail can alter the possible story—as when, at the end of *As For Me and My House*—a question of paternity shakes our very sense of whatever narrative it is we've been reading. Instead of answers we have questions. Instead of resolution we have doubt. The endings of both novels are hotly and endlessly debated. While not outlining the debate, I want to suggest that the debates themselves—is Mrs. Bentley a good woman or a wicked woman?—is David Canaan an idealist or a self-deceiving failure?—are what create "unity." We come to a Bakhtinian version of the dialogic, in which the possibility of a single or privileged voice announcing the *right* version of the narrative is talked away. The unity is created by the very debate that seems to threaten the unity.

Do the provinces or does the federal government deserve the revenue from oil? Was Riel the hero, or was it really Gabriel Dumont? Why is the expression "the CPR" a curse in western Canada?

Given the failure of ends, of goals—and it's interesting to look at the hesitancy built into the ends of Canadian novels—process becomes more important than end. The novel that acts out this concern for process with greatest effect might well be Margaret Laurence's *The Diviners*.

Again, the protagonist of the novel is a writer, Morag Gunn. Morag is an orphan. She lives on geographical margins—she is born in a small town in Manitoba and when we see her writing she is in a cottage on a river in rural Ontario. She is aware of other margins—through her Celtic background she is reminded of threatened mythologies and of a language that she has in fact lost. She is a writer obsessively concerned to locate the meta-narratives of her own life and of Canada—and what she finds, over and over, is a set of contradictions, sets of variations. As an archaeologist of her own stories, she finds traces, lies, misreadings, concealments, fragments.

There is a moment in *The Diviners* that has become a touchstone passage in Canadian writing. Morag Gunn, living in London, meets a Scottish painter, Daniel McRaith. Morag had gone to London expecting to find a centre. Instead, she finds her closest friend (and lover) in an artist who is as uncertain as she about the centre. And, like her, he does his best work by remaining decentred. But Morag goes on believing she might still find a centre if she goes to Scotland, to what she believes must be her true "home." McRaith takes her there:

> McRaith points across the firth, to the north.
> "Away over there is Sutherland, Morag Dhu, where your people came from. When do you want to drive there?"
> Morag considers.
> "I thought I would have to go. But I guess I don't, after all."
> "Why would that be?"
> "I don't know that I can explain. It has to do with Christie. The myths are my reality. Something like that. And also, I don't need to go there because I know now what it was I had to learn here."
> "What is that?"
> "It's a deep land here, all right," Morag says. "But it's not mine, except a long long way back. I always thought it was the land of my ancestors, but it is not."
> "What is, then?"
> "Christie's real country. Where I was born."
> McRaith holds her hand inside his greatcoat pocket. Around them the children sprint and whirl. (318-19)

One of the important elements in meta-narratives is the story of the place and moment of origin. In the American story we hear of the apparently infinite crowd that was aboard the *Mayflower*, we hear of the moment in July 1776 when there seems to have been no opposition at all to the impulse toward revolution and, regrettably, little toleration for peoples who want to emulate that moment. In Canada we cannot for the world decide when we became a nation or what to call the day or days or, for that matter, years that might have been the originary moments. If we can't be united, we can't be disunited. Our genealogy is postmodern. Each move of a generation back into time doubles the number of ancestors instead of refining itself toward a sacred moment. (I remember vividly, as a student, hitting on Lord Raglan's *The Hero*, and for the first time being made aware of the mathematics of genealogy.) Morag Gunn is there but she isn't there; she isn't there but she's there. Margaret Laurence attempts some counting of ancestral sources—and her heroine gets stories from the official histories, from the mouths of the veterans who actually fought in the trenches, from the survivors of the trek from the Scottish villages, from her Métis lover in Manitoba, from the professor of English to whom she is married for a while, from her own daughter who has songs of her own to sing. The abundance, the disunity, is her saving unity. Christie Logan is indeed of and in the "real country" of Canadian art and story. He is a garbage man who "reads" what he finds in the nuisance grounds, and as such he is the ultimate archaeologist of that old new place called Canada.

The attempt at allowing versions of narrative might explain the extreme intertexuality of Canadian culture. Where the impulse in the US is usually to define oneself as American, the Canadian, like a work of postmodern architecture, is always quoting his many sources. Our sense of region resists our national sense. I hear myself saying, I'm from *western* Canada. Or, even beyond that—because I was born in Alberta and now live in Manitoba—people ask me, seriously, if I think of myself as an Albertan or a Manitoban. We maintain ethnic customs long after they've disappeared in the country of origin. We define ourselves, often, as the cliché has it, by explaining to Americans that we aren't British, to the British that we aren't Americans. It may be that we survive by being skilful shape-changers. But more to the point, we survive by working with a low level of self-definition and national definition. We insist on staying multiple, and by that strategy we accommodate to our climate, our economic situation, and our neighbours.

Morag Gunn works this experience through by encountering the many versions of herself as artist, ranging from shaman and prophet to fool and clown. In Canadian writing there is little sense of a privileged self at the centre. Contrast Morag Gunn in *The Diviners* with Jay Gatsby in F. Scott Fitzgerald's *The Great Gatsby*. Fitzgerald's hero, we are told, springs from the Platonic concept of himself. Morag Gunn springs from a multiplicity of stories.

At the centre of any meta-narrative is a traditional hero. Canadians, uncertain of their meta-narratives, are more than uncertain of their heroes. We have no "dearly loved" leaders. The Fathers of Confederation tend to be an anonymous bunch. When Canadian TV producers tried to find an equivalent of America's frontier hero Daniel Boone, they came up with Radisson and Groseilliers. How they thought they would make a single hero out of that pair of look-alike fur thieves I don't know.

The struggle with the concept of hero illuminates much about the faltering meta-narrative in Canadian life. The western story, in Canada as in the US, seems to offer the best possibility for a fresh and genuine story. In the American west, the "free" or the "criminal" figure becomes heroic—the cowboy or the outlaw. In the Canadian west, the figure of authority is often the fictional protagonist. A remarkable number of school teachers ride into town—in the fiction not only of a comic writer like W.O. Mitchell but also in the near-tragic writings of Gabrielle Roy or in a novel like Martha Ostenso's *Wild Geese*. In this kind of fiction the authority figure as good guy ends up being treated parodically. The best example is Sinclair Ross's *As For Me and My House*. In that novel the "stranger" who "violates" the order of the town is the new minister, Philip Bentley. We first see him when he is unpacking. Or rather, when he is sleeping instead of unpacking. It is obvious from the first page of the story that his wife has the faster gun-hand. "He hasn't the hands for it," Mrs. Bentley says. "I could use the pliers and hammer twice as well myself . . ." (3).

Philip is white-faced and tight-lipped, quick, mostly, at drawing shut the door—of his study or of the bedroom. In this truly magnificent novel, the potential hero, Philip, has his role usurped by his nameless wife, the endlessly fascinating woman who, by quietly keeping a diary, creates the work of art that her artist-minister-husband cannot create. Perhaps the TV producers were right in looking for a doubled hero in the Canadian psyche. They might have fared better, however, had they turned to Louis Riel and Gabriel Dumont, those paired leaders who in their division of action and meditation, gun and book, act out the disunity that becomes our dance of unity.

Rudy Wiebe tried to find a single hero in the great Plains Cree leader of the nineteenth century, Big Bear, and in a way he succeeds profoundly. Big Bear refused to be baptized and he refused to settle his people on a reserve. In his refusals, in his resistance to the temptations, he resisted a whole new set of meta-narratives. In a sense he became the archetypal Canadian by refusing to become a Canadian. The divisions within him became the mark of his unified "Canadianness." Wiebe makes of Big Bear a powerful and attractive figure who in his defeat asserts his values—and the stories that carry those values. Again, here, it is the authority figures—the Queen's representatives, the agents of the Eastern Canadian government—who ride in from the east and begin to parody what they claim to stand for. In this new world, the old stories break down. The systems of law, being used to take the land away from the Indians, become a parody of law. The systems of writing, up against the elaborate oral codes and traditions of the Indians, become a parody. Justice itself becomes a parody of justice. And yet the parodic forms, in their single-mindedness and in their greed, triumph; in the final inversion the forces of "civilization" destroy a prospering civilization that was based on a buffalo economy and the complex interrelatedness of tribal life and geography. The railway in Wiebe's book—the iron horse of 1885—announces the arrival of a new story—of immigration, of dustbowl economics, of life and death on the reservation—and in this new story, by that ambiguous process we call art, the defeated Big Bear is transformed into an emblem of what the new story claims to cherish. In this near-hopeless separation of hero from communal behavior, the Canadian psyche, once again, both survives and flourishes. [. . .]

It is no accident that the hero of the Canadian story, often, is the artist. David Canaan, writing or not writing. Mrs. Bentley, writing about her husband's not writing or painting. Margaret Laurence's Morag Gunn, growing old, still learning. Michel Tremblay's writer, waiting to be born. In a rock-bottom situation like ours, in which the very shape of story itself falters, the artist in the act of creating art becomes the focus.

The nameless woman in Margaret Atwood's *Surfacing* is an artist, an illustrator of children's books who can't make her illustrations match the folk-tales she's trying to illustrate. A second character in *Surfacing*, David, back in the fifties wanted to be a minister and tried selling Bibles door-to-door to put himself through theological seminary. Now he's trying to make a film, with his friend Joe. At the end of the story, the nameless heroine exposes their film and drops it into a lake. By the end of the story, she has mated with Joe, who is on the way to becoming a bear-like creature, and she *might* be pregnant. The story becomes that minimal for Atwood. In making that minimal statement, she has become for many the quintessential *Canadian*, not just the Canadian artist. She locates our story by not finding it. The missing father is the central metaphor in *Surfacing*, the central metaphor in a failed and successful quest that is full of cryptic messages and languages that yield up their meaning by not speaking. Again, all is periphery and margin, against the hole in the middle. We are held together by that absence. There is no centre. This disunity is our unity.

I can suggest other novels that deal with the same paradox or strategy. Michael Ondaatje's *Coming through Slaughter*, the story of a black American jazz musician, Buddy Bolden, who left behind no record of his music. Alice Munro's *Lives of Girls and Women*, the growing-up into artist of Del Jordan, a girl in a small town in Ontario, born into the silence of a small town, learning the fragments of story that make her life cohere. The *künstlerroman* is basic to the Canadian search for and rejection of meta-narrative. Audrey Thomas's *Latakia,* the search of a woman writer that takes her back to the place where the alphabet is supposed to have developed, only to discover the chaos of unreadable maps, languages she can't understand, an archaeological site that yields up only a bewildering multitude of fragments.

Let me end, however, by glancing at one meta-narrative that has asserted itself persistently in the New World context—and that is the myth of the new world, the garden story. The dream of Eden.

That dream, and the falling into fragments of the dream, haunts Canadian writers from nineteenth-century figures like Thomas C. Haliburton, berating his fellow Nova Scotians for their failures, from Susanna Moodie, arriving from England into Quebec and Ontario, to Stephen Leacock, making his comic readings of life in a small town, to contemporary writers like myself. It haunted the politicians like Sir John A., building his railway in the name of a slogan (from sea to sea); like Louis Riel, proclaiming his Métis nation; like Tommy Douglas, again in the west, announcing the formation of a socialist party; to John Diefenbaker of Saskatchewan, dreaming his further dream of the Canadian north.

Perhaps it is the novelist Frederick Philip Grove who most tellingly explores that Eden dream. He was a German novelist, Paul Greve, who faked his suicide and managed his own rebirth as a Canadian writer, as a teacher, living on the prairies of Louis Riel. In his novel *Settlers of the Marsh,* he takes his characters from Sweden and Germany and England, from the United States and Ontario, to the promised new world of Manitoba. Grove, in that setting, shows that life in the new world meant mind-numbing and body-breaking work. And, more than that, he shows, before our eyes, the collapse of the stories the settlers of the marsh brought with them. In the opening of the story, two Swedish immigrants are walking through a blizzard, lost. The narrator tells us: "Both would have liked to talk, to tell and to listen to stories of danger, of being lost, of hairbreadth escapes: the influence of the prairie snowstorm made itself felt. But whenever one of them spoke, the wind snatched his word from his lips and threw it aloft" (16).

Perhaps the literal word is being dispersed, as Lyotard would have it, "in clouds of narrative language elements. . . ."

In this silence the two men are unhooked from their old stories, and from the unified world-view (whatever its virtues and vices) that those stories allowed. There, on the old hunting-grounds of Louis Riel's Métis, delivered to this place by railway, the two immigrants enter into the Canadian story. And the hero is, again, two, as if the disunity is so radical that it physically splits the hero. And yet, out of that division comes the discovery of unity.

The unnaming allows the naming. The local pride speaks. The oral tradition speaks its tentative nature, its freedom from the authorized text.

Notes

1. Tenth Annual Conference of the British Association for Canadian Studies, Edinburgh, 9-12 April 1985.

Works Cited

Laurence, Margaret. *The Diviners.* Toronto: McClelland, 1974.

Lyotard, Jean-François. *The Postmodern Condition: A Report on Knowledge.* Trans. Geoff Bennington and Brian Massumi. Minneapolis: U of Minnesota P, 1984.

Ross, Sinclair. *As For Me and My House.* 1941. Toronto: McClelland, 1957.

Grove, Frederick Philip. *Settlers of the Marsh.* 1925. Toronto: McClelland, 1966.

8

"'Circling the Downspout of Empire': Post-Colonialism and Postmodernism"*

Linda Hutcheon

The subject of Daphne Marlatt's phrase "circling the downspout of Empire" is "[C]anadians," and she is not alone in seeing Canada as still caught up in the machinations of Empire and colony, imperial metropolis and provincial hinterland (see Monk 14). Irving Layton once defined "Anglo-Canadian" in these terms:

> A native of Kingston, Ont,
> —two grandparents Canadian
> and still living
>
> His complexion florid
> as a maple leaf in late autumn,
> for three years he attended
> Oxford
>
> Now his accent
> makes even Englishmen
> wince, and feel
> unspeakably colonial. (Scott and Smith 75)

Whatever truth there may be in these accusations of *neo*-colonialism, there are many others who are coming to prefer to talk about Canada in terms of *post*-colonialism, and to place it in the context of other nations with which it shares the experience of colonization. In much recent criticism, this context has also come to overlap with that of post-modernism. Presumably, it is not just a matter of the common prefix or of the contemporaneity of the two enterprises. In literary critical circles, debates rage about whether the post-

* *ARIEL* 20.4 (1989): 149-75; rpt. *Past the Last Post: Theorizing Post-Colonialism and Post-Modernism*, ed. Ian Adam and Helen Tiffin (Calgary: U of Calgary P, 1990), 167-89. [Editor's note: I have used the *Past the Last Post* version as my copy text for this essay.]

colonial *is* the post-modern or whether it is its very antithesis (see Tiffin, "Post-Colonialism").

Part of the problem in deciding which camp to belong to is that in many of these debates the term post-modernism is rarely defined precisely enough to be more than a synonym for today's multinationalist capitalist world at large. But it *can* have a more precise meaning. The architecture which first gave aesthetic forms the label "postmodern" is, interestingly, both a critique of High Modern architecture (with its purist ahistorical embracing of what, in effect, was the modernity of capitalism) and a tribute to its technological and material advances. Extending this definition to other art forms, "post-modern" could then be used, by analogy, to describe art which is paradoxically both self-reflexive (about its technique and material) and yet grounded in historical and political actuality. The fiction of writers like E.L. Doctorow, Graham Swift, Salman Rushdie, Michael Ondaatje, Toni Morrison, and Angela Carter might provide examples. I have deliberately included here writers who would be categorized by others as either post-colonial or feminist in preference to the label "post-modern." While I want to argue here that the links between the post-colonial and the post-modern are strong and clear ones, I also want to underline from the start the major difference, a difference post-colonial art and criticism share with various forms of feminism. Both have distinct political agendas and often a theory of agency that allow them to go beyond the post-modern limits of deconstructing existing orthodoxies into the realms of social and political action. While it is true that post-colonial literature, for example, is also inevitably implicated and, in Helen Tiffin's words, "informed by the imperial vision" ("Post-Colonialism" 172), it still possesses a strong political motivation that is intrinsic to its oppositionality. However, as can be seen by its recuperation (and rejection) by both the Right and the Left, post-modernism is politically ambivalent: its critique coexists with an equally real and equally powerful complicity with the cultural dominants within which it inescapably exists.

Those cultural dominants, however, are shared by all three forces. As Gayatri Spivak notes: "There is an affinity between the imperialist subject and the subject of humanism" (202). While post-colonialism takes the first as its object of critique and post-modernism takes the second, feminists point to the patriarchal underpinnings of both. The title of a recent book of essays on colonial and post-colonial women's writing pinpoints this: *A Double Colonization* (Petersen and Rutherford). Feminisms have had similar impacts on both post-modern and post-colonial criticism. They have redirected the "universalist"—humanist and liberal—discourses (see Larson) in which both are debated and circumscribed. They have forced a reconsideration of the nature of the doubly colonized (but perhaps not yet doubly de-colonized) subject and its representations in art (see Donaldson). The current post-structuralist/post-modern challenges to the coherent, autonomous subject have to be put on hold in feminist and post-colonial discourses, for both must work first to assert and affirm a denied or alienated subjectivity: those radical post-modern challenges are in many ways the luxury of the dominant order which can afford to challenge that which it securely possesses.

Despite this major difference between the post-modern and the post-colonial—which feminisms help to place in the foreground and which must always be kept in mind—there is still considerable overlap in their concerns: formal, thematic, strategic. This does not mean that the two can be conflated unproblematically, as many commentators seem to suggest (Pache; Kröller, "Postmodernism"; Slemon, "Magic"). Formal issues such as what is called "magic realism," thematic concerns regarding history and marginality, and discursive strategies like irony and allegory are all shared by both the post-modern and the post-colonial, even if the final uses to which each is put may differ (cf. During 1985, 369). It is not a matter of the post-colonial *becoming* the post-modern, as one critic has suggested (Berry 321), but rather that the manifestations of their (different, if related) concerns often take similar forms; for example, both often place textual gaps in the foreground but their sites of production differ: there are "those produced by the colonial encounter and those produced by the system of writing itself" (Slemon, "Magic" 20), and they should not be confused.

The formal technique of "magic realism" (with its characteristic mixing of the fantastic and the realist) has been singled out by many critics as one of the points of conjunction of post-modernism and post-colonialism. Its challenges to genre distinctions and to the conventions of realism are certainly part of the project of both enterprises. As Stephen Slemon has argued, until recently it has been used to apply to Third World literatures, especially Latin American (see Dash) and Caribbean, but now is used more broadly in other post-colonial and culturally marginalized contexts to signal works which encode within themselves some "resistance to the massive imperial centre and its totalizing systems" (Slemon, "Magic" 10; also "Monuments"). It has even been linked with the "new realism" of African writing (Irele 70-71) with its emphasis on the localized, politicized and, inevitably, the historicized. Thus it becomes part of the dialogue with history that both post-modernism and post-colonialism undertake. After modernism's ahistorical rejection of the burden of the past, postmodern art has sought self-consciously (and often even parodically) to reconstruct its relationship to what came before; similarly, after that imposition of an imperial culture and that truncated indigenous history which colonialism has meant to many nations, post-colonial literatures are also negotiating (often parodically) the once tyrannical weight of colonial history in conjunction with the revalued local past. The post-modern and the post-colonial also come together, as Frank Davey has explained, because of the predominant non-European interpretation of modernism as "an international movement, elitist, imperialist, 'totalizing,' willing to appropriate the local while being condescending toward its practice" (119).

In post-modern response, to use Canadian examples, Margaret Atwood rewrites the local story of Susanna Moodie, Rudy Wiebe that of Big Bear and Louis Riel, George Bowering that of George Vancouver. And in so doing, all also manage to contest the dominant Eurocentric interpretation of Canadian history. Despite the Marxist view of the post-modern as ahistorical— because it questions, rather than confirms, the process of History—from its roots in architecture on post-modernism has been embroiled in debates and dialogues with the past (see Hutcheon). This is where it overlaps significantly with the post-colonial (Kröller, "Politics" 121) which, by definition, involves a "recognition of historical, political, and social circumstances" (Brydon 7). To say this is not to appropriate or recuperate the post-colonial into the post-modern, but merely to point to the conjunction of concerns which has, I think, been the reason for the power as much as the popularity of writers such as Salman Rushdie, Robert Kroetsch, Gabriel Garcia Marquez, and so many others.

At this thematic and structural level, it is not just the relation to history that brings the two *posts* together, there is also a strong shared concern with the notion of marginalization, with the state of what we could call ex-centricity. In granting value to (what the centre calls) the margin or the Other, the post-modern challenges any hegemonic force that presumes centrality, even as it acknowledges that it cannot privilege the margin without acknowledging the power of the centre. As Rick Salutin writes, Canadians are not marginal "because of the quirkiness of our ideas or the inadequacy of our arguments, but because of the power of those who define the centre" (6). But he too admits that power. The regionalism of magic realism and the local and particular focus of post-modern art are both ways of contesting not just this centrality, but also claims of universality. Post-modernism has been characterized as "that thought which refuses to turn the Other into the Same" (During 1987, 33) and this is, of course, where its significance for post-colonialism comes in. In Canada, it has been Québecois artists and critics who have embraced most readily the rhetoric of this post-colonial liberation—from Emile Borduas in 1948 to *Parti Pris* in the 1960s. However real this experience of colonization is in Québec, there is a historical dimension here that cannot be ignored. Québec may align itself politically with francophone colonies such as Algeria, Tunisia and Haiti (Kröller, "Politics" 120), but there is a major political and historical difference: the pre-colonial history of the French in Québec was an imperialist one. As both Leonard Cohen's *Beautiful Losers* and Hubert Aquin's *Trou de mémoire* point out, the French were the first imperial force in what is now Canada and that too cannot be forgotten—without risking bad faith. This is not to deny, once again, the very real sense of cultural dispossession and social alienation in Québec, but history cannot be conveniently ignored.

A related problem is that post-modern notions of difference and positively valued marginality can themselves be used to repeat (in a more covert way) colonizing strategies of domination when used by First World critics dealing with the Third World (see Chow 91): the precise point at which interest and concern become imperializing appropriation is a hotly contested one. In addition some critics, of course, see post-modernism as itself the dominant, Eurocentric, neo-universalist, imperial discourse (Brydon 5; Tiffin, "Post-Colonialism" 170-72). There are no easy solutions to any of these issues raised by the perhaps uncomfortable overlap of issues between the post-modern and the post-colonial, but that in itself is no reason not to explore that problematic site of interaction.

Besides the formal and thematic areas of mutual concern that I have already mentioned, there is what could be called a strategic or rhetorical one: the use of the trope of irony as a doubled or split discourse which has the potential to subvert from within. Some have seen this valorization of irony as a sign of the "increasing purchase of post-structural codes of recognition in Western society" (Slemon, "Post-Colonial" 157), but post-structuralism can also be seen as a product of the larger cultural enterprise of post-modernism (see Hutcheon). In either case, though, as a double-talking, forked-tongued mode of address, irony becomes a popular rhetorical strategy for working within existing discourses and contesting them at the same time. Its inherent semantic and structural doubleness also makes it a most convenient trope for the paradoxical dualities of both post-modern complicitous critique and post-colonial doubled identity and history. And indeed irony (like allegory, according to Slemon) has become a powerful subversive tool in the re-thinking and re-addressing of history by both post-modern and post-colonial artists.

Since I would like to discuss this point in more detail with particular reference to Canadian art, I must first make what might seem a digression, but which is, I believe, crucial: one of the lessons of post-modernism is the need to respect the particular and the local, and therefore to treat Canada as a post-colonial country seems to me to require some specification and even explanation. This is not to deny in any way that Canada's history and what have been called the "psychological effects of a colonial past" (Keith 3) are not both very real and very important. Indeed, parts of Canada, especially the West, still feel colonized (see Harrison 208; Cooley 182). It is almost a truism to say that Canada as a nation has never felt central, culturally or politically; it has always felt what Bharati Mukherjee calls a "deep sense of marginality":

The Indian writer, the Jamaican, the Nigerian, the Canadian and the Australian, each one knows what it is like to be a peripheral man whose howl dissipates unheard. He knows what it is to suffer absolute emotional and intellectual devaluation, to die unfulfilled and still isolated from the world's centre. (Mukherjee Blaise 151)

But to say this is still not the same as equating the white Canadian *experience* of colonialism, and therefore of post-colonialism, with that of the West Indies or Africa or India. Commentators are rather too quick to call Canada a Third World (Saul 53) and therefore post-colonial culture (Slemon, "Magic" 10). Yet, they have behind them the weight of the famous pronouncement of Margaret Laurence that Canadians are Third World writers because "they have had to find [their] own voices and write out of what is truly [theirs], in the face of an overwhelming cultural imperialism" (17). While this may be true and while certainly Canadian literary "models remained those of Britain and more recently of America" (18), I cannot help feeling that there is something in this that is both trivializing of the Third World experience and exaggerated regarding the (white) Canadian. Of course Canada was politically a colony; but the consequences for white (not Native) writers today of that past are different from those for writers in Africa, India, or the Caribbean. The structural domination of Empire (see Stam and Spence 3-4)—not to mention the racial and cultural—differs considerably, as even thinking about something as obvious as economic "under-development" (Dorsinville, *Pays* 15) would suggest.

As Helen Tiffin and Diana Brydon have pointed out, there are different types of colonial conditions even within the British Empire. On the one hand, in countries like Africa and India, the cultural imposition associated with colonialism took place on "the homeground of the colonized people" (Tiffin, "Comparison and Judgement" 31; Brydon 3). On the other hand, in countries like Canada, Australia, and New Zealand, the English language and culture were transplanted (by settlers, convicts, slavemasters) to a foreign territory "where the indigenous inhabitants were either annihilated or marginalized" (Brydon 3). If Canada is any example, these settler colonies meant the near destruction of the indigenous culture (and people): it is one thing to impose one culture upon another, it is another thing practically to wipe out what existed when the colonizers appeared on the scene. From this perspective, it could be said that the British relation to the Native peoples in Canada and their culture was almost more destructive than that relation of imposition that took place in Africa or India. To relegate a culture to secondary status is not the same as making it illegal. But when Canadian culture is called post-colonial today the reference is very rarely to the Native culture, which might be the more accurate historical use of the term. The culture referred to most frequently is the English-language one of the descendants of the whole colonial settlers. (The fact that this is not quite accurate is important—given Canada's pluri-ethnicity—but I will return to that later.) Native and Métis writers are today demanding a voice (Cuthand; Armstrong; Campbell) and perhaps, given their articulations of the damage to Indian culture and people done by the colonizers (French and British) and the process of colonization, theirs should be considered the resisting, post-colonial voice of

Canada. Or perhaps the best model is that of Helen Tiffin: the aboriginal writing should be read as standing in what Richard Terdiman calls a counter-discursive relation to the settler literature, just as that settler literature stands counter-discursively against the imperial culture (Tiffin, "Post-Colonialism" 173; "Post-Colonial Literatures" 20). Nevertheless, there is still a difference in the degree and even kind of colonization endured. As Coral Ann Howells puts it:

> Colonization of the prairie was in the deepest sense a power struggle between whites and Indians over possession of the land complicated by the clash of irreconcilable values, for possession of the land meant very different things to the two parties in conflict. In [Rudy Wiebe's novel, *The Temptations of] Big Bear* the process of colonization is presented in precisely these terms of cultural clash and eventual imperial domination. To the whites land ownership meant exclusive possession of the prairies through the signing of land treaties with the Indians which "forever extinguished, as the Prime Minister like [*sic*] to say it, all native rights."... For them land spelt economic and political power, an extension of the British Empire. For the Indians however the land was life itself, necessary to their physical, cultural and spiritual survival. (149)

This is not quite the genocide of the Caribs or Arawaks in the West Indies, but it is still something which must be considered when dealing with the specificity of *Canadian* post-colonialism (see Pons and Rocard on the Canadian Native as an issue of colonization).

This important difference in the various histories of colonialism can be seen clearly if we extend even briefly this comparison of the Canadian experience with that of the West Indies, which some also see as examples of settler colonies (although to others slavery or "exile in conditions of bondage" [McDonald 78] remains the dominant heritage). Both the Caribbean countries and Canada shared that European colonization which more or less effectively destroyed certain Amerindian cultures. In Wilson Harris's words: "this aboriginal conquest exists like a ruin of psychological premises and biases in our midst" (3). But Canada had no imported African slave labour and no indentured workers from India or China to replace them after Abolition (though the usually ignored Chinese railway workers in Canada might be a close approximation). The racial composition of the two countries has therefore been different, and so too has been the different races' sense of belonging. Indentured labourers, unlike slaves or settlers, were always considered itinerant; they never belonged to where they worked and lived. In the West Indies, the fact that these Indian servants were often poor and caste-bound contributed to the ease with which their own culture could be suppressed. While culturally a hybrid, like all post-colonized nations (Tiffin, "Post-

Colonial Literatures" 17), Canada has experienced no actual "creolization" which might have created something new out of an adaptation process within a split racial context (see Brathwaite). Without this racial mixing, Canada's colonial culture lacked some of the sense of a "civilizing" mission, but still defined itself in terms of values which can, today, be seen as British, white, middle-class, heterosexual, and male, and it passed on these values most obviously in its educational system. In her novel, *Cat's Eye*, Margaret Atwood offers a child's view of what was learned in Canadian schools in the middle of the twentieth century:

> In countries that are not the British Empire, they cut out children's tongues, especially those of boys. Before the British Empire there were no railroads or postal services in India, and Africa was full of tribal warfare, with spears, and had no proper clothing. The Indians in Canada did not have the wheel or telephones, and ate the hearts of their enemies in the heathenish belief that it would give them courage. The British Empire changed all that. It brought in electric lights. (79)

The irony of the child's perspective underlines the politics of colonialism—in Canada and in the rest of the Empire. Singing "The Maple Leaf Forever," thinking it is the Canadian content to balance singing "Rule Britannia," the young girl notices that it too is really about England: "Wolfe, the dauntless hero, came / and planted firm Britannia's flag / On Canada's fair domain" (80).

As David Arnason explains the history of this neo-colonialism, Canada was settled by "immigrants who did not regard themselves as Canadians, but as Englishmen living in a new land. The sense of history of this first generation of immigrants is the sense of history of the mother country, not of Canada" (54). As writers, these immigrants, not surprisingly, wrote in the tradition of Britain—at least until the reality of the Canadian experience began to force alterations in the inherited forms. The influx of British Loyalists at the time of the American Revolution further enforced the values of Empire. According to one view, Loyalist myths

> have encouraged us Canadians to honour colonial symbols instead of adopting our own, and to substitute for nationalism a peculiar form of coattails imperialism. Loyalist myth-makers have never been able to imagine a Canada disentangled from Britain. Perhaps this is why, for a long time after Confederation, few Canadians could think of Canada as a nation, and no longer as a mere colony. (Bell and Tepperman 79)

The nostalgia for the British Empire which was inculcated in Atwood's character has its echo in another typical cultural irony pointed out by Arun Mukherjee: the equestrian statue of King George which sits in Toronto's aptly named "Queen's Park" was brought to Canada from India "after the latter decided to discard all visual reminders of its colonial masters" (88). This example only confirms the long history of colonialism in Canada: from the *British* North America Act (passed in Westminster, not Ottawa) to the very recent repatriation of the Constitution itself. After all, until 1947, Canadians were defined as "British subjects."

This perhaps long, seeming digression is intended to make the point that one can certainly talk of post-colonialism in Canada, but only if the differences between its particular version and that of, especially, Third World nations is kept in mind. Two other distinctions must be made, however, which further condition the use of the term in a Canadian context. The first is the pluri-ethnic (and lately more multiracial) nature of Canadian society. Some of the immigrants who populate this country are not from colonized societies and they often consciously resist being labelled post-colonial. Filippo Salvatore, an Italian Canadian writer living in Québec and writing in French, states: "the defeat of the Plains of Abraham and that of the Patriotes in 1837 did not leave indelible psychic scars on me. Psychologically I am not part of a colonized people" (203). For him and others, the immigrant experience can even be seen as a reverse of that of colonization, a conscious decision to change culture (Caccia 164).

But there are other immigrants who do not share this element of choice, who come to Canada from the West Indies, Asia or Latin America and see it as "a necessarily occupied territory because land was denied somewhere else" (Davies 33). This is largely non-European immigration, and the historical and political contexts of post-colonization cannot usually be ignored, as they might in an Italian or other European perspective. The specificity of *Canadian* post-colonial culture today is being conditioned by this arrival of immigrants from other post-colonial nations. To be educated, as Atwood described, in a British-inspired school system in Canada is still different from being so educated in Jamaica, where the system is seen, by black writers who were trained in it, as even more obviously and "proudly geared towards the needs of the British economy" and as clearly maintaining "the social stratification" that denigrates the living language of the people (Allen 66). Immigrants with this experience, who then come to Canada, bring with them an extra-acute sense of colonialism which is bound to change the nature of post-colonialism in Canada itself. Witness Cyril Dabydeen's poem, "Sir James Douglas, Father of British Columbia," which opens with

You were born where I was born.
Demerara's sun in your blood,
Guiana's rain on your skin.
You came from Creole stock
taking a native wife. (41)

The Guyanese Canadian poet addresses Douglas as "part of my heritage too / despite colonialism." The piece ends with the poet pouring (demerara) sugar into his tea and "thinking if you were more Scottish / I'd be less of the tropics" (42). This is the doubled sense of post-colonialism that is part of some of the writing we now call Canadian.

There is yet one other specific factor of Canadian experience which cannot be separated from the notion of what post-colonial means to it. For years now (see Morton 150), Canadians have felt that they are being "colonized" by American capital. The use of the term "colonization" is not totally metaphoric, for Albert Memmi defined it as "above all, economic and political exploitation" (149), and there are many Canadian economic nationalists who would claim that this is precisely what the United States is doing to Canada. Even if one does not agree with the extremity of such an evaluation, it is still the case that Canadians often feel at least culturally colonized by American mass media. They also often feel somehow politically threatened by the constant reminders of the power and imperialist impulses of our neighbour to the south (for a classic Canadian view of American power, see Grant). And speaking the same language as both the real historical colonizers and the present-day would-be colonizers has created problems for Canadian writers trying to hear their own "English" tongues (Kroetsch 1; Haberly). With these additional issues of the often doubled post-colonial focus of many Canadians and the sensitivity to American imperialism, the very use of the word "post-colonial" cannot help but be a complex issue in a Canadian context.

The fact that post-modernism is alternately claimed as an invention of either Latin America or the United States (cf. Tiffin, "Post-Colonialism" 170) is interesting in this light, for it indirectly points to the intersection of the concerns of post-modernism and post-colonialism that interests me here. Both terms, whatever their geographic origins, are tethered to earlier entities— colonialism and modernism, respectively. Some Canadian artists have addressed this double tethering, most notably photographer Geoff Miles in his *Foreign Relations: Re-W/riting a Narrative in Parts.* A series of texts and photographic images "about" colonial relations, this work offers a view of Canada, not as the Third World, but certainly also not as the First. In his catalogue, Miles notes that to discuss the photograph as a post-modern art object in Canada is "to do so within the confines of colonialism and the colonising power of the gaze of the other(s). For is it not true that we are in the unique position of being colonised by three gazes all at once; that of France, Britain, and the United States" (2). Neither post-modernism nor post-colonialism can go backwards; both by definition contest the imperialist devaluing of the "other" and the "different." But Miles feels that the discourse of photography in Canada is still very much caught within the limits of the colonial and the modernist. But in a way this also describes *any* post-colonial or post-modern art, insofar as both (as the very semantic composition of the adjectives suggests) operate in terms of that which they oppose: both contest from within. The question Miles asks himself is one which has a number of possible answers: "How do we construct a discourse which displaces the effects of the colonising gaze while we are still under its influence?" (3). These answers include, as he notes, deconstructing existing myths which support the discourses of colonialism (including modernism) and constructing different ones to take their place. They would also include irony—that strategic trope that allows a work to address a culture from within, while still articulating some challenge.

When I began this discussion of irony as a discursive strategy of both post-modernism and post-colonialism, I suggested that, not unlike allegory, irony is a trope of doubleness. And doubleness is what characterizes not just the complicitous critique of the post-modern, but, by definition, the twofold vision of the post-colonial—not just because of the obvious dual history (Slemon, "Magic" 15) but because a sense of duality was the mark of the colonial as well. Doubleness and difference are established by colonialism by its paradoxical move to enforce cultural sameness (JanMohamed 62) while, at the same time, producing differentiations and discriminations (Bhabha, "Signs" 153). This is the doubleness often represented in the metaphor of Prospero and Caliban (Mannoni; Dorsinville, *Caliban*; for a critique of this see Baker, especially 190-96, and Donaldson). It is the doubleness of the colonial culture imposed upon the colonized (Meyers vii). But it is also the doubleness of the colonized in relation to the colonizer, either as model or antithesis (Memmi 140). As Raymond Williams has argued, however, all national literatures develop in this sort of way—up to a point: from imitation of a dominant pattern to assimilation or internalization of it (see also Marchak 182), but then to a stage of open revolt where what was initially excluded by the dominant pattern gets revalorized (121-28). Is the last one here the post-colonial stage, as most critics suggest? If so, then it can still be argued that its revolt continues to operate within the power field of that dominant culture, no matter how radical its revalorization of its indigenous culture (Tiffin, "Post-Colonialism" 172). This is why irony, the trope that works from within a power field but still contests it, is a consistently useful strategy for post-colonial discourse.

Nevertheless, Homi Bhabha has argued in a series of influential articles that irony and mimicry are the modes of the colonialist, not the post-colonial: "The discourse of post-Enlightenment English colonialism often speaks in a tongue that is forked, not false" and this, he feels, is the strategy of "colonial power and knowledge" ("Of Mimicry" 126). Bhabha sees irony as appropriating the colonized Other, and implicitly therefore as part of the ambivalence and hybridity that characterize the colonial ("Representation" 93; "Signs" 154; "The Other Question" 18) in what both Edward Said and Albert Memmi have seen as its inescapable and complex mutual interrelations with the colonized. In Memmi's words: "The bond between colonizer and colonized is thus destructive and creative" (89). Without denying any of this doubleness of the experience and literature of colonization, it is still possible to see a different and consequent doubleness as characterizing the post-colonial: what has been called its "bicultural vision" (Parameswaran 241) or "metaphysical clash" (Tiffin, "Comparison and Judgement" 32; see, too, "Comparative Methodology" 29). And the way post-colonial critics talk about this literature suggests the potential importance of irony as the subversive force operating from within: "the challenge is to use the existing language, even if it is the voice of a dominant 'other'—and yet speak through it: to disrupt . . . the codes and forms of the dominant language in order to reclaim speech for oneself" (New, *Dreams* x). Irony is one way of doing precisely this, a way of resisting and yet acknowledging the power of the dominant. It may not go the next step—to suggest something new—but it certainly makes that step possible. Often combined with some sort of self-reflexivity, irony allows a text to work within the constraints of the dominant while placing those constraints *as constraints* in the foreground and thus undermining their power.

On the level of language, irony becomes one of the chief characteristics of what Bharati Mukherjee calls the "step-mother tongue" in which post-colonial writers write, "implying as it does the responsibility, affection, accident, loss, and secretive roots-quest in adoptive-family situations" (Mukherjee Blaise 147). Irony is thus one way of creatively modifying (JanMohamed 84; New, "New Language" 363) or even twisting the language so as to signal the "foreignness" of both the user and her/his experience. W.H. New has traced, as one common thread in Commonwealth literature, the *sense* of irony, the sense of being caught between two worlds: "Though dualities abound in the ironist's world, the stances he may take range from parody and innuendo through sarcasm and self-disparagement to absurdity and nihilism. . . . At its best, the ironic stance provokes a serious deliberation into the problems that led to dualities in the first place" (New, *Among Worlds* 3). This involves a reviewing of colonial and post-colonial history through the doubled lenses of ironic defamiliarization: in Canada, Cohen's *Beautiful Losers* remains perhaps the most powerful example of this process. The contradictions and heterogeneous dualities that make up the post-colonial experience also resonate with the paradoxes and multiplicities of the post-modern and, in both, irony seems to be a preferred trope for the articulation of that doubleness. The post-modern challenges to humanist universals come together with post-colonial contestings provoked by statements like A.J.M. Smith's famous valorization of those Canadian poets who "made an effort to escape the limitations of provincialism or colonialism by entering into the universal civilizing culture of ideas" (xxiv). Such a description can today be seen as pure neo-colonialism, looking as it does to Arnoldian standards for validation, standards which have been argued to be anything but universal—but rather the product of specifically nineteenth-century British, middle-class, white, male values (Belsey).

Because irony is also the trope of the unsaid, it becomes as well a possible way to encode a subtext which will deflect the risks of "[f]ull visibility and accessibility . . . [which] constitute an inherent danger for the colonized" (Weir 61). As Lorraine Weir argues, irony

> in the hands of those who exercize genuine power is very different from the same device in the hands of those classified as powerless. Among those whose basic communication may frequently depend upon the skilled use and reception of ironic utterance—that is, among the powerless irony will be all the more powerful. The Irish, as is commonly known, are masters of irony and invective; so is the primary community of women. (67)

Joining women and the Irish here would be ironic post-colonial writers as obvious as Narayan and Rushdie, each in his different way, and others perhaps less immediately obvious: Ruth Prawer Jhabvala (see Gooneratne 65-78) or Ngugi and Tayib Salih (Said 54).

Irony is the trope of the redeployable and the refracted as well as simply of the double, but doubleness seems to provide fertile ground for its usage. This makes Canada—as a post-colonial nation (in the very specific sense offered above) and as part of a general post-modern culture—rich terrain indeed:

> *Canada est omnis divisa in partes duo:* all Canada is divided into two parts. We used to have Upper and Lower Canada, but, with the settling of the plains beyond Ontario, this division is now expressed as East and West. There's also North and South and lots of divisions not based on geography: a political division between the Provincial and Federal governments; an economic one between the have and have-not provinces; a sectorial one between industrial regions and agricultural; a linguistic one between English and French. And so on. (Pechter 291)

But the multiplicity of these dualities does not always make the often resulting ironies easy to interpret, for these are frequently double-directed ironies. For example, James Reaney's poem, "The Royal Visit" (in Barbour and Scobie 58), uses repetition to signal irony: the repeated line that both those in Stratford, Ontario, who were slighted by not being presentable and thus presented to royalty and those who did not manage to see the Queen because the train moved too quickly through the town would remember the event "to their dying day." But is the irony directed against colonial royalists in Canada? against an inculcated neo-colonial mentality? against royalty for not caring enough for those who cared for them? or against all of these simultaneously? What about the subtle, self-reflating Canadian ironies of Miriam Waddington's "Back at York University" (271-72) where the narrator confronts the dual colonization of Canadian culture:

I am walking back
to an English colony,
watch me change into
an American aspiration,
look, I'm whispering into
a Canadian answer-box . . .

But neither Waddington nor Reaney are usually considered post-modern writers, and so it is hard to see from these passing examples where irony actually marks the overlapping of concerns for which I have been arguing. But in order to show that, instead of looking to the writing of Atwood, Ondaatje, Kroetsch or other writers in Canada who are generally seen as both post-colonialist and post-modern, I would like to change media and investigate briefly the intersection of the post-colonial with the post-modern in Canadian visual art and film which are usually labelled as post-modern, but which I think ought to be viewed in the light of post-colonialism as well, especially in their use of irony in the negotiation of the aesthetic and historical heritage within which they work.

Some Canadian artists *do* see themselves as working within the bounds of a historically determined colonialism. London artist Greg Curnoe writes: "the artists who are original, who break out of the colonial mode, are the ones who really affect our culture . . . because they develop out of their whole background" (quoted in Théberge 17). None of Smith's universalism for Curnoe! Post-colonial art, he implies, would be that which derives directly from its own local and particular situation. This too is a tenet of post-modernism, of course. Another example of the kind of artist who might be simultaneously post-colonial and post-modern is Charles Pachter. Like many other Canadians (such as Margaret Atwood and Joyce Wieland), Pachter's time in the United States seems to have sharpened his sense of what constitutes both the historical and current nature of colonialism in Canada. His 1972 series of paintings and prints on the theme of *Queen and Moose* chooses deliberately provocative subjects and forms: the Queen as the symbol of nostalgic neo-colonialism meets the Ur-cliché of the Canadian wilderness experience. His ironic portrayals and situations explode both myths, or rather, he makes them implode under their own accumulated cultural weight.

The entire question of Canadian identity has become a kind of playground—or battlefield—for the post-modern as well as the post-colonial defining of "difference" and value. As Laura Mulvey has written:

The question of Canadian national identity is political in the most direct sense of the word, and it brings the political together with the cultural and ideological issues immediately and inevitably. For the Canada delineated by multinationals, international finance, U.S. economic and political imperialism, national identity is a point of resistance, defining the border fortifications against exterior colonial penetration. Here nationalism can perform the political function familiar in Third World countries. (10)

Mulvey argues that Geoff Miles's work, *The Trapper's Pleasure of the Text*, deconstructs the Canadian identity and reduces it to its male, Anglo-Saxon and capitalist defining essences. And it would seem to be irony that triggers and even enables this deconstruction. The title alone, with its incongruous juxtaposition of a well-known work by Roland Barthes and the notion of a trapper, sets up the possibility for irony. The trapper here is the original European, white, male traveller, exploiting nature for financial gain, who made colonization possible in Canada. But in conjunction with the photograph (of a street scene devoid of people except for the shadow of the photographer), the person who captures the visual image is also a trapper: also a white male, he has just returned from studying in England; he too exploits external reality for potential financial gain (if he can sell his photographs). Like the trapper of old, he not only captures "reality" but fixes it and in that sense destroys its "life." This too is a form of metaphoric colonization, a taking over through representations. As Mulvey writes: "the metaphor ironizes and parodies the way that photographic aesthetics have apotheosized the decisive moment (the kill) and consequently the 'Trapper' himself as hero" (10). Further ironies result from the text which accompanies the visual image: one, positioned near the photographer's shadow, reads "Standing above it all / he sensed the power / of his position." The preying and the voyeuristic are clearly not absent from this awareness of position. On the other side, away from the shadow, we read: "The text needs its shadow! / This shadow is a bit of ideology, / a bit of representation, a bit of subject." And, of course, a shadow can, by definition, only ever be a bit of a subject and a bit of a representation. Without a shadow, that is, without a self-reflexively revelatory doubling, the text is in danger of replacing the photograph as a transparent realist medium presuming direct access to the "real." The deliberate echoing of Barthes, from the title to these texts, also recalls Barthes's own autobiographical and complex ironic use of photographs and text in both *Roland Barthes by Roland Barthes* and *Camera Lucida: Reflections on Photography*. In Miles's work too, the viewer must respond actively to decipher ironies and construct meanings in the relation of text to image. The post-colonial "Trapper" and the post-modern "Pleasure of the Text" overlap within the problematics of ironic doubleness.

The same dualities or perhaps, more accurately, the same unreconciled and unresolved contradictions that characterize both the post-modern and the post-colonial can be seen in Joyce Wieland's political film trilogy, *True Patriot Love*, a title whose echo of "O Canada" immediately places in the foreground the significance of her Canadianness to her exploration of the inter-section of the aesthetic and the political in these films. The first, *Rat Life and Diet in North America*, was made when Wieland was living in New York in 1968. But it is also subtly concerned with historical as well as current colonialism, for it is a loving parody of Beatrix Potter narratives. It is about the rebellion of a group of rats (actually gerbils in the film) against the oppression of New York and the Vietnam War. These "political prisoners" escape to Canada where they live on an organic co-op farm. Some critics have argued that this idealistic and naïve view of Canada shows Wieland to be "removed from the political mainstream" (Magidson and Wright 39), but perhaps it depends on *whose* political mainstream. What such a view misses are the ironies that per-haps only Canadians would notice: ironies of disjunction between the real and the ideal Canada, and ironies resulting from the view that, for a Canadi-an, even a less than ideal Canada might be preferable to the United States— a point American critics might be forgiven for missing.

The second film, *Reason over Passion* (1967-69) is an ironic reworking of the conventions of the travel documentary. It portrays the Canadian landscape as recorded by a hand-held camera through the windows of trains and cars. There are also freeze-frame pictures of the face of Pierre Trudeau, the man who uttered the rationalist statement that gives Wieland her title. This mate-rial is rephotographed from a moviola to get a grainy effect that self-reflex-ively serves to introduce an immediately noticeable visible mediation between the recording and the recorded. The images are accompanied by a variety of machine noises, a female voice, and 537 printed permutations of the title's letters, as selected by reason's instrument—a computer. This reappropriation of the landscape of Canada as the subject of art is a political and cultural state-ment of the value of the local and the particular over the universal and the eternal. It is not, as some critics have suggested, a nostalgic move, but a post-modern and post-colonial challenging that both contests nostalgia and post-modernly mixes elegy with exaltation in the viewing of the land. And it is the ironic juxtaposition of the title, the Trudeau shots, and the soundtrack with the landscape, as well as the self-reflexive mode of recording, that makes this double contesting possible.

The third film, *Pierre Vallières*, is the most overtly political, as its title sug-gests, for it is a parody of the documentary portrait. Its three parts link Québec colonization and search for liberation with that of women. The fixed camera frames the Québec revolutionary Vallières's mouth from which come the words we hear: thirty-three minutes of monologue with subtitles. After a while the moustached mouth with its crooked, discoloured teeth goes beyond suggesting the paradoxical revolutionary folk hero and working-class victim imaged as one (see Rabinovitz, "Films" 168-69) to imply almost a kind of sex-inverted, ironic *vagina dentata*, the terror of which informs the messages of women's liberation as well as Québec decolonization in the soundtrack.

Many of these same national and gender ironies are picked up in her 1971 National Gallery retrospective, also called *True Patriot Love/Véritable Amour Patriotique*. The entire show was set up to feel like a country fair, perhaps in itself signalling a feminist subversion of the honorific retrospective format. She even sold bottles of a perfume she created, called "Sweet Beaver: The Perfume of Canadian Liberation." The beaver as sweet here suggests more than a "nostalgic longing for a Canadian wilderness past" (Rabinovitz, "Issues" 40). As a symbol of Canada, the beaver is "sweet" because it is both pleasurable and innocent, but also because it was an appealing lure to European fur-traders and colonizers, first, and then to American capital. As medievalists also know well, the beaver (*castor*) has traditionally in the West represented a gentle (male) beast and the secretions of its scent glands were considered important to medicine— while serving the beaver as a mode of sexual attraction. In various versions of myth, when hunted, the beaver is said to bite off its own testicles (mistaken for scent glands) and thus escape with its life. Wieland's Canadian beaver may also be self-mutilating but safe, attracting but medicinal. The link between castration and *castor* is also an evident one offering another form of safety, this time from sexual vices and sins. But, as a number of critics have noted, *today* this image also cannot help connoting pornographic reductions of women as well: "Canada's history as a land raped and colonized by England and then by the United States parallels women's history of oppression" (Rabinovitz, "Issues" 40). Moreover, by ironically, if indirectly, pointing to the capitalist and patriarchal representations of women (in both pornography and in advertising—she did make the perfume a commercial object), Wieland adds another level of irony: perfume here is the very femininely coded medium that delivers a message which defies the trivialization it seems to invite. Perfume has traditionally been used to enhance women's sexual attraction to men, but here the "sweet" lure is loaded! The feminist, the environmentalist and the Canadian nationalist ironies here are at one and the same time post-modern and post-colonial.

Such is also the case in Fastwürms's installation, *Father Brébeuf's Fugue State*. According to medical psychology, a "fugue state" is a state wherein awareness of identity seems to disappear. This work politicizes and historicizes—and thereby ironizes—this term in relation to the spiritual conquest of North America, which was the first step in the French colonization of Canada's aboriginal peoples and the destruction of their identity. Using industrial materials to create post-modern ironic incongruities in the representation of historical objects, this work suggests the juxtaposition of the colonizing quest of the Jesuit missionaries with the resistance of the Native peoples, including their torture of Father Jean de Brébeuf in 1649. Tarpaper walls and fluorescent lights implicitly signal the loss and indeed the total destruction of one culture, the one close to nature; a charred wooden cross suggests the survival, despite many trials, of the other. As one commentator describes another part of the installation: "Heaped onto a pile of consumer kitsch and junk goods of Western culture are a few cobs of Indian corn and a complete deer skeleton, the leg bones of which prop up a barbecue grill topped with a steak—the stake of colonization" (Fischer 12). But it is also, most ironically and horrifically, the stake at which Brébeuf was burned—or barbecued. Yet the cross remains, however charred, and all that is left of the Native culture is bones. This is the loss of identity suggested by the title's fugue state: Brébeuf's loss of the memory of the act of colonization and its subsequent destruction of the identity of *others*.

The art of Geoff Miles, Joyce Wieland and Fastwürms, each in its own way, confronts the amnesia of colonialism through the memory of post-colonialism. And all three use the discursive strategy of irony to underline the political dimension of that confrontation. But in each case, the contesting is done from within the dominant discourse, as may be inevitable given the structure of the trope of irony. The post-*colonial* is therefore as implicated in that which it challenges as is the post-*modern*. Critique may always be complicitous when irony is its primary vehicle. For this reason, I would disagree with one important part of Simon During's particular definition of post-colonialism as "the need, in nations or groups which have been victims of imperialism, to achieve an identity uncontaminated by universalist or Eurocentric concepts and images" (1987, 33). Most post-colonial critics would oppose this as an essentialist, not to say simplifying, definition, and I would have to agree with them that the entire post-colonial project usually posits precisely the impossibility of that identity ever being "uncontaminated": just as the *word* post-colonialism holds within it its own "contamination" by colonialism, so too does the culture itself and its various artistic manifestations, in Canada as elsewhere. Colonies might well speak "unreflectingly," as Dennis Lee has suggested (54), but the *post*-colonial has at its disposal various ways of subverting from within the dominant culture—such as irony, allegory, and self-reflexivity—that it shares with the complicitous critique of post-modernism, even if its politics differ in important ways. I return to this last point once again to emphasize the difference that the use of irony by both underlines. The post-colonial, like the feminist, is a dismantling but also constructive political enterprise insofar as it implies a theory of agency and social change that the post-modern deconstructive impulse lacks. While both "post-"'s *use* irony, the post-colonial cannot *stop* at irony, as Ihab Hassan's exposition of the trope's post-modern features in the end suggests:

> *Irony*. This could also be called, after Kenneth Burke, perspectivism. In the absence of a cardinal principle or paradigm, we turn to play, interplay, dialogue, polylogue, allegory, self-reflection—in short, to irony. This irony assumes indeterminacy, multivalence; it aspires to clarity, the clarity of demystification, the pure light of absence. We meet variants of

it in Bakhtin, Burke, de Man, Jacques Derrida, and Hayden White. And in Alan Wilde we see an effort to discriminate its modes: "mediate irony," "disjunctive irony," and "postmodern" or "suspensive irony" "with its yet more racial vision of multiplicity, randomness, contingency, and even absurdity." Irony, perspectivism, reflexiveness: these express the ineluctable recreations of mind in search of a truth that continually eludes it, leaving it with only an ironic access or excess of self-consciousness. (506)

WORKS CITED

Allen, Lillian. "A Writing of Resistance: Black Women's Writing in Canada." Dybikowski et al. 63-67.

Arnason, David. "Icelandic Canadian Literature." Balan 53-66.

Armstrong, Jeannette C. "Writing from a Native Woman's Perspective." Dybikowski et al. 55-57.

Atwood, Margaret. *Cat's Eye.* Toronto: McClelland, 1988.

Baker, Houston A., Jr. "Caliban's Triple Play." *Critical Inquiry* 13.1 (1986): 182-96.

Balan, Jars, ed. *Identification: Ethnicity and the Writer in Canada.* Edmonton: Canadian Institute of Ukrainian Studies, University of Alberta, 1982.

Barbour, Douglas and Stephen Scobie, eds. *The Maple Laugh Forever: An Anthology of Comic Canadian Poetry.* Edmonton: Hurtig, 1981.

Bell, David and Lorne Tepperman. *The Roots of Disunity: A Look at Canadian Political Culture.* Toronto: McClelland, 1979.

Belsey, Catherine. *Critical Practice.* London and New York: Methuen, 1980.

Berry, Reginald. "A Deckchair of Words: Post-colonialism, Post-modernism, and the Novel of Self-projection in Canada and New Zealand." *Landfall* 40 (1986): 310-23.

Bhabha, Homi K. "Of Mimicry and Man: The Ambivalence of Colonial Discourse." *October* 28 (1984):125-33.

—. "The Other Question—The Stereotype and Colonial Discourse." *Screen* 24.6 (1983): 18-36.

—. "Representation and the Colonial Text: A Critical Exploration of Some Forms of Mimeticism." *The Theory of Reading.* Ed. Frank Gloversmith. Brighton: Harvester, 1984. 93-122.

—. "Signs Taken for Wonders: Questions of Ambivalence and Authority Under a Tree Outside Delhi, May 1817." *Critical Inquiry* 12.1 (1985): 144-65.

Brathwaite, Edward Kamau. *The Development of Creole Society in Jamaica 1770-1820.* Oxford: Oxford UP, 1978.

Brydon, Diana. "The Myths that Write Us: Decolonising the Mind." *Commonwealth* 10.1 (1987): 1-14.

Caccia, Fulvio. "The Italian Writer and Language." Trans. Martine Leprince. Pivato 153-67.

Campbell, Maria. *Halfbreed.* Halifax: Goodread Biographies, 1973.

Chow, Rey. "Rereading Mandarin Ducks and Butterflies: A Response to the Postmodern Condition." *Cultural Critique* 5 (1986-87): 69-93.

Cooley, Dennis. *The Vernacular Muse: The Eye and Ear in Contemporary Literature.* Winnipeg: Turnstone, 1987.

Cuthand, Beth. "Transmitting Our Identity as Indian Writers." Dybikowski et al. 53-54.

Dabydeen, Cyril. *This Planet Earth.* Ottawa: Borealis, 1979.

Dash, J. Michael. "Marvellous Realism: The Way Out of Negritude." *Caribbean Studies* 13.4 (1974): 57-77.

Davey, Frank. *Reading Canadian Reading.* Winnipeg: Turnstone, 1988.

Davies, Ioan. "Senses of Place." *Canadian Forum* 727 (April 1983): 33-34.

Donaldson, Laura E. "The Miranda Complex: Colonialism and the Question of Feminist Reading." *Diacritics* 18.3 (1988): 65-77.

Dorsinville, Max. *Caliban Without Prospero: Essay on Quebec and Black Literature.* Erin, ON: Press Porcépic,1974.

—. *Le Pays natal: essais sur les littératures du Tiers Monde et du Québec.* Dakar: Nouvelles Editions Africaines, 1983.

During, Simon. "Postmodernism or Postcolonialism?" *Landfall* 39.3 (1985): 366-80.

—. "Postmodernism or Post-colonialism Today." *Textual Practice* 1.1 (1987): 32-47.

Dybikowski, Ann, Victoria Freeman, Daphne Marlatt, Barbara Pulling, Betsy Warland, eds. *In the Feminine: Women and Words/Les femmes et les mots* (*Conference Proceedings* 1983). Edmonton: Longspoon, 1985.

Fastwürms. *Father Brébeuf's Fugue State* (1983). Canada Council Art Bank, Ottawa.

Fischer, Barbara. *Perspective 88: Fastwürms.* Catalogue, AGO, 17 August-26 October 1988.

Gooneratne, Yasmine. *Diverse Inheritance: A Personal Perspective on Commonwealth Literature.* Adelaide: Centre for Research in the New Literatures in English, 1980.

Grant, George. "Canadian Fate and Imperialism." *Technology and Empire: Perspectives on North America.* Toronto: Anansi, 1969. 61-78.

Haberly, David T. "The Search for a National Language: A Problem in the Comparative History of Postcolonial Literatures." *Comparative Literature Studies* 11.1 (1974): 85-97.

Harris, Wilson. "The Phenomenal Legacy." *Literary Half-Yearly* 11.2 (1970): 1-6.

Harrison, Dick. *Unnamed Country: The Struggle for a Canadian Prairie Fiction.* Edmonton: U of Alberta P, 1977.

Hassan, Ihab. "Pluralism in Postmodern Perspective." *Critical Inquiry* 12.3 (1986): 503-20.

Howells, Coral Ann. "Re-Visions of Prairie Indian History in Rudy Wiebe's *The Temptations of Big Bear* and *My Lovely Enemy*." Pons and Rocard 145-54.

Hutcheon, Linda. *A Poetics of Postmodernism: History, Theory, Fiction.* London and New York: Routledge, 1988.

Irele, Abiola. "Parables of the African Condition: A Comparative Study of Three Post-Colonial Novels." *Journal of African and Commonwealth Literature* 1 (1981): 69-91.

JanMohamed, Abdul R. "The Economy of Manichean Allegory: The Function of Racial Difference in Colonialist Literature." *Critical Inquiry* 12.1 (1985): 59-87.

Keith, W.J. *Canadian Literature in English.* London and New York: Longman, 1985.

Kroetsch, Robert. "A Canadian Issue." *Boundary 2* 3.1 (1974): 1-2.

Kröller, Eva-Marie. "The Politics of Influence: Canadian Postmodernism in an American Context." *InterAmerican Literary Relations.* Ed. M.J. Valdes. Vol. 3. New York: Garland, 1985. 118-23.

—. "Postmodernism, Colony, Nation: the Melvillean Texts of Bowering and Beaulieu." *University of Ottawa Quarterly* 54.2 (1984): 53-61.

Larson, Charles R. "Heroic Ethnocentrism: The Idea of Universality in Literature." *American Scholar* 42 (1973): 463-75.

Laurence, Margaret. "Ivory Tower or Grassroots?: The Novelist as Socio-Political Being." *A Political Art: Essays in Honour of George Woodcock.* Ed. William H. New. Vancouver: U of British Columbia P, 1970. 15-25.

Lee, Dennis. "Cadence, Country, Silence: Writing in Colonial Space." *Boundary 2* 3.1 (1974): 151-68.

McDonald, Avis G. "How History Hurts: Common Patterns in Australian and West Indian Fiction." *Queen's Quarterly* 96.1 (1989): 78-93.

Magidson, Debbie and Judy Wright. "True Patriot Love." *Art and Artists* 8.7 (1973): 38-41.

Mannoni, O. *Prospero and Caliban: The Psychology of Colonization.* 1950. New York: Praeger, 1964.

Marchak, Patricia. "Given a Certain Latitude: A (Hinterland) Sociologist's View of Anglo-Canadian Literature." *In Our Own House: Social Perspectives on Canadian Literature.* Ed. Paul Cappon. Toronto: McClelland, 1978. 178-205.

Marlatt, Daphne. *How Hug a Stone.* Winnipeg: Turnstone, 1983.

Memmi, Albert. *The Colonizer and the Colonized.* 1957. New York: Orion, 1965.

Meyers, Jeffrey. *Fiction and the Colonial Experience.* Totowa, NJ: Rowman and Littlefield, 1973.

Miles, Geoff. *Foreign Relations: Re-W/riting a Narrative in Parts.* Catalogue, Gallery 44.

Monk, Philip. "Colony, Commodity and Copyright Reference and Self-Reference in Canadian Art." *Vanguard* 12.5-6 (1983): 14-17.

Morton, W.L. *The Canadian Identity.* 1961. Toronto: U of Toronto P, 1972.

Mukherjee, Arun P. "South Asian Poetry in Canada: In Search of a Place." *World Literature Written in English* 26.1 (1986): 84-98.

Mukherjee Blaise, Bharati. "Mimicry and Reinvention." *The Commonwealth in Canada.* Ed. Uma Parameswaran. Calcutta: Writers Workshop Greybird, 1983. 147-57.

Mulvey, Laura. "Magnificent Obsession." *Parachute* 42 (1986): 6-12.

New, William H. *Among Worlds: An Introduction to Modern Commonwealth and South African Fiction.* Erin, ON: Press Porcépic, 1975.

—. *Dreams of Speech and Violence: The Art of the Short Story in Canada and New Zealand.* Toronto: U of Toronto P, 1987.

—. "New Language, New World." *Awakened Conscience: Studies in Commonwealth Literature.* Ed. C.D. Narasimhaiah. New Delhi: Sterling, 1978. 360-77.

Pache, Walter. "The Fiction Makes Us Real: Aspects of Postmodernism in Canada." *Gaining Ground: European Critics on Canadian Literature.* Ed. Robert Kroetsch and Reingard H. Nischik. Edmonton: NeWest, 1985. 64-78.

Parameswaran, Uma. "Amid the Alien Corn: Biculturalism and the Challenge of Commonwealth Literary Criticism." *World Literature Written in English* 21.1 (1982): 240-53.

Pechter, Edward. "Of Ants and Grasshoppers: Two Ways (or More) to Link Texts and Power." *Poetics Today* 9.2 (1988): 291-306.

Petersen, Kirsten Holst and Anna Rutherford, eds. *A Double Colonization: Colonial and Post-Colonial Women's Writing.* Mundelstrup, Denmark: Dangaroo, 1986.

Pivato, Joseph, ed. *Contrasts: Comparative Essays on Italian Canadian Writing.* Montreal: Guernica, 1985.

Pons, X. and M. Rocard, eds. *Colonisations: Rencontres Australie-Canada.* Toulouse: Université de Toulouse-Le Mirail, 1985.

Rabinovitz, Lauren. "Issues of Feminist Aesthetics: Judy Chicago and Joyce Wieland." *Women's Art Journal* 1.2 (1980-81): 38-41.

—. "The Films of Joyce Wieland." *Joyce Wieland.* Toronto: AGO; Key Porter Books, 1987. 117-20, 161-79.

Said, Edward W. "Intellectuals in the Post-Colonial World." *Salmagundi* 70-71 (1986): 44-64.

Salutin, Rick. *Marginal Notes: Challenges to the Mainstream.* Toronto: Lester and Orpen Dennys, 1984.

Salvatore, Filippo. "The Italian Writer of Quebec: Language, Culture and Politics." Trans. David Homel. Pivato 189-206.

Saul, John Ralston. "We Are Not Authors of the Post-Novel Novel." *Brick* (Winter 1988): 52-54.

Scott, F.R. and A.J.M. Smith, eds. *The Blasted Pine: An Anthology of Satire, Invective and Disrespectful Verse.* Rev. ed. Toronto: Macmillan, 1967.

Slemon, Stephen. "Magic Realism as Post-Colonial Discourse." *Canadian Literature* 116 (1988): 9-23.

—. "Monuments of Empire: Allegory/Counter-Discourse/Post-Colonial Writing." *Kunapipi* 9.3 (1987):1-16.

—. "Post-Colonial Allegory and the Transformation of History." *Journal of Commonwealth Literature* 23.1 (1988): 157-68.

Smith, A.J.M., ed. *The Oxford Book of Canadian Verse in English and French.* Toronto: Oxford UP, 1960.

Spivak, Gayatri Chakravorty. *In Other Worlds: Essays in Cultural Politics.* New York and London: Routledge, 1988.

Stam, Robert and Louise Spence. "Colonialism, Racism, and Representation." *Screen* 24.2 (1983): 2-20.

Théberge, Pierre. *Greg Curnoe.* Ottawa: National Gallery of Canada, 1982.

Tiffin, Helen. "Commonwealth Literature and Comparative Methodology." *World Literature Written in English* 23.1 (1984): 26-30.

—. "Commonwealth Literature: Comparison and Judgement." *The History and Historiography of Commonwealth Literature.* Ed. Dieter Riemenschneider. Tübingen: Günter Narr, 1983. 19-35.

—. "Post-Colonial Literatures and Counter-Discourse." *Kunapipi* 9.3 (1987): 17-34.

—. "Post-Colonialism, Post-Modernism and the Rehabilitation of Post-Colonial History." *Journal of Commonwealth Literature* 23.1 (1988): 169-81.

Waddington, Miriam. *Collected Poems.* Toronto: Oxford UP, 1986.

Weir, Lorraine. "Toward a Feminist Hermeneutics: Jay Macpherson's *Welcoming Disaster.*" *Gynocritics: Feminist Approaches to Canadian and Quebec Women's Writing/Gynocritiques: Démarches féministes à l'écriture des Canadiennes et Québécoises.* Ed. Barbara Godard. Toronto: ECW, 1987. 59-70.

Wieland, Joyce, dir. *Rat Life and Diet in North America.* 1968.

—. dir. *Reason Over Passion.* 1967-69.

—. dir. *Pierre Vallières.* 1972.

Williams, Raymond. *Marxism and Literature.* Oxford: Oxford UP, 1977.

9

"THE WHITE INUIT SPEAKS: CONTAMINATION AS LITERARY STRATEGY"*

Diana Brydon

My title is inspired by the coincidental appearance of the Inuit as symbolic figure in two important Canadian novels published in 1989, Kristjana Gunnars' *The Prowler* and Mordecai Richler's *Solomon Gursky Was Here*. By echoing the influential American ethnographic text *Black Elk Speaks*, I mean to highlight the assumptions about cultural purity and authenticity that post-modernism and post-colonialism, and these two texts, both use and challenge. *Black Elk Speaks* itself is now being recognised as a white man's construct, fusing traditional Lakota with Christian philosophy—a hybrid rather than the purely authentic of the anthropologist's dreams (Powers). Unlike those who deplore a perceived loss in authenticity in Black Elk's cultural contamination, Gunnars and Richler explore the creative potential of such cross-cultural contact. For them, as for the bilingual Canadian poet Lola Lemire Tostevin, "the concept of contamination as literary device" would seem to be appealing. Tostevin argues that "Contamination means differences have been brought together so they make contact" (13).

Such a process defines the central activities of post-modernism and post-colonialism—the bringing of differences together into creative contact. But this is also where they part company. For it is the nature of this contact—and its results—that are at issue. For post-colonial writers, the cross-cultural imagination that I am polemically calling "contamination" for the purposes of this article, is not just a literary device but also a cultural and even a political project. Linda Hutcheon ("'Circling the Downspout'") in this collection[1] points out that post-colonialism and feminism have "distinct political agendas and often a theory of agency that allow them to go beyond the post-modern limits of deconstructing existing orthodoxies into the realms of social and political action." In contrast, she argues, "post-modernism is politically ambivalent" (72). At the same time, however, she concludes that the post-colonial is "as implicated in that which it challenges as is the post-*modern*" (88). This assertion depends on a leap from the recognition that the post-colonial is "contaminated" by colonialism (in the word itself and the culture it signifies)

---

* *Past the Last Post: Theorizing Post-Colonialism and Post-Modernism*, ed. Ian Adam and Helen Tiffin (Calgary: U of Calgary P, 1990), 191-203.

to the conclusion that such "contamination" necessarily implies complicity. It is this notion I would like to explore more fully in the rest of this paper.

If we accept Hutcheon's assertion that post-modernism is politically ambivalent, what are the implications of such a theory? There are at least two that interest me here. Firstly, what enables this ambivalence? Post-modernism takes on a personality; it becomes a subject, human-like in its ability to express ambivalence. The functions of the author, declared dead by post-structuralist theory, resurface in post-modernism and in the post-modernist text through the concept of ambivalence. The authority of the post-modernist text comes from this ambivalence, this ability to see all sides, to defer judgement and to refuse agency. Secondly, what are the effects of this ambivalence? It would seem to suggest that action is futile; that individual value judgements are likely to cancel each other out; that one opinion is as good as another; that it would be futile and dishonest to choose one path above any other; that disinterested contemplation is superior to any attempt at action. In effect, then, ambivalence works to maintain the status quo. It updates the ambiguity so favoured by the New Critics, shifting their formalist analysis of the text's unity into a psychoanalysis of its fissures, and their isolation of text from world into a worldliness that cynically discounts the effectiveness of any action for social change.

To refer to contradictions instead of a fundamental ambivalence places the analysis within a political rather than a psychoanalytical framework. Post-modernism and post-colonialism often seem to be concerned with the same phenomena, but they place them in different grids of interpretation. The name "post-modernism" suggests an aestheticising of the political while the name "post-colonialism" foregrounds the political as inevitably contaminating the aesthetic, but remaining distinguishable from it. If post-modernism is at least partially about "how the world dreams itself to be 'American'" (Stuart Hall qtd. in Ross xii), then post-colonialism is about waking from that dream, and learning to dream otherwise. Post-modernism cannot account for such post-colonial resistance writing, and seldom attempts to.

Much of my work over the past decade has involved documenting the contradictions of Canadian post-colonialism. Reading Canadian literature from a post-colonial perspective, recognizing Canadian participations in empire and in the resistance to empire, one quickly encounters some of the limitations of post-modernist theory in accounting for Canadian texts, even for those apparently post-modernist in form. Because Linda Hutcheon is one of Canada's preeminent theorists of the post-modern, this essay engages with her work first of all as a way of posing some of the problems I see when the post-colonial and the post-modern are brought together.

Despite post-modernism's function as a problematising mode, several assumptions central to imperial discourse survive unchallenged in the work of its defenders. These include an evolutionary model of development, a search for synthesis that relies on a revival of the notion of authenticity, and an insistence on judging a work on its own terms alone as if there were only one true reading. A post-colonial reading would reject such assumptions; post-modernist readings affirm them under the guise of a disinterested objectivity.

I am aware here of entering disputed territory. The quarrels over the meaning of postmodernism are well documented elsewhere in this book [*Past the Last Post*] and in numerous others. Post-colonial criticism has its own disputes, with a scantier and more recent documentation. I would distinguish the post-colonial criticism developed by Ashcroft, Griffiths and Tiffin in *The Empire Writes Back* from that developed by the U.S.-based Jameson, Gates and Spivak, which to my mind suffers from some of the same assumptions as does post-modernism.

1. THE EVOLUTIONARY MODEL

In "'Circling the Downspout'" Hutcheon writes that "[t]he current post-structuralist/post-modern challenges to the coherent, autonomous subject have to be put on hold in feminist and post-colonial discourses, for both must work first to assert and affirm a denied or alienated subjectivity: those radical post-modern challenges are in many ways the luxury of the dominant order which can afford to challenge that which it securely possesses" (72-73). There are several problems with this statement. The first is the notion that there is a single evolutionary path of literary development established by the European model. Secondly, there is the idea of a norm of subjectivity also established by the European model. Thirdly, there is the implied assumption that poetical commitment (to the liberation of nation or women), even in non-European countries, must necessarily express itself through a literary realism that presents a unified subject along the nineteenth century European model. And finally, it seems to demean literary criticism as a "luxury," something nonessential that not all societies really need, as if critique is not a necessary component for culture or identity building.

These assumptions are so strongly embedded in our western culture that even texts challenging such notions are read to confirm them. Consider Jamaica Kincaid's *Annie John*, a complex metafictional work challenging notions of a unified subjectivity that is often read as a traditional *bildungsroman* consolidating a simple achievement of just such a selfhood. Yet as Simon Gikandi argues, "Caribbean women writers are concerned with a subject that is defined by what de Laurentis calls 'a multiple, shifting, and often self-contradictory identity, a subject that is not divided in, but rather at odds, with language'" (14). This is the kind of subject whose exploration Hutcheon argues must be "put on hold" in feminist and post-colonial writing, yet in fact we find it in many of these texts, if we read them with the openness we bring to European fictions.

2. The Search for Synthesis

In expressing her unease with the use of post-colonial to describe the settler and multicultural contemporary cultures of Canada, Hutcheon suggests that perhaps Native culture "should be considered the resisting, post-colonial voice of Canada" (76-77). This search for the authentic Canadian voice of post-colonialism mirrors the title of her book on post-modernism in Canada, *The Canadian Postmodern*. Just as we saw a unitary subjectivity being affirmed in the evolutionary model, so we see a unified voice or style being advocated here. Although Hutcheon here identifies Robert Kroetsch as "Mr Canadian Postmodern" (*Postmodern* 183), I would argue that there are several Canadian post-modernisms just as there is more than one Canadian post-colonial voice. A term may have multiple, subsidiary meanings without losing its usefulness in indicating a general category.

Hutcheon's assumption that the post-colonial speaks with a single voice leads her to belabour the necessity of resisting the totalising application of a term that in her analysis would blur differences and deny the power relations that separate the native post-colonial experience from that of the settlers. Certainly turning to the post-colonial as a kind of touristic "me-tooism" that would allow Canadians to ignore their own complicities in imperialism would be a serious misapplication of the term. Yet, as far as I know, discussions of Canadian post-colonialism do not usually equate the settler with the native experience, or the Canadian with the Third World. The kind of generalisations that Richard Roth criticises in Abdul JanMohammed's work do tend to totalise in this way, but this kind of work always ignores countries like Canada. To my mind, Hutcheon gets it backwards when she writes: "one can certainly talk of post-colonialism in Canada, but only if the differences between its particular version and that of, especially, Third World nations is kept in mind" (79). The drawing of such distinctions is the whole point of talking about post-colonialism in Canada. The post-colonial perspective provides us with the language and the political analysis for understanding these differences. The danger is less that Canadians will rush to leap on the victim wagon than that they will refuse to recognize that they may well have some things in common with colonised people elsewhere.

Hutcheon's argument functions as a sort of straw man that misrepresents the post-colonial theoretical endeavour as practised in relation to Canada, deflecting attention away from its radical potential. Her argument demonstrates that in our care to respect the specificity of particular experiences we run another risk, that of a liberal pluralism which uses the idea of different but equal discourses to prevent the forming of alliances based on a comparative analysis that can perceive points of connection. Consider the following statement from *The Canadian Postmodern*: "If women have not yet been allowed access to (male) subjectivity, then it is very difficult for them to contest it, as the (male) post-structuralist philosophers have been doing lately. This may make women's writing *appear* more conservative, but in fact it is just *different*" (5-6). By positing female writing as "just different" from the male norm, Hutcheon erases the power differential she has been trying to establish, while reaffirming the male as the norm and the experimental as more advanced than and superior to the conservative. It sounds like special pleading for the second-rate, while on the surface it reaffirms the liberal myth of society formed from a plurality of equal differences.

Her assertion of Canadian difference from other post-colonial experiences functions in a similar way. The focus on uniqueness denies us the insights to be derived from careful comparison. Far from separating it from other post-colonial nations, Canada's pluri-ethnic composition allows for points of connection with some experiences elsewhere which when analysed comparatively may yield insights into how power operates, other than by sheer force, in our own fairly comfortable world. Far from totalising, a post-colonial analysis can identify structural patterns of oppression and the moves that coopt difference to maintain oppression as well as the strategies for resisting it.

Hutcheon suggests in "'Circling the Downspout'" that "Canada has experienced no actual 'creolization' which might have created something new out of an adaptation process within a split racial context" (78). What about the Metis, and the literature now being created by Metis writers? What about a writer like Tostevin, equally at home in English and French? At a less literal level, what about the metaphorical creolization of novels like *The Prowler* and *Solomon Gursky Was Here*? Most of the rest of this essay concerns itself with challenging this claim.

3. THE CULT OF AUTHENTICITY

Paul Smith suggests that post-modernist discourse replaces the "conflictual view and the comic view of the third world" with a "cult of authenticity" (142). This seems to be what is happening with Hutcheon's assertion that only Canada's native peoples may claim to speak with an authentic post-colonial voice. Such an assertion connects her approach to post-colonialism to that of Fredric Jameson which produces a first world criticism respectful of a third world authenticity that it is believed his own world has lost. But what are the effects of such a "cult of authenticity"? Meaghan Morris concludes her analysis of *Crocodile Dundee* with the statement that "[i]t is hardly surprising, then, that the figure of the colonial should now so insistently reappear from all sides not as deprived and dispossessed by rapacity but as the naive spirit of plenitude, innocence, optimism—and effective critical 'distance'" (124). The post-modernist revisionings of the colonial and post-colonial that Smith and Morris discuss function to defuse conflict, denying the necessity of cultural and political struggle, and suggesting that tourism is probably the best model for cross-cultural interaction.

Hutcheon's argument that Canada's native peoples are the authentic postcolonial voice of the nation, with its implication that descendents of settlers and immigrants represent at best a contaminated post-coloniality, conforms to this post-modernist model. To challenge it, as Hutcheon knows, is fraught with difficulties because authenticity has also been used by colonial peoples in their struggles to regain power over their own lives. While post-colonial theorists embrace hybridity and heterogeneity as the characteristic post-colonial mode, some native writers in Canada resist what they see as a violating appropriation to insist on their ownership of their stories and their exclusive claim to an authenticity that should not be ventriloquised or parodied. When directed against the Western canon, post-modernist techniques of intertextuality, parody, and literary borrowing may appear radical and even potentially revolutionary. When directed against native myths and stories, these same techniques would seem to repeat the imperialist history of plunder and theft. Or in the case of *The Satanic Verses*, when directed against Islam, they may be read as sullying the dignity of a religion that prides itself on its purity.

Although I can sympathise with such arguments as tactical strategies in insisting on self-definition and resisting appropriation, even tactically they prove self-defeating because they depend on a view of cultural authenticity that condemns them to a continued marginality and an eventual death. Whose interests are served by this retreat into preserving an untainted authenticity? Not the native groups seeking land rights and political power. Ironically, such tactics encourage native peoples to isolate themselves from contemporary life and full citizenhood.

All living cultures are constantly in flux and open to influences from elsewhere. The current flood of books by white Canadian writers embracing Native spirituality clearly serves a white need to feel at home in this country and to assuage the guilt felt over a material appropriation by making it a cultural one as well. In the absence of comparable political reparation for past appropriations such symbolic acts seem questionable or at least inadequate. Literature cannot be confused with social action. Nonetheless, these creole texts are also part of the post-colonial search for a way out of the impasse of the endless play of post-modernist difference that mirrors liberalism's cultural pluralism. These books, like the post-colonial criticism that seeks to understand them, are searching for a new globalism that is neither the old universalism nor the Disney simulacrum. This new globalism simultaneously asserts local independence and global interdependencies. It seeks a way to cooperate without cooption, a way to define differences that do not depend on myths of cultural purity or authenticity but that thrive on an interaction that "contaminates" without homogenising.

Darlene Barry Quaife's *Bone Bird* is one of the most interesting of these new creole texts. Aislinn Cleary, part-white and part-native, learns to reach out to others through her initiation into a mixture of local Vancouver Island native spiritual practice and her grandmother's beliefs, brought with her as a refugee from Mexico fleeing the aftermath of Pancho Villa's thwarted rebellion. Her friendship with two tree planters temporarily working in town acquaints her with the stories of other refugees: Hugh's Chinese mother fleeing the Second World War in the Pacific and Ivan's Polish mother fleeing the same war in Europe. Hugh is researching and documenting historical and cultural links between China and the West Coast of America that might explain the similarities he has discovered between certain artistic symbols. He and Aislinn need each other to complete this work. The "bone bird" metamorphoses as a spiritual guide, leading Teodora, Aislinn's grandmother, out of despair into new life and directing Aislinn toward new journeys with Hugh, and as "the scavenger," mascotting the unemployed loggers of Aislinn's town toward new lives elsewhere. The political realities of a colonial economy where a logging operation can first destroy the material bases of the native culture and then that of the settler culture logging the trees by shutting down the single industry company town are at the heart of this narrative. They are at once part of a global system of exploitation and a specifically evoked particular experience, with its own smells, sights, sounds, pleasures and pains. The text records these accurately, with love and anguish, but it directs its quest for spiritual values toward the alliances that can survive, resist, and renew. The only advocate of cultural purity is Aislinn's racist, and very ill, English mother, a war bride who did not know that her Canadian husband was part-Indian until it was too late to turn back.

4. JUDGING THE WORK ON ITS OWN TERMS

Hutcheon's conclusion to her *Poetics of Postmodernism* admits the "limited" aims of post-modernism and its "double encoding as both contestatory and complicitous" (230). She acknowledges that "I would agree with Habermas that this art does not 'emit any clear signals,'" but adds that its saving grace is that "it does not try to." It cannot offer answers, "without betraying its anti-totalizing ideology" (231). I have suggested that it does surreptitiously offer answers—in ambivalence itself, in the relativity of liberal pluralism, in the cult of authenticity that lies behind its celebration of differences. But is it true that answers necessarily totalise? Are these the only alternatives? Is Hutcheon here asking enough of the post-modernist text? Or is she even asking the most interesting or the most important questions? Isn't the effect of such a conclusion to preserve the status quo and the myth of an objectivity that itself totalizes? Can we legitimately ask more of a text than it asks of itself? Postcolonial criticism suggests that we can.

5. READING THE WHITE INUIT

To read Kristjana Gunnars' *The Prowler* and Mordecai Richler's *Solomon Gursky Was Here* is to enter two very different literary experiences. Both nod to post-modernist antecedents (Gunnars to Grass's *Tin Drum* and Richler to Márquez's *One Hundred Years of Solitude*) and employ post-modernist techniques (fragmenting narrative, doubling incidents, metafictional commentary, interrupted chronology, mixing of modes), but in *The Prowler* these techniques are integral to the way the text makes its meaning whereas in *Solomon Gursky* they are entertaining excrescences on a tale almost Dickensian in its fundamental faithfulness to a realist's investment in character and story.

Far from surrendering the author's authority, Richler delights in his control, duplicating it within the text in the story of Solomon Gursky's/Sir Hyman Kaplansky's manipulation of Moses Berger. Here the author plays his reader as a fisherman plays a fish, the fish gladly seizing the hook of narrative in return for the pleasure of the quest. *The Prowler* abandons such myths of control in search of an equal partnership between writer and reader, both prowlers seeking to transgress the boundaries of traditionally delimited territories and seeking to subvert the linearity and predicability of traditional plots with their winners and their losers. *The Prowler* puts as much distance as possible between the writer as prowler and the idea of an author God in control of the story. Prowling the borders, silences and dead ends of stories, reader and writer nonetheless come together to share a point of view, to discern emergent patterns, and to make choices about how we make meaning in the world.

These reading experiences are different in the power they allocate to writer and reader, and in the distance they are willing to travel to question dominant assumptions about the way the world works and whether or not it is possible to change it to make it a better place. Richler's is finally a conservative vision and Gunnars' a radical one. Nonetheless, both texts insist that the reader must move beyond a post-modernist ambivalence into a world of moral decision making. Neither Gunnars nor Richler offer answers, but their texts do make value judgements and encourage their readers to make them too. Although they recognize inevitable complicities, they choose contestation; they discover free spaces for resistance; they introduce love and freedom into worlds of pain and hatred. In their work, post-modernist devices serve post-colonial ends. Although the experience of reading these two books is very different, they offer similar visions of the marginalised, similar questionings of myths of purity and authenticity, similar affirmations of cultural contamination, and similar insistences on the political agency that characterizes the post-colonial. These similarities, I would suggest, derive from the particular circumstances of a Canadian post-coloniality that is not indigenous but in the process of becoming so.

Just as the North functions for many non-Northerners as a final frontier, so the Inuit can seem a last symbol of cultural integrity. Both Gunnars and Richler explode these myths of North and Northerners. For them the North is an archetypal colony and the people who inhabit the North find their identity in dispute between those committed to maintaining an ideal of cultural purity and those who favour cultural interaction.

The Prowler explains that "White Inuit" are Icelanders, Northerners who survive on a diet of fish in a country with a history of multiple colonisations. As "White Inuit" their identity is already hybrid, privileged by race and underprivileged by location. The narrator's already hybrid identity as white Inuit is further complicated by different parental legacies, by language, by class, and by changes in the power structures governing her island as well as shifts in her geographical location. Her response to such endless discriminations of difference is to multiply the contaminations: "The solution was to study more languages. I would learn French and German, Faeroese and Inuit. I would confuse them all" (Section 133). If language determines identity, multiply the identities; confuse the categorisers; transgress the limits imposed on identity. She will be a boundary-crosser, a border-prowler. Cultural purity, the myth of her homogenous Icelandic society, is not possible even there.

But neither is it possible to be all things to all people. To speak Danish and English is not to betray her Icelandic identity, but to ask questions such as "Why has there been such a long history of starvation?" (Section 44) is to begin to recognise that "it is not possible to sympathize with all sides at once. When you choose your allegiances, I thought, you ally yourself with the one who suffers" (Section 142). Such an alliance entails drawing connections between political realities and private lives, between military occupations and imperial control on the one hand and the shortage of food and shelter on the other, between comfort in Denmark and the United States and suffering in Iceland.

The text's post-modernist celebration of multiplicities—"I imagine a story that allows all speakers to speak at once, claiming that none of the versions is exactly a lie" (Section 68)—is complicated by its recognition that "human psychology is determined by politics. And politics is determined by diet. That is, those who eat best win" (Section 155). Material realities ground the text's utopian desire for surfeit in the remembrance of a manipulated scarcity. Nonetheless, *The Prowler* chooses to end with an image of hope, rewriting the story of Noah's Ark as an Icelandic myth of a new beginning with a communal welcoming after the disaster of the Second World War. This Ark contains the mothers and fathers of future generations, returning Icelanders enriched by their contact with the outside world.

Richler too reappropriates the story of Noah's Ark in multiple rewritings that turn the doomed ship Erebus of the Franklin expedition into an ark that enables the survival of his mythical Jewish explorer Ephraim Gursky. Gursky takes as his emblem the raven that disappointed Noah on the Biblical ark but that represents a survivor trickster figure for North American Native mythologies. The raven, who "speaks in two voices" (500), provides an alternative creation myth to that of Genesis for Ephraim's grandson Solomon. Solomon's son Henry meets his death on what his neighbours term "Crazy Henry's Ark," and his son Isaac only survives through an act of cannibalism that appears to symbolise Richler's view of father/son relations in this text. Despite the cultural contaminations of Richler's Ark of origins, it remains throughout its transformations a purely masculine process that limits its celebration of cultural hybridity.

Ephraim introduces Jewish customs into Inuit practice, to the confusion of anthropologists and historians seeking cultural authenticity in the far North. Richler's comic invention of "The McGibbon Artifact," "the only Eskimo carving of what was clearly meant to represent a kangaroo" (61) makes a serious political point reiterated throughout the text, that the movements of peoples and interactions of cultures that have characterized the twentieth century have taken place as part of the military expansion of capital, but that there is always a space for resistance, for eluding control and surprising the enemy. Ephraim Gursky beats the convict system that built the British empire in the nineteenth century; Solomon Gursky beats the capitalists at their own game in the twentieth. The multiple colonial childhoods that Kaplansky/Gursky/ Raven invents to entertain his British guests draw the reader's attention to the structural similarities produced by the expansion of empire even as the stories function for his listeners as isolated instances of a titillating authenticity.

Solomon, the archetypal wandering Jew who survived prohibition in Canada and the Holocaust in Europe "didn't die of old age," Moses suspected, "but in the Gulag or a stadium in Latin America" (550-51). He becomes the spirit of resistance to oppression in all its guises, changing shapes as fast as his enemies, always one step ahead of those who would betray the human spirit. The danger in such tales is the homogenizing of differences into the repetition of a single narrative, and the elimination of collective action in favour of the myth of the superhuman individual whose triumphs can easily be used to justify the continued oppression of the rest of us. Its strength lies in its insistence that individual lives do matter, that each of us can make a difference, a point brought home by the book's title *Solomon Gursky Was Here*. The survival of the surprising Mr. Morrie and the rejuvenation of Moses further support such a reading as do other elements in the text.

Using the recurrent post-colonial metaphor of the colony as the empire's garbage dump, both Gunnars and Richler explore what it means to live in a place that is powerless to refuse others' refuse, what others have refused. Iceland is where other countries dump their lepers. "They did not think people on this remote island counted" (Section 41). Canada is where the British dump "the effluvium of their slums" (Richler 81). Both novels affirm, however, that such apparent disadvantages may be turned to advantage. Gunnars' narrator muses on how North America "turns out to be a place where major defects go unnoticed" (Section 149). A weakness elsewhere may be turned into a strength here. (This is a premise explored at more length in Bharati Mukherjee's *Jasmine*.) Similarly, Richler's Moses muses: "If Canada had a soul . . . then it wasn't to be found in Batoche or the Plains of Abraham or Fort Walsh or Charlottetown or Parliament Hill, but in The Caboose and thousands of bars like it that knit the country together from Peggy's Cove, Nova

Scotia to the far side of Vancouver Island" (64). In other words, that elusive Canadian essence is not to be found in historic defeats, military battles or the parliamentary process, but in the survival of working class communal culture at the local level throughout the land. The "effluvium" of British slums bring a tough cultural specificity to Canada that Britain rejected but our writers now embrace. This turning the tables on those who think they have you where they want you, this transvaluation of values is part of the post-colonial literary strategy that clears a space for history's silenced ones to speak. Strength comes not from victimhood, from what one has been denied, but from a reevaluation of what one has.

Richler's embrace takes in the ugly racism as well as the moral probity of the Bert Smiths whom he has Solomon see as the "essence" of this country (74). Bert Smith, like Moses's arch enemy Professor Hardy, believes in cultural purity but finds himself defeated as the "true north, strong and free" of the national anthem yields to Richler's celebration of a "mongrelized" nation (79-80). In a delightfully understated ironic reversal, just when Smith and his landlady, Mrs. Jenkins, think they have finally parted company, Richler shows us Mrs. Jenkins unconsciously seeing with Smith's eyes and Smith unconsciously speaking in Mrs. Jenkins' voice (444-45). For all their stubborn opposition to each other's point of view, they have inevitably contaminated one another through the proximity in which they have lived. Despite themselves, their horizons have broadened and they have grown in the process.

Both Richler and Gunnars retain the utopian dream of the quest for a just society, and locate that quest in the contaminations of cross-cultural exploration. Both write out of positions specifically located in the current debate about multiculturalism in Canada: Richler as a male, Canadian-born Jew and Anglophone Quebecker; Gunnars as a female, Icelandic immigrant to the Canadian West for whom English is not a first language. Both vigorously dispute any residual faith in the possibility of cultural authenticity. Both show how colonial relations permeate some European and North American experiences. It is not possible to postulate a Them and Us based on geography or the nation-state alone. These texts work to "resuscitate" the local referent from "the coma induced by typecasting" (Roth 249), showing how post-modernisms and post-colonialisms are themselves riddled by differences that nonetheless may be understood through a double-pronged analysis that looks for the workings of power in specific conditions.

Perhaps the clearest difference between a post-modernist practice and a post-colonial practice emerges through their different uses of history. As Hutcheon points out, "[h]istoriographic metafiction acknowledges the paradox of the *reality* of the past but its *textualized accessibility* to us today" (*Poetics* 114). Without denying that things happened, post-modernism focuses on the problems raised by history's textualized accessibility: on the problems of representation, and on the impossibility of retrieving truth. Post-colonialism, in contrast, without denying history's textualized accessibility, focuses on the reality of a past that has influenced the present. As a result of these different emphases, post-modern fiction takes liberties with what we know of the facts of the past much more freely than does post-colonial fiction. Richler's improbable introduction of fictional characters into historical narrative has more in common with the methods of a Sir Walter Scott than a D.M. Thomas. Neither he nor Gunnars deny that different versions of specific events will circulate, but they are interested in the effects of historical happenings: the effects of invasion, of military occupation, of food blockades, of revolution.

More than this, they do not hesitate to suggest that some interpretations carry greater validity than others: lies may be distinguished from truths; false values from valid ones. Gunnars writes: "Reading *Morgunbladid*, the Icelandic daily, I saw the population of the island was being reassured. The American Base, it said, is not a nuclear base. Some months later in Canada I happened upon an American military map. Iceland, it showed, *is* a nuclear base" (Section 30). Richler provides a diary entry showing Kaplansky asking his French neighbours who came to the dinner parties put on by the German officers occupying his house during the Second World War. One neighbour sobs in reply: "We had no choice but to accept his invitations. It was awful. His father was a pork butcher. He had no manners. He didn't even know that Pouilly-Fumé is not a dessert wine" (515-16). Here Richler relies on our knowledge of the Holocaust to "place" these values. Richler's most sympathetic characters need to believe that a writer should not be bought, that not everything can be turned into a commodity, even in a commodity culture. *The Prowler* believes that "the text desires to be true" (Section 69). Near its end, its narrator admits "That the text has been prowling in the reader's domain. Telling itself and then interpreting itself. . . . The text is relieved that there are no borders in these matters" (Section 164). In other words, neither author is willing to surrender the agency that Hutcheon sees as characterizing the post-colonial but not the post-modern. Their recognition of complicities does not make them complicit.

As Stephen Slemon points out in this collection [*Past the Last Post*], "Western post-modernist readings can so over-value the anti-referential or deconstructive energies of postcolonial texts that they efface the important recuperative work that is also going on within them" (7). Those deconstructive energies are at work in these two novels, but it is the recuperative power, which they seek to energize for their readers and their Canadian culture, that most distinguishes them. And it is this power that a post-colonial reading can help us to understand. The white Inuit are speaking. Who is listening?

Notes

1. [Editor's note: Brydon is referring to the collection in which this article originally appeared, *Past the Last Post.* Page references to Gikandi's and Slemon's articles

are to that collection; page references to Hutcheon's article are keyed to this volume.]

WORKS CITED

Adam, Ian, and Helen Tiffin, eds. *Past the Last Post: Theorizing Post-Colonialism and Post-Modernism.* Calgary: U of Calgary P, 1990.

Ashcroft, Bill, Gareth Griffiths and Helen Tiffin. *The Empire Writes Back: Theory and Practice in Post-Colonial Literatures.* London: Routledge, 1989.

Black Elk, and John G. Neihardt. *Black Elk Speaks.* 1961. Lincoln: U of Nebraska P, 1979.

Gates, Henry Louis, ed. *Race, Writing and Culture.* Chicago: U of Chicago P, 1986.

Gikandi, Simon. "Narration in the Post-Colonial Moment: Merle Hodge's *Crick Crack Monkey*." Adam and Tiffin 13-20.

Gunnars, Kristjana. *The Prowler.* Red Deer: Red Deer College P, 1989.

Hutcheon, Linda. *The Canadian Postmodern: A Study of Contemporary English-Canadian Fiction.* Toronto: Oxford UP, 1988.

—. "'Circling the Downspout of Empire.'" Adam and Tiffin 167-89.

—. *A Poetics of Postmodernism: History, Theory, Fiction.* London: Routledge, 1988.

Jameson, Fredric. "Third World Literature in an Era of Multinational Capitalism." *Social Text* 15 (1986): 65-88.

Morris, Meaghan. "Tooth and Claw: Tales of Survival and *Crocodile Dundee*." Ross 105-27.

Powers, William. "When Black Elk Speaks, Everybody Listens." *Social Text* 24 (1990): 43-56.

Quaife, Darlene Barry. *Bone Bird.* Winnipeg: Turnstone, 1989.

Richler, Mordecai. *Solomon Gursky Was Here.* Markham: Viking, 1989.

Ross, Andrew, ed. *Universal Abandon?: The Politics of Post-Modernism.* Minneapolis: U of Minnesota P, 1988.

—. Introduction. *Universal Abandon?* vii-xviii.

Roth, Richard. "The Colonial Experience and Its Post-Modern Fate." *Salmagundi* 84 (Fall 1989): 248-65.

Slemon, Stephen. "Modernism's Last Post." Adam and Tiffin 1-11.

Smith, Paul. "Visiting the Banana Republic." Ross 128-48.

Spivak, Gayatri Chakravorty. *In Other Worlds: Essays in Cultural Politics.* London: Methuen, 1987.

Tostevin, Lola Lemire. "Contamination: A Relation of Difference." *Tessera* (Spring 1989): 13-14.

10

"English Canada's Postcolonial Complexities"*

Donna Bennett

By Canadian history also is to be understood one history, not one French and one British, but the entire history of all Canada. There are not two histories, but one history, as there are not two Canadas, or any greater number, but one only. Nor are there two ways of life, but one common response to land and history expressed in many strong variants of the one, it is true, but still one in central substance. The reason for this is that the history of Canada after 1760 is only a continuation and extension of the history of Canada before 1760. There is but one narrative line in Canadian history.

 —W.L. Morton, "The Relevance of Canadian History" (88-89)

I: Canadian Literature and the Postcolonial Model

Conversations about Canadian politics, society and culture, if not saccharine accounts of the joys of multiculturalism, are full of complaint about the divisive nature of certain policies; they seem to begin and end as a "lament for a slain chieftain," the postcolonial dream of a unified, perhaps dualist, Canadian nation felled by the intrigue or ambitions of warring clans—the "French," the "ethnics," the "westerners," the "Anglo-Celts."

 —Robert F. Harney, "So Great a Heritage as Ours" (228)

Discussions of literature in terms of a colonial mentality, colonial discourse, and the need for decolonization have lately been gathered together into a field of critical inquiry that has come to be known as postcolonialism.[1] Although *postcolonial* has been around as a convenient period term (especially for such things as American furniture and architecture) since early in the century, a more general postcolonial dialogue, arising out of the massive wave of colonies coming to independence after World War II, is a recent development. Use of a postcolonial perspective as a way of looking at literary studies began in the late 1970s among Australian critics.[2] An early example of this postcolonial approach to literary and cultural criticism can be seen in the spe-

---

* *Essays on Canadian Writing* 51/52 (1993/94): 164-210.

cial 1977 postcolonial literature issue of the Australian journal *New Literature Review*, which "grew out of a series of postgraduate seminars held at the Australian National University in 1976" (Ashcroft 4). The emphases that have come to characterize postcolonial criticism are evident there; the editor of the journal, W.D. Ashcroft, writes:

> Through an ability to write in a common language, albeit the language of an oppressor, writers of vastly disparate cultures have demonstrated the universality of an impulse for liberation that Westerners have usually only recognised in their own intellectual revolutions.
>
> In colonial and post-colonial literature in English we see how the amorphous political concept of imperialism has revealed itself in the quite specific concerns of individual freedom. . . . [T]he historical experience [of oppression] has proved a vital catalyst in post-colonial literature's considerations of the nature of human experience. (3)

Postcolonial criticism moved more generally into critical discourse in the mid-eighties and gained wider attention after the 1989 publication of Ashcroft, Gareth Griffiths, and Helen Tiffin's survey *The Empire Writes Back: Theory and Practice in Post-Colonial Literatures* (1989). But its impact on Canadian literary studies was not felt much before the nineties. In 1990, Balachandra Rajan concluded a survey article, "Scholarship and Criticism," for a new volume of *Literary History of Canada*, by calling for the practice of such a criticism:

> Commonwealth scholarship [in Canada] also has not as yet responded sufficiently to studies of the relationship between dominance and discourse, of which Edward W. Said's *Orientalism* (1978) is a pioneering example. Exploration of this relationship has made it evident that freeing itself within the imposed discourse is only the first stage in the emancipation of the subjected voice. The second is to free itself from that discourse. Post-colonial literature may now be at the second stage. If so, a different and less familiar kind of scholarship may be required to address its problems. (151)[3]

Similarly, Terry Goldie concluded his 1991 review of *The Empire Writes Back* by describing the work as a good introduction to postcolonial practice and adding, "I hope more Canadians—and more important, Canadianists—will join" (204).

In fact, the practice of postcolonial criticism had already begun in Canada. Although the papers presented at a 1986 conference in Ottawa on literary theory in Canada (subsequently published as *Future Indicative: Literary Theory and Canadian Literature*) show no impact of either Said or postcolonial theory, beginning around 1988, and increasing sharply after the publication of *The Empire Writes Back*, there has been a growing use of a postcolonial model as a context for Canadian writing.[4] In 1991 and 1992, postcolonial approaches were frequently employed in Canadian criticism.[5] Postcolonialism offers a powerful and attractive model for Canadian criticism, one that will undoubtedly have an impact on the future of our critical discourse.

Clearly Canada does emerge out of a history that allows it and its literature to be thought of as postcolonial. Compared to a country such as the United States, which has sometimes been called the world's first postcolonial nation, Canada seems newly postcolonial; because it remained a colony during the height of nineteenth-century nation building and imperial expansion, it has had a longer and more intense experience of the colonial condition. But as soon as we identify Canada as *postcolonial*, we realize that the exact application of the term is unclear. *Postcolonial* suggests a historical period, but in current use the term lacks a clear terminus a quo and terminus ad quem.[6] Since most postcolonial critics make assumptions about resistance to inherited discourse,[7] is what we are now calling the postcolonial condition something built into the first moment of colonization—brought about by the colonists' inherent resistance to thinking of their land, and themselves, as ruled by distant others?[8] Or does a country become postcolonial only at the moment of political independence? Indeed, can a country or a people ever completely throw off past coloniality and claim to have become—or to have recovered— an authentic and essential self? And if so, when?

In postcolonial discussions, this problem of period is often seen as an aspect of a larger and perhaps irresolvable paradox: Does resistance to a dominant external discourse mean a continuing acknowledgement of the superior power of that discourse?[9] But even in the literal terms of political history the independence of Canada as a colony is particularly difficult to date. Officially Canada ceased to be a British colony in 1867, but its complete independence has only been achieved since that time and by increments.[10] It is this problem of transition from imperial subject to autonomous state that Pelham Edgar referred to in 1912 when he wrote: "The problems affecting Canadian literature are peculiar to all the outlying dependencies of our Empire, and are in part shared by the United States, though our neighbours have the advantage of being a distinct nation, whereas we are neither, as yet, a nation nor quite an empire" (111).

Period is not the only problem. Place can also be ambiguous in discussions of postcoloniality. In English studies, *postcolonial* has become a more acceptable way of describing the former colonies of England—that is, it is a desirable replacement for the adjective *commonwealth*. More generally, the term is being employed to refer to all of the former colonies of European nations. (But this usage is not uniform; it has not been widely accepted in Latin American studies, for example.)[11] As well—and we will explore this in some detail later—the term can also be used internally, as a way of discussing a group of people *within* a country who have a sense of a separate identity and cohesion. Linda Hutcheon pointed out one such group when she observed that "when Canadian culture is called post-colonial today the reference is very rarely to the Native culture, which might be the more accurate historical use of the term" (76). More than a way of specifying time and place, postcolonialism has become a loose conceptual field, or an attitude.[12]

The larger ideas shaping postcolonialism have themselves not been stable. In particular, the idea of nation (and therefore of nationalism) causes a problem. The authors of *The Empire Writes Back* argued that "all post-colonial studies continue to depend upon national literatures and criticism. The study of national traditions is the first and most vital stage of the process of rejecting the claims of the centre to exclusivity" (17). But *nation* has come under attack from other critical schools. In Canada, Frye spoke as early as 1965 about our writers as having entered "a world which is post-Canadian, as it is post-American, post-British, and post everything except the world itself" (18); and discussions of going beyond nationalism in Canadian literature have been frequent since the beginning of the eighties.[13] Recently Diana Brydon has spoken of using postcolonial theory in the teaching of Canadian poetry as a way to break down a national approach: "Such a focus can change our understanding of Canadian poetic traditions, shifting attention from continuity to disruption and from homogeneity to heterogeneities" (81).

Postcolonialism, therefore, does not seem to define a precise field of inquiry. Variously historical, political, and ideological, more prescriptive than descriptive, *postcolonial* assumes its meaning and function as a term inside larger fields of discourse. Perhaps what we can most safely say at the outset is the following. Postcolonialism is a point of view that contains within it a basic binarism: it divides our way of thinking about a people into two parts, as colonial opposed to postcolonial.[14] *Colonial* denotes a way of seeing that accepts the imperial point of view, while *postcolonial* is a viewpoint that resists imperialism—or relationships that seem imperialistic. The people of a colony (or even of a former colony) are the mother country's possessions so long as they are colonials; the system for appropriating and maintaining the colony is colonialism. Thus, to speak of postcolonialism is to focus attention on those who have sought independence and who view the imperial country's proprietary claims as invalid.

As a body of theoretical statements, postcolonial concerns have from the beginning been shaped by, and have interacted with, deconstructive and poststructuralist theory and with theories of resistance writing. The most significant debate within postcolonialism has been about the role of poststructuralism (often treated as equivalent to postmodernism); while poststructuralism has been seen by some as threatening to the emergence of a postcolonial identity, almost all postcolonial studies have shown awareness of, and benefited from, poststructuralist (and other contemporary) critiques of race, class, and gender. Theory and writing that identifies itself as postcolonial, therefore, have often emphasized the view that, before authentic native expressions can be glimpsed, much less put in place, externally imposed narratives, mythologies, values, and perspectives need to be stripped away. Colonial identity has to be decreated in order for postcolonial identity to flourish. However, in constructing their field of inquiry, many postcolonial critics—especially those who, like the authors of *The Empire Writes Back*, emphasize the linkage of postcolonialism with national identity—have implicitly created a history for their enterprise that assumes that though the term *postcolonialism* may be relatively new the pattern of thinking it expresses is not; *postcolonial* is thus a description that can be applied to a body of already existing literary responses to, and critical dialogues about, colonialism and its cultural effects. Hidden in such historicizing presumptions is the assumption that at some point postcolonial attitudes existed in more limited (less deconstructive) ways than they do in the current era—and that postcolonial writing is therefore also a way of referring to the political, social, and cultural developments characteristic of previously colonized regions as they sought for, and took on, varying degrees of self-recognition and an autonomous status.

Conceived that way, postcolonialism allows one to focus on the cultural work those nations have done, or needed to do, in order to give birth to, or revitalize, autonomous cultures in regions previously dominated by externally imposed ways of perceiving, understanding, and responding. To describe a country as postcolonial in this sense could simply be to imply a coming of age, or a coming into identity. Thus, early stages in postcolonial criticism (or what can retrospectively be identified as postcolonial criticism) might be those that emphasized the telling of previously neglected or suppressed narratives—especially those that affirmed a distinct cultural identity (often understood as arising out of the narratives of personal identity told within the newly emerging culture)—and the depiction in poetry, drama, and fiction of unrecorded details, as a way of showing the local as it once existed or as it actually exists. This is the kind of postcolonialism emphasized by Stephen Slemon in "Modernism's Last Post":

> Whereas a post-modernist criticism would want to argue that literary practices such as these expose the constructedness of *all* textuality . . . an *interested* post-colonial critical practice would want to allow for the positive production of oppositional truth-claims in these texts. It would retain for post-colonial writing, that is, a mimetic or referential purchase to textuality, and it would recognize in this referential drive the operations of a crucial strategy for survival in marginalized social groups. (5)

Aware of the divergence of this statement from the frequent emphasis on the postcolonial task as resisting or deconstructing a prior hegemonic discourse, Slemon continues:

> This referential assumption would appear to make what I am calling a post-colonial criticism radically fractured and contradictory, for such a criticism would draw on post-structuralism's suspension of the referent in order to read the social "text" of colonialist power and at the same time would reinstall the referent in the service of colonized and post-colonial societies. (5)

In his 1987 essay "Canadian (Tw)ink: Surviving the White-Outs," Gary Boire begins by outlining this kind of constructive postcolonialism—but it serves in that piece as a straw man, a target for the doubled postcolonial resistance that is described in the second part of his paper.

The Empire Writes Back finds Canadian postcolonialism implicit in statements made by Robert Kroetsch and Dennis Lee in the first half of the seventies. In fact, one could read an inchoate postcolonialism out of the whole history of the Canadian literary and cultural dialogue. Canada's first novel, Frances Brooke's *The History of Emily Montague* (1769), provides a critique of the inhibiting effects of colonialism in its ironic treatment of Captain William Fermor's procolonialism. The limits a colonial mentality imposes on literary production are reflected upon in critical statements as early as Sir Daniel Wilson's 1858 review of Charles Sangster's *The St. Lawrence and the Saguenay* ("However much taste and refinement may be displayed in such echoes of the old thought and fancy of Europe, the path to success lies not in this direction for the poet of the new world" [134]) and Edward Hartley Dewart's 1864 introductory essay to his anthology of Canadian poetry ("Our colonial position, whatever may be its political advantages, is not favourable to the growth of an indigenous literature" [xiv]). By the mid-twentieth century, E.K. Brown's *On Canadian Poetry* (1943) and Northrop Frye's Canadian essays had given such prominence to discussions of the colonial mentality as a stultifying aspect of Canada's inheritance that the topic almost became a critical trope.

The seventies saw a shift within Canada from one kind of postcoloniality—the belief that the values and topics of the new land must be recognized to help affirm its independent existence and indigenous ways of being—to the more resisting response that has been central in recent postcolonial theory. This change is apparent in two statements made by Robert Kroetsch. Talking with Margaret Laurence in 1970, he said: "In a sense, we haven't got an identity until somebody tells our story. The fiction makes us real" ("Conversation" 63). But in the opening of his 1974 essay "Unhiding the Hidden"—written after extended contact with American theorist William Spanos's Heideggerian "destructive" criticism[15]—Kroetsch wrote: "At one time I considered it the task of the Canadian writer to give names to his experience, to be the namer. I now suspect that on the contrary, it is his task to un-name" (17).

However, this more deconstructive kind of postcolonialism is not entirely new to Canada. Though it may not have been fully articulated before Dennis Lee's important 1972 essay "Cadence, Country, Silence: Writing in Colonial Space,"[16] the need for members of the settlement culture to resist—and especially to silence or deconstruct—the pull of empire is dramatized in fiction as early as Hugh MacLennan's *Barometer Rising* (1941). In that novel, the disastrous 1917 Halifax explosion opens a cultural space in much the same way as a psychological breakdown in Margaret Atwood's 1972 novel *Surfacing* "clear[s] a space" for the protagonist (177). But the need to name into existence should not be opposed to the need for unnaming: it is better to understand these as complementary sides of any postcolonial development.[17] Each describes something about today's complex world in which no culture is ever pure and in which the arrival of political autonomy means neither an automatic erasure of old colonial structures nor an immediate understanding of the former colony's innate characteristics.

II: Postcolonial Demographics

The complication of time meeting space in literary theory and historiography, with its attendant clash of the "pure" and the "hybrid," is well illustrated by the contradictions that have arisen in the Canadian situation. In Canada, where the model of the "mosaic" has been an important cultural determinant, Canadian literary theory has, in breaking away from European domination, generally retained a nationalist stance, arguing for the mosaic as characteristically Canadian in contrast to the "melting-pot" of the U.S.A. But the internal perception of a mosaic has not generated corresponding theories of literary hybridity to replace the nationalist approach. Canadian literature, perceived internally as a mosaic, remains generally monolithic in its assertion of Canadian difference from the canonical British or the more recently threatening neo-colonialism of American culture.

—Bill Ashcroft, Gareth Griffiths, and Helen Tiffin,
The Empire Writes Back (36)

What I would like to do is consider the range of possibilities, historically as well as in the present, that emerge when we ask questions about the postcolonial history of Canadian literature. If we attempt to dilate and unpack the model of postcolonialism, with reference to some of the literature's historical specifics, we might be able to see just where it is useful and where it is limited. After all, Canada seems an ideal laboratory for the study of postcolonial writing: it was formed by the interactions of three distinct cultures—the aboriginal, the French, and the English. Each of these cultures was deeply affected by colonialism, and each has writers who identify themselves as members of these originary groups and who explicitly deal with the problems of colonial dominance and the difficulties of finding identity after having been subordinated to another culture. But Canada's postcolonial relationships are not simply defined by its founding history or even confined to its borders. Canadians have also examined another de facto colonial or postcolonial relationship: Canada's interaction with the United States. Discussing the way Canadian writers and critics have, over a period of time, brought Canadian literature into existence and learned to conceive of it as having autonomy is hardly new. And such exploration is still neither exhausted nor unprofitable. But when we frame the coming into being of Canadian writing as a postcolonial topic it does look somewhat different. At the same time, we must be cautious with our use of postcolonial approaches: as we shall see, it is important that we not lose sight of the range of postcolonial choices in a nation as diversified as Canada. Because of this complexity, Canada not only provides material for postcolonial analysis, it also supplies a site on which the postcolonial model itself can be tested and refined.

* * *

As an organized polity, Canada began as New France, a settlement colony established by France. When, with the Treaty of Paris of 1763, France ceded the colony to the English, it became part of British North America, a colony inside an alien colonial structure. Although French Canada has now been adrift from its mother country for well over two centuries, it still has a habit of looking to France for validation, and it may, therefore, be thought of as existing in that uneasy relationship with an original European parent that often characterizes postcolonialism. Yet an identification of French Canada as postcolonial in its relationship to France is obviously misleading and becomes the first point at which we encounter the problems of applying a postcolonial model in Canadian studies. The "postness" of its colonial experience dates, more than anything else, from its first resistance to the imposition of British colonial status, a resistance that, as long as French Canada remains inside Canada, may never be completely successful. Because it is by means of its relationship first to England and then to English Canada that French Canada has defined itself as a society refusing colonial dominance, the affirmation of a Euro-French heritage may actually be an anticolonial act of resistance for a French-Canadian writer, rather than one of lingering coloniality. In fact, because French-Canadian literature celebrates a heritage that has roots in New France and in France and that resists the power and influence of English Canada, with its British heritage, French Canada combines the features of a postcolonial culture that was once politically connected to an imperial power, but is now free to define its own nature, with those of a subaltern culture that is constrained by the ongoing presence of an occupying power.[18]

The divided nature of the Canadian national literary canon is one reflection of the depth of the political and linguistic separation of French and English Canada. Few writers and their works are known widely enough by members of both literary communities—or by general readers—for there to be an identifiably national or corporate Canadian literature. A few critics do comfortably bridge the two cultures, but most of these tend to refrain from statements that explicitly—or even implicitly—suggest the existence of a unified bicultural (or transcultural) Canadian canon.

This separation between French and English literatures is only one of many fractures that characterize the nation's literature. Canada has now seen the emergence of a substantial body of literature by the third of Canada's three founding peoples, writers who identify themselves as descendants of Canada's Native population—a group without memory of any other home country. In their desire to maintain or recover a sense of self-identity, members of this group may have less in common with French-and English-Canadian writers than with writers from indigenous postcolonial societies, such as India or Nigeria, that were formally occupied by imperial nations. However, Canadian Native cultures (there is, of course, no single Native culture) also share some concerns with the culture of French Canada, for they are not postcolonial in the sense of having clearly passed from a period of being dominated to one of being free of the dominant culture. At the same time, both French and English Canada, while they may be postcolonial to a dominant Other, have played, and continue to play, the role of imperial power to Native culture.[19] This is Boire's point in "Canadian (Tw)ink." Taking for granted the postcoloniality of the settler culture in Canada, he argues that both its literature and criticism have ignored the erasure of the Native that its colonization depended upon:

> Most striking in [F.R.] Scott's poem ["Laurentian Shield"], in much nationalist writing of the period, and especially in academic commentaries on this writing, is what may be termed the "Boer syndrome" of Canadian decolonization. The liberating dialectic formulated by the modernists in Canada has but one essential focus: the interaction of colonialist and empire. It is a dialectic that concentrates not so much on the colonized at the hands of the colonizer, but on the experience the recolonizer enjoys at the expense of the twice-colonized. There is little awareness of the colonialist's own colonization of indigenous peoples, virtually no guilt at rendering entire cultures invisible through the heroical act of naming a found land. (224)

Though Natives and their cultures have long been subject matter in Canadian literature,[20] Native literature was chiefly oral for most of its history, and until recently little written work by Natives has been gathered into a literary canon. Today the vitality of Native literature, much of it contemporary, is apparent in collections such as *All My Relations: An Anthology of Contemporary Canadian Native Fiction*, edited by Thomas King for McClelland and Stewart in 1990, and *An Anthology of Canadian Native Literature in English*, edited by Daniel David Moses and Terry Goldie for Oxford University Press in 1992.[21] If not yet canonical, recent literary works by Native Canadians—such as the extraordinary plays by Tomson Highway—are beginning to be read or seen by a wide national audience. As most of it is in English, Canadian Native writing becomes the kind of postcolonial literature that is created by an invaded people and written in the language of the invaders, a literature that must find a way to create within that language an authentic alternative discourse.[22]

But is the relationship of Native culture to those of French and English Canada, or even the relationship of Canadian Francophone culture to Anglophone culture, truly postcolonial? When the imperial relationship is no longer defined by distance—by the tension between imperial centre and colonial margin—is it truly imperial, even though it emerges out of colonial practices and thus may be thought of as postcolonial in some sense? Is exploitation by a government seated elsewhere the same as suppression by a dominant group that finds itself occupying the same territory as the exploited peoples? Or is this second conflict better understood as an unequal competition for a home ground, a civil rather than a colonial struggle? While the answers are not simple, for the purposes of my argument, I will rely on the fact that at least one of the groups in each relationship conceives of it in ways that make a postcolonial approach usable. And because both French Canadians and Natives hold English Canada at least partially responsible for their colonial subjugation, English Canada has played an oddly doubled role: subjected to an imperial power, it has also been an agent of that power in the control it has exercised over populations within Canada's boundaries. That double agency of English Canada—the way it has been both dominant and subaltern—suggests just how radically the ground begins to shift whenever we approach English-Canadian literature as the product of a postcolonial people.[23] [. . .]

IV: No One Culture

It was the view of the royal commission, shared by the government and, I am sure, by all Canadians, that there cannot be one cultural policy for Canadians of British and French origin, another for the original peoples and yet a third for all others. For although there are two official languages, there is no official culture, nor does any ethnic group take precedence over any other. No citizen or group of citizens is other than Canadian. . . . [A]dherence to one's ethnic group is influenced not so much by one's origin or mother tongue as by one's sense of belonging to the group, and by what the commission calls the group's "collective will to exist."

—Pierre E. Trudeau,
"Announcement of Implementation of Policy of Multiculturalism within Bilingual Framework" (House of Commons, 8 Oct. 1971)

Another way in which postcolonial concerns are reproduced within Canada becomes apparent when we look at the individuals of non-British origins who came from their homelands into English Canada between Confederation and World War II. During the first big wave of post-Confederation immigration, between the 1890s and World War I, groups of northern and eastern Europeans settled the Canadian Prairies,[24] an area that had, up to this time, remained largely undeveloped agriculturally. The rural European immigrants—many were German speakers, Ukrainians, or Scandinavians—tended to establish whole rural communities. They were, initially, cut off linguistically from Canadian culture, and remained so for generations. Unlike the Celtic and American settlers in Ontario, these Europeans were also generally excluded from the English power structures that grew up around the larger towns and cities where the new arrivals from Eastern Canada and the United Kingdom tended to settle during this period.

Those attitudes we have been identifying with postcoloniality usually arise out of claims upon the land; that is, postcolonial groups either see themselves as indigenous, as is the case with Native Canadians, or else, like the French and English Canadians, they view themselves as a founding settlement people with claims based on their development, usually through agriculture, of a geographically defined area. Those who settled the Prairies—regardless of their national origin—felt this second kind of claim. They saw themselves as no less a founding people than the French, the English, and the Natives. Thus, while there is, as I have already suggested, something like an internal postcolonialism arising from regional anxieties about cultural and political exclusion, its sources ought to be understood as more than a sense of regional otherness. The differences felt by Prairie Westerners are produced by the fact that so many residents had ancestors who came to the area neither directly from Britain nor from Eastern Canada. In the three Prairie provinces, between twenty and thirty-seven percent of the population are descended northern and eastern Europeans, and they share this area with a large number of people who came to settle there directly from America. These settlers brought a new kind of postcolonialism into English-language Canada because they eventually asserted a kind of separatist claim on cultural identity different from that of the Québécois or even the Natives. These differences in background affect this region both politically and culturally, and they have prompted, in concert with the changes taking place in Ontario in the first decades of the twentieth century, a reconsideration of what the Canadian identity should be.

In the aftermath of World War I, and following various disputes over diplomatic sovereignty, many English Canadians had grown disillusioned with the idea of an identity to be found inside anything like a "Vaster Britain," and longed instead for a more independent—a more postcolonial—sense of Canada. The increased need for this Canadian sense of self was exacerbated by the new, cheap American media that began to flood Canada just after the war.[25] In the 1920s, the recently arrived non-British immigrants appeared to offer one way of creating this postcolonial, particularly Canadian, identity. Although the established policy of Anglo-conformity[26] did not really abate, a modifying idea did emerge: Canadian identity would be a hybrid of British and European culture, and the older English sense of self would be enriched by the perspectives that these Europeans now imported with them.[27]

This idea brought into existence another—albeit temporary—kind of internal postcoloniality. New immigrants were encouraged to contribute something of their heritage as a way of creating the new national culture. Thus the postcolonial needs of the society as a whole invited at least a limited expression of the differences that these new citizens from non-English cultures brought with them. This opportunity for immigrants to shape the culture was, however, conceived of as a transitory phase, because newcomers would not only modify the culture of Canada but would also themselves be modified and Canadianized—both by the settlement experience itself and by their exposure to the culture already in place in the new country.

The result for Canadian literature of this new openness to European settlers is evident with the appearance, in the twenties, of the first important books in English from writers such as Frederick Philip Grove (an emigrant from Germany), Martha Ostenso (who was born in Norway), and Laura Goodman Salverson (who was born in Canada but spoke only Icelandic until she was ten). These were works that not only revealed the realities of contemporary settlement life but also recorded new ways of experiencing a frontier. Widely read by British Canadians, these new writers were not perceived as concerned with questions of immigrant or ethnic identity but accepted into the mainstream because they were recording a settlement experience common to all Canadian immigrants—an experience that may have been increasingly distant to many English-Canadian readers from southern Ontario and farther east, but one that seemed, nonetheless, to help articulate what it meant to be Canadian. Even though English Canadians accepted them as Canadian, these writers had a distinct approach to storytelling that has in turn shaped the development of English-Canadian fiction and poetry. In particular, because they drew on a Continental realist tradition, Grove and

Ostenso created powerful novels of pioneer life on the Prairies that captured distinctively Canadian settings and situations while employing an aesthetics that increased the gulf between Canadian literary writing and the works then coming out of British and international modernism.

Thus this postcolonial longing for a distinct Canadian identity and culture that would blend Continental European and British characteristics was in fact realized in Canadian literature at this time, even though it was not recognized as such; the distinct kind of Prairie realism that emerged was influenced by writing that had its origins in Europe as well as by the starkness of Prairie life. Prairie realism and the writing that evolved out of it is indicative of a post-colonial development in which region becomes so distinctive that it asserts proprietary rights to a part of national identity and also affects canonical standards, in this case playing a role in displacing poetry from the centre of the Canadian canon.[28]

* * *

Though the writing of English-speaking Canadians of non-British origins became visible in the 1920s, ethnically identified writers and works did not really emerge until the poetry of A.M. Klein began to appear in the thirties. Critics who write about Klein's poetry often quote Ludwig Lewisohn, who called Klein both "the first contributor of authentic Jewish poetry to the English language," and "the first Jew to contribute authentic poetry to the literatures of English speech" (v). But it is worth noticing how these statements each locate Klein outside the Canadian canon. Should we think of Klein as a Jewish poet? Or as an English poet? Or can we claim him, after all, as a Canadian poet? And does it matter? European born and American based, Lewisohn undoubtedly saw his locating Klein in the larger English tradition as a claim on universal standards and therefore a validation of Klein's worth—but it is against the need for such validations that postcolonialism defines itself. However, for Lewisohn to describe Klein as one who has broken free in a way that permits him to write an "authentic Jewish poetry" in the non-Jewish language of English is to see Klein as a poet capable of finding an authentic voice within an alien discourse, a project that has been understood as central to postcolonial writing.

Still, that description of Klein also directs our attention to an identity that is external to the postcolonial nation—and at the same time, internal to it. Klein's move from the "Jewish poetry" of his earlier books to the "Canadian poetry" he wrote after 1945—which, when collected in *The Rocking Chair and Other Poems* (1948), won him the Governor General's Award—is therefore an act with larger cultural significance. On one hand, Klein may have felt, after the shocks of World War II, that he wanted to write with less ethnic affiliation. But, on the other hand, as he made plain at the time, he saw his new subject

matter as a way of connecting Jewish identity with what we would now understand as the postcolonial dimensions of his society:

> For an interval I have abdicated from the Hebrew theme which is my
> prime mover to look upon the French Canadian in this province: we
> have many things in common: a minority position; ancient memories;
> and a desire for group survival. Moreover the French Canadian enjoys
> much—a continuing and distinctive culture, solidarity, *land*—which I
> would wish for my own people. (qtd. in Caplan 149)

In any case, Klein's claiming of a literary space within Canadian writing for
identifiably ethnic writing helped to create room for other Jewish writers—
the poet Irving Layton in the forties and after, and the novelists Henry Kreisel
(*The Rich Man* [1948]), Mordecai Richler (*Son of a Smaller Hero* [1955]), and
Adele Wiseman (*The Sacrifice* [1956])—as well as for writers, such as Hun-
garian-born John Marlyn (*Under the Ribs of Death* [1957]), who produced literary works that recorded perceptions and perspectives from outside the
Anglo-Celt and Jewish traditions. The work of such explicitly ethnic writers,
along with the appearance of autobiographical narratives that called attention to the ethnicity of already established writers (in particular, Salverson's
Confessions of an Immigrant's Daughter [1939]), opened up to Canadian readers a detailed sense of non-British life in Canada for the first time.

Perhaps because of the way such writing prepared the ground, and because
of the changed cultural atmosphere in Canada after World War II, the literary contributions of the most recent wave of immigrants to Canada have been
considerable. Although Anglo-conformity has never been completely abandoned, Canada's official policy of multiculturalism, instituted in 1971, has
provided immigrants with a great deal more cultural autonomy. Unlike the
earliest non-British settlers, who learned, with respect to the dominant English-Canadian culture, to repress or hide their distinct cultures, and unlike
those in the first half of the twentieth century, who found that they could
express their differences carefully, recent immigrants have been encouraged
to see culture and individual expression as distinct from, but not threatening
to, the preexisting politics and economic practices of English Canada. Officially, so long as these new immigrants adapt to Canadian law and commerce
and gain enough facility in English to function in everyday transactions, they
are allowed to maintain—and even to encourage the growth of—their old
culture, which is now referred to by such terms as *heritage.*

Hence the construction of ethnic identity increasingly comes to play a role
within Canada that resembles the role Canada plays as a postcolonial nation.
This freedom to continue in the cultural traditions of one's homeland has
not resulted in the continued development of a blended culture that English
Canadians once envisioned. One result has been that since the 1960s recent

immigrants have powerfully influenced English-Canadian literature, not by becoming assimilated, nor by creating some slight modification of English-Canadian culture, but by producing major literary works that have challenged the traditional shape of the Canadian canon. A measure of the role being played by these new writers in Canadian literary culture may be seen in the fact that in 1991 and 1992 the winners of the fiction category of the Governor General's Awards came from their midst: Rohinton Mistry for *Such a Long Journey* and Michael Ondaatje for *The English Patient*. (Perhaps even more remarkable is the fact that the English translation of a novel previously published in Czech, Josef Škvorecký's *The Engineer of Human Souls*, won the award in 1984.) The effect of the appearance of such books was touched upon in a recent statement made by Ven Begamudré:

> Among my contemporaries, Rohinton Mistry holds a special place. His short-story collection *Tales from Firozsha Baag* [1987] marked a turning point in Canadian literature precisely because most of it is not set in Canada. Without meaning to, he gave other writers of our generation permission: not to write about Canada yet be Canadian writers. (11)[29]

The new multiethnic writing that has emerged in contemporary Canada is a rich mix that not only includes the Italian-Canadian poetry of Mary di Michele and Pier Giorgio Di Cicco and fiction of Nino Ricci, and the work of writers with roots in the Caribbean community such as Austin Clarke, Dionne Brand, and Neil Bissoondath, but has also made room for, and celebrated, the work of refugee writers such as George Faludy and Škvorecký. This is a literature that, in its accounts of immigrant experience and cultural otherness, may resonate with Canada's preexisting postcolonial condition partly because the ethnic writers' backgrounds are often already postcolonial. These writers from other postcolonial countries now find themselves relocated within a new postcolonial society. As well, there are parallels to the narratives of writers from countries that were once officially colonies in the work of writers, such as Faludy and Škvorecký, who have been displaced from Eastern Europe and who write about resistance to Nazi and Soviet dominance.

The poems and narratives produced by recent immigrants to Canada speak to the culture at large because these individuals are both settlers full of hope and refugees in an alien environment. Their stories may therefore be seen as having continuity in a cultural fabric begun by the early English settlers, who had come to Canada because they lacked money; and the Scots, who had been thrown off their lands; and the Irish, forced to find another country or starve; and the Chinese, indentured by necessity to a life in another country. In 1970, Margaret Atwood created, in *The Journals of Susanna Moodie*, a poetic sequence that makes Susanna Moodie a central figure in what we now understand to be one kind of postcolonial struggle—to feel at one with a new place and to find an adequate means of expressing that relationship. In an often cited remark from the afterword, Atwood describes Moodie's personal history as an image of a generalizable Canadian displacement, observing: "We are all immigrants to this place even if we were born here . . . we move in fear, exiles and invaders" (62). The immigrant's story of exile and loss (found in such works as *Running in the Family*, Michael Ondaatje's 1982 chronicle of his family history in Ceylon) can be transformed into a postcolonial myth as exile is turned into belonging and loss into gain (this process takes place in works such as Ondaatje's 1987 novel *In the Skin of a Lion*, where the nearly forgotten story of immigrants becomes that of the synthesis that created twentieth-century Toronto). In the larger context of Canadian literature, readers may feel that the exploration of otherness in such stories, often part of an examination of a master-servant relationship in which struggle is always necessary to stave off a loss of self-identity, becomes almost allegorical because it offers so many parallels to the struggles that have long existed within Canada and that Canada faces as a postcolonial nation.

Some immigrant writers, such as those whose origins are in Italy or elsewhere in western Europe, may not have the postcolonial perspective of writers from former colonies (or from the former Soviet bloc), but they contribute in their own way to something that resembles a postcolonial dialogue, because they tell us of the struggle faced by all immigrants to another country, and of how, even in an officially multicultural country, one's old culture, and thus one's identity, is always marginalized or under threat. Another language shuts out an original one, new ways of living wear away the old, and one's children no longer understand the claims of a home that lies elsewhere. To become an immigrant is thus always to become in some way colonized. The condition of being engaged in a struggle to keep an established identity in the ocean of a new culture may not be a truly postcolonial one,[30] but it is often spoken of in terms that are congruent with postcolonial concerns. For example, William Boelhower observed, in *Canadian Literature* in 1988, that ethnic writing in Canada sees itself as searching for space for its own discourse in competition with "a cultural politics shaped by the internal dynamics of a centring and centralized order of official discourse" (172).

The disorientation of the western European immigrant in North America contributes to the larger narratives of alterity being told in Canada today.[31] In addition, the last twenty years have seen the emergence of other groups of writers who, though they are not immigrants, are not of British origin. Canada's multiculturalism policy, as well as enabling newly arrived immigrants to maintain external cultural ties, has encouraged the literary expression of those groups who have maintained separate ethnic identities although their ancestors arrived in Canada before mid-century, Canadians whose cultures have long been present, though relatively silent. Books from these groups are also rapidly entering the Canadian canon: novels such as Joy Kogawa's *Obasan*

(1981), about the World War II displacement of Japanese Canadians, and Sky Lee's 1990 reconstruction of four generations of life in Vancouver's China-town, *Disappearing Moon Cafe*, are now frequently taught in surveys of English-Canadian fiction and written about in critical journals. In contrast to narra-tives by non-British immigrants, theirs is a kind of ethnic writing that focuses on the postcolonial condition of belonging to two cultures *within* the same country—that is, on what it means to identify oneself both as Canadian and as a person from a culture that exists as a de facto colony, a marginal group that is no longer as closely related to the mother country as it would appear to be to outsiders, or even as it might claim.

In describing how successfully these ethnic works of literature have, in the current generation, found a broader readership, I do not mean to suggest that English-Canadian writing has become the blended culture idealized ear-lier in the century. Difference is still important and, for some ethnic writers, endangered by contact with Anglo Canada, difference is a necessity. Because differentiation is so much a part of this ethnic writing, it may actually act as a countervailing force to English Canada's conceiving of itself as a postcolonial culture. The texts produced by members of these groups may direct our attention, on one hand, to postcolonial experiences that lie outside of Cana-da (as Mistry's do), or, on the other hand, call our attention to the need to come to terms with old identities within the Canadian milieu (as Lee's do), with the result that the dynamic in which the emerging *nation* seeks defini-tion apart from its imperial parent becomes relatively unimportant. Because the cultural references of these newest writers are often larger than national, they are producing work that challenges the nationalist assumptions built into the earliest form of the postcolonial model, and they may be moving Canada a step beyond the postcolonial to a true postnationalism.

One would not, however, want to overstate this case. Some ethnic writers (such as Kogawa and Bissoondath) have reservations about multiculturalism, and their narratives focus on the individual's desire for a place within the emerging postcolonial Canadian identity rather than on its margins, chal-lenging its existence: *Obasan* dramatizes the error made by a Canadian wartime government that resulted in the internment or relocation of *Canadi-ans*, and shows the reader how that error arose from the persistent misper-ception of Japanese-Canadians as Japanese. *Disappearing Moon Cafe* is told from the perspective of a fourth-generation Chinese Canadian who seeks to escape a community that has become too turned in on itself and who is ready to take her place within (but not simply be assimilated into) the larger web of Canadian society, largely by articulating the forces that restricted the previous generations from doing so. Ondaatje has gone out of his way to call attention to his sense that his writing is a product of Canadian experience, education, and background and, in his *In the Skin of a Lion*, has given to Toronto and to the rural Ontario landscape a quality of heroic myth not previously found in the work of any other Canadian writer. Perhaps what we need to recognize is that the history of Canadian literature and criticism tells us that Canada has become—and perhaps it always was, in its own way—a more individualistic country than the United States. Frye's famous question—"Where is here?"— is no longer a geographical question (it never really was) but one of group identity: "*Who* is here?"

In the history of Canadian writing, that question has had no single answer.

V: The Centre That Did Not Hold: English-Canadian Literature in Fragments?

> Canada . . . has become a place where the demise of meta-narratives has brought out the relevance of the marginal, the local, and the heteroglossia of texts that do not privilege master narratives. The issue of appropriation of an other's story in the literary work, which has stirred such recent controversy, is part of this mistrust for national unity and identity. Unity and identity at whose expense? is one of many questions being asked by writers who reject any definition of "Canadian" that cannot accommodate the multiplicity and plurality of voices, texts, and readers that do not merge into a unified whole.
>
> —Roy Miki,
> "The Future's Tense: Some Notes on Editing, Canadian Style" (189)

I began this essay with an epigraph from W.L. Morton, who insisted that there was only one Canada. But what a postcolonial perspective underlines is that at no point in its history has there been only one Canada—and therefore there has never been only one canon or tradition or literature. Although at times the influence of the British canon on education and criticism has been very strong, Canadian literature has always contained within it marginalized groups asserting perspectives that pull away from the centre.

Of the multiple Canadian postcolonialisms I have suggested, many arise from relationships in which groups seek to add to, and shape, Canada's national culture. But the anxiety that Roy Miki expresses—a fear that defining national culture may erase "the multiplicity and plurality of voices"— results in another kind of internal postcolonialism, one in which the whole must be resisted by its parts. Plurality has become important in Canada both because the government has de-emphasized culture as a source of Canadian identity and because Canada, like the United States, has countered the economic effects of a relatively low birthrate through a high level of immigration,[32] producing not only a plural culture but also one in which plurality is ever increasing. The pattern that characterizes today's constant influx of new immigrants is different from that created by the massive immigrations at earlier points in Canadian history (periods of high immigration followed by periods of relative demographic stability); high levels of immigration are now perceived of as a permanent facet of Canadian cultural life. Given the continual cultural change that new immigration brings, and the fact that many of the new immigrants are not from western European backgrounds, Canada's policy of multiculturalism, combined with its destabilization of the relationship between culture, politics, and economics, has undoubtedly been a benign way of ensuring that these newcomers are accommodated.

However, multiculturalism has its limitations. For example, to understand it as an antiracist policy, as some have taken it to be, may be an error: multiculturalism does encourage some understanding between cultures, but it also keeps cultures separate and allows them to be identified as Other.[33] By institutionalizing multiculturalism, Canada has encouraged identity through alterity. In doing so, it has effectively institutionalized marginality, an action that is always associated with postcolonialism.[34] Do such developments mean that Canada no longer has, and no longer needs, a national culture? As a country that has been, and remains, subject to powerful decentring forces, Canada reflects the tension always present in postcolonialism, which, even as it sets up resistance to the imperial centre, begins to construct an identity that threatens to become a new centre.

The way these centripetal and centrifugal tendencies have interacted in English Canada can be seen in the long critical debate over thematicism. The thematic approach, which dominated Canadian criticism from the late sixties to the mid-seventies, can now be understood as part of Canada's postcolonial drive to construct an autonomous national identity by identifying a coherent culture that exists apart from (and, in a work such as *Survival*, as a counter to) the imperial centre, a centre that, from the end of World War II until the end of the seventies, was progressively redefined as America rather than Britain.[35] It is paradoxical, therefore, that Frank Davey, in "Surviving the Paraphrase," the 1976 essay that first brought thematic criticism into disfavour, attacked the method under the banner of anticolonialism.[36] Miki now sees thematic criticism as part of "an insurgent nationalism that attempted to construct a 'usable tradition' to fill the void left by the loss of the centred structure called 'Canada'" (189):

> [T]heme as a critical device displaying the apparent unity, or the sameness, of a diversity of works, provided a methodological tool for a nationalist criticism, and perhaps it was useful in a specific phase of Canadian literature. . . . [T]he demise of thematic criticism with its nationalist objective [was] an inevitability. (191)

Given this new antinationalism, which has replaced the earlier concern with colonialism, the dimension of postcolonial criticism that pulls towards cultural or national unity is now often regarded with suspicion—even though Canadian culture may remain endangered by the pervasiveness of American media, and even though nationalism still has its vigorous proponents.[37] But writers and critics such as Miki, concerned about the erasure of regional and ethnic differences, feel more threatened today by a monolithic Canadian identity than by any external dominance:

> The issue of open form extends beyond the historic frame of the "New American" poetics of Charles Olson and others. It includes, in contemporary writing, those writers who work within de-stabilized and ex-centric language forms which disrupt the centrality of the autonomous lyric voice in a great deal of CanLit. (184)

What statements such as these make clear is how rapidly things have changed in the three years since Balachandra Rajan described Canadian criticism as having "not as yet responded sufficiently to studies of the relationship between dominance and discourse," and called for "a different and less familiar kind of scholarship." Rajan, believing that there are two stages to postcoloniality—the first of which is "the emancipation of the subjected voice" within the discourse, while the second is the movement to the outside of, and the freeing of the voice from, that discourse—claimed that we needed a new approach if we were to take that second step (151). It is undoubtedly something like this second step that is envisioned by postcolonial critics such as Boire, who feels the solution to the erasure of Native history is to bring into existence a Canadian criticism that will respond to Michel Foucault's call for the systematic dismantling of "a comprehensive view of history and . . . [of any] retracing the past as a patient and continuous development" (qtd. in Boire 232). Or those such as Diana Brydon, who has moved from a conservative postcolonial view of the continuities of the relationship between the new nation and its European parent (in 1982), through a postcoloniality that accepts the idea of a hybrid literature (in 1988), to a desire to turn away from national "continuity to disruption and from homogeneity to heterogeneities." Thus, for many of its practitioners, despite its roots in the formative stages of new nations, and its interest in those stages, postcolonial criticism has become profoundly anti-nationalistic.

I would argue that what Rajan's statement is based on, and what underlies statements by many of these critics, is a conceptual framework that has its roots in those great nineteenth-and twentieth-century metanarratives of Darwinism, Marxism, and Freudianism. Postcolonialism internalizes an evolutionary model; it envisions a passing through progressive stages of unfreedom to freedom and of blindness to enlightenment. In consequence, many make the assumption that not only is a postcolonial perspective necessary—and superior to the less enlightened views it replaces—but that a newer kind of postcolonialism is also emerging that is superior to all others. The danger of such evolutionary assumptions is that they produce a doctrinaire criticism, one that resembles a belief system. (Of course, the temptation to testify to one's faith is not limited to critical essays conducted under the rubric of postcolonialism.)

Such criticism may seek to close down dialogue and to turn examinations of positions taken into attacks on the individuals who take those positions. But, having begun by seeking space within a dominant discourse, postcolonialism should not impose a new dominant discourse. Nor should it tell those who disagree with it (some of whom are among the formerly silenced) that they must be quiet. If we seek heterogeneity, we ought to guard against the new homogeneity.

Perhaps part of the problem with seeing postcolonialism as a progressive model stems from the fact that postcolonial approaches are more useful for identifying differences and tracing out the dynamics of power than for recognizing and valuing similarities and accommodations, whether they be those of groups or of individuals. At some level, postcolonial critics may, therefore, begin to assume that value comes from defining a force as hostile and responding to it: they may take contestation as the only valid methodology and practice. If we treat only some of the routes to autonomy as legitimate, if we make marginality and resistance our only measures of authenticity, then we limit the questions we can ask and predetermine the answers we will receive.

A postcolonial criticism can function in Canada in complex ways. Although the authors of *The Empire Writes Back* may have felt, writing in 1989, that Canada, and its literary culture, "remains generally monolithic in its assertion of Canadian difference from the canonical British or the more recently threatening neo-colonialism of American culture" (36), I would argue that theirs was a partial view of Canada's postcolonial aspect, and that a Canadian monolith has never really existed and certainly does not exist now. Asking postcolonial questions of English-Canadian literature can be productive so long as we do not impose a single kind of postcolonialism, and so long as we do not presume that the postcolonial perspective is the only way to frame one's vision. The postcolonial model invites us to see—and gives us a new way of seeing—the play of tensions within Canadian culture as well as the tensions between Canada's culture and that of any external centre. Perhaps what it finally helps us to see is that here is a collection of cultures within the *idea* of English Canada, not so much a mosaic as a kaleidoscope, an arrangement of fragments whose interrelationships, while ever changing, nevertheless serve–by virtue of their container, we might say—not only to influence what we see when we look through the glass, but also to affect the placement of the other elements in the array.

Notes

1. I wish to thank the members of the Works in Progress in English group at the University of Toronto for their helpful comments on an early version of this essay.

2. Australian postcolonial criticism followed two developments in the Australian teaching curriculum—the reassessment, after 1959, of the place of Australian literature, and the decision, in the 1970s, to locate Australian literature within the context of South Pacific literatures (a development given impetus by the reaction against American and Australian involvement in Vietnam).

3. In his survey of recent Canadian criticism (through 1988), Peter Dale Scott, emphasizing marginality and emergence as central concerns for Canadian critics, also pointed out the lack of Said's impact, observing, "one might have expected that Edward Said would be one American critic whom Canadian critics would find especially congenial" (32).

4. Diana Brydon used the term earlier (she may have been the first Canadian critic to employ it), in her 1982 essay "Tradition and Post-Colonialism: Hugh Hood and Martin Boyd," published in the interdisciplinary journal *Mosaic* 15.3: 1-15— but in that essay *postcolonialism* doesn't carry the weight of associations with counterdiscourse and resistance that it later takes on. (Brydon's point is almost the obverse: she wants to emphasize the potential of European traditions for postcolonial writers.) The first extended analysis of Canadian literature in what has become the dominant postcolonial model seems to be Gary Boire's 1987 essay "Canadian (Tw)ink: Surviving the White-Outs." Other essays that appeared before *The Empire Writes Back* are Stephen Slemon's "Magic Realism as Post-Colonial Discourse," *Canadian Literature* 116 (1988): 9-24, Linda Hutcheon's "'Circling the Downspout of Empire,'" and Diana Brydon's "The White Inuit Speaks"; these last two appeared in a 1988 special issue of *Ariel*, later expanded and reprinted as *Past the Last Post: Theorizing Post-Colonialism and Post-Modernism* (1990) [Editor's note: Brydon's article did not appear in the 1988 *ARIEL* issue]. One indication of this transitional moment in the emergence of a postcolonial approach in Canadian criticism is the fact that W.H. New's 1987 study *Dreams of Speech and Violence: The Art of the Short Story in Canada and New Zealand* makes some moves towards, but no explicit use of, postcolonial theory (the body of the book is made up of close textual discussions shaped by structuralist-influenced narratology); however, in a 1988 essay entitled "W.H. New: *Dreams of Speech and Violence* and Postcolonial Criticism in Canada," Leslie Monkman discussed *Dreams of Speech and Violence* as a demonstration of New's moving the field of Canadian criticism beyond "a narrow nationalism" and into postcolonial discourse (*World Literature Written in English* 28: 91-96), while in 1989 Helen Tiffin read New's text explicitly, and somewhat distortingly, as an example of postcolonial theory ("Subversion," *Canadian Literature* 121: 131-33).

5. See, for example, *Canadian Literature* 128 (1991), which contains Dorothy Seaton's essay "The Post-Colonial as Deconstruction: Land and Language in Kroetsch's 'Badlands,'" and a review by Boire ("Possible Storms") characterizing postcolonial societies as resistance cultures. *Canadian Literature* 132 (1992), a special issue entitled *South Asian Connections*, contains three (out of eleven) essays and at least two reviews that use postcolonial approaches. In one, Boire

describes Bharati Mukherjee's *Jasmine* as *"the* paradigmatic 'postcolonial' narrative; it is *the* story that 'tells' Euro- and Americo-centricity back into itself by reversing readerly (read Anglo-American) expectations, by including all that is usually excluded, by bringing inside what is usually left outside" (160). See also Neil Querengesser, "Canada's Own Dark Heart: F.R. Scott's 'Letters from the Mackenzie River,'" *Essays on Canadian Writing* 47 (1992): 90-104, and Diana Brydon, "Reading Dionne Brand's 'Blues Spiritual for Mammy Prater.'" Sylvia Söderlind's 1991 book *Margin/Alias: Language and Colonization in Canadian and Québécois Fiction* is the first full-length study in Canada to make use of the postcolonial model (chiefly in its introduction and conclusion).

6. Social scientists and historians have tended to use *postcolonial* more strictly as a period term, for the era following independence. However, it is now coming to signify anticolonial sentiments prior to, as well as after, independence.

7. Helen Tiffin describes postcolonialism as "a set of discursive practices, prominent among which is *resistance* to colonialism, colonialist ideologies, and their contemporary forms and subjectificatory legacies" (vii). Cf. Söderlind: "In current critical terminology, postcolonial writing is, or at least should be, subversive, and cultural marginality is often seen as a precondition for subversion. . . . A methodology attentive to the subversive potential of postcolonial literatures must by necessity subscribe to a view of language which allows for resistance" (4).

8. This resistance could be assumed to be present whether the colonists were indigenes, on whom a colonial rule had been imposed, or settlers, who had brought the structures of empire with them, because it would arise from the bond with the land that superseded the claims of, and the ties to, the imperial country. Although the first or first few generations of settlers would not have a bond as strong as that of the Native peoples, over time, particularly if the settlers were not directly connected to the power structure of the mother country, this bond could become strong.

9. Söderlind, for example, maintains that "The term postcolonialism may seem self-explanatory and neutral; its application is, in fact, here as in most criticism, limited to the literature produced in former colonies that assumes a position of resistance to the metropolis. Its use thus indicates a critical stance that probably overlooks a great deal and may well be based on an imperialist assumption that any writing of importance produced by former subjects must be focused on their contestatory relationship to the absent master" (6).

10. For example, it was not until the Imperial Conference of 1926 that Canada and other dominions were recognized as equal in status to Britain; the Statute of Westminster (11 Dec. 1931) granted Canada's Parliament full legal freedom. The statute excepted certain areas, however, and in these Canada remained subordinate to Britain. It was only with the 1949 amendment to the Supreme Court Act that the Judicial Committee of the British Privy Council ceased to be Canada's last court of appeal. And it was not until 1982 that Canada brought

home its constitution. (It is significant that doing so necessitated an act of the British Parliament: the requirement it annulled—that approval of the British Parliament be obtained for any Canadian constitutional changes—may have been only pro forma, but it was a legal requirement nonetheless because, until this historical moment, the basis for all Canadian law and government remained a single piece of British legislation, the British North America Act of 1867.)

11. In Canada, the question of place is doubly complicated because there is also some confusion over the locus of empire. Do French Canadians exist in a post-colonial relationship to France and do English Canadians define themselves against England? I will turn to this question in part II.

12. Ashcroft, Griffiths, and Tiffin address the problem of time and place by writing: "We use the term 'post-colonial' . . . to cover all the culture affected by the imperial process from the moment of colonization to the present day" (2). But, as W.H. New enquires, "If 'post' covers everything since European/non-European contact, then when, except conceptually, is 'pre'?" (3). Moreover, such a way of defining *postcolonial* fails to distinguish between what are usually understood as postcolonial cultural activities and those of individuals and groups whose sentiments are procolonial or neocolonial.

13. See, for example, the 1981 special issue (14.2) of *Mosaic* entitled *Beyond Nationalism: The Canadian Literary in Global Perspective*.

14. It *is* possible to think of *precolonial* as a third term—in the sense it is already used in history and art history, to refer to the societies of the indigene prior to the arrival of Europeans.

15. Kroetsch and Spanos founded *Boundary 2: A Journal of Postmodern Literature* in 1972, a point at which Spanos was just beginning to formulate his influential Heideggerian aesthetics (given full expression in the 1976 special Heidegger issue [4.2] of *Boundary 2*). Concerning Spanos's use of Heidegger, Vincent B. Leitch writes: "Understood as destructive interpretation, Heidegger's readings work to free texts of reified perspectives and canonical commentaries. . . . [They become] performances of unconcealing, of the happening of truth" (239).

16. Kroetsch may have also been influenced in his change of emphasis by this essay, which he reprinted in the special Canadian issue (3.1) of *Boundary 2* that he edited in 1974.

17. Dorothy Seaton suggests that there are actually *two* possible alternatives to post-colonial naming. As well as the construction of counterdiscourses, she argues that there is a more radically deconstructive possibility, a response that "embraces instead the endless strangeness of both land and discourse, interrogating the very capacity of discourse to constitute the land" (77). She notes, however, that this "distinction between counter-discursive and deconstructive efforts is somewhat artificial, each movement sharing strategies and effects with the other" (88).

18. For more discussion of the place of contemporary French-Canadian writing in the contexts I am raising, see Söderlind, especially her introduction and two concluding chapters.

19. See Barbara Godard for a discussion of Native literature in the context of "resistance literature . . . produced within a struggle for decolonization" (199).

20. See Leslie Monkman, *A Native Heritage: Images of the Indian in English-Canadian Literature* (Toronto: U of Toronto P, 1981); the essays in *The Native in Literature,* ed. Thomas King, Cheryl Calver, and Helen Hoy (Toronto: ECW, 1987); and Terry Goldie, *Fear and Temptation: The Image of the Indigene in Canadian, Australian, and New Zealand Literatures* (Kingston: McGill-Queen's UP, 1989).

21. The title of that volume, however, suggests that it functions as a supplement to Oxford's earlier *An Anthology of Canadian Literature in English* (1983), of which only the revised edition (1990) contains the work of a writer who emerged from Native culture (E. Pauline Johnson, a figure who was anthologized earlier in the century but subsequently dropped from the canon).

22. The argument was advanced by several postcolonial theorists in the eighties that the use of the language of empire (usually English) is one of the characteristics of, and problems for, postcolonial cultures. In Native literature, the question of language choice, and especially of the formation of an alternative discourse that is intended to exist inside a dominant one, is frequently signalled by the inclusion of passages in Native languages within English-language works.

23. This complexity becomes greater still when a Canadian such as Sara Jeannette Duncan comes to dwell in another, different sort of colony. Recently, both Misao Dean, in her book on Duncan, *A Different Point of View* (McGill-Queen's UP, 1991), and in an essay, "The Paintbrush and the Scalpel: Sara Jeannette Duncan Representing India" (*Canadian Literature* 132 [1992]: 82-93), and Jennifer Lawn, in "'The Simple Adventures of Memsahib' and the Prisonhouse of Language" (*Canadian Literature* 132 [1992]: 16-30), have used postcolonial perspectives to look at the fiction Duncan produced while living in India. Each concludes that although Duncan occupied a position safely inside the imperial regime in India, she was to some degree able to define a position within her writing that was "consciously in opposition to the definitions imposed by imperialist culture" (Dean 89).

24. Although southern Europeans also immigrated to Canada during this period, in smaller numbers, they tended to locate themselves in the cities of eastern Canada and thus to join a large population. Their history of absorption into Canadian life is typical; living initially in city ghettos, they either had to remain isolated from their new culture or forgo Old World cultural support. Urban ghetto communities, however distinct, have tended to have less visible impact than ethnically coherent rural communities.

25. See Mary Vipond's essay "Canadian Nationalism and the Plight of Canadian Magazines in the 1920s." Regarding the metaphor I have used in the sentence to which this note is attached, Vipond remarks: "Canadians always seemed to

use aquatic metaphors—deluge, flood, tidal waves—to describe the influx of American popular culture. Perhaps most expressive of all was W.L. Grant, who remarked that American influences seemed to 'seep in underground like drainage'" (44).

26. English-Canadian Anglo-conformity is a species of that colonial normalization that shows up in every colony. The inheritance and standards of the mother country are presumed to be appropriate to the colonial culture. Although such conformity permeates the colony's social, political, aesthetic, and economic spheres, it is most noticeable in the educational structure and curricula. (In English-Canadian schools, until relatively recently, most of the history and literature taught was British; Canadian history and literature were only a small element within these disciplines.) Anglo-conformity not only affects non-British immigrants but it is also a marker for all English Canadians, long after Confederation, of their coloniality.

27. See Howard Palmer, "Reluctant Hosts: Anglo-Canadian Views of Multiculturalism in the Twentieth Century," *Readings in Canadian History: Post-Confederation,* ed. R. Douglas Francis and Donald B. Smith, 2nd ed. (Toronto: Holt, 1986): 185-201.

28. See Bennett 141-46.

29. This question of whether Canadian literature must be set in, and therefore reflect, Canada is a typical feature of postcolonial dialogues and one that has been responded to in various ways, from Lighthall's concerns about sacrificing quality in order to find poems that reflected Canadian circumstances to the nationalist grumblings over the 1972 Governor General's Award going to a novel, Robertson Davies's *The Manticore,* that takes place in Switzerland.

30. It is worth remembering that the parallels can be distorting. It is a simplification to see the immigrant as existing in a postcolonial relationship to the new nation because it treats the immigrant group (or even the individual immigrant) as a potentially autonomous colony unto itself. Where postcolonialism originally based its claims on the authenticity of indigenous experience, the culture left behind now becomes the only authentic one, and must be rescued from the imperial pressures of the place to which the immigrant has come.

31. Of course, some writers resist definitions in terms of otherness by creating literary works that maintain the cultural perspective of their origins. Writers such as Faludy and Mistry do not write of their immigrant experience, or do so only occasionally; instead they tell of the life they knew before they immigrated. For such writers, Canada is not—or not yet—the place of the imagination but the safe haven from which they can record their narrative of displacement.

32. This goal, first stated in 1947 by Mackenzie King ("The objective of Canada's immigration policy must be to enlarge the population of the country"), was reiterated by John Diefenbaker in 1959 in his National Development Policy (in which he called for immigration at an annual rate of between 0.75 and 1.25%

of Canada's total population) and in the 1966 White Paper on Immigration formulated under Lester Pearson. For details see Chris Taylor, "Demography and Immigration in Canada: Challenge and Opportunity," *Canadian Mosaic: Essays on Multiculturalism*, ed. A.J. Fry and Ch. Forceville (Amsterdam: Free UP, 1988): 45-63. Robert Harney's essay "'So Great a Heritage as Ours': Immigration and the Survival of the Canadian Polity" provides a very useful general discussion of these policies, the purposes they have been asked to serve, and the myths that have sometimes driven them. Notice that, while Canada's overall population has increased little during this period because of a large out-migration, the proportion of newcomers into society has grown substantially.

33. This warning has several times been sounded by writers (and others) in the multicultural community. See, for example, Arnold Harrichand Itwaru in the introduction to *The Invention of Canada: Literary Text and the Immigrant Imaginary* (Toronto: TSAR, 1990) especially 16-18, as well as the analysis of multicultural policies as texts in Smaro Kamboureli, "The Technology of Ethnicity: Law and Discourse," *Open Letter* 8th ser. 5-6 (1993): 202-17. A rich discussion of the large questions surrounding multiculturalism as a concept can be found in the long essay by the Canadian philosopher Charles Taylor, published, with commentaries by four American academics, as *Multiculturalism and "The Politics of Recognition"* (Princeton: Princeton UP, 1992).

34. Tamara Palmer suggests that even though "the story, the Fiction" in ethnic writing "is a cathartic rite of adaptation, a means of linking old and new, past and present, its profound duality is never quite overcome; rather, it remains in the ironic tone and related metafictional self-awareness that are the product of marginality. Paradoxically, perhaps this very marginality is what ultimately makes this Fiction so much a part of the evolving Canadian literary tradition whose characteristic mode, as a number of critics have pointed out, is the ironic one— a mode that expresses a profound awareness, based in marginality, of emanating from a post-colonial cultural space in which reality is problematic because there are differing, hierarchical versions of it" (113). For further discussion of the interplay of marginality and ethnicity in Canadian writing, see Linda Hutcheon, "'The Canadian Mosaic: A Melting Pot on Ice': The Ironies of Ethnicity and Race," *Splitting Images: Contemporary Canadian Ironies* (Toronto: Oxford UP, 1991): 47-68.

35. I plan to consider this development of Canada's postcolonial identity in the context of American-Canadian relations (in which resistance plays a more central role than previously) in another essay.

36. Davey argued that the critics who practiced thematic criticism did so because they didn't think Canadian literature could measure up to international standards: "The motivations of thematic criticism strike one as essentially defensive. . . . A declared motive has been to avoid evaluative criticism. . . . An even more important but undeclared motive appears to have been to avoid treating Canadian writing as serious literature" (6-7).

37. There is no sign of a return to the intense cultural nationalism of the sixties
and seventies, but the renewed anxieties in the cultural communities resulting
from the Canada-U.S. Free Trade Agreement (which has been replaced by the
trilateral North American Free Trade Agreement) and the general neglect of
the arts during the Mulroney years, have kept some cultural nationalists (such
as Rick Salutin, columnist for the *Globe and Mail*) in the arena. As well, two
recent books have returned to prominence the argument about Canada becoming a political and economic colony of America—Mel Hurtig's *The Betrayal of
Canada* (Toronto: Stoddart, 1991) and Lawrence Martin's *Pledge of Allegiance:
The Americanization of Canada in the Mulroney Years* (Toronto: McClelland, 1993).

WORKS CITED

Adam, Ian, and Helen Tiffin, eds. *Past the Last Post: Theorizing Post-Colonialism and
Post-Modernism.* Calgary: U of Calgary P, 1990.

Ashcroft, Bill [W.D.], Gareth Griffiths, and Helen Tiffin. *The Empire Writes Back: Theory and Practice in Post-Colonial Literatures.* London: Routledge, 1989.

Ashcroft, W.D. Introduction. *New Literature Review* (1977): 3-4.

Atwood, Margaret. Afterword. *The Journals of Susanna Moodie.* Toronto: Oxford UP,
1970. 62-64.

—. *Surfacing.* Toronto: McClelland, 1972.

Begamudré, Ven. "Greetings from Bangalore, Saskatchewan." *Canadian Literature* 132
(1992): 8-14.

Bennett, Donna. "Conflicted Vision: A Consideration of Canon and Genre in English-Canadian Literature." *Canadian Canons: Essays in Literary Value.* Ed. Robert
Lecker. Toronto: U of Toronto P, 1991. 131-49.

Boelhower, William. "Italo-Canadian Poetry and Ethnic Semiosis in the Postmodern
Context." *Canadian Literature* 119 (1988): 171-78.

Boire, Gary. "Canadian (Tw)ink: Surviving the White-Outs." *Essays on Canadian Writing* 35 (1987): 1-16.

Brown, E.K. *On Canadian Poetry.* Rev. ed. 1944. Ottawa: Tecumseh, 1973.

Brydon, Diana. "Reading Dionne Brand's 'Blues Spiritual for Mammy Prater.'" *Inside
the Poem: Essays and Poems in Honour of Donald Stephens.* Ed. W.H. New. Toronto:
Oxford UP, 1992. 81-87.

Caplan, Usher. *Like One That Dreamed: A Portrait of A.M. Klein.* Toronto: McGraw-Hill,
1982.

Davey, Frank. "Surviving the Paraphrase." *Surviving the Paraphrase: Eleven Essays on
Canadian Literature.* Winnipeg: Turnstone, 1983. 1-12.

Dean, Misao. "The Paintbrush and the Scalpel: Sara Jeannette Duncan Representing
India." *Canadian Literature* 132 (1992): 82-93.

Dewart, Edward Hartley. Introductory essay. *Selections from Canadian Poets with Occasional Critical and Biographical Notes and an Introductory Essay on Canadian Poetry.*
1864. Literature of Canada: Poetry and Prose in Reprint. Toronto: U of Toronto P,
1973. ix-xix.

Edgar, Pelham. "A Fresh View of Canadian Literature." *University Magazine* 11 (1912): 479-86. Rpt. in *The Search for English-Canadian Literature: An Anthology of Critical Articles from the Nineteenth and Early Twentieth Centuries.* Ed. Carl Ballstadt. Toronto: U of Toronto P, 1975. 110-17.

Frye, Northrop. Conclusion. *Literary History of Canada: Canadian Literature in English.* Ed. Carl F. Klinck. Toronto: U of Toronto P, 1965. 821-49.

Godard, Barbara. "The Politics of Representation: Some Native Canadian Women Writers." *Canadian Literature* 124-25 (1990): 183-225.

Goldie, Terry. "Textual Replacing." *Canadian Literature* 131 (1991): 202-04.

Harney, Robert F. "'So Great a Heritage as Ours': Immigration and the Survival of the Canadian Polity." *If One Were to Write a History . . . : Selected Writings.* Ed. Pierre Anctil and Bruno Ramirez. Toronto: Multicultural History Society of Ontario, 1991. 227-69.

Hutcheon, Linda. "'Circling the Downspout of Empire.'" Adam and Tiffin 167-89.

Kroetsch, Robert. "A Conversation with Margaret Laurence." *Creation.* Ed. Kroetsch. Toronto: New, 1970. 53-63.

——. "Unhiding the Hidden: Recent Canadian Fiction." 1974. *Robert Kroetsch: Essays.* Special issue of *Open Letter* 5th ser. 4 (1983): 17-21.

Leitch, Vincent B. *Deconstructive Criticism: An Advanced Introduction.* New York: Columbia UP, 1983.

Lewisohn, Ludwig. Foreword. *Hath Not a Jew . . . .* By A.M. Klein. New York: Behrman, 1940. v-viii.

Lighthall, William Douw. Introduction. *Songs of the Great Dominion: Voices from the Forests and Waters, the Settlements and the Cities of Canada.* Ed. Lighthall. London: Walter Scott, 1889. xxi-xxxvii.

Lower, Arthur M. *Colony to Nation: A History of Canada.* 5th ed. Toronto: McClelland, 1977.

MacLulich, T.D. *Between Europe and America: The Canadian Tradition in Fiction.* Toronto: ECW, 1988.

Miki, Roy. "The Future's Tense: Some Notes on Editing, Canadian Style." *Open Letter* 8th ser. 5-6 (1993): 182-96.

Morgan, Henry James. "Literature." *Dominion Annual Register, 1882.* Rpt. in *Towards a Canadian Literature: Essays, Editorials and Manifestos.* Ed. Douglas M. Daymond and Leslie G. Monkman. Vol. 1. Ottawa: Tecumseh, 1984. 65-70. 2 vols.

Morton, W.L. "The Relevance of Canadian History." *The Canadian Identity.* 2nd ed. Toronto: U of Toronto P, 1972. 88-114.

New, W.H. "The Very Idea." Editorial. *Canadian Literature* 135 (1992): 2-11.

Palmer, Tamara J. "Mythologizing the Journey to and from Otherness: Some Features of the Ethnic Voice in Canadian Literature." *From "Melting Pot" to Multiculturalism: The Evolution of Ethnic Relations in the United States and Canada.* Ed. Valeria Gennaro Lerda. Rome: Bulzoni, 1990. 91-113.

Rajan, Balachandra. "Scholarship and Criticism." *Literary History of Canada: Canadian Literature in English.* Ed. Carl F. Klinck. Vol. 4 [ed. W.H. New]. Toronto: U of Toronto P, 1990. 133-58. 4 vols. 1976-90.

Scott, Peter Dale. "The Difference Perspective Makes: Literary Studies in Canada and the United States." *Essays on Canadian Writing* 44 (1991): 1-60.

Seaton, Dorothy. "The Post-Colonial as Deconstruction: Land and Language in Kroetsch's 'Badlands.'" *Canadian Literature* 128 (1991): 77-89.

Slemon, Stephen. "Modernism's Last Post." Adam and Tiffin 1-11.

Söderlind, Sylvia. *Margin/Alias: Language and Colonization in Canadian and Québécois Fiction.* Toronto: U of Toronto P, 1991.

Stewart, Ian. "New Myths for Old: The Loyalists and Maritime Political Culture." *Journal of Canadian Studies* 25.2 (1990): 20-43.

Tiffin, Helen. Introduction. Adam and Tiffin vii-xvi.

Trudeau, Pierre E. "Announcement of Implementation of Policy of Multiculturalism within Bilingual Framework." Canada. Parliament. House of Commons. *Debates.* 28th Parliament. 3rd sess. Vol. 8 (13 Sept. 1971-19 Oct. 1971). Ottawa: Queen's Printer, 1971. 8545-46. Statement was made on 8 Oct.

Vipond, Mary. "Canadian Nationalism and the Plight of Canadian Magazines in the 1920s." *Canadian Historical Review* 58 (1977): 43-63.

Wilson, Sir Daniel. "Review of Sangster's *The St. Lawrence and the Saguenay.*" *An Anthology of Canadian Literature in English.* Ed. Russell Brown and Donna Bennett. Vol. 1. Toronto: Oxford UP, 1982. 132-35. 2 vols.

PART IV
SETTLER-INVADER POSTCOLONIALISM

11

"Unsettling the Empire: Resistance Theory for the Second World"*

Stephen Slemon

My argument here comprises part of what I hope will become a larger meditation on the practice of "post-colonial criticism," and the problem it addresses is a phenomenon which twenty-five years ago would have seemed an
embarrassment of riches. The sign of the "post-colonial" has become an especially valent one in academic life (there are even careers to be made out of
it), and like feminist theory or women's studies programs a decade ago, the
area is witnessing an enormous convergence within it of diverse critical practices and cultural forces. We are now undergoing an important process of
sorting through those forces and tendencies, investigating where affiliations
lie and where they cross, examining the political and pedagogical goals of the
area, and re-negotiating basic issues such as where our primary "material" of
study and of intervention lies. What I want to do in this paper is take a position within this process of questioning—but because this *is* a process, I want
also to advance this position as provisional and temporary, a statement in
search of that clarifying energy which emerges at the best of times out of
friendly discussion and collegial exchange.

In specific terms, what I want to do in this paper is address two separate
debates in critical theory, and then attempt to yoke them together into an
argument for maintaining within a discourse of post-colonialism certain textual and critical practices which inhabit ex-colonial settler cultures and their
literatures. The textual gestures I want to preserve for post-colonial theory
and practice are various and dispersed, but the territory I want to reclaim for
post-colonial pedagogy and research—and reclaim *not* as a unified and indi-
visible area but rather as a groundwork for certain modes of anti-colonial
work—is that neither/nor territory of white settler-colonial writing which
Alan Lawson has called the "Second World."

The first debate concerns the *field* of the "post-colonial." Is the "post-colonial" a synonym for what Wallersteinian world-systems theory calls the periphery in economic relations? Is it another way of naming what other discourses
would call the Third and Fourth Worlds? Is it a name for a discursive and representational set of practices which are grounded in a politics of anti-colo-

* *World Literature Written in English* 30.2 (1990): 30-41.

nialism? Or is the term post-colonial simply another name for the old Commonwealth of literary activity—a synonym for such unfortunate neologisms as "the new literatures in English," or what Joseph Jones in a fleeting moment of unitary hopefulness wanted to call "Terranglia," or what the Modern Languages Association of America in its continuing moment of exclusionary and yet proprietorial backyardism still wants to call "English Literatures Other than British and American"?

The second debate I want to address concerns the nature of literary *resistance* itself. Is literary resistance something that simply issues forth, through narrative, against a clearly definable set of power relations? Is it something actually *there* in the text, or is it produced and reproduced in and through communities of readers and through the mediating structures of their own culturally specific histories? Do literary resistances escape the constitutive purchase of genre, and trope, and figure, and mode, which operate elsewhere as a contract between text and reader and thus a set of centralizing codes, or are literary resistances in fact necessarily *embedded* in the representational technologies of those literary and social "texts" whose structures and whose referential codes they seek to oppose?

These questions sound like definitional problems, but I think in fact they are crucial ones for a critical industry which at the moment seems to find these two central terms—"post-colonial" and "resistance"—positively shimmering as objects of desire and self-privilege, and so easily appropriated to competing, and in fact hostile, modes of critical and literary practice. Arun Mukherjee makes this point with great eloquence in "Whose Post-Colonialism and Whose Postmodernism?"—asking what specificity, what residual grounding, remains with the term "post-colonial" when it is applied indiscriminately to both Second- and Third-World literary texts. The term "resistance" recently found itself at the centre of a similar controversy, when it was discovered how very thoroughly a *failure* in resistance characterized some of the earlier political writing of the great theorist of *textual* resistance, Paul de Man. Both terms thus find themselves at the centre of a quarrel over the kinds of critical taxonomies that will be seen to perform legitimate work in articulating the relation between literary texts and the political world; and to say this is to recognize that critical taxonomies, like literary canons, issue forth from cultural institutions which continue to police what voices will be heard, which *kinds* of (textual) intervention will be made recognizable and/or classifiable, and what *authentic* forms of post-colonial textual resistance are going to look like. These debates are thus institutional: grounded in university curricula, and *about* pedagogical strategies. They are also about the question of authenticity itself: how a text emerges from a cultural grounding and speaks to a reading community, and how textual ambiguity or ambivalence proves pedagogically awkward when an apparatus called "English studies" recuperates various writing practices holistically as "literatures," and then deploys them wholesale towards a discourse of inclusivity and coverage.

The first debate—the question of the "post-colonial"—is grounded in the overlapping of three competing research or critical fields, each of which carries a specific cultural location and history. In the first of these fields, the term "post-colonial" is an outgrowth of what formerly were "Commonwealth" literary studies—a study which came into being *after* "English" studies had been liberalized to include "American" and then an immediate national or regional literature (Australian, Canadian, West Indian), and as a way of mobilizing the concept of national or geographical *difference* within what remains a unitary idea of "English." The second of these critical fields, in contrast, employs the term "post-colonial" in considering the valency of subjectivity specifically within Third- and Fourth-World cultures, and within black, and ethnic, and First-Nation constituencies dispersed within First-World terrain. The institutionalizing of these two critical fields has made possible the emergence of a third field of study, however, where nation-based examinations of a variable literary Commonwealth, or a variable literary Third World, give way to specific analyses of the discourse of colonialism (and neo-colonialism), and where studies in cultural representativeness and literary mimeticism give way to the project of identifying the kinds of anti-colonialist resistance that can take place in literary writing.

The past few years have therefore witnessed an extraordinary burgeoning of "post-colonial" criticism and theory, largely because the second and third of these pedagogical fields have at last gained hold within the First-World academy. "Post-colonial" studies in "English" now finds itself at a shifting moment, where three very different critical projects collide with one another on the space of a single signifier—and what will probably be a single course offering within an English studies programme. Not surprisingly, this situation has produced some remarkable confusions, and they underpin the present debate over the specificity of the "post-colonial" in the areas of literary and critical practice.

The confusion which concerns me here is the way in which the *project* of the third "post-colonial" critical field—that is, of identifying the scope and nature of anti-colonialist resistance in writing—has been mistaken for the project of the second critical field, which concerns itself with articulating the literary nature of Third- and Fourth-World cultural groups. For whereas the first and second of these post-colonial critical fields work with whole nations or cultures as their basic units, and tend to seek out the defining characteristics under which *all* writing in that field can be subsumed, the third critical field is concerned with identifying a social force, colonialism, and with the attempt to understand the resistances to that force, *wherever* they lie. Colonialism, obviously, is an enormously problematical category: it is by definition transhistorical and unspecific, and it is used in relation to very different kinds of cultural oppression and economic control. But like the term "patriarchy," which shares similar problems in definition, the concept of colonialism, to this third critical field, remains crucial to a critique of past and present power relations in world affairs, and thus to a specifically *post*-colonial critical practice which attempts to understand the relation of literary writing to power and its contestations.

This mistaking of a pro-active, anti-colonialist critical project with nation-based studies in Third- and Fourth-World literary writing comes about for good reason—for it has been, and always will be, the case that the most important forms of resistance to any form of social power will be produced from within the communities that are most immediately and visibly subordinated by that power structure. But when the idea of anti-colonial resistance becomes *synonymous* with Third- and Fourth-World literary writing, two forms of displacement happen. First, *all* literary writing which emerges from these cultural locations will be understood as carrying a radical and contestatory content—and this gives away the rather important point that subjected peoples are sometimes capable of producing reactionary literary documents. And secondly, the idea will be discarded that important anti-colonialist literary writing can take place *outside* the ambit of Third- and Fourth-World literary writing—and this in effect excises the study of anti-colonialist Second-World literary activity from the larger study of anti-colonialist literary practice.

In practical terms, this excision springs in part from a desire to foreclose upon a *specific* form of "Commonwealth" literary criticism. For a small number of old-school "Commonwealth" critics, comparative studies across English literatures did indeed promise the renewal through "art" of that lost cross-cultural unity which a capricious twentieth-century history had somehow denied for Britain and the empire. And so this excision provides an effective way of figuring one important objective of post-colonial criticism: and that is the rejection of neo-colonialist, Eurocentrist, and late capitalist purchase in the practice of post-colonial literary analysis.

This excision also springs from a rather healthy recognition that—as Linda Hutcheon has recently put it—the experience of colonialism, and therefore of post-colonialism, is simply *not* the same in, say, Canada as it is in the West Indies or in Africa or in India. As Fourth-World literary writing continually insists, Second- and Third-World cultures do not inhabit the same political, discursive, and literary terrains in relation to colonialism. The excision of Second-World literary writing from the field of the "post-colonial" therefore figures the importance of cultural *difference* within post-colonial criticism and theory—even if that difference is conscripted to the service of what remains at heart an extended nation-based critical practice founded on a unitary model and on the assumption of equivalent (as opposed to, say, "shared") cultural and literary experience within a positivist and essentialist "post-colonial" sphere.

Nevertheless, I want to argue, this conflating of the projects of the second and third post-colonial critical fields, and the consequent jettisoning of Second-World literary writing from the domain of the post-colonial, remains—in the Bloomian sense—a "misreading," and one which seems to be setting in train a concept of the "post-colonial" which is remarkably purist and absolutist in tenor. Tim Brennan, one of the most interesting of the newly emerging US-based, First-World critics in the post-colonial field, has been an enormously forceful proponent for this conflation of the second and third post-colonial critical projects—for the refiguration of the post-colonial literary terrain as "the literature not of the 'colonies' but of the 'colonized'" (5)—and he puts the argument for this position as follows:

> [Writers such as] Nadine Gordimer or John Coetzee of South Africa, along with others from the white Commonwealth countries, while clearly playing [a] mediating role [between colonizer and colonized], are probably better placed in some category of the European novel of Empire because of their compromised positions of segregated privilege within colonial settler states. They are too much like the fictional "us" of the so-called mainstream, on the inside looking out. (35-36)

Brennan's argument is actually more complex than this quotation suggests, for it hangs upon an extremely suggestive category called "the novel of Empire," which in another discussion would need to be unpacked. But for my purposes here, his argument is useful because it makes visible the fact that the foundational principle for this particular approach to the field of post-colonial criticism is at heart a simple binarism: the binarism of Europe and its Others, of colonizer and colonized, of the West and the Rest, of the vocal and the silent. It is also a centre/periphery model with roots in world-systems theory—and as so often happens with simple binary systems, this concept of the post-colonial has a marked tendency to blur when it tries to focus upon ambiguously placed or ambivalent material. In what seems to be emerging as the dominant focus of post-colonial literary criticism now—especially for literary criticism coming out of universities in the United States—this blurring is everywhere in evidence in relation to what world-systems theory calls the field of "semi-periphery," and what follows behind it is a radical foreclosing by post-colonial criticism on settler/colonial writing: the radical ambivalence of colonialism's middle ground.

This foreclosing most commonly takes the rather simple form of stark forgetfulness, of overlooking the Second World entirely as though its literature and its critical traditions didn't even exist. An example of this forgetfulness is provided by Laura Donaldson in her otherwise scrupulously researched article in *Diacritics* entitled "The Miranda Complex." Here Donaldson argues that while the trope of Prospero and Caliban has been done to death in anti-colonialist criticism (and here she relies upon an article by Houston Baker published in *Critical Inquiry* as her authority), the trope of Miranda and Caliban—the trope of the Anglo-European daughter in the multiple interpella-tions of both colonialism and patriarchy—has been "virtually ignored" (68) by literary criticism. From a Second-World perspective, however, what *really* remains "virtually ignored"—in a gesture so common as to be symptomatic of much of the US-based, First-World "post-colonial" critical practice—is that body of critical work, published in Second-World critical journals by scholars such as Diana Brydon and Chantal Zabus, which discusses the Miranda-Cal-iban trope precisely in the terms Donaldson's article calls for. In cases like this, where *Diacritics* cites *Critical Inquiry*, Donaldson cites Baker, the academ-ic star-system of First-World criticism inscribes itself wholesale into post-colo-nial studies, and a large and important body of astute anti-colonial literary critical work ends up simply getting lost in the move.

A more important form of this foreclosing process, however, is under-scored by a much more substantive critical concern: and that is to preserve the concept of cultural *difference* in the critical articulation of literary post-colonialism. Arun Mukherjee's article, for example, advances in exemplary form the argument that "post-colonial" studies in literary resistance inher-ently totalize dissimilar cultures when they consider the resistances to colo-nialism of both imperialism's "white cousins" and its black, colonized sub-jects. Specifically, Mukherjee argues, this critical practice dangerously overlooks "realist" writing from the Third and Fourth Worlds, and ends up privileging the kind of post-colonial writing which takes resistance to colo-nialism as its primary objective. The argument for a post-colonial critical prac-tice here, of course, has nothing to do with the kind of wilful forgetfulness which characterizes Donaldson's misreading; but it does promulgate a mis-reading of its own, I would argue, in mistaking the *project* of anti-colonialist criticism with the kind of nation-based descriptive criticism which character-izes the first post-colonial critical field I have been discussing. Here, I suspect, the conflation between the second and third post-colonial critical fields has become so naturalized that the *specific* project of the third post-colonial field seems no longer recognizable: the project of articulating the forms—and modes, and tropes, and figures—of anti-colonialist textual resistance, *wherev-er* they occur, and in *all* of their guises. A more damaging critique of the kind of critical practice Mukherjee objects to, I think, lies in the propensity of anti-colonialist critics (like myself) to overlook the range of anti-colonialist ges-tures which inhabit First-World, or imperial, writing itself.

At any rate, the new binaristic absolutism which seems to come in the wake of First-World accommodation to the fact of post-colonial literary and cultur-al criticism seems to be working in several ways to drive that trans-national region of ex-colonial settler cultures away from the field of post-colonial lit-erary representation. The Second World of writing within the ambit of colo-nialism is in danger of disappearing: because it is not sufficiently pure in its anti-colonialism, because it does not offer up an experiential grounding in a common "Third-World" aesthetics, because its modalities of *post*-coloniality are too ambivalent, too occasional and uncommon, for inclusion within the field. This debate over the scope and nature of the "post-colonial," I now want to argue, has enormous investments in the second debate I want to discuss in this paper, for in fact the idea of both literary and political *resistance* to colonialist power is the hidden term, the foundational concept, upon which *all* these distinctions in the modality of the "post-colonial" actually rest.

The debate over literary resistance is in fact a very complicated one, and criticism offers a seemingly endless set of configurations for the kinds of reading and writing practices which a theory of resistance might possibly comprise. In order to simplify this debate, however, I want to suggest that in rudimentary form the idea of literary resistance collapses into two general movements or concepts, each of which contains important distinctions that I won't address here.

The first concept of resistance is most clearly put forward by Selwyn Cudjoe in his *Resistance and Caribbean Literature* and by Barbara Harlow in her *Resistance Literature*. For Cudjoe and Harlow, resistance is an act, or a set of acts, that is designed to rid a people of its oppressors, and it so thoroughly infuses the experience of living under oppression that it becomes an almost autonomous aesthetic principle. *Literary* resistance, under these conditions, can be seen as a form of contractual understanding between text and reader, one which is embedded in an experiential dimension and buttressed by a political and cultural aesthetic at work in the culture. And "resistance literature," in this definition, can thus be seen as that category of literary writing which emerges as an integral part of an organized struggle or resistance for national liberation.

This argument for literary "resistance" is an important one to hold on to—but it is also a strangely untheorized position, for it fails to address three major areas of critical concern. The first is a political concern: namely, that centre/periphery notions of resistance can actually work to *reinscribe* centre/periphery relations and can "serve an institutional function of securing the dominant narratives" (Sharpe 139). The second problem with this argument is that it assumes that literary resistance is simply somehow *there* in the literary text as a structure of intentionality, and *there* in the social text as a communicative gesture of pure availability. Post-Lacanian and post-Althusserian theories of the *constructedness* of subjectivity, however, would contest such easy access to representational purity, and would argue instead that resistance is grounded in the *multiple* and *contradictory* structures of ideological interpellation or subject-formation—which would call down the notion that resistance can *ever* be "purely" intended or "purely" expressed in representational or communicative models. The third problem with this argument is that it has to set aside the very persuasive theory of power which Foucault puts forward in his *The Archaeology of Knowledge*: the theory that power *itself* inscribes its resistances and so, in the process, seeks to contain them. It is this third objection, especially, which has energized the post-structuralist project of theorizing literary resistance—and in order to clarify what is going on in that theatre of critical activity I want to focus especially on Jenny Sharpe's wonderful article in *Modern Fiction Studies* entitled "Figures of Colonial Resistance."

Sharpe's article involves a reconsideration of the work of theorists such as Gayatri Spivak, Homi Bhabha, Abdul JanMohamed, and Benita Parry, each of whom has worked to correct the critical "tendency to presume the transparency" of literary resistance in colonial and post-colonial writing (138), and who collectively have worked to examine the ways in which resistance in writing must go beyond the mere "questioning" of colonialist authority. There are important differences in how all of these theorists define literary resistance, but the two key points Sharpe draws out are, first, that you can never *easily* locate the sites of anti-colonial resistance—since resistance itself is always in some measure an "effect of the contradictory representation of colonial authority" (145) and never simply a "reversal" of power—and secondly, that resistance itself is therefore never *purely* resistance, never *simply* there in the text or the interpretive community, but is always *necessarily* complicit in the apparatus it seeks to transgress. As Sharpe puts it: "the colonial subject who can answer the colonizers back is the product of the same vast ideological machinery that silences the subaltern" (143); and what she is saying here, basically, is that a *theory* of literary resistance *must* recognize the inescapable partiality, the incompleteness, the untranscendable *ambiguity* of literary or indeed *any* contra/dictory or contestatory act which employs a First-World medium for the figuration of a Third-World resistance, and which predicates a semiotics of *refusal* on a gestural mechanism whose first act must always be an acknowledgement and a *recognition* of the reach of colonialist power.

Sharpe's argument, that is, underscores the way in which literary resistance is necessarily in a place of ambivalence: between systems, between discursive worlds, implicit and complicit in both of them. And from this recognition comes the very startling but inevitable claim—made most spectacularly by Tim Brennan in his book on *Salman Rushdie and the Third World*—that the Third-World resistance writer, the Third-World resistance text, is necessarily self-produced as a doubly-emplaced and *mediated* figure—Brennan's term is "Third-World Cosmopolitan"—between the First and the Third World, and *within* the ambit of a First-World politics.

This brings me at last to the central thesis of my paper, which begins with the observation that there is a contradiction within the dominant trajectory of First-World post-colonial critical theory here—for that same theory which argues persuasively for the necessary *ambivalence* of post-colonial literary resistance, and which works to emplace that resistance squarely *between* First- and Third-World structures of representation, *also* wants to assign "Second-World" or ex-colonial settler literatures unproblematically to the category of the literature of empire, the literature of the First World, precisely *because* of its ambivalent position within the First-World/Third-World, colonizer/colonized binary. Logically, however, it would seem that the argument being made by Spivak, Bhabha, Sharpe, and others about the ambivalence of literary and other resistances—the argument that resistance texts are necessarily double, necessarily mediated, in their social location—is in fact nothing less than an argument *for* the emplacement of "Second-World" literary texts within the field of the "post-colonial": for if there *is* only a space for a *pure* Third- and Fourth-World resistance outside the First-World hegemony, then *either* you have to return to the baldly untheorized notion which informs the first position in the debate over literary resistance, *or* you have to admit that at least as far as writing is concerned, the "field" of the genuinely *post*-colonial can never *actually* exist.

It is for this reason, I think, and not because of some vestigial nostalgia for an empire upon which the sun will never set, that many critics and theorists have argued long and hard for the preservation of white Australian, New Zealander, southern African, and Canadian literatures within the field of comparative "post-colonial" literary studies. At bottom, the argument here is the one which Alan Lawson made at The Badlands Conference in Calgary in 1986: namely, that in order to avoid essentialism and to escape theoretical absolutism, we might profitably think of the category of the settler cultures of Australia, Canada, southern Africa, and New Zealand as inhabiting a "Second World" of discursive polemics—of inhabiting, that is, the space of dynamic *relation* between those "apparently antagonistic, static, aggressive, [and] disjunctive" (68) binaries which colonialism "settles" upon a landscape: binaries such as colonizer and colonized, foreign and native, settler and indigene, home and away. Lawson is careful to note that such a doubleness or ambivalence in emplacement is by no means an exclusive domain or prerogative for "Second-World" writing, and by no means an essentialist category governing *all* activity going on within the settler literatures. Rather, the "Second World"—like the third of the three "post-colonial" critical fields I have been discussing—is at root a *reading position*, and one which is and often has been taken up in settler and ex-colonial literature and criticism. The "Second World," that is, like "post-colonial criticism" itself, is a critical manoeuvre, a reading and writing action; and embedded within it is a theory of communicative action akin in some ways to Clifford Geertz's thesis about "intermediary knowledge," or Gadamer's theory of an interpretive "fusion of horizons." "The inherent awareness of both 'there' and 'here' and the cultural ambiguity of these terms," writes Lawson, "are not so much the boundaries of its cultural matrix, nor tensions to be resolved, but a space *within* which [the Second-World, post-colonial literary text] may move *while* speaking" (69). Lawson's definition of literary representation in the discursive "Second

World" thus articulates a figure for what many First-World critical theorists would correctly define as the limits and the condition of *post-colonial* forms of literary resistance. The irony is that many of those same First-World critics would define that "post-colonial" as exclusively the domain of the Third and Fourth Worlds.

But what perhaps marks a *genuine* difference in the contestatory activity of Second- and Third-World post-colonial writing, I now want to argue, is that the *illusion* of a stable self/other, here/there binary division has *never* been available to Second-World writers, and that as a result the sites of figural contestation between oppressor and oppressed, colonizer and colonized, have been taken *inward* and *internalized* in Second-World post-colonial textual practice. By this I mean that the *ambivalence* of literary resistance itself is the "always already" condition of Second-World settler and post-colonial literary writing, for in the white literatures of Australia, or New Zealand, or Canada, or southern Africa, anti-colonialist resistance has *never* been directed at an object or a discursive structure which can be seen as purely external to the self. The Second-World writer, the Second-World text, that is, has always been complicit in colonialism's territorial appropriation of land, and voice, and agency, and this has been their inescapable condition even at those moments when they have promulgated their most strident and most spectacular figures of post-colonial resistance. In the Second World, anti-colonialist resistances in literature must necessarily *cut across the individual subject*, and as they do so they also, necessarily, contribute towards that theoretically rigorous understanding of textual resistance which post-colonial *critical* theory is only now learning how to recognize. This ambivalence of emplacement is the *condition* of their possibility; it has been since the beginning; and it is therefore scarcely surprising that the ambivalent, the mediated, the conditional, and the radically *compromised* literatures of this undefinable Second World have an enormous amount yet to tell to "theory" about the nature of literary resistance.

This *internalization* of the object of resistance in Second-World literatures, this internalization of the self/other binary of colonialist relations, explains why it is that it has always been Second-World *literary* writing rather than Second-World *critical* writing which has occupied the vanguard of a Second-World post-colonial literary or critical *theory*. Literary writing is *about* internalized conflict, whereas critical writing—for most practitioners—is still grounded in the ideology of unitariness, and coherence, and specific argumentative drive. For this reason, Second-World *critical* writing—with some spectacularly transgressive exceptions—has tended to miss out on the rigours of what, I would argue, comprises a necessarily ambivalent, necessarily contra/dictory or incoherent, anti-colonialist *theory* of resistance. In literary documents such as De Mille's *Strange Manuscript* or Furphy's *Such Is Life*, to name two nineteenth-century examples, or in the "re-historical" fictions of writers such as Fiona Kidman, Ian Wedde, Thea Astley, Peter Carey, Kate Grenville, Barbara Hanrahan, Daphne Marlatt, Susan Swan, and Rudy Wiebe—to name only a *few* from the contemporary period—this necessary *entanglement* of anti-colonial resistances within the colonialist machineries they seek to displace has been consistently thematized, consistently worked *through,* in ways that the unitary and logical demands of critical argumentation, at least in its traditional genres, have simply not allowed.

A fully adequate version of the argument I am making here would attempt to show in detail how at least one of these Second-World fictional texts manages to articulate a post-colonial or anti-colonial reading for resistance. For the purposes of the larger debate I am attempting to address, however, it may prove more useful to close with two subsidiary arguments about post-colonial critical practice, and then to open the floor—if one can do that in writing—to the kinds of critical cross-questioning which the field of post-colonial research and teaching at present needs to engage with.

The first point concerns a loss that I think we sustain if we hold too nostalgically to an expanded but at heart nation-based model of post-colonial criticism—whether that model applies to a "Commonwealth" or to a "Third- and Fourth-World" constituency. If "post-colonial literature" becomes a term for designating an essential unitariness in the lived experience of different and dispersed peoples, all of the critical problems which accrue around nationalist models of critical definition—the hegemonic force of the concept of "nation," for example, and the necessary blindness that the concept settles upon the internally marginalized—will simply be carried forward into a new object of study, and we will be constrained to replay in our field all of the debates that have troubled each one of the positivist categories of period and place that comprise traditional English studies. Our object of attention will be differentiated from that of other areas by the usual categories, but our field, in essence, will remain an add-on discipline, a marker of the infinite ability of traditional English studies to accommodate national and historical difference within its inherently liberal embrace. We have a chance, however, to employ our field more radically: we can use it to raise questions about the kinds of work literary documents perform in culture, and we can use it to question the discourses of inclusivity and "coverage" which have so often been deployed within English studies to depoliticize literary writing and to obscure the struggle for power which takes place within textual representation.

The second and final point I want to make concerns the way in which our interest in multiple, racially mixed, gendered and engendered, national and trans-national post-colonial literatures not only carries us inescapably into the theatre of colonialist and neo-colonialist power relations, but also carries us into the figurative domains of other modes of power as they appear in and are contested through the field of literary writing. Post-colonial texts are *also* concerned with the problem of privilege through racism and patriarchy, also at work contesting the kinds of hierarchical exclusion which operate through homophobia, and nationalism, and adultism; and in part this means that the debate over the post-colonial field and over the question of anti-colonialist literary resistance will never tell us everything about the struggles for power that actually take place under colonialism's baleful gaze. Rather, this debate tells us that all of our negotiations for change—in literature and criticism, in pedagogy, in immediate political engagement—are marked by provisionality and partiality, and are bounded by an historical specificity that does not simply translate itself into other theatres of social contestation. But more encouragingly, it also hints to us of the presence of figural activity for agency and resistance going on in cultural places we have somehow been taught to ignore. We need to specify our resistances to power, but we need also to recognize the ubiquity of resistances and to understand their incompleteness, their strengths, their losses and their gains. "There is another world, but it is in this one," quotes Lawson. There is also a *second* world of post-colonial literary resistance, but it inhabits a place—a place of radical ambivalence—where too much post-colonial criticism in the First World has so far forgotten to look.

WORKS CITED

Brennan, Timothy. *Salman Rushdie and the Third World: Myths of the Nation.* London: Macmillan, 1989.

Brydon, Diana. "Re-writing *The Tempest.*" *World Literature Written in English* 23.1 (1984): 75-88.

Cudjoe, Selwyn R. *Resistance and Caribbean Literature.* Athens: Ohio UP, 1980.

Donaldson, Laura E. "The Miranda Complex: Colonialism and the Question of Feminist Reading." *Diacritics* 18.3 (1988): 65-77.

Foucault, Michel. *The Archaeology of Knowledge.* Trans. A.M. Sheridan Smith. New York: Pantheon, 1972.

Harlow, Barbara. *Resistance Literature.* New York and London: Methuen, 1987.

Hutcheon, Linda. "'Circling the Downspout of Empire': Post-Colonialism and Post-modernism." *ARIEL* 20.4 (1989): 149-75.

Lawson, Alan. "A Cultural Paradigm for the Second World." The Badlands Conference on Canadian and Australian Literatures. U of Calgary. 29 Aug. 1986. *Australian-Canadian Studies* 9.1-2 (1991): 67-78.

Mukherjee, Arun. "Whose Post-Colonialism and Whose Postmodernism?" *World Literature Written in English* 30.2 (1990): 1-9.

Sharpe, Jenny. "Figures of Colonial Resistance." *Modern Fiction Studies* 35 (1989): 137-55.

Zabus, Chantal. "A Calibanic Tempest in Anglophone and Francophone New World Writing." *Canadian Literature* 104 (1985): 35-50.

12

"Postcolonial Theory and the 'Settler' Subject"*

Alan Lawson

As I see it, postcolonial theory manifests two quite different impulses that remain in perpetual tension within its strategies and its trajectories. As, "essentially," a theory of difference, postcolonialism articulates itself through an insistence on the representation, inscription, and interpretation of the particular, the local, that which is not the same. It resists universals. But, as a mode of analysis and historicocultural explanation, as a heuristic polemic, postcolonialism forever desires to become another grand narrative, another of the Great Explanations.

This essay records my current place on the arc of this oscillation between the empirical and the transcendental. I want to tilt back a little from what is often said to be a present postcolonialist predilection for the Great Explanation toward a reassertion of the particular. I argue here for the ethical as well as the hermeneutical value of locating a particular kind of postcolonial site— the "settler" subject. This is not only a reading strategy of some value but a political and ethical necessity. To overlook the particularity of the settler site, to collapse it into some larger and unspecified narrative of empire or metropolis, or even to exclude it from the field of the postcolonial altogether, is to engage in a strategic disavowal of the actual processes of colonization, a self-serving forgetting of the entangled agency of one's history as a subject with that of the displaced Native/colonized subject.

But empiricisms must take account of their frames. I suggest specifically that the colonial project is recognizable in the valorized narratives (and narrative forms) in which our ambiguously postcolonial cultures characterize themselves and their tendentious histories. I presume, as a postcolonial comparativist, that by reading putatively similar cultures we can recognize those characterizations as paradigms of nation-narration and perhaps as modes and structures of determi/nation. This paper draws its perceptions, then, from an engagement with Canadian, Australian, New Zealand, and South African literatures as literatures of what is tendentiously called settlement.

There have been many typologies and taxonomies of the imperialized world[1]: I am proposing this one in order to achieve more highly differentiat-

---

* *Essays on Canadian Writing* 56 (1995): 20-36.

ed readings of particular kinds of cultures and their texts. My taxonomy specifically refuses what is sometimes said to be the collapsing of all post-colonial cultures into a single category. I want to enable the investigation of one particular kind of postcolonial site as part of a project to distinguish different kinds of postcolonial subject positions. My proposal takes a polemical reading position that finds a peculiar power *within* a radical relatedness, in the negotiation between those agonistic, static, disjunctive, and apparently overdetermining binaries that have inscribed and reinscribed the cultural condition of postcolonial communities.

I therefore engage with some recent debates on and in the postcolonial field—specifically, about postcolonial studies and about the valorized modalities of postcoloniality. My principal motivation is to argue for the specific valency of the kind of writing/reading that can go on in what I have elsewhere called the "Second World" (Slemon, Lawson)—which is more or less that part of colonial space occupied by the postimperial, so-called settler colonies. I will also briefly make an argument that postcolonial criticism, like other major modes of criticism, has its own temporality, a particular set of historical and institutional locations, its own ideological sites, and hence a specific archaeology and bibliography. The archival narrative of this argument would be that there has been a strong tradition of resistance to (or, more generally, engagement with) the power of particular imperial discourses since very early in the colonial period. We need to learn how to identify those resistances, to recognize the names by which they identified themselves. This is analogous to some feminist attempts to identify earlier feminisms and to locate the distinctive address of their particular sites of resistance. It has not been adequate for some time to speak of an unhyphenated, singular feminism. I would also suggest that it is not adequate to speak of a single, unmodified, unspecified post-colonialism: indeed, it would undermine the fundamental political motivation of postcolonialism (as a theory of difference) to do so. Like gender, race (and other nominations of cultural difference, such as nationality or settler status) is culturally rather than biologically determined. Hence, I present an argument for a particular kind of reading that might take place in that Second World, a kind of reading that acknowledges, but with a very precise inflection, what Homi K. Bhabha has called the "double inscription" of colonial space ("Signs" 150). The Second World, that which is always more than two, exerts its own particular kind of leverage on certain Western notions of epistemology and hence of narrative and textuality.

Stephen Slemon has argued that one of the most contested of contemporary critical territories is that of the postcolonial. The point I want to take further is that in the competition for the newly valorized term "postcolonial," some critics (especially within the US academy) have foreclosed on a particularly valuable site of critical reading and textual resistance. The exclusion of the so-called settler colonies has become something of a shibboleth in some postcolonial practice. The slippage from "Third World" to "postcolonial," a collapsing of the one into the other, is, if not always easy to document, one of the gestures of the field—at least in some (usually metropolitan) quarters (see Brennan; McClintock; Mukherjee; Robbins; Shohat; and Williams and Chrisman, "Colonial"). In explicitly or implicitly enacting this exclusion, they have bracketed off from examination the very place where the processes of colonial power as negotiation, as transactions of power, are most visible. That foreclosing risks capitulating to the notion of the operation of imperialism as a one-way imposition of colonial power from above, thereby reinscribing the moment of imperialism's discursive capture of history. In doing so, those critics overlook the fact that the colonial "moment" (as in physics) is a transaction of forces, a relationship—unequal, certainly, but a relationship nonetheless. Colonial power is a product of all vectors in the system, and we prevent its interrogation if we occlude any one of them. As Slemon observes, this exclusion of settler cultures unreflectingly reinscribes the familiar "binarism of Europe and its Others, of colonizer and colonized, of the West and the Rest, of the vocal and the silent" (143). Critiques of postcolonial theory have noted that locating resistance *either* in the contradictions of the colonialist text *or* in an essentialist Third World consciousness serves to conceal the actual operations of resistance (see Parry). But it is not often recognized that doing so continues to recirculate the self-serving Eurocentricity (or US imperialism) of the binary operation of power in the overarching reductionist conception of the world as, once again, Europe and its other. This overlooking effectively oversees Europe's other others. "[D]o we not," in Alice A. Jardine's memorable phrase, "run the danger of (belatedly) developing nothing but the negative of the Great Western Photograph?" (39).

Indeed, one is tempted to speculate about the motivation for the sometimes overdetermined repudiation of invader-settler postcolonialism in the US academy. The anxiety that it reveals may derive from what outsiders often recognize as a desire in US nation-narration to forget its own colonizing status in favour of a more urgent attention to recent problems of race: African-American, Chicano, et cetera. The effacement of the US First Nations (a term that will take much longer to take root in the discursive politics of America than it has in Canada) is part of the same politics that wishes to efface other invader-settler colonies from the domain of the postcolonial, and this is because these settler colonies might remind the US of the repressed memory of its own historical circumstance and of its painful and tricky need to negotiate its own idealized constructions of origin.

We need to attend more comprehensively to the different ways in which imperialism interpellated the full range of its subjects so that we can explore the particular investitures of power, both material and discursive, that postcolonial readings unmask and unravel. The subjects of empire have been subjected to many different forms of address: it is precisely these differences that must be recovered in the current battle over the institutional locations of postcoloniality.

To speak merely of postcolonial resistance without specifying the particular cultural/historical materiality in which it is called into being is to speak in/differently. The Second World postcolonial subject does not simply resist a discursive power that is (or has been) imposed from outside. In writing back against the representations of experience of "this" place, this subject opposes that which is internal to itself in a dual sense—its own history of apprehensions and its own history of representations. The New Zealand critic Patrick Evans has usefully observed that "All colonies begin as words" (18). This reminds me of a suggestive pun made by Ross Chambers: "what is mediated can always be re-mediated" ("Fables" 1).

The foundational literary-critical arguments about the relation of the processes of colonization to language are in fact quite old. The argument may, in some forms, have risked an unproblematized conception of language, but it is nevertheless important to see that it has a genealogy, or else, like imperialism itself, we risk "emptying the field," creating a critical *terra nullius*, a new Virgin Land ready for occupation, effecting a genesis amnesia. The general outlines of the argument about the relation between the colonial condition and the operations of the imperial language can be traced from D.E.S. Maxwell's 1964 article "Landscape and Theme," through various suggestions by W.H. New, Dennis Lee, and Robert Kroetsch, to the work of more recent (and more often cited) colonial discourse analysts as diverse as Homi K. Bhabha, Edward W. Said, Gayatri Chakravorty Spivak, and Peter Hulme. The irreducible base of the argument about the relation between colonialism and language is the assumption that "colonial" is not just a period of history but an operation of discourse. As an operation of discourse, colonialism interpellates colonial subjects and incorporates them (substantially by the mechanism of inscription) in a system of representation. They become what Annamaria Carusi has usefully called "subject-effects," the "subject as a discursive instance which is the effect of a variety of structures or discursive practices" (104). The colonized subject is thus caught by both interpellation and inscription. In this way, the colonizing subject can assume the authority of "speaking for" just as, in so many historical narratives (as I will discuss later), the settler "stands in" for the Indigene. They are always already written by that system of representation. Hulme's formulation of colonial discourse is useful: it is "an ensemble of linguistically-based practices unified by their common deployment in the management of colonial relationships" (2). In this sense, postcolonialism is driven by an engagement with the power that remains in the discourse. It cannot, then, cease at those historic moments of independence.

Because the postcolonial situation is always already mediated, it is forever in the process of being re-mediated. The corollary of Chambers's pun is that the remedy will always be incomplete. This is something that most Canadians (except Brian Mulroney) who voted on the constitutional referendum instinctively understood. Settler cultures are, as Joanne Tompkins argues, sites of rehearsal, or (re)negotiation. They are liminal sites at the point of negotiation between the contending authorities of Empire and Native.

The settler subject is, in a sense, the very type of the nonunified subject *and* the very distillation of colonial power, the place where the operations of colonial power as *negotiation* are most intensely visible. Formed by the worldview of post-Enlightenment Europe, the subject's involvement with colonial space is figured as epistemological crisis. In almost endless repetition, colonial space is figured as lack, absence, emptiness, a ". . . space [that] cannot hear" (Atwood 11); as Dorothy Seaton points out in "Colonising Discourses: The Land in Australian and Western Canadian Exploration Narratives," colonial space is figured as outside discourse, a place of nonmeaning, a place of chaos that threatens the coherence of the subject ("what does he change into" [Atwood 19]; "The moving water will not show me / my reflection" [Atwood 11]). Colonial experience is therefore deconstructive of the coherence of European epistemology. For epistemological reasons, then, but also for professional ones, the colonial explorer had to empty the land of prior signification—what is already known cannot be discovered, what already has a name cannot be named. For the settler, too, the land had to be empty. Empty land can be settled, but occupied land can only be invaded. So the land must be emptied so that it can be filled, in turn, with both discourse and cattle.

But evacuating the land of prior discursive and human occupation is also strategic in the ethical and legal domains, as Australia's High Court formally recognized on 3 June 1992 in the famous Mabo case (see Borch). In a landmark decision, the High Court concluded two things: the doctrine of *terra nullius*, which had been used for two centuries in British and Australian law to deny Native land claims, was itself untenable—the land was indeed not empty at the moment of "settlement"; and, at least in certain places, a form of Native title had not been, as the judgement puts it, "extinguished."

But other evacuations are more in the domain of narrative and metaphor. The "frontier," the "north," and (in Australia) the "centre" are still popularly and even academically referred to as empty spaces (over which cruise missiles may be tested). These tropes are persistent devices, thoroughly installed in our cultural metaphysics and our discourses, of clearance and removal, of effacement. But they are, therefore, also paradoxical reminders of the extent to which the project of settlement (which is a project of displacement *and* replacement) has fallen short. As Chris Prentice points out, that which is logically prior cannot be expelled in a single moment (51).

Settler postimperial cultures are suspended between "mother" and "other," simultaneously colonized and colonizing. Bhabha reminds us that "the colonial presence is always ambivalent, split between its appearance as original and authoritative and its articulation as repetition and difference . . . . To recognize the *différance* of the colonial presence is to realize that the colonial text occupies that space of double inscription . . ." ("Signs" 150). I deploy Bhabha's observation that "the colonial text occupies that space of double inscription" in a particular way within the frame of the Second World to refer to the endlessly problematic double inscription within the Second World subject of authority and authenticity.

If we put that double inscription of authority and authenticity together with the notion that the cultures of the Second World are both colonizing and colonized, we can see that there are always two kinds of authority and always two kinds of authenticity that the settler subject is *con/signed* to desire and disavow. The settler subject is signed, then, in a language of authority and in a language of resistance. The settler subject enunciates the authority that is in colonial discourse on behalf of the imperial enterprise that he—and sometimes she—represents. The settler subject represents, but also mimics, the authentic imperial culture from which he—and, more problematically, she—is separated. This is mimicry in Bhabha's special sense since the authority is enunciated on behalf of, but never quite as, the imperium: that authority is always incomplete, as the Cree chief Big Bear, in Rudy Wiebe's novel *The Temptations of Big Bear* (1973), recognizes. Out of that which is "*almost the same but not quite*" emerges the menace of "the repetitious slippage of difference and desire" (Bhabha, "Of Mimicry" 130, 131). In Western art, popular culture, history, fiction, and even postcolonial theory, mimicry seems always to be in the pathetic or scandalous performance of the colonized. However, I argue that in settler cultures, mimicry is a necessary and unavoidable part of the repertoire of the settler.

The settler subject also exercises authority over the Indigene and the land while translating his (but rarely her) desire for the Indigene and the land into a desire for Native authenticity in a long series of narratives of psychic encounter and indigenization. And in reacting to that subordinacy, that incompleteness, that sign of something less, the settler mimics, appropriates, and desires the authority of the Indigene: the menacing "not quite" is here more dangerous. This time it is not resistance but oppression or—worse—effacement. In a seminar in Melbourne, Georgina Williams, a Koori (southeastern Australian Aboriginal) activist, made the powerful observation that "There's a sense of urgency among those people buying up Aboriginal paintings because there may not be anyone left to paint them soon because they're killing themselves off." This refocuses for us the old tripled dreams of the settler situation: effacement (of Indigenous authority) and appropriation (of Indigenous authenticity). First, the effacement of the Indigene, the evacuation of the land: they're dying out, they have recessive genes, they have no resistance to disease or alcohol (that is, it's not the settlers who kill them, it's physiology, biology, the laws of science); they hang themselves in prison (it's their culture[2]); she or he (Trugernanna in Tasmania, Shawnandithit in Newfoundland[3]) is the last of her or his tribe (it's historical "progress"). The frequent scientific observation of the "dying race" in the nineteenth century enabled a narrative of ethical indigenization in which the settler simply assumed the place of the disappearing Indigene without the need for violence (or, of course, the designation "invader"). *We Are Going* (1964) is the ironic (but frequently misread) title of the first volume of poetry by an Aboriginal Australian, Kath Walker (who from 1988 until her death in 1993 used her tribal name, Oodgeroo Noonuccal). The "vanishing race" trope has been described in some detail by Leslie Monkman (65-95), Terry Goldie (148-69), and Daniel Francis (11-82); in South Africa, such narratives circulate around the Bushmen; in New Zealand and southern Africa, "history" records *pre*settlement displacements and exterminations. As Goldie rightly notices, these "'last of his tribe' lament[s]" (159) are crucial strategies in the replacement of the Indigene with forms of white indigeneity such as the pioneer, the Mountie, the woodsman, a process he has usefully called "indigenization" (13). Second, the discovery and display of "authentic" Aboriginal art as a signifier of a recoverable, authentic Indigenous culture enables the effacement of any catastrophic intervention by the settler. It is as though the invasion never "took place."

The third settler dream captured in Williams's insight is the desire to inherit the Natives' spiritual "rites" to the land, something which is figured in James Fenimore Cooper's "The Leatherstocking Tales" as well as numerous settler narratives in Canada, Australia, southern Africa, and New Zealand. This desire is also expressed in the sentimentalization of the mixed-race figure who enacts a slippage between the white desire and the Native right, white "civilization" and Native "elemental energy." All of these figure an unacknowledged recognition of Native authority.

There is also a complex chain of signification between desire for indigenized identity, spirituality, and land and desire for Aboriginal women which needs to be explored.[4] The settler's desire to stand in for the Native produces the inadmissible desire for miscegenation,[5] what in South Africa is often known as the "taint." The insertion of the settler self into the (physical and discursive) space of the Indigene is simultaneously characterized by desire and disavowal. The movement into indigenous space must be asymptotic: indigeneity must be approached but never touched. This produces in the settler an anxiety of proximity. The self-indigenizing settler has to stop just short of going completely native and, therefore, is frequently represented as sexless. "He" must stand just in front of, but not exactly in the place of, the Indigene. The need, then, is to *dis*place the other rather than *re*place him; but the other must remain to signify the boundary of the self, to confirm the subjectivity of the invader-settler. The other, as a consequence of this "almost but not quite" move, is therefore always in some sense present, ready (like Freud's "uncanny") for its return. The boundaries of civilizations (like discourses) are sometimes startlingly porous.

The Second World narrative, then, has a double teleology: the suppression or effacement of the Indigene, and the concomitant indigenization of the settler, who, in becoming more like the Indigene whom he mimics, becomes less like the atavistic inhabitant of the cultural homeland whom he is also reduced to mimicking. The text is thus marked by counterfeitings of both emergence and origination. The settler subject-position is both postimperial and post-colonial; it has colonized and has been colonized: it must speak of and against both its own oppressiveness and its own oppression. As Dennis Lee writes about the problem of language in colonial space, "To speak unreflect-ingly in a colony, then, is to use words that speak only alien space. . . . And to reflect further is to recognise that you and your people do not in fact have a privileged authentic space just waiting for words; you are, among other things, the people who have made an alien inauthenticity their own" (54). He then concludes that "the impasse of writing that is problematic to itself is transcended only when the impasse becomes its own subject, when writing accepts and enters and names its own condition as it is naming the world" (57). In the settler postcolonial situation, utterance always addresses—wit-tingly or unwittingly—both of its antecedent authorities/authenticities. In speaking back against the imperium, in the interests of its own identity poli-tics, the settler site of enunciation will always tend to reappropriate the posi-tion of all of those others with and against whom it has mediated that imper-ial power. It is important to stress that the term "Second World" also has a strategic function. It draws attention to the bifocality, bivocality, and double-ness and duplicity of the "in between" condition of subjects in the settler colonies. As empire's supplement, the settler "subject-effect" (Carusi 104) will, in any figural or textual location, have its unavoidable ambivalence exposed.

To theorize the settler in the way that I am attempting might have two ben-efits. First, it draws attention to the term settler as a (tendentious) discursive phenomenon and foregrounds the slippage from invader to peaceful settler as a strategy within the project of imperialism. Second, using Second World against the Eurocentred order of worlds with which Fredric Jameson has been associated (see "Third-World") might be a way of changing the assump-tions of that unilinear cosmology altogether, and of releasing it from the asymmetrical recirculation of power within the self-serving binarism. My sug-gestion is to recognize the Second World of the settler as a place caught between two First Worlds, two origins of authority and authenticity: the orig-inating world of Europe, the imperium, as source of the Second World's prin-cipal cultural authority; and that other First World, that of the First Nations, whose authority the settlers not only effaced and replaced but also desired. (This perception is triggered by the very canny insistence of Canadian Native peoples on being called *First* Nations.) To each of these First Worlds, the set-tlers are secondary—indeed, supplementary. Of course, that secondariness reminds us that the settler was also the go-between for the European First World with the strategically named Third; the settler acted as a mediator rather than as a simple transmitter of imperialism's uncomfortable mirroring of itself. Colonial space, then, is occupied by vectors of difference. The in between of the settlers is not unbounded space but a place of negotiation; colonialism is a relation, an unequal one but no less a relation for that. The boundaries of civilization are especially porous.

This is not to repeat the arithmetical fallacies—it does not seek to produce a new hierarchy of cultural dominance and subalternity in a numerical sequence of worlds, nor does it subscribe to the notion that oppressions can be added up, cumulated as in the dubious notion of "double colonization." Each system of dominance interpellates its subjects differently: these can be added to but not added up.[6] My project here is instead part of an attempt to specify the cultural address. The subject is always differentiated—made an object of difference—within each and every economy of representation within which she/he is found. The subject is always (variously) interpellated in and by several unequal systems of representation that each partly and partially specify the subject's address. We need to identify, then, for any histori-cized, gendered, culturally specific site of enunciation, the prior sites whose authority either licenses the utterance or provokes the resistance, the contra/diction. The address of the settler is toward both the absent(ee) cultural authority of the imperium and the effaced, recessive cultural authority of the Indigene.

Second World cultural space, then, is colonizing and colonized, both doubly inscribed and doubly absent (in that resistance and effacement). This might allow us to begin to read the history of Second World criticism differently, to do a cultural history of readings. One cartography from which to work would be to identify the motivating resistances in postcolonial criticism as proceeding from those doubly inscribed authorities I have just described. This might enable us to see certain practices of the inscription of national identity as resistances to the operations of the discourses of the imperial within variously specified cultural domains. But we could also see those practices as simultaneously reinscribing the other kind of authority, the authority they exercise over the Indigene on behalf of—but never as—the imperial. In this double move, we might recognize the resistance in nationalisms while recognizing their concomitant containment. It might be in that simultaneous mediation of power that we can see, too, how nationalist criticism can be co-opted by those imperial institutions.

National identity is a form of identity politics: it is formulated as a strategy of resistance toward a dominant culture. The dominant culture was, for those in the former British Empire, that of Greater Britain; more recently, the dominant culture has become, for the citizens of many more nations, the global-izing tendency of the international politics, popular culture, and academic politics of the United States, or the more dispersed, moving target of multinational capital. Identity politics asserts the *id-entity* of the group as a form of opposition to other, more powerful groups who have access to more privileged speaking positions. In order to do this, identity politics asserts the uniqueness and the homogeneity of the group in the hope that its undivided (if specious) unity will empower it against the apparent seamlessness of the hegemonic discourse. In the foundations of cultural nationalism, then, we can identify one vector of difference (the difference between colonizing subject and colonized subject: settler-Indigene) being replaced by another (the difference between colonizing subject and imperial centre: settler-imperium) in a strategic disavowal of the colonizing act. The national is what replaces the indigenous and in doing so conceals its participation in colonization by nominating a new colonized subject—the colonizer or invader-settler.

This cartography of Second World cultural space might also enable us to map the shift in the study of national literatures away from examinations of representations of self—national identity as identity politics—toward examinations of representations of the nation's other—paradigmatically, but not exclusively, representations of the Indigene. In terms of the resistance to the dual inscriptions, it is a shift in anxieties about mediation from the mother to the other. So, in part, the history of a postcolonial criticism may be seen as a continuous cycle between what Bhabha calls "Counter-narratives of the nation that . . . disturb those ideological manoeuvres through which 'imagined communities' are given essentialist identities" ("DissemiNation" 300). What motivates this cycle is the dual inscription of authority and authenticity and the need to resist each inscription of it, the desire to avoid both "[r]epression and cooption" (Chambers, *Room* 3), to forestall the tendency of resistance to become recontainment.

Identifying the different names for cultural resistance in postcolonial criticism and in its cousins, Commonwealth and national-literatures criticism, might also be undertaken. In Canada and Australia, the practice of postcolonial criticism has been, since the mid-nineteenth century, marked by its engagement with, and resistance to, the power embedded in particular imperial institutional discourses of the literary. This might be analogous to the way in which we now recognize that certain postcolonial literary texts write back against or subvert imperial master texts (see Brydon; and Tiffin) and/or to the way in which they resist the codes of apprehension and signification embedded in literary discourse by colonialist descriptions and formulations of colonial space.

A mapping of postcolonial criticism depends upon recognizing that criticism works through protocols licensed from time to time by its particular, cited site of enunciation within institutions that are themselves highly vectored and historically mediated. These protocols function as euphemisms, as decorous ways of speaking, not so much the unspeakable but that which it is disempowering to speak in certain places or at certain times.

So in 1950s and 1960s Canadian and Australian criticism, for example, resistance and politics were frequently thematized as "identity," thus metaphorizing the humanist concerns of New Criticism. In the critical and institutional protocols of the period, this was how a cultural politics could be spoken. Writing about identity was a way of dealing with the dual inscription of authority in the Second World by expressing a desire for its unification within the "person" of national selfhood. But this critical strategy also reinscribed imperial authority by its imbrication in the metaphors of "parent and child" and "maturation," metaphors that always privileged the imperial and refigured colonial subordinacy. In Canada (and to a lesser extent, Australia and New Zealand), thematic criticism sought ways of figuring the text as a manifestation of a deep cultural narrative. This contributed a sense of cultural wholeness, a unity, and, in the battles for institutional recognition, a curricular coherence. Certainly, thematic criticism tended to be ahistoric, but in doing so it avoided the "evolutionary fallacy" (Stevenson 399) that presumes that literatures develop *ab ovo* and always move toward maturity by solving each of their ideological, formal, and modal problems in turn, once and for all. By drawing attention to tropes and motifs that recur in colonial and postcolonial texts, thematic criticism had its own way of showing the return of the colonial moment in the coded languages of a culture. It is profoundly disabling to overlook the resistive insights of an earlier mode of critical practice, since this, as Benita Parry points out in a slightly different context, "severely restricts (eliminates?) the space in which the colonized can be written back into history" (39).

Incompatible geometries cannot be smoothed over into what Houston Baker refers to as "an uninflected space of difference" (2); not all differences are the same. The postcolonialism of the metropolitan East Asian intellectual is not the same as that of the rural Ugandan, nor is the postcolonialism of the Aboriginal Australian the same as that of the white Canadian, nor (even) is the postcolonialism of the Native Canadian the same as that of the Native American, the New Zealand Maori, or the Australian Aborigine. But the settler subject does not disappear in this project of difference; rather, she/he emerges from the material and textual enactments and enunciations of imperial power as a central site of investigation of the actual operations of colonial power. And colonial power is, as Bhabha has been showing us, the sum total of the power that is wielded in the colonial situation—not merely the imposition of imperial power from above and centre. To read the moment of imperialism in that unilinear fashion is simply to reconquer the colonial subject.

Global capitalism can be a pretty terrifying place for those of us who do not inhabit the great and powerful places of the earth; the "borderless economy" (Iyer 58) of subjectivity and culture, which is the effect of academic or political attempts to reduce the postcolonial world to one singularity or another, is an even more deeply oppressive place. As Jameson remarked at the New York MLA Convention in 1992, "the national is not an empty term . . . nation operates as a brake on transnational non-accountable decentred decision-making. . . . It is a sign of the finitude of the national unit, a way of feeling the sharp pang of powerlessness" ("National Intellectuals"). This is an old, familiar, and necessary recognition to those who live outside the centres of cultural authority, who have worked out their "pangs of powerlessness" in self-reflexive nationalisms, but who are also prepared to acknowledge their own particular postcoloniality as subjects with a particular discursive history, as subjects necessarily "in between."

Notes

1. For accounts of these, see Low; and Ashcroft, Griffiths, and Tiffin 1-2, 6-7, chap. 1.
2. In Australia, a Commission of Enquiry into Aboriginal Deaths in Custody was conducted from 1986 to 1989 by Justice Muirhead. It investigated over one hundred deaths of Aboriginal people who died while in prison or in police custody between 1980 and 1988; the most common means of death was hanging. The commission investigated, with considerable research and input from Aboriginal groups, the cultural and historical background of the phenomenon.
3. According to received history, Truganini (Trugernanna) was the last of the Tasmanian Aborigines. After the official genocide of her compatriots, she died in 1888. In fact, there are many people of Tasmanian Aboriginal descent, and the extraordinary difficulty that they have had in proclaiming their existence testifies to the vigour and persistence of colonialist historical discourse. While the genocide of the Beothuks of Newfoundland was less systematic, it was actually more comprehensive: the last Beothuk, Shawnandithit, died in 1829.
4. See Goldie 63-84.
5. I am grateful to J.M. Coetzee for a suggestive discussion on this point.
6. I am indebted to a comment Bhabha made on an earlier draft of this paper for this insight.

WORKS CITED

Ashcroft, Bill, Gareth Griffiths, and Helen Tiffin. *The Empire Writes Back: Theory and Practice in Post-Colonial Literatures.* New Accents. London: Routledge, 1989.

Atwood, Margaret. *The Journals of Susanna Moodie.* Toronto: Oxford UP, 1970.

Baker, Houston. "Of Ramadas and Multiculturalism." *MLA Newsletter* 24.2 (1992): 2-3.

Bhabha, Homi K. "DissemiNation: Time, Narrative, and the Margins of the Modern Nation." *Nation and Narration.* Ed. Bhabha. London: Routledge, 1990. 291-322.

— . "Of Mimicry and Man: The Ambivalence of Colonial Discourse." *October* 28 (1984): 125-33.

— . "Signs Taken for Wonders: Questions of Ambivalence and Authority under a Tree outside Delhi, May 1817." *Critical Inquiry* 12 (1985): 144-65.

Borch, Merete Falck. "Eddie Mabo and Others and the State of Queensland, 1992: The Significance of Court Recognition of Landrights in Australia." *Kunapipi* 14.1 (1991): 1-12.

Brennan, Tim. "Cosmopolitans and Celebrities." *Race and Class* 31.1 (1989): 1-19.

Brydon, Diana. "Re-Writing *The Tempest.*" *World Literature Written in English* 23.1 (1984): 75-88.

Carusi, Annamaria. "Post, Post and Post: Or, Where Is South African Literature in All This?" *Past the Last Post: Theorizing Post-Colonialism and Post-Modernism.* Ed. Ian Adam and Helen Tiffin. London: Harvester, 1991. 95-108.

Chambers, Ross. "Fables of the Go-Between." *Literature and Opposition.* Ed. Chris Worth, Pauline Nestor, and Marko Pavlyshyn. Clayton, Austral.: Centre for Comparative Literature and Cultural Studies, Monash U, 1994. 1-28.

— . *Room for Maneuver: Reading (the) Oppositional (in) Narrative.* Chicago: U of Chicago P, 1990.

Evans, Patrick. *The Penguin History of New Zealand Literature.* Auckland: Penguin, 1990.

Francis, Daniel. *The Imaginary Indian: The Image of the Indian in Canadian Culture.* Vancouver: Arsenal, 1992.

Goldie, Terry. *Fear and Temptation: The Image of the Indigene in Canadian, Australian, and New Zealand Literatures.* Kingston: McGill-Queen's UP, 1989.

Hulme, Peter. *Colonial Encounters: Europe and the Native Caribbean, 1492-1797.* London: Methuen, 1986.

Iyer, Pico. "The Empire Writes Back." *Time* 8 Feb. 1993: 54-59.

Jameson, Fredric. "National Intellectuals and World Literary History." Div. on Literary Criticism, MLA Convention. New York, 29 Dec. 1992.

— . "Third-World Literature in the Era of Multinational Capitalism." *Social Text* 15 (1986): 65-88.

Jardine, Alice A. *Gynesis: Configurations of Woman and Modernity.* Ithaca: Cornell UP, 1985.

Kroetsch, Robert. "Death Is a Happy Ending: A Dialogue in Thirteen Parts." With Diane Bessai. *Figures in a Ground: Canadian Essays on Modern Literature.* Ed. Diane Bessai and David Jackel. Saskatoon: Western Producer Prairie, 1978. 206-15.

— . "Reciting the Emptiness." *The Lovely Treachery of Words: Essays Selected and New.* Toronto: Oxford UP, 1989. 34-40.

— . "Unhiding the Hidden: Recent Canadian Fiction." *Journal of Canadian Fiction* 3.3 (1974): 43-45.

Lawson, Alan. "A Cultural Paradigm for the Second World." *Australian-Canadian Studies* 9.1-2 (1991): 67-78.

Lee, Dennis. "Cadence, Country, Silence: Writing in Colonial Space." *Boundary 2* 3 (1974): 151-68.

Low, D.A. "Lion Rampant." *Journal of Commonwealth Political Studies* 2 (1963-64): 235-52.

Maxwell, D.E.S. "Landscape and Theme." *Commonwealth Literature: Unity and Diversity in a Common Culture.* Ed. John Press. Extracts from the Proc. of a Conference at the U of Leeds, 9-12 Sept. 1964. London: Heinemann, 1965. 82-89.

McClintock, Anne. "The Angel of Progress: Pitfalls of the Term 'Post-Colonialism.'" Williams and Chrisman, eds. 291-304.

Monkman, Leslie. *A Native Heritage: Images of the Indian in English-Canadian Literature.* Toronto: U of Toronto P, 1981.

Mukherjee, Arun P. "Whose Post-Colonialism and Whose Postmodernism?" *World Literature Written in English* 30.2 (1990): 1-9.

New, W.H. *Among Worlds: An Introduction to Modern Commonwealth and South African Fiction.* Erin, ON: Porcepic, 1975.

—. "New Language, New World." *Awakened Conscience: Studies in Commonwealth Literature.* Ed. C.D. Narasimhaiah. New Delhi: Sterling, 1978. 361-77.

—. "Re: Visions of Canadian Literature." *Literary Criterion* 19.3-4 (1984): 23-47.

Parry, Benita. "Problems in Current Theories of Colonial Discourse." *Oxford Literary Review* 9.1-2 (1987): 27-58.

Prentice, Chris. "Some Problems of Response to Empire in Settler Post-Colonial Societies." *De-Scribing Empire: Post-Colonialism and Textuality.* Ed. Chris Tiffin and Alan Lawson. London: Routledge, 1994. 45-58.

Robbins, Bruce. "Colonial Discourse: A Paradigm and Its Discontents." *Victorian Studies* 35.2 (1992): 209-14.

Said, Edward W. *Orientalism.* London: Routledge, 1978.

Seaton, Dorothy. "Colonising Discourses: The Land in Australian and Western Canadian Exploration Narratives." *Australian-Canadian Studies* 6.2 (1989): 3-14.

Shohat, Ella. "Notes on the 'Post-Colonial.'" *Social Text* 31-32 (1992): 99-113.

Slemon, Stephen. "Unsettling the Empire: Resistance Theory for the Second World." *World Literature Written in English* 30.2 (1990): 30-41.

Spivak, Gayatri Chakravorty. *In Other Worlds: Essays in Cultural Politics.* New York: Routledge, 1988.

—. *The Post-Colonial Critic: Interviews, Strategies and Dialogues.* Ed. Sarah Harasym. New York: Routledge, 1990.

Stevenson, Lionel. "Literature in an Emerging Nation." *South Atlantic Quarterly* 64 (1965): 394-400.

Tiffin, Helen. "Post-Colonial Literatures and Counter-Discourse." *Kunapipi* 9.3 (1987): 17-34.

Tompkins, Joanne. "'The Story of Rehearsal Never Ends': Rehearsal, Performance, Identity in Settler Culture Drama." *Canadian Literature* 144 (1995): 142-61.

Williams, Georgina. "The Spiritual Reunification of Aboriginal People." La Trobe U. English Seminars. Melbourne, 16 Sept. 1992.

Williams, Patrick, and Laura Chrisman. "Colonial Discourse and Post-Colonial Theory: An Introduction." Williams and Chrisman, eds. 1-20.

—, eds. *Colonial Discourse and Post-Colonial Theory: A Reader.* New York: Harvester Wheatsheaf, 1993.

13

"Reading Postcoloniality, Reading Canada"*

Diana Brydon

I. Combatting a Double Erasure

Although all living cultures undergo recurrent reinvention, the contemporary rethinking of Canada has been exacerbated by constitutional negotiations around the Meech Lake and Charlottetown Accords and the recent referendum in Quebec, as well as by challenges to official multiculturalism and its secondary status within Canada's bicultural model of nationhood, challenges launched by Quebec separatists, First Nations groups, and people of colour during the 1980s. This current renegotiating of Canada and Canadianness takes place within a postcolonial context not always fully understood or recognized by either participants or analysts. This issue of *Essays on Canadian Writing*[1] aims to make that context more visible so that its implications for our future can be more clearly seen. The following essays explore Canada's colonial history and intellectual heritage, its mapping of space, and its self-representations through language and image, in order to clarify what is at stake in current battles over the redefinition of Canada and the scope of postcolonial studies.

These debates about Canadian nationhood and the relevance of postcolonialism, though often seen as distinct, are in fact connected in ways that are important for Canadians to understand. The focus of this volume is academic and literary, but the range of discussion involves understanding how Canadians see themselves and their world and how they are equipped (by their education and their history) to deal with the difficult moral and practical problems posed by decolonization at the end of the twentieth century. These two academic disciplines—Canadian literary criticism and postcolonial literary studies—have both been made possible by decolonization, and they have been formed within its determining context, but their different trajectories have only occasionally crossed paths without establishing influential connections. Canadian literary history has been written and Canadian literary canons have been formed without extended attention to postcolonial issues. The history of Canadian contributions to postcolonial studies is now being erased from both Canadian literary history and current accounts of postcolo-

---

* *Essays on Canadian Writing* 56 (1995): 1-19.

nialism. The politics and implications of that double erasure are my concern here.

Postcolonial theory is currently proliferating at a bewildering rate, so that it now seems preferable to substitute the plural form for the singular. To write of postcolonial theories is to recognize the multiplicity and fundamental incompatibility of much that now passes under the rubric of postcolonial. Debates about the proper definition of the field and its appropriate mission are charged with excitement and sometimes acrimony. A strong shared sense that these things matter and are worth contesting has resulted in little agreement as yet about the history, scope, and boundaries of the field.

But many of the sharpest debates centre on the problem of how to situate and evaluate the cultural production of invader-settler colonies such as Canada, Australia, and New Zealand.[2] This collection addresses that issue, simultaneously testing the limits of the discursive address of postcolonial theories and of Canadian literary histories, canons, and criticism. The volume has been shaped around the belief that postcolonial frames of interpretation are most enabling when they facilitate distinctions between different orders of colonial experience, rather than, on the one hand, conflating Third World and invader-settler societies as equally victimized or, on the other, banishing settler colonies from the sphere of "properly" postcolonial subject matter.

In *Post-National Arguments: The Politics of the Anglophone-Canadian Novel since 1967*, Frank Davey sees contemporary English-Canadian fiction as signalling the arrival of the postnational state. This collection seeks a larger context for what Davey calls the "postnational," trying to understand it within the context of Canadian literary culture's struggling with postcolonial dilemmas, including a colonial heritage insufficiently acknowledged in our national histories and criticism. Canada has not yet produced equivalents to Bob Hodge and Vijay Mishra's postcolonial reading of Australian identity in *Dark Side of the Dream: Australian Literature and the Postcolonial Mind*, which reads the cultural productions of white settlers and Aboriginal peoples in terms of their cross-cultural contacts under colonialism, nor to Ross Gibson's more postmodern and discontinuously postcolonial reading of Australian culture in *South of the West: Postcolonialism and the Narrative Construction of Australia*. These important books situate current Australian cultural debates within larger postcolonial and postmodern contexts. This collection of essays makes no attempt to replicate their arguments by producing Canadian equivalents because the Australian debate is culturally specific to Australia. Canadian imperatives take us in different directions, and certainly away from grand phrases like the postcolonial moment, the postcolonial mind, or the postcolonial intellectual. It is useful, however, to consider why such initiatives have not happened in Canada, and to look at where our own scholarly interests have been concentrated instead. For example, Julia V. Emberley's *Thresholds of Difference: Feminist Critique, Native Women's Writings, Postcolonial Theory* concentrates on the cross-illuminations of feminist and postcolonial theories, but leaves the problem of invader-settler postcolonialism unresolved to concentrate instead on what she (following Paul Tennant) terms the "internal colonialism" (131) of Native peoples. More problematically, she assumes that postcolonial theory is exclusively metropolitan and Third World in its origins, ignoring Canadian and Commonwealth contributions to its development.

The focus of this collection falls on the mutual cross-interrogation of postcolonial and Canadian discursive formations, fields usually constructed as separate domains of investigation. Within Canadian literary studies, this kind of serious engagement with the implications of postcolonial theory for Canadian thinking has been rare. Yet there are antecedents for this volume that are in danger of being forgotten, as metropolitan critics rewrite the history of postcolonialism to designate metropolitan origins for a discipline that in fact had multiple heterogeneous beginnings within different colonial, postcolonial, and metropolitan locations.

II. POSTCOLONIALISM IN CANADA

The history of postcolonial work in Canadian literary studies is discontinuous. It is marked by a series of aborted starts and little sustained dialogue in print, even though key transitional figures, such as W.H. New, worked simultaneously within the two fields. That double placement, far from working as an advantage, may well have led to an underestimation of New's importance as an orienting figure in the shaping of both fields. His *Among Worlds: An Introduction to Modern Commonwealth and South African Fiction*, published in 1975, has not yet received due acknowledgement for its reorientation of the disciplinary orthodoxies of its time. Its originality and continued relevance seem to have been dismissed because of its Canadian origins and the modesty of its presentation.

Donna Bennett's article "English Canada's Postcolonial Complexities" begins to document a history of postcolonialism in Canada, but her account can only be partial partly because that history has been truncated and its documentation scattered. Too many gaps still remain in the historical record. In addition, there will inevitably be disagreements over the nuances of interpretation. I would take issue with her dating and her acceptance of foreign origins for postcolonial practices in Canada. She argues that "Use of a postcolonial perspective as a way of looking at literary studies began in the late 1970s among Australian critics," and that "its impact on Canadian literary studies was not felt much before the nineties" (107-08). My own experience in the field has been different. There were earlier initiatives, but they appeared to lead to dead ends, at least for a time, and now they are in danger of being forgotten.

Earlier accounts of these developments (which Bennett does not cite) provide different genealogies. In their introduction to *Australian/Canadian Liter-*

atures in English: Comparative Perspectives, Russell McDougall and Gillian Whitlock identify an institutionalized beginning for postcolonial literary studies in the dialogue between Australian and Canadian critics that was originally encouraged by the establishment of the "Dominions Project" of the Humanities Research Council of Canada in the 1950s (4), and they locate discussions of literary affinities even earlier, in the late nineteenth century. Their narrative is closer to my own experience of developments in the field. They point out that after the comparative initiatives of the 1950s and early 1960s, "a monocultural perspective has been ascendant" (9), but that new challenges to that ascendancy were launched in the late 1970s and early 1980s.

That monocultural perspective ensured that few Canadianists read beyond a narrow definition of their discipline, often ignoring work published overseas or in journals devoted to comparative perspectives or to other national literatures dealing with colonialism and its aftermath. The result has been limiting in many ways. Bennett's article is timely in reiterating the argument for Canada's suitability as "an ideal laboratory for the study of postcolonial writing" (113-14), a point she appears to have derived from Sylvia Söderlind. But we need to ask why earlier statements of this position, such as R.T. Robertson's "Another Preface to an Uncollected Anthology: Canadian Criticism in a Commonwealth Context" (1973), John Moss's 1975 editorial in the *Journal of Canadian Fiction*, or my article "Australian Literature and the Canadian Comparison" (1979), appear to have led nowhere. Bennett provides a preliminary narrative of Canadian work in this field and a justification for it, but she cannot provide a full account of the range of debate that animated thinking about postcolonialism in Canada before the "postcolonial" became internationally recognized by metropolitan centres because the relevant material is scattered, sometimes out of print, and demands a fuller history than an article can accomplish.

Bennett argues that postcolonialism entered Canadian awareness only in the late 1970s and early 1980s. This is true of the term in its present expanded usage, but not of the concept, nor of an analysis attentive to identifying colonial mentalities and complicities as well as resistant and alternative, non-repressive agendas. These were alive much earlier. Several Canadian critics describe their personal introductions to the field through Commonwealth criticism in *A Shaping of Connections: Commonwealth Literature Studies—Then and Now* (1989), a collection edited by Hena Maes-Jelinek, Kirsten Holst Petersen, and Anna Rutherford. In "Reading for Resistance in the Post-Colonial Literature," an essay in that volume, Stephen Slemon presents a sophisticated history of how Commonwealth literary criticism became postcolonial, describing convincingly the ways in which an "enabling 'disobedience'" (113) to New Criticism led Commonwealth practitioners into postcolonialism and arguing that "what has changed here is the *modality* of our critical practice, not its *key signature*" (113).

Arun Mukherjee, in her introduction to her important book *Towards an Aesthetic of Opposition: Essays on Literature, Criticism, and Cultural Imperialism* (1988), a collection of articles published between 1984 and 1987, argues yet another postcolonial position from a location loosely within the Commonwealth field, which affords her what she terms "space for an alternative point of view" (8). This article has now been reprinted in an expanded form as part of her new book entitled *Oppositional Aesthetics: Readings from a Hyphenated Space* (1994). Another theoretically inflected trajectory brought Tony Wilden to postcolonialism, a journey he narrates in his unjustly neglected analysis of Canadian colonialism entitled *The Imaginary Canadian* (1980). Both Mukherjee and Wilden interrogate the institution of English studies, Mukherjee from a Third World position and Wilden from a poststructuralist one. My point here is that the debate not only began earlier but was more fully developed, and expressed a wider range of options, than Bennett's account, which assumes a foreign origin for postcolonial thinking, acknowledges.

My own first encounter with postcolonial theory came in 1968, when I read Frantz Fanon's *The Wretched of the Earth* in my first-year history class at the University of Toronto. In a 1972 graduate class in Commonwealth literature at the University of Toronto, taught by Jim Howard, we used Fanon's *Black Skin, White Masks* to provide our interpretive frame for theoretical analysis. This would still be considered an impeccably postcolonial approach. Albert Memmi's *The Colonizer and the Colonized* and *Dominated Man*, available in English in 1965 and 1968, were also read during this period in Quebec and English Canada as speaking directly to Canadian experiences. They were part of the Canadian discursive framework for understanding the world during the late 1960s and early 1970s.

Histories that identify Edward Said as the initiator of postcolonial analysis engage in a dangerous forgetting of these precursors. To suggest, as Linda Hutcheon does in "Eruptions of Postmodernity: The Postcolonial and the Ecological," that Leonard Cohen's *Beautiful Losers* (1966) "offered a vision of what (twenty-five years later) postcolonial theorists call the complexities of the interdependence of colonizer and colonized" (158) is to forget how central such issues were to the climate in which Cohen wrote. Postcolonial theorizing did not begin twenty-five years later. Although Bill Ashcroft, Gareth Griffiths, and Helen Tiffin, the authors of *The Empire Writes Back: Theory and Practice in Post-Colonial Literatures*, argue that postcolonial thinking, in terms of resistance to imperialism and imperial discursive structures, began with the imposition of colonialism, such postcolonial resistance began to attract metropolitan attention in the period after the end of World War II, as formerly colonized countries regained or first established their formal independence. Certainly Memmi spoke of the "implacable dependence" (ix) of colonizer and colonized in the preface to *The Colonizer and the Colonized*, published in French in 1957 (possibly echoing Sartre's account of anti-Semite and Jew), and Fanon exhaustively psychoanalysed the condition in *Black Skin, White Masks*, published in French in 1952. Cohen brought such analysis into dialogue with Canadian concerns in *Beautiful Losers* in a way that some literary critics of the time were able to recognize, even if, as Hutcheon argues, disciplinary orthodoxies steered them away from such insights.

While Hutcheon is certainly correct in recognizing that Northrop Frye's formalist theories carried more academic prestige in the 1960s than did postcolonial reading strategies, these other theoretical options were being offered at the University of Toronto even in those years of Frye's ascendance, if only in courses in history and Commonwealth literature. Influenced by them, I travelled to Australia in 1973 to begin my Ph.D. in a deliberate search for an expanded comparative framework that could adapt Fanon's and Memmi's insights to the Canadian settler-society context. I was inspired as well by John Pengwerne Matthews's careful historical and comparative work in *Tradition in Exile*, and I knew that other Canadians, such as Jack Healy and Bruce Nesbitt, had preceded me.

The continuity I am identifying between earlier criticism of Canadian colonialism and current postcolonial critiques is largely an English-Canadian phenomenon. Jonathan Hart points out that "'Postcolonial theory' is a term now taken for granted in English but not used in other languages such as French" (71). Little dialogue has ensued between the English-Canadian postcolonialism identified here and the anticolonial struggles of Quebec. As Caroline Bayard argues in presenting her reasons for producing "a book about critical discourse in both Canadas" ("Languages" 9), "by and large each critical discourse has been smugly turned towards its own sources of methodological vitality, its own developments, rather than exploring one another's sources or which features it might share with others" (9). She herself has shown, in her article "From *Nègres blancs d'Amérique* (1968) to Kanesatake (1990): A Look at the Tensions of Postmodern Quebec," how analyses of intersections of postmodernism and postcolonialism could bridge this gap. Investigations of shared Eurocentric and Orientalist inheritances may also help bridge this critical divide between Quebec and the rest of Canada. One such promising collaborative venture is Jocelyne Doray and Julian Samuel's coedited book *The Raft of the Medusa: Five Voices on Colonies, Nations and Histories*, which explicitly addresses the implications of postcolonial analysis for understanding Quebec and English Canada.

In arguing for a more expanded historical record of postcolonialism in Canada, one that can account for the work of these earlier critics and teachers, I am asserting that there is a specifically English-Canadian mode of reading Canada and postcoloniality against one another that has formed a kind of "subjugated knowledge" (to put it in Foucauldian terms) that runs throughout our literary history despite our repeated forgettings. R. Radhakrishnan describes the contradictory formation of such subjugated knowledges: "they have always existed in history, but in the domain of theory they have been written out of effective existence. Within the auspices of the dominant theory their very historical and material reality has been dehistoricized and rendered nonexistent" (63-64). I have engaged here with Bennett's and Hutcheon's articles because by beginning to retrieve these knowledges, they have initiated a dialogue I hope this volume can continue. Their work in remembering histories that had been rendered nonexistent now enables us to ask what investment Canadianists might have had in furthering a process of forgetting.

The answer may lie in part in the unresolved contradictions of Canada's invader-settler inheritance. Non-Native Canadians have moved from denying to acknowledging guilt for the invasion and theft of First Nations lands, but that move is easier than recognizing current, continued complicity in imperialist patterns of domination, both epistemological and economic. Guilt is a paralysing and self-indulgent emotion. It excuses inaction and creates a paradoxical kind of pleasure in self-recrimination. To acknowledge complicity, in contrast, is far more threatening. It is easy to cast oneself as the victim of one's identity as an oppressor and to use that new identity as an excuse for continued inaction and even self-congratulation for one's inaction. Paradoxically, guilt allows some English Canadians to continue to feel like victims even when they have decided that they are no longer the colonized (as Margaret Atwood assumes English Canadians are in *Survival: A Thematic Guide to Canadian Literature*) but are now the colonizer (from the Native perspective). It is much harder to imagine oneself outside the binary of oppressor versus oppressed, as complicit in a system that can be analysed and changed, in which it is not too late to make a difference.[3] Postcolonial criticism in Canada has approached this awareness of complicity several times, but we have always drawn back from the precipice it has revealed before us: the possibility, indeed the necessity, of initiating a radical change in the way our society is organized and understood. This kind of postcolonialism does not allow Canadians to be merely observers, academic students of a phenomenon that happens elsewhere. This kind of postcolonialism is about all of us: whether we have inherited identities as First Nations, Métis, Québécois, invader-settler, immigrant, or "ethnic." If we wish to understand the complexities of these emerging postcolonialisms, then we must proceed with the postcolonial analysis of invader-settler societies.

In her essay in this volume, Sylvia Söderlind's assessment that Canada's claim to postcoloniality constitutes our "moral luck" addresses a self-congratulatory tone inherent in some postcolonial rhetoric, but conflates the tone with the substance of the argument. Postcolonial reading strategies confer neither moral superiority nor inferiority on either the critic or the subject matter; rather, postcolonial reading strategies attend to the material conditions in which the critic finds herself, conditions that are seldom morally clear cut. Like political correctness, post-colonialism is being characterized as a humourless, vanguardist "belief system" (Bennett 126) in ways that delegitimate its justifiable demands for change. This kind of oversimplification of a complex phenomenon, like Bennett's assertions that "postcolonial criticism has become profoundly anti-nationalistic" and that "Postcolonialism internalizes an evolutionary model . . ." (126), strikes me as a misrepresentation that fails to recognize the genuinely different assumptions and values, starting points and goals, that postcolonial criticism is employing.

On the contrary, much postcolonial criticism identifies such evolutionary models with colonialist habits of mind, seeing decolonization as a process of rupture with imperialist oppositions between tradition and modernity and with imperialist assumptions about progress, the nature of change, and the meaning of cultural maturity. While it is true that a certain strain of cosmopolitan postcolonialism remains suspicious of nationalisms of any kind, many more postcolonial critics, perhaps best represented by Aijaz Ahmad in *In Theory: Classes, Nations, Literatures*, are insisting that there are many different kinds of nationalisms, all of which need to be understood in context. My understanding of postcolonial theory is that it requires us to pay very careful attention to the category of nation and the many different kinds of nationalism to which the nation may call us at different times. Such an interpellation may be especially fraught in a country such as Canada, where it has never been possible to forget that our national identity is neither unified nor natural but something we work at reinventing and protecting every day. The implications for Quebec, as Marvan Hassan notes, are equally complex (90-93).

III. SETTLER-COLONY POSTCOLONIALISM

The most extended arguments for the inclusion of invader-settler societies within the postcolonial field have appeared in Ashcroft, Griffiths, and Tiffin's *The Empire Writes Back*, in Slemon and Tiffin's *After Europe*, in Brydon and Tiffin's *Decolonising Fictions*, and in key articles by Alan Lawson and Stephen Slemon. Arguments against their inclusion appear as throwaway remarks in many places but receive consolidated expression in some of the introductory material to the selections in *Colonial Discourse and Post-Colonial Theory: A Reader*, edited by Patrick Williams and Laura Chrisman.

These objections deserve close scrutiny. Williams and Chrisman list two major obstacles to describing countries such as Canada as postcolonial: first, because of "their implication in contemporary capitalism," and second, because of their "historical relation" to colonialism (4). From my perspective, these two conditions provide compelling reasons for including the analysis of Canadian culture within postcolonial studies. Colonialism and imperialism fuelled the development of capitalism; their relation requires examination to be understood. Similarly, if postcolonialism does not investigate the range of historical relations of colonies to colonialism, it will never gain a full perspective on colonialism and how to counter its negative effects. I believe that postcolonialism proves itself most useful as a locally situated, provisional, and strategic attempt to think through the consequences of colonialism and to imagine nonrepressive alternatives to its discursive regime. To me, it is an activist and interventionary politics and a thinking process more than a static object of inquiry. To argue, as do Söderlind and Bennett, that postcolonialism must always be "subversive" and limited to adopting a "position of resistance to the metropolis" (Söderlind 4, 6) is, however, to oversimplify potentially more complex relations.

A similar equating of postcolonialism with resistance to the metropolis appears to inform the generalizations that Williams and Chrisman provide to support their exclusion of Canada from the postcolonial field. Of Canada, Australia, and New Zealand, which they describe in a racialized discourse as "the former white settler colonies," they write:

> That these were not simply colonies was formally recognised at the time by Britain in granting them Dominion status. Economically and politically, their relation to the metropolitan centre bore little resemblance to that of the actual colonies. They were not subject to the sort of coercive measures that were the lot of the colonies, and their ethnic stratification was fundamentally different. Their subsequent history and economic development, and current location within global capitalist relations, have been very much in a metropolitan mode, rather than a (post-)colonial one. (4)

In this passage, the nominating of authentic and inauthentic colonies is central to the editors' designation of an authentic postcolonial project. (Söderlind's *Margin/Alias: Language and Colonization in Canadian and Québécois Fiction* employs a similar opposition between what she terms "a real postcolonial situation—in Africa" [7] and the Canadian adoption of the marginalized position of the postcolonial as a postmodern "alias.") In Williams and Chrisman's naming, the authentic colony is implicitly defined as poor, nonwhite, and resistant, and the inauthentic as rich, white, and complicit. They define the Canadian kind of colony out of existence by characterizing its development as the opposite of that presumed for those unnamed colonies that they term "the actual colonies" (4). Ironically, withholding the status of "authentic" colonialism from countries such as Canada makes the editors complicit in the continuing denial and marginalization of Native people's experience of colonialism as well as of the invader-settler and immigrant experiences. This disqualification of Canadian colonialism seems to contradict the editors' earlier definition of colonialism as "the conquest and direct control of other people's land" (2). It also makes it harder for all Canadians to identify and combat the particular kinds of postcolonial experience they are currently undergoing as they watch their economy shrink, jobs disappear, and cultural sovereignty erode.

The generalizations that Williams and Chrisman employ to disqualify settler colonies from the postcolonial domain are disconcertingly vague. The grounds of their argument shift quickly, so that dominion status slides into metropolitan before our eyes. Yet clearly, if dominion status means anything, it marks a colonial, that is a nonmetropolitan, positioning that is historically specific to the invader-settler societies, and it marks not their founding (as Williams and Chrisman imply) but their first step toward postcolonial status.

The ahistorical bias of using Canada's dominion status, a temporary state, to freeze it forever outside the postcolonial is a tactic that this volume seeks particularly to challenge. Postcolonialism is neither a thing nor an essentialized state; rather, it is a complex of processes designed to circumvent imperial *and* colonial habits of mind. If we can reclaim the specificity and historical situatedness of the dominion model, however, it could prove helpful in distinguishing settler-colonial patterns of decolonization from those achieved in other kinds of colonies. Jim Davidson's coining of the term "de-dominionisation" for distinguishing Australian and Canadian moves to independence seems helpful in refining the terminology we need to distinguish these different types of development.

The problem with Williams and Chrisman's formulation of the postcolonial, in contrast, is its ahistorical assignment of absolute difference and its rigid exclusivity. They can imagine only one kind of colony and one pattern of colonization. It may be that colonial discourse theory's reliance on self/other distinctions makes such exclusivity almost inevitable. An unresolvable opposition is developing between those postcolonialisms that seek to challenge binary modes of thinking as implicitly imperialist and those postcolonialisms that continue to operate within binary models. Again and again in this latter criticism, one finds two recurring claims: an insistence on clinging to the binary of colonizer/colonized and the naming of a resistant postcolonialism as postcolonialism's only authentic expression. Complicit forms of colonialism become almost unthinkable within this model. As Slemon argues,

> the new binaristic absolutism which seems to come in the wake of First-World accommodation to the fact of post-colonial literary and cultural criticism seems to be working in several ways to drive that trans-national region of ex-colonial settler cultures away from the field of post-colonial literary representation. The Second World of writing within the ambit of colonialism is in danger of disappearing . . . because it does not offer up an experiential grounding in a common "Third World" aesthetics, because its modalities of *post*-coloniality are too ambivalent,

too occasional and uncommon, for inclusion within the field. ("Unsettling" 144-45)

Following Slemon's observations, this volume examines the "ambivalent," "occasional," and "uncommon" modalities of Canadian colonialism and postcolonialism. To ignore these, in my view, would be to misunderstand contemporary Canadian problems and consequently err in proposing solutions. This debate about terminology and the scope of the postcolonial involves more than skirmishing over professional turf. It has social-policy and political implications as well as specifically disciplinary repercussions within the university. Writing about national liberation and culture, Amilcar Cabral suggests that "it is much less difficult to dominate and continue dominating a people whose culture is similar or analogous to that of the conqueror" (60). "Conqueror" would strike many as an exaggeration of the status of the transnational corporations based mainly in the United States who currently dominate cultural production and transmission in Canada, yet the truth is that Canadian culture, despite its similarity in many ways to British and American cultures, does display many of the signs of a dominated culture. The few Canadian movies that manage to get produced seldom get necessary distribution and exposure to meet their costs; the Canadian radio, television, and book industries are foreign-dominated. Our understanding of these issues is obscured if we fail to recognize Canada's colonial history and its neocolonial present. If postcolonial analysis can foreground these, then it will serve an important purpose. But it can only illuminate Canadian histories and contradictory complicities if its range is extended beyond what the West finds exotic and entrancingly other.

Given such problems in defining the scope of the postcolonial, many have wondered if it is a term worth fighting for. Does it help critics understand current Canadian debates about multiculturalism, racism, postmodernism, and appropriation of voice, or does it obscure these issues through homogenizing and universalizing a metaphorized marginality to such an extent that these problems can be made to disappear, at least from the domain of theoretical discussion? To those who would equate the postcolonial simply with official decolonization or the end of the colonial, the term itself raises some new problems that seem to obscure our ability to make useful distinctions between types of colonialism, postcolonialism, and decolonization, and impede our understanding of the roles of racism or continued forms of domination under neocolonialism. These objections are shrewdly rehearsed by Anne McClintock in "The Angel of Progress: Pitfalls of the Term 'Post-Colonialism,'" yet she also points out that thinking around postcoloniality has inspired much valuable work and its usefulness is far from exhausted.

Debates about terminology provided material for an entire subfield within Commonwealth literary studies for decades before "postcolonial" emerged as the preferred term with the publication of *The Empire Writes Back*. Those discussions, like the newer ones around postcolonialism, serve more to clarify fissures and problems within the field than to lead to agreement around its focus and methodology. Part of the problem lies in the range of meanings assigned to "the postcolonial," which can designate a subject matter, a period, or a methodology, none of which has yet been satisfactorily established.

IV. Testing the Limits

In response to this currently fluid state of potential postcolonial applications, this issue [of *ECW*] has been organized to canvass the entire range of the field while zeroing in on particularly suggestive problems of context, text, or reading strategy. [. . .]

It is possible to argue that the collection as a whole provides a flexible but ultimately bounded definition of what the postcolonial means (and could mean) within the specifically Canadian context. Whereas Williams and Chrisman argue that Canadian development has taken metropolitan forms, McClintock makes an opposite (and to me a more compelling) argument that Canada has not yet undergone decolonization and is unlikely to soon (295), though in Davidson's terms Canada has been "de-dominionised." If postcolonial analysis can help us understand this situation, then its value will be proved. More than fashionable lip service to "resistance" and "subversion," we need a historically grounded criticism that can help us understand contemporary inequities in order to combat them effectively. At the same time, however, we must listen carefully to critics who see postcolonialism itself as a new form of imperialism, a new language for obscuring an understanding of racisms, or merely a form of postmodernism. These point to the potential within postcolonial studies to reinstall the very oppressions they are seeking to oppose.

In soliciting these essays, I was looking for debate more than consensus. My aim was to provide a cross section of the kind of work being done in and on Canada within postcolonial contexts right now. The contributors do not always agree with one another. In this context, such diversity of opinion is probably more a strength than a weakness. The volume as a whole reinforces McClintock's call for "a *proliferation* of historically nuanced theories and strategies . . . which may enable us to engage more effectively in the politics of affiliation, and the currently calamitous dispensations of power" (303). In organizing this collection, I have proceeded on the assumption, articulated by Bennett, that "Asking postcolonial questions of English-Canadian literature can be productive so long as we do not impose a single kind of postcolonialism, and so long as we do not presume that the postcolonial perspective is the only way to frame one's vision" (127). There are limits to the postcolonial reading strategy, as with any other approach, including the

Canadianist, but there are also strengths on which we are only beginning to draw. This volume begins to test those limits.

If there is a point of agreement among the contributors to this volume beyond this shared commitment to engagement in the debate, it probably lies in the belief that we need "to make a stronger distinction between the post-colonialism of settler and non-settler countries" (Mishra and Hodge, "What Is Post(-)Colonialism?" 288) if we are to hold to the term at all and make it mean something particular to Canadians. To strengthen these distinctions about kinds of power relations within the postcolonial frame seems more helpful than to deny the participation of invader-settler colonies in these heterogeneous postcolonial formations. [. . .]

As a reflection of the current state of Canadian literary criticism's post-colonial participation, this collection shows an eclectic array of influences but also some important paths of divergence from the way the field is developing in Britain and the United States. The Australian-authored *The Empire Writes Back* is cited more often than metropolitan-based theorists, though as several articles show, its reception is far from uncritical. What we do have in this collection is a fundamental rethinking of the earlier pieties constructing English-Canadian settler nationalism and a questioning of the ways in which the traditional disciplinary structures of English, history, and geography participated in the construction of a Canadian nationalism that both occluded and celebrated its colonizing role. [. . .] The goal throughout is a commitment to establishing and sustaining difference: the differences that make Canada Canada, *and* the differences that continue to challenge that national formation of an immigrant, capitalist culture on usurped land.

Notes

1. [Editor's note: This essay was originally published as the introduction to a special issue of *ECW* entitled "Testing the Limits: Postcolonial Theories and Canadian Literature," edited by Diana Brydon. At various points, the article makes reference to the *ECW* issue as "this collection" and "this volume."]

2. For many years, Canada was described as a settler colony. In the late 1980s, postcolonial critics modified the description to "settler-invader" in order to remind readers that, from the point of view of indigenous peoples whose lands were taken, "settlement" was in fact an invasion. I have reversed the terms here, to "invader-settler," to shift the emphasis from two opposing historical narratives and to stress that the narrative of settlement in itself occludes and denies the prior fact of invasion. Instead of adding the modifier "invader" to the prior narrative of the victor, which celebrated settlement, priority should in fact be given to the initial fact of invasion.

3. For a thorough analysis of this disabling guilt, see Perreault.

WORKS CITED

Ahmad, Aijaz. *In Theory: Classes, Nations, Literatures.* London: Verso, 1992.

Ashcroft, Bill, Gareth Griffiths, and Helen Tiffin. *The Empire Writes Back: Theory and Practice in Post-Colonial Literatures.* New Accents. London: Routledge, 1989.

Bayard, Caroline. "From *Nègres blancs d'Amérique* (1968) to Kanesatake (1990): A Look at the Tensions of Postmodern Quebec." *World Literature Written in English* 30.2 (1990): 17-29.

——. "The Languages of Critical Discourse in Canada and Quebec 1880-1980." *100 Years of Critical Solitudes: Canadian and Québécois Criticism from the 1880s to the 1980s.* Ed. Bayard. Toronto: ECW, 1992. 9-23.

Bennett, Donna. "English Canada's Postcolonial Complexities." *Essays on Canadian Writing* 51-52 (1993-94): 164-210.

Brydon, Diana. "Australian Literature and the Canadian Comparison." *Meanjin* 38 (1979): 154-65.

Brydon, Diana, and Helen Tiffin. *Decolonising Fictions.* Sydney: Dangaroo, 1993.

Cabral, Amilcar. "National Liberation and Culture." Williams and Chrisman 53-65.

Davey, Frank. *Post-National Arguments: The Politics of the Anglophone-Canadian Novel since 1967.* Toronto: U of Toronto P, 1993.

Davidson, Jim. "The De-dominionisation of Australia." *Meanjin* 38 (1979): 139-53.

Emberley, Julia V. *Thresholds of Difference: Feminist Critique, Native Women's Writings, Postcolonial Theory.* Toronto: U of Toronto P, 1993.

Fanon, Frantz. *Black Skin, White Masks.* Trans. Charles Lam Markmann. New York: Grove, 1967.

——. *The Wretched of the Earth.* Trans. Constance Farrington. New York: Grove, 1963.

Gibson, Ross. *South of the West: Postcolonialism and the Narrative Construction of Australia.* Bloomington: Indiana UP, 1992.

Hart, Jonathan. "Traces, Resistances, and Contradictions: Canadian and International Perspectives on Postcolonial Theories." *Arachnè* 1.1 (1994): 68-93.

Hassan, Marvan. "On and around the Raft." With Will Straw. *The Raft of the Medusa: Five Voices on Colonies, Nations and Histories.* Ed. Jocelyne Doray and Julian Samuel. Montreal: Black Rose, 1993. 89-112.

Hodge, Bob, and Vijay Mishra. *Dark Side of the Dream: Australian Literature and the Post-colonial Mind.* Australian Cultural Studies. North Sydney: Allen, 1991.

Hutcheon, Linda. "Eruptions of Postmodernity: The Postcolonial and the Ecological." *Essays on Canadian Writing* 51-52 (1993): 146-63.

Lawson, Alan. "A Cultural Paradigm for the Second World." *Australian-Canadian Studies* 9.1-2 (1991): 67-78.

Maes-Jelinek, Hena, Kirsten Holst Petersen, and Anna Rutherford, eds. *A Shaping of Connections: Commonwealth Literature Studies — Then and Now.* Sydney: Dangaroo, 1989.

McClintock, Anne. "The Angel of Progress: Pitfalls of the Term 'Post-Colonialism.'" Williams and Chrisman 291-304.

McDougall, Russell, and Gillian Whitlock. *Australian/Canadian Literatures in English: Comparative Perspectives*. Melbourne: Methuen, 1987.

Memmi, Albert. *The Colonizer and the Colonized*. Trans. Howard Greenfeld. New York: Orion, 1965.

——. *Dominated Man*. New York: Orion, 1968.

Mishra, Vijay, and Bob Hodge. "What Is Post(-)Colonialism?" Williams and Chrisman 276-90.

Moss, John G. Editorial. *Journal of Canadian Fiction* 3.4 (1975): 1-2.

Mukherjee, Arun P. *Towards an Aesthetic of Opposition: Essays on Literature, Criticism, and Cultural Imperialism*. Stratford, ON: Williams, 1988.

New, William H. *Among Worlds: An Introduction to Modern Commonwealth and South African Fiction*. Erin, ON: Porcépic, 1975.

Perreault, Jeanne. "White Feminist Guilt, Abject Scripts, and (Other) Transformative Necessities." *Colour: An Issue*. Ed. Roy Miki and Fred Wah. Spec. issue of *West Coast Line* 13-14 (1994): 226-38.

Radhakrishnan, R. "Toward an Effective Intellectual: Foucault or Gramsci?" *Intellectuals: Aesthetics, Politics, Academics*. Ed. Bruce Robbins. Cultural Politics 2. Minneapolis: U of Minnesota P, 1990. 57-99.

Robertson, R.T. "Another Preface to an Uncollected Anthology: Canadian Criticism in a Commonwealth Context." *Ariel* 4.3 (1973): 70-81.

Slemon, Stephen. "Reading for Resistance in the Post-Colonial Literature." Maes-Jelinek, Petersen, and Rutherford 100-15.

——. "Unsettling the Empire: Resistance Theory for the Second World." *World Literature Written in English* 30.2 (1990): 30-41.

Slemon, Stephen, and Helen Tiffin, eds. *After Europe: Critical Theory and Post-Colonial Writing*. Sydney: Dangaroo, 1989.

Söderlind, Sylvia. *Margin/Alias: Language and Colonization in Canadian and Québécois Fiction*. Toronto: U of Toronto P, 1991.

Wilden, Tony. *The Imaginary Canadian*. Vancouver: Pulp, 1980.

Williams, Patrick, and Laura Chrisman, eds. *Colonial Discourse and Post-Colonial Theory: A Reader*. New York: Columbia UP, 1994.

PART V

FIRST NATIONS SUBJECTS

14

"GODZILLA VS. POST-COLONIAL"*

Thomas King

I grew up in Northern California, and I grew up fast. I don't mean that I was raised in a tough part of town where you had to fight to survive. I was raised in a small town in the foothills, quite pastoral in fact. I mean I grew up all at once. By my first year of high school, I already had my full height, while most of my friends were just beginning to grow.

We had a basketball team at the high school and a basketball coach who considered himself somewhat of an authority on the subject of talent. He could spot it, he said. And he spotted me. He told me I had a talent for the game, and that I should come out for the team. With my size, he said, I would be a natural player. I was flattered.

I wish I could tell you that I excelled at basketball, that I was an all-star, that college coaches came to see me play. But the truth of the matter is, I wasn't even mediocre. Had I not been so very young and so very serious, I might have laughed at my attempts to run and bounce a ball at the same time. Certainly most everyone who saw me play did.

Now before you think that my embarrassment in basketball was the fault of an overzealous coach, you have to remember that we both made more or less the same assumption. The coach assumed that because I was tall, I would be a good player. And once the coach called my height to my attention and encouraged me, I assumed the same thing. We spent the rest of our time together trying to figure out why I was so bad.

Just before the first game of my second season, I tore my knee, mercifully ending my basketball career. My experience taught me little about basketball, but it did teach me a great deal about assumptions.

Assumptions are a dangerous thing. They are especially dangerous when we do not even see that the premise from which we start a discussion is not the hard fact that we thought it was, but one of the fancies we churn out of our imaginations to help us get from the beginning of an idea to the end.

Which brings me, albeit by a circuitous route, to post-colonial literature. I am not a theorist. It's not an apology, but it is a fact. So I cannot talk to the internal structure of the theory itself, how it works, or what it tells us about the art of language and the art of literature. Nor can I participate to any great

*   *World Literature Written in English* 30.2 (1990): 10-16.

extent in what Linda Hutcheon calls "the de-doxifying project of postmodernism."

But having played basketball, I can talk about the assumptions that the term post-colonial makes. It is, first of all, part of a triumvirate. In order to get to "post," we have to wend our way through no small amount of literary history, acknowledging the existence of its antecedents, pre-colonial and colonial. In the case of Native literature, we can say that pre-colonial literature was that literature, oral in nature, that was in existence prior to European contact, a literature that existed exclusively within specific cultural communities.

Post-colonial literature, then, must be the literature produced by Native people sometime after colonization, a literature that arises in large part out of the experience that is colonization. These particular terms allow us to talk about Native literature as a literature that can be counterpoint to Canadian literature, a new voice, if you will, a different voice in the literary amphitheatre. I rather like the idea of post-colonial literature, because it promises to set me apart from the masses and suggests that what I have to offer is new and exciting. But then again, I rather liked the idea of playing basketball, too.

I said at the beginning that I was not a theorist and was not going to concern myself with how post-colonialism operates as a critical method. But I am concerned with what the term says about Natives and Native literature and the initial assumptions it makes about us and our cultures.

When I made that rather simplistic comparison between pre-colonial and post-colonial, I left out one of the players, rather like talking about pre-pubescence and post-pubescence without mentioning puberty. My apologies. It was a trick to make you think I was going to say something profound, when, in fact, I was going to make the rather simple observation that in the case of pre- and post-pubescence and pre- and post-colonial, the pivot around which we move is puberty and colonialism. But here, I'm lying again. Another trick, I'm afraid, for in puberty's case, the precedent, the root, and the antecedent are, at least, all part of a whole, whereas in the case of colonialism—within a discussion of Native literature—the term has little to do with the literature itself. It is both separate from and antithetical to what came before and what came after.

Pre-colonial literature, as we use the term in North America, has no relationship whatsoever to colonial literature. The two are neither part of a biological or natural cycle nor does the one anticipate the other, while the full complement of terms—pre-colonial, colonial, and post-colonial—reeks of unabashed ethnocentrism and well-meaning dismissal, and they point to a deep-seated assumption that is at the heart of most well-intentioned studies of Native literatures.

While post-colonialism purports to be a method by which we can begin to look at those literatures which are formed out of the struggle of the oppressed against the oppressor, the colonized and the colonizer, the term itself assumes that the starting point for that discussion is the advent of Europeans in North America. At the same time, the term organizes the literature progressively suggesting that there is both progress and improvement. No less distressing, it also assumes that the struggle between guardian and ward is the catalyst for contemporary Native literature, providing those of us who write with method and topic. And, worst of all, the idea of post-colonial writing effectively cuts us off from our traditions, traditions that were in place before colonialism ever became a question, traditions which have come down to us through our cultures in spite of colonization, and it supposes that contemporary Native writing is largely a construct of oppression. Ironically, while the term itself—post-colonial—strives to escape to find new centres, it remains, in the end, a hostage to nationalism.

As a contemporary Native writer, I am quite unwilling to make these assumptions, and I am quite unwilling to use these terms.

A friend of mine cautioned me about this stridency and pointed out that postcolonial is a perfectly good term to use for that literature which is, in fact, a reaction to the historical impositions of colonialization. She suggested I look at Maria Campbell's *Halfbreed* and Beatrice Culleton's *In Search of April Raintree* as examples of works for which the term is appropriate. She further suggested that post-colonial was not such a simple thing, that much of what I was concerned with—centres, difference, totalizing, hegemony, margins—was being addressed by post-colonial methodology. If this is true, then it is unfortunate that the method has such an albatross—as the term—hanging around its neck. But I must admit that I remain sceptical that such a term could describe a non-centred, non-nationalistic method.

If we are to use terms to describe the various stages or changes in Native literature as it has become written, while at the same time remaining oral, and as it has expanded from a specific language base to a multiple language base, we need to find descriptors which do not invoke the cant of progress and which are not joined at the hip with nationalism. Post-colonial might be an excellent term to use to describe Canadian literature, but it will not do to describe Native literature.

As a Native writer, I lean towards terms such as tribal, interfusional, polemical, and associational to describe the range of Native writing. I prefer these terms for a variety of reasons: they tend to be less centred and do not, within the terms themselves, privilege one culture over another; they avoid the sense of progress in which primitivism gives way to sophistication, suggesting as it does that such movement is both natural and desirable; they identify points on a cultural and literary continuum for Native literature which do not depend on anomalies such as the arrival of Europeans in North America or the advent of non-Native literature in this hemisphere, what Marie Baker likes to call "settler litter." At the same time, these terms are not "bags" into which we can collect and store the whole of Native literature. They are, more properly, vantage points from which we can see a particular literary landscape.

Two of these terms are self-apparent: tribal and polemical. Tribal refers to that literature which exists primarily within a tribe or a community, literature that is shared almost exclusively by members of that community, and literature that is presented and retained in a Native language. It is virtually invisible outside its community, partly because of the barrier of language and partly because it has little interest in making itself available to an outside audience. In some cases, tribes—the Hopi come to mind—take great pains in limiting access to parts of their literature only to members of their immediate community. Polemical refers to that literature either in a Native language or in English, French, etc. that concerns itself with the clash of Native and non-Native cultures or with the championing of Native values over non-Native values. Like Beatrice Culleton's *In Search of April Raintree,* Maria Campbell's *Halfbreed,* D'Arcy McNickle's *The Surrounded* and *Wind from an Enemy Sky,* and Howard Adams' *Prison of Grass,* polemical literature chronicles the imposition of non-Native expectations and insistences (political, social, scientific) on Native communities and the methods of resistance employed by Native people in order to maintain both their communities and cultures.

The terms interfusional and associational are not as readily apparent. I'm using interfusional to describe that part of Native literature which is a blending of oral literature and written literature. While there are contemporary examples that *suggest* the nature of interfusional literature—some of the translations of Dennis Tedlock and Dell Hymes work along with those of Howard Norman in *The Wishing Bone Cycle*—the only complete example we have of interfusional literature is Harry Robinson's *Write It on Your Heart.*

The stories in Robinson's collection are told in English and written in English, but the patterns, metaphors, structures as well as the themes and characters come primarily from oral literature. More than this, Robinson, within the confines of written language, is successful in creating an oral voice. He does this in a rather ingenious way. He develops what we might want to call an oral syntax that defeats readers' efforts to read the stories silently to themselves, a syntax that encourages readers to read the stories out loud.

The common complaint that we make of oral literature that has been translated into English is that we lose the voice of the storyteller, the gestures, the music, and the interaction between storyteller and audience. But by forcing the reader to read aloud, Robinson's prose, to a large extent, avoids this loss, re-creating at once the storyteller and the performance.

Yeah, I'll tell you "Cat With the Boots On."
Riding boots on.
That's the stories, the first stories.
There was a big ranch, not around here.

That's someplace in European.

Overseas.

That's a long time, shortly after the "imbellable" stories.

But this is part "imbellable" stories.

It's not Indian stories.

This is white people stories,

       because I learned this from the white people.

Not the white man.

The white man tell his son,

       that's Allison—John Fall Allison.

White man.

He is the one that tell the stories to his son.

His son, Bert Allison.

His son was a half Indian and a half white,

       because his mother was an Indian.

And his father was a white man.

So his father told him these stories.

But he told me—Bert Allison.

So he told me,

       "This is not Indian stories.

       White man stories."

You understand that?

This metamorphosis—written to oral, reader to speaker—is no mean trick, one that Robinson accomplishes with relative ease. More important, his prose has become a source of inspiration and influence for other Native writers such as Jeannette Armstrong and myself.

Associational literature is the body of literature that has been created, for the most part, by contemporary Native writers. While no one set of criteria will do to describe it fully, it possesses a series of attributes that help to give it form.

Associational literature, most often, describes a Native community. While it may also describe a non-Native community, it avoids centring the story on the non-Native community or on a conflict between the two cultures, concentrating instead on the daily activities and intricacies of Native life and organizing the elements of plot along a rather flat narrative line that ignores the ubiquitous climaxes and resolutions that are so valued in non-Native literature. In addition to this flat narrative line, associational literature leans towards the group rather than the single, isolated character, creating a fiction that de-values heroes and villains in favour of the members of a community, a fiction which eschews judgements and conclusions.

For the non-Native reader, this literature provides a limited and particular access to a Native world, allowing the reader to associate with that world without being encouraged to feel a part of it. It does not pander to non-Native expectations concerning the glamour and/or horror of Native life, and it especially avoids those media phantasms—glitzy ceremonies, yuppie shamanism, diet philosophies (literary tourism as one critic called them)—that writers such as Carlos Castenada and Lynn Andrews have conjured up for the current generation of gullible readers.

For the Native reader, associational literature helps to remind us of the continuing values of our cultures, and it reinforces the notion that, in addition to the usable past that the concurrence of oral literature and traditional history provides us with, we also have an active present marked by cultural tenacity and a viable future which may well organize itself around major revivals of language, philosophy, and spiritualism.

Two of the better examples of associational literature are Basil H. Johnston's *Indian School Days* and Ruby Slipperjack's *Honour the Sun.* Each creates an Indian community, Johnston at a Jesuit boarding school, Slipperjack in northern Ontario. The novels themselves describe daily activities and the interaction of the community itself, and, aside from the first-person narrator, no one character is given preference over another.

Because *Indian School Days* is about a boarding school, we might well expect to see a sustained attack on this particularly colonial institution, and, while Johnston does on occasion criticize the expectations that the Jesuits have for their Native wards, he defuses most of the conflicts by refusing to make easy judgements and by granting responsibility and choice to both the Jesuits and the Native boys. The boys are not portrayed as hapless victims, and the Jesuits are not cast as uncaring jailers. Particularly telling are the concerted efforts made by the clerics and the students to care for the very young students, "babies" as Johnston calls them, who "seldom laughed or smiled and often cried and whimpered during the day and at night." While the older boys tried to act "as guardians or as big brothers," the burden of care "fell on the young scholastics, who had a much more fatherly air than the senior boys in Grades 7 and 8."

Ruby Slipperjack concerns herself with an isolated Native community in northern Ontario. Written in the form of a diary, the book follows the everyday life of an extended family. The book has no pretense at plot nor is there a desire to glorify traditional Native life. The story is told in simple and unassuming prose that focuses on relationships:

> There are seven of us in the family, four girls and three boys. My oldest brother got married and went away a long time ago. My other brother, Wess, spends most of his time at the cabin on our old trapline. The rest of us girls are all here. We live in a one-room cabin our father built before he died. Mom got someone to make a small addition at the back a couple of years ago. That's where she sleeps with our little brother,

Brian. Brian was just a little baby when my father died and he's about six years old now. The rest of us sleep in the main room on two double beds and a bunk bed.

Three other kids live with us. Mom looks after them because their parents left their home. I guess three more doesn't make much difference aside from the fact the food and clothes have to stretch a little further. The father came to see them once. I heard Mom say that she has never gotten a penny for their keep. Their mother has never come. Actually, I am closer to them than to my own sisters, since mine are gone all winter. Maggie and Jane have become my regular sisters and Vera and Annie are my special sisters when they are home in the summer.

Within the novel, the narrator neither posits the superiority of Native culture over non-Native culture nor suggests that the ills that beset the community come from outside it. Her brother's tuberculosis, John Bull's violent rampages, and the mother's eventual alcoholism are mentioned and lamented, but they are presented in a non-judgemental fashion and do not provide an occasion for accusation and blame either of non-Native culture at large or the Native community itself.

Both books provide access to a Native world, but the access is not unlimited. It is, in fact, remarkably limited access. While Johnston hints at some of the reasons why Indian parents allow their children to be placed at St. Peter Claver's, he does not elaborate on the complex cultural dynamics that have helped to maintain these schools. Much of this is hidden, as are the Native communities outside the school from which the students come. While Slipperjack appears more forthright in her description of the family and the community, she refuses to share with us the reasons for the narrator's mother's alcoholism, the cause of John Bull's violent behaviour, and the reasons for the narrator's leaving the community. In the end, what is most apparent in these two books is not the information received but the silences that each writer maintains. Non-Natives may, as readers, come to an association with these communities, but they remain, always, outsiders.

Now it goes without saying that creating terms simply to replace other terms is, in most instances, a solipsistic exercise, and I do not offer these terms as replacements for the term post-colonial so much as to demonstrate the difficulties that the people and the literature for which the term was, in part, created have with the assumptions that the term embodies.

Unlike post-colonial, the terms tribal, interfusional, polemical, and associational do not establish a chronological order nor do they open and close literary frontiers. They avoid a nationalistic centre, and they do not depend on the arrival of Europeans for their *raison d'être*.

At the same time, for all the range they cover, they do not comfortably contain the work of such Native writers as Gerald Vizenor and Craig Kee Strete.

Vizenor's postmodern novels *Darkness in St. Louis Bearheart* and *Griever: An American Monkey King in China* and Strete's short story collections of surreal and speculative fiction *The Bleeding Man* and *If All Else Fails* cross the lines that definitions—no matter how loose—create.

And it may be that these terms will not do in the end at all. Yet I cannot let post-colonial stand—particularly as a term—for, at its heart, it is an act of imagination and an act of imperialism that demands that I imagine myself as something I did not choose to be, as something I would not choose to become.

15

"Semiotic Control: Native Peoples in Canadian Literature in English"*

Terry Goldie

If the image of native peoples in Canadian literature is analyzed in semiotic terms, the signifier, the literary image, does not lead back to the implied signified, the racial group usually termed Indian or Amerindian, but rather to other images.[1] This phenomenon could be seen as simply another version of Jacques Derrida's analysis of semiosis, which might be termed the Quaker Oats box view of the sign. The person on the box is holding a box with a picture of the same person holding a box with a picture of the same person holding a box . . . The root image cannot exist, for there must always be another image on the box being held, no matter how small. In the same way, each signifier can refer only to another signifier. Any implied signified is unreachable.

But the signifier can be quite precise in itself. John Berger's *Ways of Seeing* states as follows of the visual image:

> An image is a sight which has been recreated or reproduced. It is an appearance, or a set of appearances, which has been detached from the place and time in which it first made its appearance and preserved—for a few moments or a few centuries. (9-10)

A literary representation might seem less absolute, but the indigene in literature is similarly a reified preservation, an extreme example of the law noted by Edward Said in *Orientalism*: "In any instance of at least written language, there is no such thing as a delivered presence, but a *re-presence*, or a representation" (21). Each representation of the indigene is a signifier for which there is no signified except the image. The referent has little purpose in the equation. In the context of the indigene, the unbreachable alterity between signifier and signified is never what many have claimed, an abstruse philosophical concept with nihilist tendencies, but an important aspect of the "subjugated knowledges" to which Michel Foucault refers in *Power/Knowledge* (81). The valorization of the image is defined by a process in which the signified is signifier, in which representation is Image.

---

* *Studies on Canadian Literature: Introductory and Critical Essays,* ed. Arnold E. Davidson (New York: MLA, 1990), 110-23.

Yet there is a significant hidden connection between text and reality. In *Orientalism* Said suggests that what is important in Western representations of Eastern culture is not the approximation of presence that seems to be the intention but rather the conformity of the works to an ideology called orientalism. Said studies not the reality the works seem to represent, the truths they claim to depict, but the reality of the texts and their ideology, and of the ideology of the authors and their culture. In the case of Canadian native peoples, creative literature is but one of the more visible reflections of a process that permeates our culture, even those aspects of it that seem most removed from native peoples. For instance, I am "writing" this line on a computer purchased from Beothuck Data Systems, named for the now-extinct indigenes of Newfoundland.

The reality of the ideology is shaped by the reality of invasion and oppression. Eric R. Wolf comments on the creation of "race":

> Racial designations, such as "Indian" or "Negro," are the outcome of the subjugation of populations in the course of European mercantile expansion. The term *Indian* stands for the conquered populations of the New World, in disregard of any cultural or physical differences among native Americans. (380)

But the details and even the major events of the conquest are not significant factors in the image of the native. History awarded semiotic control to the invaders. Since then the image of native peoples has functioned as a constant source of semiotic reproduction, in which each textual image refers to those offered before. The image of "them" has been "ours."

This analysis attempts to reveal the semiotic limitations of various texts, particularly of those that have been said to provide "positive" or "realistic" views of native peoples. I seek Pierre Macherey's "ideological horizon" (132), the concealed but omnipresent ideology controlling the text. Yet in identifying that horizon, in deconstructing that center of control, I must recognize that I cannot avoid asserting my own center, as a white Canadian male of a certain age. Like any other critic I must recognize that, in Yeats's words, "The centre cannot hold."

The shape of the signifying process as it applies to native peoples is formed by a certain semiotic field; the images function within its boundaries. A few associations suggest the area: war dance, war whoop, tomahawk, and dusky. The native is a semiotic pawn on a chessboard controlled by the white signmaker; yet the individual signmaker, the individual player, can move these pawns only within certain prescribed areas. To extend the analogy, the textual play between white and native is a replica of the black and white squares. The basic dualism, however, is not good and evil, although it is often argued to be so, as in Abdul R. JanMohamed's "Economy of Manichean Allegory":

"The dominant model of power—and interest—relations in all colonial societies is the manichean opposition between the putative superiority of the European and the supposed inferiority of the native" (63). In some early and many contemporary texts the opposition is, rather, between the "putative superiority" of the indigene and the "supposed inferiority" of the white. A white teacher in Philip Kreiner's *People like Us in a Place like This* explores the northern barrens with his Indian friend, Elijah Sealhunter: "I feel pulled out of myself. And what I like best about being out there by the bay is that I know it's not my place to be out there. I know that if Elijah wasn't there, and I was, I would die" (31). The white alien is given life by the prophet-natural hunter. As with Said's Oriental Other, positive and negative images are swings of the pendulum:

> Many of the earliest Oriental amateurs began by welcoming the Orient as a salutary *dérangement* of their European habits of mind and spirit. The Orient was overvalued for its pantheism, its spirituality, its stability, its longevity, its primitivism, and so forth. . . . Yet almost without exception such over-esteem was followed by a counter-response: the Orient suddenly appeared lamentably underhumanized, antidemocratic, backward, barbaric, and so forth. (150)

Said's "overvalued" is present in the short passage from Kreiner, but even there the "counter-response" is always implied.

The complications extend beyond racial opposition, as noted by Sander Gilman:

> Because there is no real line between self and the Other, an imaginary line must be drawn; and so that the illusion of an absolute difference between self and Other is never troubled, this line is as dynamic in its ability to alter itself as is the self. This can be observed in the shifting relationship of antithetical stereotypes that parallel the existence of "bad" and "good" representations of self and Other. But the line between "good" and "bad" responds to stresses occurring within the psyche. Thus paradigm shifts in our mental representations of the world can and do occur. We can move from fearing to glorifying the Other. We can move from loving to hating. (18)

The problem is not the negative or positive aura associated with the image but rather the image itself. As the passage from Kreiner suggests, the Other is of interest only to the extent that it comments on the self, a judgment that could correctly be applied to the present study, concerned primarily not with native peoples but with the image of the native, a white image.

This image is usually defined, as it is in Kreiner, in association with nature.

The explorers attempted to make their signifying process represent real experience, to create the "informational" text defined by Mary Pratt: "[T]he invisible eye/I strives to make those informational orders natural, to find them there uncommanded, rather than assert them as the products/producers of European knowledges or disciplines" (125).

Thus, to define the Indian as "natural" seems to be "natural" in Samuel Hearne's *Journey from Prince of Wales's Fort*, but it continues to be so in contemporary fiction—for instance, W.O. Mitchell's *Since Daisy Creek*. The field, that uniform chessboard, has remained, particularly in the few basic moves that the indigenous pawn has been allowed to make.

At least since Frantz Fanon's *Black Skin, White Masks* it has been a commonplace to use "Other" and "Not-self" for the white view of blacks and for the resulting black view of themselves, an assertion of a white self as subject in discourse that leaves the black Other as object. The terms are similarly applicable to the Indian and Inuk but with an important shift. They are Other and Not-self but also must become self. Gayatri Spivak, in "Three Women's Texts," examines the value of the colonized to the colonizer: "The project of imperialism has always already historically refracted what might have been the absolute Other into a domesticated Other that consolidated the imperialist self" (253). Any imperialist discourse valorizes the colonized according to its own needs for reflection.

But in Spivak's area of study, the Indian subcontinent, the imperialist discourse remains admittedly nonindigenous. India is valorized by imperialist dynamics but it "belongs" to the white realm only as part of the empire. Canadians have long had a clear agenda to erase this separation of belonging. The white Canadian looks at the Inuk. The Inuk is Other and therefore alien. But the Inuk is indigenous and therefore cannot be alien. So the Canadian must be alien! But how can the Canadian be alien within Canada? There are only two possible answers. The white culture might reject the indigene, by stating that the country really began with the arrival of the whites, an approach no longer popular but significant in the nineteenth and early twentieth centuries. Or else the white culture can attempt to incorporate the Other, in superficial gestures such as naming a firm Mohawk Motors, or in sensitive and sophisticated creative endeavors such as the novels of Rudy Wiebe.

The importance of the alien within cannot be overstated. In their need to become "native," to belong in their land, whites in Canada have required a process I have termed "indigenization," the impossible necessity of becoming indigenous. For many writers, the only chance seemed to be through the humans who are truly indigenous, the Indians and Inuit. As J.J. Healy notes in the Australian context:

The Aborigine was part of the tension of an indigenous consciousness. Not the contemporary Aborigine, not even a plausible historical one, but the sort of creature that *might* persuade a white Australian to look in the direction of the surviving race. (173)

Many Canadians have reacted strongly to other such "creatures" and to their own need to become indigenous. Of course, the majority of writers have paid little if any attention to native peoples. But the process of indigenization is complex, and each nineteenth-century reference to the white Canadian as "native" is a comment on indigenization, regardless of the absence of Indians or Inuit in those references. As Macherey states, "an ideology is made of what it does not mention; it exists because there are things which must not be spoken of" (132). In other words, absence is also negative presence, which might be opposed by the "positive absence" of a name like Beothuck Data or of texts such as Isabella Valancy Crawford's "Malcolm's Katie," written in 1884. The Indian is neither subject nor overt object of the poem, but natural phenomena are often represented through overtly "Indian" metaphors, an apparent attempt to "indigenize" the text.

Said notes a number of what he terms "standard commodities" associated with the Orient. Two commodities that appear to be standard in the economy created by the semiotic field of the Indian and Inuk in Canadian literature are sex and violence. They are poles of attraction and repulsion, temptation by the sensual maiden and fear of the fiendish warrior. Often the two poles are found in the same work; in John Richardson's *Wacousta*, the warrior constantly attacks, but the maiden helps the white to avoid that attack. They are emotional signs, semiotic embodiments of primal responses. Could one create a more appropriate signifier for fear than the treacherous redskin? He incorporates the terror of an impassioned, uncontrolled spirit of evil. He is strangely joined by the Indian maiden, who tempts the being chained by civilization toward the liberation of free and open sexuality, not untamed evil but unrestrained joy. Following the pattern noted in Gilman's *Difference and Pathology*, "the 'bad' Other becomes the negative stereotype; the 'good' Other becomes the positive stereotype. The former is that which we fear to become; the latter, that which we fear we cannot achieve" (20). Added to this construction is the alien's fear of the warrior as hostile wilderness—this new, threatening land—and the arrivant's attraction to the maiden as restorative pastoral—this new, available land. The absent Indian and Crawford's Indianized poem might also be seen in this context. The general sign of fear leads to an indigenization that excludes the indigene. Temptation promises an indigenization through inclusion.

An intriguing yet unanswerable question is whether the depiction of the Indian leads to an emphasis on sex and violence or whether desire for the frissons of sex and violence suggests the Indian. For instance, through the first part of Joseph Howe's "Acadia" (written in the 1830s), the image of the Indian approximates the noble savage but includes a stridently gory scene of the massacre of a pioneer family, in which the Indian appears as demonic savage par excellence. The interest seems more in violence than in the Indian. Or the motivation to include the Indian might be generic, the epic shape of "Acadia." The poem presents a vision of the founding of a nation, and the Indian must fit. Thus before the arrival of the whites, the noble Indian provides an extended history for the greatness of Nova Scotia. After the whites take over, Indian treachery becomes a justification to direct the readers' empathy to the invaders rather than to those recently presented as an indigenous aristocracy. Similarly, in contemporary confessional lyrics, the sexuality of the Indian becomes a means of exploring personal and societal guilt, as in Al Pittman's "Shanadithit."

A mixture of values is present in that part of Hearne's narrative known as "The Coppermine Massacre." With himself, or his first-person persona, as physical focus, Hearne's apparently factual account presents the sexual and the violent indigenes in the same passage but with a clear split in gender and also in race. The delicate native maiden (the usual sexual focus in literature of the eighteenth, nineteenth, and much of the twentieth century) who comes toward him is the Inuit woman. This image of sexual attraction meets the repulsive violence of the demonic male, the Indians. Until well into the twentieth century the male native was almost always violence, never sex. A major change occurs, however, in novels such as Margaret Laurence's *Diviners* and Susan Musgrave's *Charcoal Burners*, in which a native male embodies a sexual attraction that the white female uses to liberate herself.

A third important commodity is orality, the associations raised by the indigene's speaking, nonwriting, state. The writers' sense of native peoples as having completely different systems of understanding, different epistemes, is based on an often undefined belief that cultures without writing operate within a different dimension of consciousness. In earlier works, white writers often deemed this a symptom of inferiority or, as in Ralph Connor's *Patrol of the Sundance Trail*, a sign of the demonic orator. Both the good and the bad sides of orality are usually presented as aspects of the natural. In Duncan Campbell Scott's poem "The Height of Land," for example, a "long Ojibwa cadence" rises from the land (55).

The philosophical base of the positive representations of natural orality found throughout twentieth-century literature is found in Walter Ong's *Orality and Literacy*:

> The fact that oral peoples commonly and in all likelihood universally consider words to have magical potency is clearly tied in, at least unconsciously, with their sense of the word as necessarily spoken, sounded, and hence power-driven. (32)

The orality of the native is seen to provide a connection to the inner world of humanity, unlike the alienating distance of the literary. In a self-reflexive denigration typical of much contemporary literature, texts such as *Spirit Wrestler*, James Houston's portrait of the Inuit, express ambivalence about the validity of writing through an elevation of the indigene's orality, represented as Said's "delivered presence."

The Indian narrator is often an important element of orality, especially in recent fiction. The representation of the text as the product of an Indian voice creates a "presence" by appearing to change the Indian from object to subject. W.P. Kinsella's Indian stories, such as those in *Dance Me Outside*, are all "told" by Silas Ermineskin. As in many other representations of minority cultures, humor arises from misperceptions of the majority culture: Silas interprets a white expression for pregnancy, "one in the oven," as a "kid in the stove" (84). Houston's historical novel *Eagle Song* uses a more sophisticated narration: "Hunters must be, oh, so careful later not to let women hear what happens on the whaling grounds, so, listener, remember, tell women nothing of these words you hear from me" (137). The narrator establishes an oral context with a clear ethnographic definition.

Representations of native language extend orality in a different direction. Perhaps the most superficial instance of this occurs in naming. At one level the conflict might be between true and false, between an Indian name that symbolizes Indian culture and an imposed white name that produces a false identity. A more significant element is asserted in A.M. Klein's poem "Indian Reservation," which states that references to nature put "fur on their names to make all live things kin" (295). It is as if a different semiotic field appears, not the field in which the writer places the indigene, but the field in which the indigene places the white and, presumably, himself or herself. There is thus a continuum, from early texts that use a few native words heavily glossed, to *Eagle Song*, in which Nootka terms are defined only by context. A simple record of indigene language might be considered more limited in its representation of the indigenous consciousness than a text in which the indigene is narrator, but its apparent absolute adherence to the indigenous semiosis could suggest that an even greater bridge has been touched if not crossed. Unlike the indigenous narrator, the white reader—and perhaps author—can barely penetrate the meaning. The narrator of Rudy Wiebe's *My Lovely Enemy* laments his inability to gloss this text:

> I don't speak Cree, I should do this properly but I don't, in the oral tradition remembering the past date by date is no Indian tradition, how can a white man find any fact beyond the story memory of a language he doesn't talk unless he tries to trace say one name of one person through all the white documents he can find, letters, diaries, notes, travel books, white gossip in the unlikeliest places you can dig from the nineteenth century? (43-44)

Yet the attempt at penetration seems essential. There is a realization that the indigenous language must be incorporated in order to connect with the power that the indigene represents.

The inclusion of Indian "speech" seems to constitute a prime example of Mikhail Bakhtin's "Discourse in the Novel":

> These distinctive links and interrelationships between utterances and languages, this movement of the theme through different languages and speech types, its dispersion into the rivulets and droplets of social heteroglossia, its dialogization—this is the basic distinguishing feature of the stylistics of the novel. (*Dialogic* 263)

Bakhtin sees dialogization as creating an important tension in fiction: "Every utterance participates in the 'unitary language' (in its centripetal forces and tendencies) and at the same time partakes of social and historical heteroglossia (the centrifugal, stratifying forces)" (272).

This suggests a positive view of the process, in which the "self" of the white text includes the Indian "Other" within its vision while at the same time representing the "social and historical" vision of the Other. Bakhtin goes so far as to call it "*another's speech in another's language*" (324). In opposition I would suggest that the image of the Indian is an example of the negative confluence of the centripetal and centrifugal Other. It is centripetal because always subject to the system of white texts. The Indian voice found in Canadian fiction "lives" only in that fiction. It is centrifugal because that Indian always reaches out to a semiotic field that has defined the image before its inclusion in the fluctuations of the individual text. The novel of the 1980s re-presents the extant image. The process is "stratifying" in a particularly pernicious sense.

There are many variants to the power of the oral Indian, such as taciturnity as the obverse of the orator's inflated diction. W.D. Lighthall provides a delightful combination of the two in *The Master of Life*: "Thou sayest 'Ugh!'" (127). The potential of this cliché is explored more extensively in *Wacousta*, which employs "the low and guttural 'ugh!'" "an assentient and expressive 'ugh!'" and an "almost inaudible 'ugh!'" within the space of three pages. These are said to indicate "astonishment," "approbation," and "eagerness," respectively (113-15). Many contemporary texts emphasize the power of silence. Mel Dagg writes in "Sunday Evening on Axe Flats": "She wraps herself in layers of silence, travelling outside herself, waiting" (*Same Truck* 44). In Sid Stephen's "She Says Goodbye to Mr. Cormack" silence surpasses even time for the last Beothuck woman:

> her tongue
> is even now becoming stone,
> dense with silence
> and hard with meaning. (n.p.)

Through the hardening comes the fluidity, the ability to overcome the restraints of linear, logical, white interpretation. Orality becomes the land, becomes presence, and mystically becomes the silent invocation of the consciousness, the vision, of Other.

Orality thus leads to a fourth commodity, mysticism, in which the native becomes a sign of oracular power, either malevolent, in most nineteenth-century texts, or beneficent, in most contemporary ones. Just as many early texts suggest orality to be inferior, so indigenous beliefs constitute so many absurd superstitions. If such beliefs did represent a different dimension of consciousness, it was not worth achieving, and certainly not equal to white doctrine. Egerton Ryerson Young's *Winter Adventures of Three Boys in the Great Lone Land* refers to the Indian's transformation from the "degradation and superstition of a cruel paganism into the blessedness and enjoyment of a genuine Christianity and an abiding civilization" (79).

For other texts, however, particularly in the twentieth century, an alien space is attractive. In Wiebe's *Temptations of Big Bear*, probably still the most resonant fictional representation of the native in Canadian literature, the mystical sensitivity of the hero validates the Christian overtones of the title, in opposition to the white culture and representatives of the Christian church. In Fred Bodsworth's *Sparrow's Fall*, the Christian hymn of the title, with its claim that God protects each creature of nature, interferes with the natural order of the north, in which the Indian, Jacob, must kill to survive. But when Jacob finds himself far from home, his belief system works as he leaves a propitiatory caribou skull: "In this strange land there would be other spirits he didn't know, and they would be pleased at this respect for them that Jacob was showing" (151). In an interesting semiotic variant, the inadequacies of the author's culture, which offers little "true" knowledge through its own popular beliefs (in which the distancing Quaker Oats box leaves divine power beyond reach), is met by an indigenous belief system (usually quite asystemic) that offers a Presence to exceed even the presence of orality.

Spivak has commented on the "soul-making" agenda of imperialist missionaries (Address). They intended to take indigenous peoples who teetered between the absolute material and the false antiphenomenal and make new creations who would possess the reality of the Christian noumenal. But in many of the texts in this study, what the white needs is not to instill spirit in the Other but to gain it from the Other. Through the indigene the white character gains soul and the potential of becoming rooted in the land. An appropriate pun is that only by going native can the European arrivant become native. Often in such narratives the Otherness of the indigene is first heightened, as in the use of an indigenous semiotic field. A similar process is the defamiliarization of common aspects of white culture. When Indians are presented as having an intricately metaphorical "iron horse" view of a train, for instance, it makes the Indians doubly Other. They are Other because the white perceives them as such and also because their own perception is so clearly that of Other.

Often, however, as in the Beothuck poems of Sid Stephen and Al Pittman, or in Margaret Atwood's novel *Surfacing*, the Other is not living Indians but art or even just memories of tribes long obliterated—Indian presence but no present Indians. This temporal split is a fifth commodity in the semiotic field of the indigene, the prehistoric. Historicity, in which the text makes an overt or covert statement on the chronology of the culture, shapes the indigene into a historical artifact, a remnant of a golden age that seems to have little connection to contemporary life. Golden age assumptions underlie the choice of genre in the various nineteenth-century heroic tragedies with native heroes, such as Charles Mair's *Tecumseh* (published in 1886). Robert Kroetsch's novel *Badlands* makes a specific comment on the prehistoric when the archaeologists find the Indian girl among the dinosaur bones: "her cabin of bones, her fossil tipi" (144).

Johannes Fabian's *Time and the Other* states of anthropology: "It promoted a scheme in terms of which not only past cultures, but all living societies were irrevocably placed on a temporal slope, a stream of time—some upstream, others downstream" (17). When native peoples, perceived to be of the "early," remain in Canadian society, which is of the "late," degradation is shown to be inevitable. A corollary of the temporal split between the golden age and contemporary decadence is a tendency to see native culture as either true, pure, and static or else not really of that culture. Wayland Drew's *Wabeno Feast* eulogizes the past Indian but begins and ends with a contemporary Indian drunk. The only other Indian in "time present" is a prostitute.

Through the commodities the white acquires Indian—"acquires," not "becomes." To "become Indian" is an absurdity or even madness, as Kroetsch's *Gone Indian* suggests. "Go native" is necessary, "gone native" is not. Some psychologists might diagnose even acquisition as a rejection of self for not-self. The typical narrative pattern must modify such a theory, however. The indigene is acquired; the white is not abandoned. Usually the connection is made through some form of sexual contact—in earlier works, a white male with a native female; in recent works, often the reverse. But in the majority of works of both types, the contact is followed by the death of the indigene. In *The Diviners*, Jules, a Métis sex object, acts as a "shaman," but removes himself after he has mystically transformed Morag, and then dies. He leaves part of himself in the form of their daughter, Pique, who might be seen as the fruition of native-white contact but could also be viewed as one more step in a deracinating chain. As much less of an Indian, although often lamenting that fact, she is another aspect of historicity. Her father is the dying Indian, a central figure in the semiosis associated with the golden age.

A variety of factors are involved in incorporating the native for the page, but still more are added when the genre requires that the native be corporeally present, in the theater. There must be presence in the theater, although the presence is that of the actors and not of the author. If the pawn is played by a white actor in disguise, signifying processes are at work, similar to those in the novel. If a native actor is used, the cross-cultural leap in which the white author creates the lines and the context for the indigene's speech might seem a beneficial erasing of boundaries, but it might also be considered a means of hiding some necessary distinctions. In the original 1967 production of George Ryga's *Ecstasy of Rita Joe*, the late Canadian actor Dan George, best known for his appearance in the film *Little Big Man*, began his rise to fame. His presence validated a noble savage stereotype of an order seldom seen in contemporary white culture. A novel can only attempt the Bakhtinian illusion of representing "another's voice." The dramatic text makes it possible for another's voice to speak the Other as described by the white self. Dan George's role as signifier of "reality" just made the limits of the image more acceptable. As long as the semiotic field exists, as long as the shapes of the standard commodities change but the commodities remain the same, the chess match can vary but there is still a definable limit to the board. The necessities of indigenization can compel white players to participate in the game, but they cannot liberate the pawn.

The chessboard analogy might in the end seem a diminution of the issue. It emphasizes the distance between the sign, the image of the native in Canadian literature, and the referent, the native peoples of Canada, but it perhaps deemphasizes the contradictions of the chessboard of Canadian political reality. If, as Derrida claims, there is nothing outside the text, then the image of the native is the clearest textualization of the erasure of native sovereignty in Canada. At a time when native self-government is a major issue in Canadian politics, a recognition of the manipulations of white indigenization in literature might be a stimulus to the reinstatement of the indigenous.

Notes

1. This paper provides a sketch of a theoretical approach used in my book *Fear and Temptation* and thus examples are kept to a minimum. The comments refer specifically to Canadian literature in English, but the majority of the assertions are applicable to a number of analogous literatures, most obviously Canadian in French and United States but also Australian and New Zealand and various South American literatures. To look beyond the "Indian" context, South African literature also fits, with J.M. Coetzee's *Waiting for the Barbarians* a perfect example of the valorization of the semiotic field of the indigene. For a general comparison, the ideological framework of Robert F. Berkhofer's *White Man's Indian* is different from the present study, but the conclusions are similar.

Works Cited

Atwood, Margaret. *Surfacing.* Toronto: McClelland, 1972.

Bakhtin, Mikhail. *The Dialogic Imagination: Four Essays.* Trans. Caryl Emerson and Michael Holquist. Ed. Holquist. Austin: U of Texas P, 1981.

Berger, John. *Ways of Seeing.* London: BBC, 1972.

Berkhofer, Robert F. *The White Man's Indian: Images of the American Indian from Columbus to the Present.* New York: Vintage, 1979.

Bodsworth, Fred. *The Sparrow's Fall.* Toronto: Doubleday, 1967.

Coetzee, J.M. *Waiting for the Barbarians.* Markham, ON: Penguin, 1982.

Connor, Ralph [Charles W. Gordon]. *The Patrol of the Sundance Trail.* Toronto: Westminster, 1914.

Crawford, Isabella Valancy. *The Collected Poems.* 1905. Toronto: U of Toronto P, 1972.

Dagg, Mel. *Same Truck Different Driver.* Calgary: Westlands, 1982.

Derrida, Jacques. *Of Grammatology.* Trans. Gayatri Chakravorty Spivak. Baltimore: Johns Hopkins UP, 1976.

Drew, Wayland. *The Wabeno Feast.* Toronto: Anansi, 1973.

Fabian, Johannes. *Time and the Other: How Anthropology Makes Its Object.* New York: Columbia UP, 1983.

Fanon, Frantz. *Black Skin, White Masks.* Trans. Charles Lam Markmann. St. Albans, Eng.: Paladin, 1970.

Foucault, Michel. *Power/Knowledge: Selected Interviews and Other Writings 1972-1977.* Trans. Colin Gordon et al. Ed. Gordon. New York: Pantheon, 1980.

Gilman, Sander. *Difference and Pathology: Stereotypes of Sexuality, Race and Madness.* Ithaca: Cornell UP, 1985.

Goldie, Terry. *Fear and Temptation: The Image of the Indigene in Canadian, Australian and New Zealand Literatures.* Montréal: McGill-Queen's UP, 1989.

Healy, J.J. *Literature and the Aborigine in Australia 1770-1975.* St. Lucia: U of Queensland P, 1978.

Hearne, Samuel. *A Journey from Prince of Wales's Fort in Hudson's Bay to the Northern Ocean Undertaken by Order of the Hudson's Bay Company for the Discovery of Copper Mines, a North West Passage &c. in the Years 1769, 1770, 1771, & 1772.* 1795. Edmonton: Hurtig, 1971.

Houston, James. *Eagle Song: An Indian Saga Based on True Events.* New York: Harcourt, 1983.

— . *Spirit Wrestler.* Toronto: McClelland, 1980.

Howe, Joseph. *Poems and Essays.* 1874. Toronto: U of Toronto P, 1973.

JanMohamed, Abdul R. "The Economy of Manichean Allegory: The Function of Racial Difference in Colonialist Literature." *Critical Inquiry* 12.1 (1985): 59-87.

Kinsella, W.P. *Dance Me Outside.* Ottawa: Oberon, 1977.

Klein, A.M. *Collected Poems.* Ed. Miriam Waddington. Toronto: McGraw Ryerson, 1974.

Kreiner, Philip. *People like Us in a Place like This.* Ottawa: Oberon, 1983.

Kroetsch, Robert. *Badlands.* Don Mills, ON: New, 1975.

—— . *Gone Indian.* Toronto: New, 1973.

Laurence, Margaret. *The Diviners.* Toronto: McClelland, 1974.

Lighthall, W.D. *The Master of Life: A Romance of the Five Nations and of Prehistoric Montreal.* Toronto: Musson, 1908.

Macherey, Pierre. *A Theory of Literary Production.* Trans. Geoffrey Wall. London: Routledge, 1978.

Mair, Charles. *Dreamland and Other Poems; Tecumseh: A Drama.* 1901. Toronto: U of Toronto P, 1974.

Mitchell, W.O. *Since Daisy Creek.* Toronto: Macmillan, 1984.

Musgrave, Susan. *The Charcoal Burners.* Toronto: McClelland, 1980.

Ong, Walter. *Orality and Literacy: The Technologizing of the Word.* London: Methuen, 1982.

Pittman, Al. *Through One More Window.* Portugal Cove: Breakwater Books, 1974.

Pratt, Mary Louise. "Scratches on the Face of the Country; or, What Mr. Barrow Saw in the Land of the Bushmen." *Critical Inquiry* 12.1 (1985): 119-43.

Richardson, John. *Wacousta.* 1832. Toronto: McClelland, 1967.

Ryga, George. *The Ecstasy of Rita Joe.* Vancouver: Talonplays, 1970.

Said, Edward. *Orientalism.* London: Routledge, 1978.

Scott, Duncan Campbell. *Selected Poems.* Toronto: Ryerson, 1951.

Spivak, Gayatri Chakravorty. Address. University of Queensland, Brisbane, Australia, 1 Aug. 1984.

—— . "Three Women's Texts and a Critique of Imperialism." *Critical Inquiry* 12.1 (1985): 243-61.

Stephen, Sid. *Beothuck Poems.* Ottawa: Oberon, 1976.

Wiebe, Rudy. *My Lovely Enemy.* Toronto: McClelland, 1983.

—— . *The Temptations of Big Bear.* Toronto: McClelland, 1973.

Wolf, Eric R. *Europe and the People without History.* Berkeley: U of California P, 1982.

Young, Egerton Ryerson. *Winter Adventures of Three Boys in the Great Lone Land.*

16

"The 'Post-Colonial' Imagination"*

Lee Maracle

I feel a little like Zola, making political and now literary proclamations from within a sense of reality which other humans do not necessarily share. Here I am, one of two non-academics at a conference of English academics on "Post-Colonialism: Theory and Practice." I am the only non-degreed teacher ever hired to deliver a university program at the University of Victoria and I am the most published Native author in the country.

I remember my first words . . . the sun was gone and rain spilled from the sky. I watched my mother enter, hunkered down into her coat as though hunching her head into her shoulders would protect her from the rain and cold. She slipped off her boots and said, "It's raining pitchforks out there." I saw no pitchforks. Instead I imagined her discomfort and played about with the picture of her hunching down to protect herself from the rain. I imagined pitchforks falling from the sky, thin and sharp—painful. To some folks rain is painful, like pitchforks might be to shafts of hay.

"Between cloud and rain there are no pitchforks, only people who think they see them—right mom?" And my Mom laughed and hugged me. It was my earliest understanding of metaphor and its place in our lives. I was three and a half then. I have memories that pre-date this image, but no words were ever let go of by me, until this moment. In my mind, the image always came first, then the words were layered overtop. This process of thought still lives with me. The images come, then the words. If there are no images, then there are no words. Consequently, I understand mathematics only in terms of physics, chemistry or shopping.

I remember the first time I spoke in school. Ms. C. asked me, "Where did Dick run?" I answered, "Far from the fenceposts who locked up the grasses no one wanted to grow" and everyone laughed. It was a different kind of laugh. Ms. C. responded, "Your insolence will not get you far in life." Perhaps it was not insolence that did so much as belief, belief in my own dreamspace where my words are born.

There is a place between the sandbank and the river where silver streaks are born. This place slides along the dreamspace of the stream [which]

* *Fuse* 16.1 (1992): 12-15.

birthed it, unaware of the wonderment of its conception, the miracle of its birth and the tenuousness of its life. Fools see the silver in terms of cost and thus place no real value on it. The wise know that in the thin lines of silver live the secrets of truth—a soft whirling knowledge that calls the body to free itself of all burdens and look at the world through the dreamspace of this silver streak.

Thin is the line along the river's edge but vast is its internal life. This place spins dreams, and webs of new life are woven into whole new worlds. I live within the boundaries of this streak. Others live here with me. They are shaped by colour and difference but no one possesses the authority to disempower others on the basis of this colour and difference. In this place all are distinct, powerful and beautiful. In this place we dream new words with old themes rich in human love and promise. We strive to inspire through words, painting our dreams of change. We are the pots, the painters, the dramatists, those who really believe if we just write this one last poem, paint this one last picture, create this one last character, we can change the world . . .

In this dreamspace there are no "post-colonial conferences on literature," no "conferences on Indigenous sovereignty" and no one asks "What do you Indians want anyway?" We all know that the human spirit divine requires freedom to blossom, freedom to dream, to create and become whole. This freedom is as basic a need as is food. However, in the real world, colonialism is our condition, and so we need to have a conference such as this one.

Unless I was sleeping during the revolution, we have not had a change in our condition, at least not the Indigenous people of this land. Post-colonialism presumes we have resolved the colonial condition, at least in the field of literature. Even here we are still a classical colony. Our words, our sense and use of language are not judged by the standards set by the poetry and stories we create. They are judged by the standards set by others.

With conditions as they are, it is a luxury for me to wander into my dreamspace and conceive of "post-colonialism." A multitude of faces, all white and too numerous to name, gather around the edges of my dreamspace. If I enter despite them, their words ignite and nearly melt away the thin line of silver housing my ability to dream. Images of screaming squaws, dirty Indians and weeping women writhe along the rivers of tears we have shed over these images which continue to meet page, print and reader. And still I imagine new words to deal with old dilemmas that still stand on the way to freedom.

At dawn, when the river reaches the sea, before me my ancestors potlatch, dance and sing. There the sun keeps time with her own sense of music, and the surface of the sea transforms. On it I see a tiara of grandmothers and grandfathers. I hear words of challenge and struggle, of transformation and change and my nation's passion for these things. I see the future. The voices of George Ryga and some of the good citizens who died before me join the congregation of my ancestors and form an arc; I suffer living and envy the dead.

In the literature of this country is the search for an essential Canadian self. This is an arc created of our common voices and vision, born with each new dreamer added to this space. Born of the realization that humans hold a thread of hope, thin, stubborn and resilient. Watered by poets, story-tellers and old writers, this hope is held by all those who refuse to peer like cowardly voyeurs at the world from behind the fence posts of a colonial fort. I am inspired by all those whose spirit excites literary courage, those who recreate language, reconceive humanity not as statistics but as creative sacred beings capable of change and transformation, capable of bringing dreams from conception to birth and transformation.

In the thin arc bridging my life to the future, the roots of my life are nearly overwhelmed. The industrial revolution, the lie of it, the stagnation inherent in it, the violence and the death culture it birthed become clear. The history of this revolution and its victims has long complex tendrils of industrial waste and death; this culture which aggrandizes its authors stretches itself all over the world, winding itself around imagination, choking all those whose images have no room for it. Those who stand in awe of this industrialization process are not yet free of it. Even our dead are not free of it. We can't even imagine beyond our common colonial condition because of it.

We are the grandchildren of an abusive industrial British parent, and in fact are nowhere near a post-colonial literature. The dirty waif of Dickensian literature has become the modern "Indian" waif. Canadian writers still hover about the gates of old forts, peek through the cracks of their protective ideological walls and try to write their own yearnings for freedom from the safety of their intellectual incarceration. The colonized still hover outside the gates, dreaming of coming in while the ideological madness of this ridiculous desire hides our truer aspirations and colours our language in stilted erratic parroting of the "mother country's" tongues. Or worse, this desire paints images of coming into the fort as equals. The existence of the fort, the laws of this fort, the humanity of it are rarely questioned. Canadians must get out of the fort and imagine something beyond the colonial condition—beyond violence, rape and notions of dirty people. We must move beyond what is—re-enter our dreamspace and recreate ourselves. We must get away from the fort's door where the scent of pillage and imprisonment still terrorizes our dreams.

In George Ryga's play "The Ecstasy of Rita Joe," Rita says "no child on the road would remember you, mister." Ryga joins the congregation of my ancestors and their dreams of a life outside the fort. "No child would remember you, mister." You who clutch the gatekeys of your colonial master, acquiesce to your colonial imprisonment in language and law intended to dehumanize you can never be remembered by an innocent child. Children are forward people, they are dreamers and their memories are too innocent to recall the jailed and the jailers. Ryga knew something then . . .

I want to be able to fictionalize our lives and still hold fast to truth, yet our lives are so rich with death. Yet I fear that in storying this death in numbers so immense, with love so deep, I may not survive. I spiral down into the silver streak of solitude to find my ceremonial self. From within this bright womb I can spiral out into the world again to reconceive of place. I can stretch time. I can erase the artifice of separation that divides today from yesterday and yesterday from tomorrow. In this place all time is the same time. In this place images speak reality—paint truth in believable pictures.

In this place my self is a significant self—a self who rises swan-like to engage the rigors of loyalty and love—a self who rises eagle-like to the need for vision, a self who, wolf-like, journeys doggedly along old trails with new directions in mind, a self who sees transformation, personal and social as natural and indispensable to growth. These things inside are not things at all, but songs sung by me, my grandmother, my grandchildren and men like Ryga.

We conjure new words by understanding our different and common pasts. We cannot resolve this past unless we can come to this silver streak between river bank and sand without quarreling.

From inside this dreamspace comes my language coloured by my need for you to see me—really see me. The heart and spirit under my skin animate my need to carve images of myself on the panes of your books, never to be forgotten. Inspired by my need to experience oneness with you at the crest of an arc of our mutual construction in a language we both understand, I build my end of this arc, word by word, dream by dream.

This arc becomes the meeting place of our two worlds. The desire for this arc, this meeting place, this oneness does not negate the existence of both our worlds. The arc pre-supposes the harmony of both: not inviting the invasion or the suppression of my world by yours. It invites sharing between them.

But we are plagued by our colonial condition. Inside the fort, Canadians seem to think this arc can be built despite the disentitlement of our land, our words, our very selves. Outside the fort, we hear the laughter and feel we must shed our ancient selves, move away from our homeland and give up our words. If Canadians are locked in the fort, we are locked outside of it. Doubt rises huge and fogs the source of our creative voice, making the arc disappear. We search your institutional hallways for evidence of ourselves. But we have forgotten the trail to our ceremonial selves in the dreamspace we once occupied.

In order to resolve this colonial condition in literature we need to have Canada recognize that first it is our condition, and second, Canada needs to view this condition as unacceptable. In literature this means to move over and create a new space for us in the annals of literature in Canada. It means don't pick up a pen and imagine you need to write on my behalf or that you should. It means that those who lay claim to a place in the dreamspace of creativity must come to understand the difference between honest stretching into the world of the imagination and pirating someone else's imagination.

If you conjure a character based on your in-fort stereotypes and trash my world, that's bad writing—racist literature and I will take you on for it. If I tell you a story and you write it down and collect the royal coinage from this story, that's stealing—appropriation of culture. But if you imagine a character who is from my world, attempting to deconstruct the attitudes of yours, while you may not be stealing, you still leave yourself open to criticism unless you do it well.

Part of our colonial condition is that we are still too busy struggling in the whirl of it, paddling through the rapids of it, to be able to enter the dream-space at the edge of it. Few of us have had the time to study our remembered story. Some have no memories to ponder. But those of us who have pondered our memorized stories know we have a criteria for story.

If the speaker achieves oneness with the listener, it's a good story.

If the listener is empowered to move to this dreamspace, and re-imagine his/herself, it's a good story.

If the listener is empowered to move to this dreamspace and re-imagine oneness with humanity, earth, flora and fauna, it's a good story.

If the story enters the world from the dreamspace where all good stories are born, it's a good story.

These are my culture's standards—conscious and unconscious—and until they become standards alongside of yours, colonialism in literature will prevail.

17

"Unfolding the Lessons of Colonization"*

Marie Battiste

As the twentieth century unfolds to a new millennium, many voices and forums are converging to form a new perspective on knowledge. Many of these voices belong to the Indigenous peoples who have survived European colonization and cognitive imperialism. They represent the thoughts and experiences of the people of the Earth whom Europeans have characterized as primitive, backward, and inferior—the colonized and dominated people of the last five centuries. The voices of these victims of empire, once predominantly silenced in the social sciences, have been not only resisting colonialization in thought and actions but also attempting to restore Indigenous knowledge and heritage. By harmonizing Indigenous knowledge with Eurocentric knowledge, they are attempting to heal their people, restore their inherent dignity, and apply fundamental human rights to their communities. They are ready to imagine and unfold postcolonial orders and society.

This book [*Reclaiming Indigenous Voice and Vision*] reveals some of these voices of commitment. They emerged from the meetings of the delegates of the United Nations Working Group on Indigenous Populations, held every year in Geneva, that converged in debates and drafting sessions on Indigenous rights. In 1996, many of these committed voices gathered at the University of Saskatchewan in Saskatoon, Canada, to honour Rigaberto Menchu Tum, Chief Ted Moses, and Erica-Irene Daes, "organic" leaders in Indigenous human rights initiatives. In the intense summer days and nights of 1996, delegates from many lands—lands that colonizers called Australia, New Zealand, South America, Europe, and North America—assembled for an unprecedented honouring ceremony and a focused talking circle to seek remedies for the colonization of the minds and souls of their peoples. The participants were Indigenous teachers and scholars and non-Aboriginal "friends" or allies. In the following collection of essays, the voices of commitment and action articulate their teachings, stories, perspectives, and reflections in many different styles—passionate, scholarly, poetic, painful, practical—all of them visionary.

---

* Introduction, *Reclaiming Indigenous Voice and Vision*, ed. Marie Battiste (Vancouver: UBC P, 2000), xvi-xxx.

A significant starting point for discussing these themes was the story of the elder's box as told by Eber Hampton, a Chickasaw educator and the president of the Saskatchewan Indian Federated College, the national post-secondary educational institute of the First Nations of Canada. He told of an elder who asked him to carry a box. Thinking well of his own youthful stature, he felt proud to be chosen and agreed willingly. The elder then thrust forward what appeared to be an empty box, which puzzled him:

> His question came from behind the box, "How many sides do you see?"
> "One," I said.
> He pulled the box towards his chest and turned it so one corner faced me. "Now how many do you see?"
> "Now I see three sides."
> He stepped back and extended the box, one corner towards him and one towards me. "You and I together can see six sides of this box," he told me. (Hampton 42)

Just as the elder revealed that there is more than one perspective required to view a box holistically, the gathering revealed many perspectives on how to map and diagnose colonization, how to heal the colonized, and how to imagine and invoke a new society. In group sittings and stories told in many dialogues and related in many texts, the gathering found multiple layers of experience and knowledge about colonization that profoundly challenged us to find remedies. We began to see the many sides of our confinement, our box.

Through our sharing, listening, feeling, and analyzing, we engaged in a critique of the trauma of colonization. We examined the frameworks of meaning behind it, we acknowledged the destructiveness that it authorized, and we imagined a postcolonial society that embraced and honoured our diversity. We shared many sides of a box that we came to know more fully. We came to see colonization as a system of oppression rather than as personal or local prejudice. We came to understand that it is the systemic nature of colonization that creates cognitive imperialism, our cognitive prisons (Battiste).

Over the course of those ten days, the voices in the gathering converged to address strategies for neutralizing the systemic nature of our oppression, identifying its viral sources, and understanding how it imprisons our thoughts. Together we sought to find ways of healing and rebuilding our nations, peoples, communities, and selves by restoring Indigenous ecologies, consciousnesses, and languages and by creating bridges between Indigenous and Eurocentric knowledge. We discovered that we could not be the cure if we were the disease. Discovering the cures that will heal and restore our heritage and knowledge is an urgent agenda occupying the daily and intellectual lives of indigenous peoples. It will be the most significant problem facing Indigenous peoples in the Decade of the World's Indigenous Peoples, 1995-

2004, as Indigenous peoples around the world continue to struggle against oppression. Understanding the processes that we detected in the course of our gathering will help to unravel ethnic tensions and wars and allow humanity to rebuild society based on diversity rather than on an ancient quest for singularity.

The participants were unique representatives of their peoples who brought to the meeting diverse ecological consciousnesses, languages, and cultures, as well as similar expressions of caring and kindness. They were the first generation of Indigenous scholars accomplished in both Eurocentric and Indigenous thought, thus providing a bridge that allowed us to enter into a dialogue and translate Indigenous knowledge and heritage. Each had walked in the colonizers' moccasins, learned to speak their languages and know their methodologies, thus earning their critiques and their respect as valued leaders and resources to protect the heritages of their nations, peoples, and communities.

Led by Leroy Little Bear, an eminent Blackfoot philosopher and scholar, now retired from the University of Lethbridge and the American Indian Programs at Harvard University, we worked together to solve the mystery of the box. He enriched our analyses and imagined the possibility of a postcolonial society that would enable us to create our own sustaining and nourishing realities. He gently urged us to respect the process of developing ourselves in healing and renewing ways and to dream for those equitable and shared benefits that we felt were necessary. He led our dialogues to sharpen our insights gained from our experiences, and he helped us to confirm our commitment to forms of inquiry both timely and exacting, as we developed new networks of solidarity.

Under the Medicine Wheel processes of the northern Plains, the sessions were organized around four related themes: mapping colonialism, diagnosing colonialism, healing colonized Indigenous peoples, and imagining postcolonial visions. As we shared our thoughts in our group dialogues, we sought to address some of the essential questions of colonization. What is it in the nature of European cultures that has resulted in the oppression of so many peoples worldwide? What is it in the nature of Indigenous peoples' culture that has allowed colonization to happen? What can we do now, and what principles can we bring forward to achieve these visions from those ten days together?

The participants shared their personal and collective pain, anguish, and analyses of their experiences with colonialism. Each had experienced most or some aspects of colonization and was enmeshed in reforming colonial governments, laws, education, economies, and institutions that sought to erase their identities, languages, and cultures, creating new colonized identities that would be impoverished in the wake of violence and destruction. Each had experienced a side of the box that others had not experienced; for some of us, there were parts of the box that we could not fully access but we still felt their presence.

These sharing sessions and dialogues are enfolded within these essays, which represent modern Indigenous voices and syntheses of the experience of colonization and Indigenous thought in many styles and from many different points of view. Many of the essays contain the "orality" of Indigenous traditions, aspects that could not be changed without destroying these voices. These essays declare an Indigenous framework of meaning and of what has been destructive that is rarely shared. They provide new frameworks for understanding how and why colonization has been so pervasive among Indigenous peoples, as well as what Indigenous peoples desire and imagine as a better life in a postcolonial context. They also offer existing and new methodologies, conceptual designs, and approaches for implementing the healing and cultural restoration of Indigenous peoples across disciplines.

The writings seek to move beyond the existing Indigenous experience of colonization by liberating Indigenous thought, practices, and discourses rather than by relying on existing Eurocentric or colonial theory. Indigenous thinkers use the term "postcolonial" to describe a symbolic strategy for shaping a desirable future, not an existing reality. The term is an aspirational practice, goal, or idea that the delegates used to imagine a new form of society that they desired to create. Yet we recognized that postcolonial societies do not exist. Rather, we acknowledged the colonial mentality and structures that still exist in all societies and nations and the neocolonial tendencies that resist decolonization in the contemporary world. Such structures and tendencies can only be resisted and healed by reliance on Indigenous knowledge and its imaginative processes.

Postcolonial Indigenous thought should not be confused with postcolonial theory in literature. Although they are related endeavours, postcolonial Indigenous thought also emerges from the inability of Eurocentric theory to deal with the complexities of colonialism and its assumptions. Postcolonial Indigenous thought is based on our pain and our experiences, and it refuses to allow others to appropriate this pain and these experiences. It rejects the use of any Eurocentric theory or its categories.

The writings in this book firmly embed the fundamental concept that Indigenous knowledge exists and is a legitimate research issue. Many parts of the existing Eurocentric academy have not fully accepted this principle, arguing that there is no such thing as an Indigenous perspective. Postcolonial, Aboriginal, and postmodern scholars have had to confront this position, as they have had to confront the institutions in which they function. Most delegates from university communities were having trouble articulating the differences between these two systems of knowledge, but through the shared dialogues they became aware of the singularity of Eurocentric thought—even if some of the issues around the diversity of approaches to life and nature remained unresolved. They came to understand the prevailing authority of Eurocentric discourses and how the unreflective dominance of these discourses in academia has led to the historical and contemporary immunity to understanding and tolerating Indigenous knowledge.

Indigenous knowledge, including its oral modes of transmission, is a vital, integral, and significant process for Indigenous educators and scholars. It has been upheld by the Supreme Court of Canada as a legitimate form for understanding and transmitting Indigenous knowledge, history, and consciousness. The Supreme Court of Canada has ordered the legal profession, in *Delgamuukw v. The Queen* (1997), to include and respect Indigenous oral traditions in standards of evidence, overruling centuries of development of the British rules of evidence. The justices of the Supreme Court held that Indigenous oral traditions are legitimate sources of evidence and ordered the courts to modify rules of evidence and procedures to acknowledge and value these traditions. This decision offers a powerful analogy for the interpretive monopoly of existing standards of research scholarship. If the courts are required to consider oral traditions, then all other decision makers should likewise consider the validity of oral traditions, including oral dissemination within Aboriginal and non-Aboriginal communities, as significant sources for the distribution and dissemination of Aboriginal knowledge and scholarship.

The necessity of bringing forward Aboriginal knowledge, perspectives, and research is being increasingly felt at all levels of scholarship. In a speech to the university community, the president of the Social Sciences and Humanities Research Council of Canada aptly pointed out that the traditions of the university to "publish or perish" have been globally tested and that the new agenda for universities will need to be "go public or perish" (Marc Renaud, Sorokin Lecture, University of Saskatchewan, Saskatoon, February 4, 1999).

Indigenous scholarship, along with research that requires moral dialogue with and the participation of Indigenous communities, is the foundation for postcolonial transformation. This scholarship evolves from a need to comprehend, resist, and transform the crises related to the dual concerns of the effect that colonization has had on Indigenous peoples and the ongoing erosion of Indigenous languages, knowledge, and culture as a result of colonization. It has involved clarifying the contested interests that occur in the many disciplines and fields of thought.

Much of the focus of Indigenous scholarship in the early years was on liberal solutions that attempted to make modal adjustments to existing institutions and their modes of delivery. There has been a growing awareness of late that we need a more systemic analysis of the complex and subtle ideologies that continue to shape postcolonial Indigenous educational policy and pedagogy. The writings in this book document action-oriented research practices. These practices identify sites of oppression and emancipation. They also support the agenda of Indigenous scholarship, which is to transform Eurocentric theory so that it will not only include and properly value Indigenous knowledge, thought, and heritage in all levels of education, curriculum, and professional practice but also develop a cooperative and dignified strategy that will invigorate and animate Indigenous languages, cultures, knowledge, and vision in academic structures.

This book offers a complex arrangement of conscientization, resistance, and transformative praxis that seeks to transform the dual crises related to colonization and culture. It is constructed on the multidisciplinary foundation essential to remedying the acknowledged failure of the current Eurocentric system in addressing educational equity for Indigenous peoples, in particular the diverse groups of disempowered peoples around the world. Similarly, it recognizes that Indigenous education is not one site of struggle but multiple struggles in multiple sites. Thus, these diverse struggles cannot simply be reduced to singular, one-dimensional solutions. Interventions and transformative strategies must be correspondingly complex, and they must be able to engage with and react to the multiple circumstances and shapes of oppression, exploitation, assimilation, colonization, racism, genderism, ageism, and the many other strategies of marginalization. This collection seeks not to resolve all tensions or their complex interfaces but to acknowledge and expose their existence and to take account of the factors as they appear in multiple sites, including epistemology, curriculum, schools, and teacher education (Smith).

This book seeks to clarify postcolonial Indigenous thought at the end of the twentieth century. It is not a definitive work, but it is a good reflection. It represents the voices of the first generation of Indigenous scholars and seeks to bring those voices, their analyses, and their dreams of a decolonized context further into the academic arena. It urges an agenda of restoration within a multidisciplinary context for human dignity and the collective dignity of Indigenous peoples. It recognizes the existing right of self-determination, and it urges Indigenous peoples to promote, develop, exercise, and maintain their orders and laws and to determine their political status and pursue freely their cultural destiny within supportive social and economic development.

One Indigenous educator, Nata Inn ni Maki—Sacred Hawk Woman (Rose von Thater), has written about the knowledge and experience that she gained at the gathering:

We were bringing to conscious recognition those elements foreign to our knowing that had entwined themselves within us, sapping us of our natural strength. We were seeing the experiences that had defined our lives with new eyes. We were looking at our history, accounting for its impact, taking ourselves to the doorways of understanding, discovering new possibilities, other strategies, watching as sources of power and strength emerged to reveal themselves in a new light. From this place and from these days together we were selecting, like artists, the elements that would tell a new story, taking from the past, re-ordering the present, envisioning a future that felt very much like a vision that had been held for us until we could reach out and hold it for ourselves. (Personal communication, June 27, 1997)

Indigenous peoples worldwide are still undergoing trauma and stress from genocide and the destruction of their lives by colonization. Their stories are often silenced as they are made to endure other atrocities. Many of these Indigenous peoples were unable to attend the institute to share their stories, despite their efforts. For them and for all Indigenous peoples worldwide, we seek to initiate dialogue, advance a postcolonial discourse, and work actively for a transformation of colonial thought. It becomes our greatest challenge and our honour to move beyond the analysis of naming the site of our oppression to act in individual and collective ways to effect change at many levels and to live in a good way. These writers are actively seeking to reject the categories assigned to them and to make a difference in creating sustainable communities. Our efforts are to reveal the inconsistencies, challenge the assumptions and the taken for granted, expose the ills, and search from within ourselves and our Indigenous heritages for the principles that will guide our children's future in a dignified life. Our efforts are enfolded within the deep meaning of poet Antonio Machado's beautiful thought: "Caminante, no hay camino, se hace camino al andar" ("Traveller, there are no roads. The road is created as we walk it [together]") (as cited in Macedo 183).

Using the Medicine Wheel to guide and illustrate the interconnectedness and continuous flux of ideas, I have used the four directions of the Sacred Circle Wheel (the winds of West, North, East, and South) to characterize the divisions of this interrelated dialogue. The Medicine Wheel illustrates symbolically that all things are interconnected and related, spiritual, complex, and powerful. Indigenous writers have explained elsewhere about the teachings of the Sacred Directions (Battiste, Introduction; Calliou; Hampton). I start with the Western Door, an unlikely place for most Aboriginal people to begin their journeys, as most Aboriginal people begin their ceremonies with the East. However, my friend Eber Hampton, in "Redefinition of Indian Education," has offered his understandings of the meanings of the directions taken from within traditional ceremonies, and for me the Western Door is appropriate for the theme of mapping colonialism because the west is the direction of "Autumn, the end of summer, and the precursor of winter. On the great plains, thunderstorms roll in from the west. In Lakota cosmology, the good red road of life runs north and south and the road of death runs east and west. The coming of Western civilization (meaning western European), with its Western forms of education, to this continent was the autumn of traditional Indian education" (31). The Western Door thus begins with mapping the contours of the ideas that have shaped the last era of domination underpinning modern society and the varied faces of colonization as it is maintained in the present era. [. . .]

The Northern Door is the "home of winter." Long nights of darkness evoke feelings of struggle and cold; long winters are when our very survival is challenged. Indigenous peoples are challenged by winter, but from their experience they learn endurance and wisdom. The north, as Eber [Hampton] has pointed out, is cold and dark, with just a hint of light that makes it possible for us to hope and dream. This direction represents the theme of diagnosing colonialism. Whenever I teach my course Decolonizing Aboriginal Education, I find that my graduate students are enriched by the diagnosis of colonialism and by their own unravelling of their experience, whether they are the colonizers or the colonized. The Northern Door is the direction from which the diagnosis of colonialism emanates. It goes beyond the practice of colonial oppression to explore the unquestioned and conflicting assumptions that underpin oppressive relationships.

The Eastern Door is the direction of spring, of the sun rising. "The east is, through its association with the sunrise, a place of beginnings and enlightenment, and a place where new knowledge can be created or received to bring about harmony or right relations" (Calliou 67). In the morning, as we turn to the east, we pray for our children, our nations, and our future generations. We are conscious of how so many of our peoples have suffered through the winter, and now we look to find new ways to warm, nourish, and heal our fragile spirits. We can turn to the Earth, as Linda Hogan suggests, to find a different yield or to invoke new understandings from the collective efforts of Indigenous peoples, whether they come from political thought, constitutional reform, or international law. The Eastern Door of healing colonized indigenous peoples presents the intellectual and practical challenges to current ways of pursuing humane relationships. It is a process of healing ourselves, our collective identities, our communities, and the spirit that sustains us.

Finally, the Southern Door is "the direction of summer, the home of the sun, and the time of fullest growth" (Hampton 28). The summer resounds with the healthy sounds of our peoples as we convene to honour our teachings, our elders, and our ancestors in ceremonies and gatherings. It calls to mind long summer days and nights in dialogue and laughter and sharing around campfires, at feasts, pow wows, potlatches, and multiple ceremonies. Our traditions, as Eber has pointed out, preserve and sustain us. Thus, the final section of this book resounds with hope and anticipation as we turn to our traditions to preserve our communities, our education, our governance, and our future through focusing on the integrity of Aboriginal knowledge, systems, and their applications. It offers the foundation for reclaiming ourselves and our voice, as we *vision the Indigenous renaissance* based on Indigenous knowledge and heritage.

Raising consciousness of the struggles of oppressed Indigenous peoples throughout the world has been an intensely challenging objective but one that Erica-Irene Daes has achieved quietly and laboriously in her role as chairperson of the United Nations Working Group on Indigenous Populations. In her essay, "The Experience of Colonization Around the World," Erica introduces the theme of mapping colonization. She acknowledges that the anguished and urgent voices that she hears persistently are linked inextricably with aggression, violence, repression, and domination. These acts of oppression tear at the very spirit of individuals, denigrating the relevance and meaningfulness of their individual human lives. But being oppressed and marginalized, they are also, she notes, closest to an understanding of their oppression and to the sources of their healing and renewal. She outlines the social and psychological process of self-discovery in an emerging postcolonial world and the concomitant need for rebuilding alliances, making commitments, and holding nations accountable for their peoples. Her note of optimism is a fresh breeze on a still, hot summer day. [. . .]

Works Cited

Battiste, M. "Micmac Literacy and Cognitive Assimilation." *Indian Education in Canada: The Legacy.* Ed. J. Barman, Y. Hébert, and D. McCaskill. Vancouver: UBC P, 1986. 23-44.

—. Introduction. *First Nations Education in Canada: The Circle Unfolds.* Ed. M. Battiste and J. Barman. Vancouver: UBC P, 1995. vii-xx.

Calliou, S. "Peacekeeping Actions at Home: A Medicine Wheel Model for a Peace-Keeping Pedagogy." *First Nations Education in Canada: The Circle Unfolds.* Ed. M. Battiste and J. Barman. Vancouver: UBC P, 1995. 47-72.

Daes, Erica-Irene. "Prologue: The Experience of Colonization Around the World." *Reclaiming Indigenous Voice and Vision.* Ed. Marie Battiste. Vancouver: UBC P, 2000. 3-8.

Hampton, E. "Redefinition of Indian Education." *First Nations Education in Canada: The Circle Unfolds.* Ed. M. Battiste and J. Barman. Vancouver: UBC P, 1995. 5-46.

Hogan, Linda. "A Different Yield." *Reclaiming Indigenous Voice and Vision.* Ed. Marie Battiste. Vancouver: UBC P, 2000. 115-23.

Macedo, D. *Literacies of Power: What Americans Are Not Allowed to Know.* Boulder: Westview, 1994.

Smith, G.H. "The Development of Kaupapa Maori: Theory and Praxis." Diss, University of Auckland, New Zealand, 1997.

PART VI

Critiques of the (Canadian) Postcolonial

18

"CANADIAN (TW)INK:
SURVIVING THE WHITE-OUTS"*

Gary Boire

for Cushla Parekowhai

A fascinating yet predictable feature of much post-colonial writing is an obsession with the writing of an authentic national history. Post-colonial writers are obsessed with the *bête noire* of an imperial past; either the absence of an intelligible and acceptable history, or the oppressive presence of an unintelligible and inflicted one becomes increasingly important to them. Prompted by what Albert Wendt calls the awareness that a "society is what it remembers," many writers return repeatedly to certain post-colonial imperatives of historical revisionism: initiation, inscription, reception, rejection, reclamation, or a combination of some or all of these acts. In countries as geographically distant, but as politically similar as Canada, Australia, New Zealand, even West Africa and Azania, both modernist and post-modernist alike return compulsively to the inheritance/imposition of Eurocentric (or American) forms of historical explanation.

These "new histories," then, in their search for new futures, enter into a dialectic with a vanished (but unforgettable) world. In many cases these fictions—works like Canadian Joy Kogawa's *Obasan*, Australian John Romeril's *The Floating World*, or New Zealander Vincent O'Sullivan's *Shuriken*—take on a revelationary as well as revolutionary role. In their attempts to probe and reveal hidden elements of the national narrative, they subvert and disturb the "symmetries of the official [presumably fictional] versions" of their own pasts;[1] in so doing they fulfil Chinua Achebe's optimistic view of the writer as a social and cultural liberationist:

> There is a saying in Ibo that a man who can't tell where the rain began to beat him cannot know where he dried his body. The writer can tell the people where the rain began to beat them. After all the writer's duty . . . is to explore in depth the human condition. In Africa he cannot perform this task unless he has a proper sense of history. (8)

---

* *Essays on Canadian Writing* 35 (1987): 1-16.

Underlying this historicizing impulse, at the base of modernist attempts to reclaim colony from empire, is a faith in the social and cultural capabilities of narrative: the flesh made word, history's old words made new. To mark, to write, to erect a sign, to locate oneself within a perimeter, within the contexts of either an apparently vacant or client society: the modernist act of Crusoesque inscription orders the chaos of silence or unintelligibility. Historical narrativization places the displaced sense of a colonized settler society; it attempts to achieve priority, self-creation, origin. (As opposed, say, to a truly Derridean form of writing which always seeks to move beyond boundaries, to deconstruct priorities, origins, teleologies.)

Interestingly, current writing in Canada (both literary and academic) manifests a similar trend. In her recent essay, "Canadian Historiographic Metafiction," Linda Hutcheon remarks:

> To write history—or historical fiction—is equally to narrate, to reconstruct by means of selection and interpretation. History (like realist fiction) is *made* by its writers, even if events are made to seem to speak for themselves. Narrativization is a central form of human comprehension. As Fredric Jameson argues, it is one of the ways we impose meaning and formal coherence on the chaos of events. . . . Hayden White, for instance, sees the link between novelist and historian in their shared "emplotting" strategies of exclusion, emphasis, and subordination of elements of a story. (231-32)

Implicit in Hutcheon's statements is a view of historical narrativization as a readerly act, something I'll return to. At this point I want to consider White's contention (as paraphrased above). Any act of remembering or interpretation involves selection; any centring presupposes marginalization. The postmodern texts mentioned above (*Obasan*, *The Floating World*, and *Shuriken*) and in Hutcheon's essay, for example, subordinate inherited foregroundings of the national myth and, in a politically committed way, focus on those elements traditionally backgrounded in Canadian history's documents. The act of exclusion or subordination is performed self-consciously within an obviously leftist political dimension.

What interests me in this discussion are some of the political dimensions involved in the writing and reading of many modernist nationalistic texts—particularly works which purport to initiate "new futures," and which try to articulate Canada into a new, more intelligible imaginative existence. In what ways did the Canadian modernists define their own relationship with Canada's imperialistic past (and present)? In their heroic attempts to evolve a decolonized poetic, did they in fact construct the basis for a decolonized society? Or did they, in both simple and complex ways, help to perpetuate an already existing state of historical amnesia? I want to explore a significant, recurring exclusion from modernist constructions of the national identity: the exclusion of Canada's indigenous populations. It seems that in their attempts to valorize the here and now, the modernists (and many of their recent critics) duplicate in both their meanings and their forms many of the historical and ideological erasures of then and there. In the process of reclaiming a "real" history for Canada, they impose yet another unreality on themselves, their readers, and their invisible victims. In short, I want to ask what these significant ideological fissures in modernist narrativizations of Canada are; and, more importantly, how and why these gaps are still perpetuated in *our* reading and teaching of Canadian ink.[2]

* * *

Modernist declarations of a Canadian cultural independence are coloured both by what Michael Neill has called "the nightmare of a missing history" (41)—Birney's "lack of ghosts"—and by daydreams of a fully articulated and rosy future.[3] As Sandra Djwa has shown in "'A New Soil,'" one freedom offered by an independent seat at Versailles was the opportunity to populate what was perceived an empty space: the vast, snowy whiteness of Canada was a blank canvas in need of paint, a blank page in need of inc/k (in all senses of that pun: the tool of inscription; an incorporated, coherent body of the imagination; and a host of truly professional writers engaged in the business of identification [3-5]).

Lawren Harris illustrates the general fervour of the enterprise:

> In Canada, with little or no tradition and background, our creative individuals find new adventures in imaginative and intuitive living. The land is mostly virgin, fresh and full-replenishing. This North of ours is a source of spiritual flow which can create through us. (4)

What is perhaps now most noticeable—in the aftermath of George Ryga's *The Ecstasy of Rita Joe*, Rudy Wiebe's *The Temptations of Big Bear*, Matt Cohen's *Wooden Hunters*, even Farley Mowat's *The Desperate People*—is the fact that from the midst of these declarations of a decolonized aesthetic, paeans for an indigenous art, Canada's indigenous peoples are conspicuously absent. In the process of centring himself, the self-styled pioneering artist either marginalizes native people or renders them altogether invisible. The indigene is either submerged and drowned in the mainstream of Canadian discourse, or pushed directly to its edge. Here, in Harris, a shadow of the image of the noble savage lurks just at the periphery of the neo-romantic praise of "intuitive living" and the "source of spiritual flow." The descriptive and revealing word for absence, "virgin," implies a linguistic, and disguises a more political, form of rape.

Perhaps more illustrative is F.R. Scott's unconsciously revealing poem, "Laurentian Shield." It is structured around a number of predictable, evocative images: the MacLennanesque Odysseus figure ("nomad, no-man") which suggests both a centripetal view of the nationalist odyssey (returning to an origin) *and* the nightmare of possible state shipwreck ("no-man" in the void of the new land, persecuted by absent gods, natural forces, and foreign multinationals). Complementing this is the recurrent pattern of the blank page—"Not written on by history, empty as paper" (91)—an absence that can be made a presence by the articulating power of the decolonized writer. Scott's pregnant image of an industrial, poetical revolution evokes a sense of the gradual overlaying of the land with spoken and written forms of the European tongue (as Robinson Crusoe overlays Friday with his European language!). The poem then concludes with yet another Greek myth, Deucalion and Pyrrha—types, apparently, for the new writers who will transform the bare rocks of Canada into poetical (and industrial) children—children who will continue to echo the modernists' original words.

Scott here shares in a recurrent post-colonial modernist dilemma: the horror of the void untouched by European mythmaking, unmapped by his own culture's imagination. Like so many post-colonial writers, he calls out blindly for a set of natural symbols—a series of signs derived from the land itself. Interestingly, Scott, the political activist, then chooses a deliberately mythical form of closure for his own poem, a closure which paradoxically derives from the ancient, foreign past, while it predicts an indigenous Canadian future which, in turn, does not accommodate indigenous Canadian peoples. The paradox is furthered when the poem ends and becomes that which is identified (in the poem itself) as missing in the new land. The poem, in effect, enacts the circular pattern of renewal which it idealizes.

Most striking in Scott's poem, in much nationalist writing of the period, and especially in academic commentaries on this writing, is what may be termed the "Boer syndrome" of Canadian decolonization. The liberating dialectic formulated by the modernists in Canada has but one essential focus: the interaction of colonialist and empire. It is a dialectic that concentrates not so much on the colonized at the hands of the colonizer, but on the experience the recolonizer enjoys at the expense of the twice-colonized. There is little awareness of the colonialist's own colonization of indigenous peoples, virtually no guilt at rendering entire cultures invisible through the heroical act of naming a found land. For all its very real radicalism, Scott's poem nevertheless makes no real attempt to restructure the present through reference to a real past (something I'll return to in my discussion of MacLennan). At no point does Scott ask the introspective question of the middle ground: "What right have I to claim turangawaewae [a space to stand] in this country?" (Pearson 161). Interestingly, the entourage of academic commentators has followed suit: a fairly recent gloss on "Laurentian Shield," for example, merely reiterates uncritically the idealistic (and imperialistic) assumptions of the poetical text. When discussing the "new vision" of the Canadian landscape generated by the Group of Seven, Sandra Djwa remarks: "Although immeasurably old in geologic time, *because the land was unpeopled* it was seen as 'young' and 'virile.' Canada was a country whose face was yet to be painted, whose voice was yet to be found, whose history was yet to be written" (4; emphasis added).

One now hesitates over the curious one-sidedness of the cultural view developed in Canadian modernist writing and perpetuated by generations of admiring readers trained in New Criticism. Just as clichés such as "frontier" or "wilderness" tend to depopulate geographical spaces, this majority construction shared by readers and critics tends either to marginalize, subordinate, or altogether exclude native peoples from the voice of Canadian Identity.[4] As Scott himself argues in the poem, Canada was inarticulate, uninscribed, empty, before the introduction of the European tongue. But the image of the blank page is, after all, only one side of the sheet and, in a poem so obsessed with origin and naming, it seems curious that there is virtually no concern with the original, indigenous name of the Laurentian area itself. In the process of creating a poetical cartography—putting Canada on a map of their own—the modernists continue to work within the perimeters of the majority culture, participating in and encouraging the ideological procedure of historical erasure. As Robin Fisher, an historian of both Maori and Canadian West Coast peoples, remarks (Bruce Trigger's book may also be consulted):

> In Canada the relationship between the native Indians and the immigrant Europeans has not, until recently, been a major concern of historians. In contrast to other former British settlement colonies in Australia or Africa, the aboriginal people have been seen as a peripheral rather than a central concern in the study of Canada's past; or, as some have it, the Indian provides a "background" for Canadian history. (xi)

At this point one must begin to question precisely what political analogues correspond to, or underline, the modernists' declarations of independence: a golden-age charter of universal rights or Ian Smith's Unilateral Declaration of Independence? What, in fact, distinguishes white, middle-class Canadians from their compeers in Aotearoa, Australia, or Kanaky and Azania? (Neill originates this question by asking what distinguishes New Zealand's white settlers from those in the last three countries I have named [47].) Even more intriguing is what, if anything, distinguishes the modernists' attempts to create an original voice from yet one more layer of linguistic colonization? In their search for this initiating word, to what extent do they delude themselves and overlay an already existing language, "Endlessly repeating something we cannot [or will not?] hear" (Scott 91)? Djwa's optimistic gloss on the Group of Seven may well be counterpointed by Sydney Moko Mead in New Zealand: "the Maori people are imprisoned in the myths of the Pakeha and our prison walls are words and stories which appear to me to be as impenetrable as thick concrete walls" (37).

* * *

A work that illustrates these many problems in writing and reading examples of modernist decolonization is Hugh MacLennan's 1945 novel, *Two Solitudes*. Although generally agreed to be seriously flawed, the book has enjoyed an illustrious commercial career. It won the 1946 Governor-General's Award for fiction; it remains ensconced in university syllabuses and government book donation programmes; and it is a standard offering in British, Canadian, and American publishers' lists. Elspeth Cameron, MacLennan's biographer, has outlined the book's phenomenal sales success and quotes, as her cover blurb, some remarks of Margaret Laurence's concerning MacLennan: he is, we are told, Canada's "first truly non-colonial writer, writing faithfully out of his own perceptions of his land and his people. . . . His books will endure." In the search for the "Great Canadian Identity" (and for the writer who will tell *his* people "where the rain began to beat them"), *Two Solitudes* is promoted and distributed by a ruling majority culture as a partial embodiment of those ideals. (See Terry Sturm's discussion of book distribution as a form of continuing colonization.) Most interesting, however, in a critical way, is the fact that MacLennan's mediocre book is encouraged to endure; how—both as a written narrative and as a readerly event—it duplicates and perpetuates the ideological values of the majority culture which is itself generated by a white, English, middle-class assemblage of romantic liberal humanists. The kinds of historical amnesia outlined so far infiltrate the book so thoroughly that *Two Solitudes* is truly, as MacLennan describes it in his foreword, a novel *of* Canada—but in ways undreamt of in MacLennan's philanthropy.

Like Scott's "Laurentian Shield," the book addresses the plight of a late-settler imagination lost inside an empty and unintelligible landscape. As MacLennan remarked in a 1971 interview, "When I started writing this was an unrecognizable country to the world and to itself; somebody had to do something like this" (132). In other words, *Two Solitudes* is, like Scott's poem, a fiction *about* the necessity of its own creation: a narrative about the need for narrative. Canada again figures as a vast blankness, a literary void, the untracked new frontier.

Though decidedly set in a post-settlement society, the novel opens with a panoramic sweep of what was (in Scott's words) "Inarticulate, arctic. . . . waiting [and] wanting. . . . A tongue to shape the vowels of its productivity" (91). In his attempts to create the right context for a harmonization of *the* two cultures—French and English—MacLennan depends on an idyllic vision of geographical harmony and amplitude:

> Northwest of Montreal, through a valley always in sight of the low mountains of the Laurentian Shield, the Ottawa River flows out of Protestant Ontario into Catholic Quebec. It comes down broad and ale-coloured and joins the Saint Lawrence, the two streams embrace the pan of Montreal Island, the Ottawa merges and loses itself, and the mainstream moves northeastward a thousand miles to the sea. . . . From the Ontario border down to the beginning of the estuary, the farmland runs in two delicate bands along the shores, with roads like a pair of village main streets a thousand miles long, each parallel to the river. All the good land was broken long ago, occupied and divided among seigneurs and their sons, and then among tenants and their sons. (3)

In an ever-widening series of expansions, the narrator then moves from the farms to the forests, to the hills, and finally to the tundra where "Nothing lives . . . but a few prospectors and hard-rock miners and Mounted Policemen and animals and the flies that brood over the barrens in summer like haze. Winters make it a universe of snow" (4). Initially the passages work hard to establish a neo-romantic view of landscape, history, and settlement. As one of Lawren Harris' "creative individuals," the narrator seeks some kind of earthy analogue for his own themes: hence the deliberate (and vaguely awkward) emphasis on balance, harmonization, equilibrium. This "emplotting" emphasis, however, should alert us to its implied opposite: the "subordination" of certain "elements of the story" (Hutcheon 232). History is here couched in the fairy-tale phrase "long ago"—a phrase which distorts the full implications of Canadian settlement. (See Bruce Trigger for a more extensive treatment of this idea.) The nostalgic genealogy of *seigneur* to son, and tenant to son, disguises the actual presettlement history of the cycle: the displacement, containment, and deracination of those before. Within the scheme of a congenial patrilineal descent, Canada "begins" with a generally unexamined notion and a critically unexplored word: "occupation." An emptiness is made full, apparently, by both Europeans and their language.

This kind of erasure continues in MacLennan's conventional image of the wilderness where we discover, like Columbus, nothing except animal life (raw resources), capitalist speculators, and agents of the law—all necessities for the perpetuation of the ideologies of a post-war nation bent on its own productivity. The Indians and Inuit who *do* live on the tundra and who occupy the French-language narrativizations of Yves Theriault are nowhere to be seen. *Their* historical presence, in other words, would pull the rug out from under this recurrent illusion of blank spaces and determinant origins. The entire process of writing (and of our subsequent directed reading) erases simple historical facts, replacing them with an idyllic image of agricultural development. *Two Solitudes* exemplifies this process which recalls, rather uncomfortably, Marx's comments on the nature of remembering primitive accumulation:

> This primitive accumulation plays in Political Economy about the same part as original sin in theology. Adam bit the apple, and thereupon sin fell on the human race. Its origin is supposed to be explained when it is told as an anecdote of the past. In times long gone by there were two sorts of people; one, the diligent, intelligent, and, above all, frugal élite; the other, lazy rascals, spending their substance, and more, in riotous living. The legend of theological original sin tells us certainly how man came to be condemned to eat his bread in the sweat of his brow; but the history of economic original sin reveals to us that there are people to whom this is by no means essential. Never mind! Thus it came to pass that the former sort accumulated wealth, and the latter sort had at last nothing to sell except their own skins. And from this original sin dates the poverty of the great majority that, despite all its labour, has up to now nothing to sell but itself, and the wealth of the few that increases constantly although they have long ceased to work. Such insipid childishness is every day preached to us in the defense of property. . . . In actual history it is notorious that conquest, enslavement, robbery, murder, briefly force, play the great part. In the tender annals of Political Economy, the idyllic reigns from time immemorial. . . . As a matter of fact, the methods of primitive accumulation are anything but idyllic. (784-85)

In the novel's very opening, then, MacLennan duplicates the state processes of historical erasure *cum* romanticization. He deploys words to occupy the apparent blankness of both his country and his page, but MacLennan does not so much fill an emptiness as colonize an existing cultural history by rendering it altogether invisible. MacLennan's writing of *Two Solitudes* constitutes a horrible misreading of history itself. The process of writing Canada into existence, of rewriting the wrongs of inherited stories, necessitates a careful reading of the past. The author confronts the text of history, interprets and orders these already constituted events, and, in the process of writing, fixes history in a meaningful and coherent form. But in MacLennan's case, this interpretation involves an idyllic harmonization, an unreal fixity emblemized in Heather's paintings of the landscape. History, with all its indeterminacies and gaps, its chaotic assemblage of events, is encapsulated in an organically organized, intelligible narrative. The novel then functions as a symbol (albeit a crude one) of transcendence—precisely the historical and literary ideal posited by the New Critics in the midst of the Cold War. The paradox is that within this imaginative historicization of Canada, history itself is excluded—the real chronicle in which the indigene is exploited, marginalized, and finally removed.

Most intriguing, however, is the fact that as MacLennan's narrative proceeds, images of the indigene gradually infiltrate the text. As if counter to authorial intention, Canada's own imperialist past lurks just at the edge of the narrative: the indigene, demanding representation, *is* incorporated—but always as an image of unintelligibility, or self-projected victimization.[5] Consider, for example, a brief portrait of Captain Yardley: "The captain came into the store nearly every day and he paid cash for whatever he bought. He spoke French, but with terrible grammar and a queer accent mixed with many English words . . . worse than an Indian, Polycarpe Drouin said" (20). Ostensibly, the passage props up one of MacLennan's recurring obsessions—the harmonious, organic blending of the two races. Thirty-three years after *Two Solitudes* was published, MacLennan reminisced that "What has divided Canada in the past has not been language. . . . It has been the point of view of the élites and rulers on both sides of the linguistic fence" (291). Here Yardley enacts with Drouin the proper basis of racial interchange: a democratic, capitalist blend of both commerce and language. But, interestingly, MacLennan here perpetuates the exclusive focus of the modernist dialectic; there are only two sides to the European linguistic fence. The original languages of Canada (perhaps Scott's incomprehensible one?) appear peripherally, are mentioned off-handedly, and are thus presented as a symbol of incomprehensibility. This technique resurfaces later when Heather muses on her family: "Even if they knew of the marriage, it would still be no easier to make them understand what passed in her mind than it would be to converse with Eskimos" (348).

In all these instances, it seems, MacLennan struggles with, but cannot resolve, the moral and intellectual dilemma of whether to include that which society demands be excluded. As a result, his text offers a guilty liberal solution: the indigene is present, but only in an absent and abstract way. The recolonizing culture(s)—exemplified collectively by the figure of Ulysses, who is in turn identified with the semi-autobiographical figure of Paul—are centred, the twice-colonized rendered invisible in this "novel of Canada." George Ryga's Indian character, Jaimie Paul, points directly at this procedure when he complains: "They don't know what it's like . . . to stand in line an' nobody sees you!" (*Ecstasy* 160).

* * *

So far I've looked at three examples of Canadian modernist writing: an extract from a manifesto, a poem, and a novel. In one way or another, each text addresses the problems involved in articulating Canada to itself; in each case the writer operates within what Sandra Djwa has shrewdly identified as a neo-romantic framework, valuing intuition, a sense of the land, and the power of the word to achieve national identity. All three pieces use similar strategies of persuasion, notably a romanticized view of history and settlement, as well as Greek myths of transformation and Odyssean questing. Ultimately all three incorporate an ideal of organicism: in both their form and meanings they envisage both a society and a literary text which is organically complete, harmonious, integrated—an artefact in which the various parts work symbiotically for the common good, each in its hierarchical place. (As Terry Eagleton has fumed, it is "hardly surprising to find [this kind of] symbol, or the literary artefact as such, being regularly offered . . . as an ideal model of human society itself. If only the lower orders were to forget their grievances and pull together for the good of all, much tedious turmoil could be avoided" [*Literary Theory* 22].)

I have argued, furthermore, that this process of writing a national narrative has mimicked state processes of historical erasure. Our authors have found themselves in a state of virtual cognitive dissonance, a condition in which a choice (though a morally dubious one), once made, must be justified and rationalized at all costs. *This* process of rationalization—which idealizes organic text and society—depends on politically significant repressions in the literary process of remembering and writing the meanings of Canadian identity. The result is a curiously hygienic, socially acceptable, but historically and politically whitewashed version of Canada's own colonizations of the void. Harris and Scott perpetuate a colonizing image of blankness; MacLennan perpetuates an equally colonizing image of innocence, heroism, and romantic optimism:

> The result of these two group-legends was a Canada oddly naive, so far without any real villains, without overt cruelty or criminal memories, a country strangely innocent in its groping individual common sense, intent on doing the right thing in the way some children are, tongue-tied because it felt others would not be interested in what it had to say; loyal, skilled and proud, race-memories lonely in great spaces. (*Two Solitudes* 340)

The question, of course, is how and why these ideologically sound images are perpetuated and fostered within the Canadian academy, how the words "university syllabus" evoke the literary *and* political word "canon."

Most interesting in these modernist writings, complete as they are with mythical, cyclical, organic closures, is the fact that they share in, indeed they enact by articulating, the readerly ideals held by a majority—the white, English, controlling class. Linda Hutcheon, citing Hayden White, points out this implicit will to power contained within the forms of realist, modernist fiction:

To write either history or historical fiction is equally to raise the question of power and control. As Hayden White has remarked, "the very
claim to have discerned some kind of formal coherence in the historical record brings with it theories of the nature of the historical world
and of historical knowledge itself which have ideological implications."
The creator or discerner of that formal coherence is in a position of
power—power over facts, clearly, but also power over readers. (235)

This is a power idealized and perpetuated by generations of Canadian critics
who themselves have been colonized by yet another colonial agent: the
Anglo-American school of New Critics. This is neither the time nor place to
examine in detail the effects of foreign hiring in Canadian universities during the fifties and sixties, but it is appropriate to muse on the legacy of this
policy which continues to exert considerable influence on Canadian criticism.

Consider Djwa on Scott, Cameron or Laurence on MacLennan, or indeed,
the conventional criticism that proliferates in scholarly journals and university classrooms across Canada. What emerges in so many "appreciations" of the
Canadian modernist movement is a duplication in criticism of the same
dehistoricized ideals contained within the literary texts. The base of critical
activity is an approving, unquestioning, acceptance of New Critical standards
which constitute a depoliticized view of art as a psychological harmonization
of the social, an aesthetic resolution of opposition and conflict into an organic whole. In this sense, this kind of reading, like the writing which is its subject, serves to perpetuate rather than question the prevailing values and
beliefs of a ruling élite. It participates in what Terry Eagleton has described
as "the crisis of the critical institution," which is the fact that "criticism today
lacks all substantive social function" (*The Function* 7). Or does it? A critical
institution which mimics the ideological mimicry of texts which, in turn,
develop an ideology of apathy, does in effect perform a politically valuable,
narcotic function. It blurs our national memories, encourages us (and our
students) to prefer acquiescence to dialectic, invisibility to acknowledgement,
intellectual onanism to social action. A testament to the efficacy of this narcotic power is the easy continuation of a national myth which can disguise the
realities of class collision in Canada; Lyell Island fades inexorably into airline
advertisements: *our* Indians perform tourist-pleasing war-dances.

I'm reminded here of a particularly apropos review by Michael Wood of the
film *Pale Rider:*

American literature (and public life) is full of worries and projects concerning the wilderness, but the west is not exactly the wilderness. It is
not a troublesome piece of nature, and it is not the promised land. It is

empty land, a version of the void. That is why the Indians are so threatening—they are not supposed to be there. And that is why the settlers are so vulnerable—they have literally colonised the middle of nowhere.

Of course, this is not how most of us recall westerns. What I chiefly remember of the westerns of my childhood is John Wayne knocking Randolph Scott through the bannisters in some saloon, and the way various cowboys got on and off their horses. (268)

Of course, this is not how most of us recall Canadian history; but what is it that we do remember, especially when we read both the modernists and their commentators?

If Canadian criticism is to displace this narcosis—if it is to fulfil a truly "substantive social function"—it must begin a truly critical remembering of history, a demystified reappraisal of its own purpose in reading, and writing about, our past writing. Unless we ourselves become conscious of the historically specific forces which have shaped the content of our own ideas about history, reading, and writing, we will not be capable of comprehending the real historical and ideological forces at work within both our literature and our lives. A proper criticism must, therefore, encompass the pleas of theorists like Michel Foucault, who argues that "The traditional devices for constructing a comprehensive view of history and for retracing the past as a patient and continuous development must be systematically dismantled" (153). If we do this, then perhaps, finally, we might put to rest such persistent mythologies as that articulated by W.J. Keith: "Canada is in the process of discovering (or in some cases rediscovering) her past, her lines of continuity. It is essential that this process be not only maintained but extended" (12-13). It is essential, I would argue with Foucault, that this latter process—in any authentic search for a new future—be destroyed.

Notes

A version of this paper was first delivered to a meeting of the Association for Canadian Studies in Australia and New Zealand, at Brisbane, Australia, in May 1986.

1. I wish to thank my colleague Jonathan Lamb for this fortuitous phrase.
2. By "ideology" I mean *both* "false consciousness" and what Terry Eagleton calls "those modes of feeling, valuing, perceiving and believing which have some kind of relation to the maintenance and reproduction of social power" (*Literary Theory* 15).
3. I would like to thank my colleague Michael Neill, whose essay, cited here, influenced, and in some instances shaped, my own argument.

4. George Ryga touches on this kind of linguistic blanketing or dehumanizing in his tough and beautiful essay, "The Village of Melons":

   The designation "banana republic" is not so much derisive as it is cynical. For it implies that some people are capable only of producing bananas. Their languages, songs, what they think and feel, count for nothing. Such a dismissal of human worth may have little effect on the peoples against which it is directed, for human worth matters little in economic exploitation—either for its architects or its victims. But it is a disastrous reflection on the cultures from which it originates, for it tarnishes them with decadence and raises the spectre of another kind of eventual decline and death. (106)

5. Terry Goldie has considered this reduction of the indigene to a sign in his interesting unpublished essay. My thanks to him for allowing me to read the manuscript.

Works Cited

Achebe, Chinua. "The Role of the Writer in a New Nation." *African Writers on African Writing*. Ed. G.D. Killam. Evanston: Northwestern UP, 1973. 7-13.

Cameron, Elspeth. *Hugh MacLennan: A Writer's Life*. Toronto: U of Toronto P, 1981.

Djwa, Sandra. "'A New Soil and a Sharp Sun': The Landscape of a Modern Canadian Poetry." *Modernist Studies: Literature and Culture 1920-1940* 2.2 (1976): 3-17.

Eagleton, Terry. *The Function of Criticism: From "The Spectator" to Post-Structuralism*. London: Verso, 1984.

—. *Literary Theory: An Introduction*. Oxford: Blackwell, 1983.

Fisher, Robin. *Contact and Conflict: Indian-European Relations in British Columbia, 1774-1890*. Vancouver: U of British Columbia P, 1977.

Foucault, Michel. "Nietzsche, Genealogy, History." *Language, Counter-Memory, Practice: Selected Essays and Interviews*. Ed. Donald F. Bouchard. Trans. Donald F. Bouchard and Sherry Simon. Ithaca: Cornell UP, 1977. 139-64.

Goldie, Terry. "Semiosis and Sovereignty: Images of the Indigene in Canadian, Australian, and New Zealand Literature." Unpublished essay, 1984.

Hutcheon, Linda. "Canadian Historiographic Metafiction." *Essays on Canadian Writing* 30 (1984-85): 228-38.

Keith, W.J. "The Function of Canadian Criticism at the Present Time." *Essays on Canadian Writing* 30 (1984-85): 1-16.

MacLennan, Hugh. "The Tennis Racket is an Antelope Bone." *Conversations with Canadian Novelists: Part One*. With Donald Cameron. Toronto: Macmillan, 1973. 130-48.

—. *Two Solitudes*. Toronto: Collins, 1945.

—. "*Two Solitudes*: Thirty-Three Years Later." *The Other Side of Hugh MacLennan: Selected Essays Old and New*. Ed. Elspeth Cameron. Toronto: Macmillan, 1978. 288-99.

Marx, Karl. "The Secret of Primitive Accumulation." *Capital: A Critique of Political*

Economy. Ed. Frederick Engels. Trans. Samuel Moore and Edward Aveling. New York: Random, 1906. 784-87.

Mead, Sydney Moko. "Pakeha and Maori Now: Children of the Myths." *University of Auckland News* 14.5 (1984): 8-10; 34-38.

Neill, Michael. "Coming Home: Teaching the Post-Colonial Novel." *Islands* ns 2.1 (1985): 38-53.

Pearson, Bill. "Home." *Fretful Sleepers and Other Essays.* London: Heinemann, 1974. 159-62.

Ryga, George. *The Ecstasy of Rita Joe.* Vancouver: Talonbooks, 1970.

——. "The Village of Melons: Impressions of a Canadian Author in Mexico." *Canadian Literature* 95 (1982): 102-08.

Scott, F.R. "Laurentian Shield." *Poets Between the Wars.* Ed. Milton Wilson. New Canadian Library 5. Toronto: McClelland, 1967. 91.

Sturm, Terry. "The Neglected Middle Distance: Towards a History of Transtasman Literary Relations." *ARIEL* 16.4 (1985): 29-46.

Trigger, Bruce. *Natives and Newcomers: Canada's "Heroic Age" Reconsidered.* Montreal: McGill-Queen's UP, 1985.

Wendt, Albert. "The Novelist as Historian." Unpublished essay, 1985.

Wood, Michael. "The Cold West." *New Society* 23 Aug. 1985: 268-69.

19

"'OLGA IN WONDERLAND': CANADIAN ETHNIC MINORITY WRITING AND POST-COLONIAL THEORY"*

Enoch Padolsky

In Linda Hutcheon's article "'Circling the Downspout of Empire,'" Canada's foremost theorist of postmodernism questions the suitability of the term "post-colonial" in the Canadian context. There are ways in which this term can apply, she argues, but it is important to specify how Canada's post-coloniality differs from that of other societies. Among the distinctions to which she draws attention is "the pluri-ethnic (and lately more multiracial) nature of Canadian society." "Some of the immigrants who populate this country," she points out, "are not from colonized societies and they often consciously resist being labelled post-colonial" (79).

Hutcheon's critique is challenged by Diana Brydon, (one of Canada's most notable post-colonialists), in the very next article of this volume. Entitled "The White Inuit Speaks: Contamination as Literary Strategy," Brydon's piece attacks postmodernism's aestheticist "ambivalence" and its tendency to "defer judgement and to refuse agency" (95). Post-colonial approaches, she argues, can provide us with "the language and the political analysis" (97) for understanding Canada's post-colonial differences in a world of post-coloniality: "Far from separating it from other post-colonial nations, Canada's pluri-ethnic composition allows for points of connection with some experiences elsewhere . . ." (98). To prove her point, Brydon then goes on to a post-colonial analysis of "metaphorical creolization" in two Canadian ethnic minority texts, Kristjana Gunnars' *The Prowler* and Mordecai Richler's *Solomon Gursky Was Here.*

My interest in these two articles—whose main *champs de bataille* is in fact not ethnicity but the intersections between postmodernism and post-colonialism—is that they provide one of the rare occasions on which Canadian ethnicity *per se* has been theorized and debated within these two very dominant, very mainstream, and very internationalized discourses. The claim by Brydon that post-colonialism's "language and political analysis" can provide a basis for understanding Canada's "pluri-ethnic composition" is particularly intriguing. What does post-colonial theory have to offer to the study of Canadian ethnic minority writing? How apt are its terms of reference, its theoretical assumptions, its political positionings and its methodologies? To put it in the

* *Canadian Ethnic Studies* 28.3 (1996): 16-28.

metaphor of my title, if the Canadian Olga were to enter the Wonderland of post-colonialism, what kind of tea party should she expect?

Perhaps the first point to note about post-colonial claims to a "language and political analysis" applicable to Canadian reality is that most post-colonial theoretical discussion takes place in non-Canadian theorized space. It is true that Canadian critics such as Brydon, Stephen Slemon and others participate in this theorizing. It is also true that Canada is a post-colonial focus of attention. Even granting these points, however, it is important to ask what sort of place Canada occupies in this discourse and how Canadian "pluri-ethnicity" is handled in such discussions. To get a quick answer to these questions, what better place to look than Brydon's own acknowledged source, "the post-colonial criticism developed by Ashcroft, Griffiths and Tiffin in *The Empire Writes Back*" (96)?

Canadian references are indeed scattered throughout this post-colonial theoretical source book, but the main section that deals with Canada is the one locating it as part of a group or category called "settler colonies." Here Canada gets a quick overview (133-45) along with Australia, New Zealand and the United States (!). As for Canadian "pluri-ethnicity," it is for the most part absent in this section as elsewhere in the book. Most of the Canadian references are to mainstream British-Canadian writers and critics (see also the discussion of Findley 97-104 and "Reader's Guide—Canada" 209). At the end of the section, however, there is a short paragraph noting the "arrival in settler colony cultures of large groups of migrants" whose writing is likely to grow in importance, "especially in Canada and Australia" (145). The use of the Australian term "migrant" to refer to Canadian ethnic and racial minorities (the term "ethnicity" does not even appear in the Index) reveals the Australian contexts of the writers of this book and illustrates my earlier point about post-colonialism's non-Canadian theoretical space. Significantly, the section also contains no reference to Quebec (equally absent from the Index), and its place within the "settler colony" of Canada. A few references to Quebec can nevertheless be found here and there in the book. These occur, however, not in the context of the Canadian nation or of Canadian "pluri-ethnicity" but with comparative reference to the "Black diaspora" (24), in "French Africa, . . . Black America and the Caribbean" (32).

As for the terminology ("language and political analysis") that does receive attention in *The Empire Writes Back*, for the most part it can be traced to other parts of the British Commonwealth, to selected "Third World" critics such as Frantz Fanon and Homi Bhabha, and to European and American theoretical sources. Key terms such as "syncreticity," and its debate with "authenticity," are traced back to cultural conditions in India, Africa and the West Indies (see 30-31; 88-97). The terms "hybridity" and "creolization," which Brydon features in her article, are derived, according to the discussions in *Empire* (33 ff. and 146 ff.) from models developed by writers such as Derek Walcott, E.K. Brathwaite and Wilson Harris who were theorizing their cultural positions in response to the historically mixed colonial and post-colonial societies of the West Indies and Guyana.

The fact that post-colonial criticism draws its theoretical concepts from elsewhere and does not adequately engage non-mainstream Canadian reality would thus seem to present a fundamental problem in claiming relevance to the contexts of Canadian "pluri-ethnicity." At the very least, such a relevance could not be assumed and would need to be proved. Yet the only question that seems to arise in post-colonial discussions of Canadian materials is how to "fit" Canada into this pre-existing post-colonial theoretical framework. What is missing is any sense of the reverse process, *i.e.* that theory itself can be affected by Canada. But as Edward Said pointed out a number of years ago ("Travelling Theory"), once theories move beyond the contexts in which they were originally developed, they seem to undergo a variety of processes, stresses and changes. If this is true, then post-colonial theorists wishing to apply their international comparative models to Canadian writing need to examine not just how the theory fits the writing but also how the "new" contexts of the writing challenge and change the validity of the theory itself. And these "new" contexts, I would argue, certainly include the local pre-existing discursive frameworks that already surround the "new" culture that the travelling post-colonial theory wishes to address.

When post-colonial theory turns to Canadian ethnicity, therefore, and the discussion moves (for example, in Brydon) to Canadian ethnic minority writing and "metaphorical creolization," "hybridity," "syncreticity," "settlers" and "natives," and a host of other imported terms, it seems to me incumbent, both theoretically and practically, to point out that there is already in Canada a whole pre-existing discourse on ethnicity called "Canadian ethnic studies." Indeed, the title I have taken for this paper—"Olga in Wonderland"—is itself an allusion to this discourse, for this version of the Lewis Carroll reference was used by Canadian sociologist Wsevolod Isajiw in his presidential address to the Canadian Ethnic Studies Association in 1975. His influential article on ethnicity and technology, which appeared in *Canadian Ethnic Studies* a few years later, serves as a reminder that in Canada, long before post-colonialism and postmodernism had "discovered" Canadian "pluri-ethnicity," "hybridity" and "creolization," Canadian theoreticians in ethnic studies were already discussing Canadian ethnic and racial diversity from a broad range of perspectives, including, as Isajiw's article indicates, the processes of cultural change.

Not that the Canadian discourse of ethnic studies was ever itself "pure," "authentic" or merely "indigenous" in its approach to Canadian ethnicity. From its inception in the 1960s, Canadian ethnic studies also had its links to international discussions of the so-called "ethnic revival" and to international theories of ethnicity that changed and developed over time. Nevertheless, what is notable about Canadian ethnic studies is that over the last three decades it has continually engaged these international discussions in ways that have Canadianized theoretical issues and integrated and adapted them within extensive studies of Canadian society. Within the ethnic studies network, then, ground breaking work (far too numerous to mention here) has been carried out on virtually every ethnic and racial group in Canada, on minority and majority relations, on intersections of ethnicity and race with gender and class, on immigration, history, politics, labour relations, aging, ethnic psychology, racism, cultural change, and on a multitude of theoretical issues. And finally, it should be noted, if most of these studies have taken place within the social sciences, cultural studies, including literary ones, have also been well represented throughout the years.

It is also worth noting, in an age highly conscious of issues of representation and positioning, that a great deal of this research has been carried out by ethnic and racial minority scholars, though the contributions of (and collaborations with) majority academics are no less noteworthy. Also relevant in the Canadian context and with reference to Canadian "pluri-ethnicity," is the fact that Canadian ethnic studies has always been bilingual, with significant research and administrative participation from scholars from Quebec. *Canadian Ethnic Studies* publishes in both English and French, every article including an abstract in both languages. Finally, Canadian ethnic studies has also been to some extent a site for Canadian Aboriginal studies. In spite of (political) hesitations by some Native Canadians on topics of ethnicity and multiculturalism, the Aboriginal component of ethnic studies has nevertheless been significant, particularly because of its links to the study of other minorities in Canada. In sum, when it comes to "ethnicity" and "race" in Canada, ethnic studies has historically been *the* "location" for research. It is solidly rooted in the Canadian social context, both majority and minority, and its membership network is probably more representative, more diverse, more inter- and multi-disciplinary and more politically engaged and community oriented than most academic networks.

The existence of this considerable discourse on Canadian ethnicity and race and its absence from post-colonial discussions of Canadian "pluri-ethnicity" should certainly, in my view, give pause to any facile acceptance of post-colonial claims on Canadian ethnic realities. Indeed, the case could really be put the other way. If post-colonial critics now wish to turn their hands to topics of Canadian ethnicity, why are they not consulting the "language and political analysis" of Canadian ethnic studies? (The same is true, I might add, for other literary scholars more used to working in postmodernist contexts or in English-Canadian or French-English mainstream canons.) Yet both Hutcheon and Brydon concede the centrality, in their debate between postmodernism and post-colonialism, of a "recognition of historical, political, and social circumstances" (Brydon qtd. in Hutcheon 74). Equally, both lay claim (for postmodernism and post-colonialism respectively) to an oppositional, radical, political stance in the face of "English colonialism," "American imperialism," "today's multinationalist capitalist world at large" and other such renderings of "power" and "oppression." Yet if these practitioners want to examine "power" and "oppression" in the Canadian social framework, especially with regard to Canadian ethnicity, if they acknowledge the importance of "history, politics and social circumstances" to their criticism, how can they proceed without reference to all the detailed work carried out in Canadian ethnic studies on the history of minority groups in Canada, on the history and character of Canadian racism, on the dynamics of minority and majority relations, on gender and class implications, and on the theory and practice of Canadian multiculturalism? It seems to me that broad comparative theories which are not grounded in such detailed contexts should be regarded with circumspection. Until post-colonial critics are willing to test their theoretical concepts in the realities of Canadian experience, and until they are willing to engage seriously with pre-existing Canadian discourses on Canadian ethnic and racial diversity, no claim to a "language and political analysis" for Canadian "pluri-ethnicity" can be taken seriously.

A non-Canadian theoretical frame of reference and the absence of relevant Canadian discourses of ethnicity are, however, only some of the problems post-colonialist criticism faces in staking a claim to Canadian "pluri-ethnicity." Other difficulties can also be discerned, both in the nature of the international discourse and in specific applications of it such as can be found in Brydon's article. These also dilute the credibility of using unadapted post-colonial models with reference to Canadian ethnicity. Time being limited, I can only outline here (briefly) three or four such problem areas.

Post-colonial theory, notwithstanding Diana Brydon and *The Empire Writes Back*, does not have a single "language and political analysis" to offer. Brydon acknowledges that "post-colonial" "may have multiple, subsidiary meanings" but still defends its "usefulness in indicating a general category"(97). Arising from British Commonwealth studies in a postwar era of Third World decolonization and postmodernist and post-structuralist theory, post-colonialism has from its beginnings been pervaded with its own internal "differences." These differences include not only the well-known divide between White and non-White colonies but also the differences, in regional and national terms, inherent in world history and the world scene. It is also worth reminding post-colonialists that Britain was not the only colonial power. The shift from "English" to "english" traced in *The Empire Writes Back*, important as this may be, still does not cover the "world."

As the recent Williams and Chrisman anthology *Colonial Discourse and Post-Colonial Theory* makes evident, these differences of post-colonial multiplicity are now becoming increasingly salient. Mishra and Hodge, for example, are not alone (see also McClintock) in arguing against the inclusion of countries like Canada and Australia within post-colonial frameworks in the first place. Indeed they dismiss homogenizing arguments for their inclusion as "a hermeneutic which is vindicated by the conditions in non-[White] settler colonies, but is then used unchanged to apply to settler colonies . . ." (286). If the "neo-colonial," the "internal colonial" and the "colonial-like" are added to the picture (terms which have been introduced to add the United States and its race relations to the post-colonial discourse), then any claim to a single transcendent multi-national theoretical framework ("*the* post-colonial perspective" [Brydon 97; my emphasis]) becomes even more diffuse. (This diffuseness, by the way, is one of the features of "traveling theory" that Said outlines.) The conclusion I would draw, therefore, is that the more post-colonial *theory* becomes post-colonial *theories*, the weaker the claim for any general post-colonial "language and political analysis" becomes, and the more crucial each local, group or national social discourse becomes in working comparatively and internationally.

Yet post-colonial theory (at least in many versions) tends to undervalue the local, the group and the nation. The anti-discursive strategies of much post-colonial analysis, moving from imperial centres to marginalized peripheries, have tended to look across nations, regions, and races and therefore, ideologically, have tended to be anti-nationalist. Thus, for example, Homi Bhabha argues: "National quests for cultural self ratification and hence origination replicate imperial cognitive processes, reinvoking their values and practices in an attempted constitution of an independent identity . . . the construction of the 'essentially' Nigerian or the 'essentially' Australian invokes exclusivist systems which replicate imperial universalist paradigms" (qtd. in Tiffin 36). In a similar vein, the *Empire* authors specifically target Canadian literary theory because "the internal perception of a mosaic has not generated corresponding theories of literary hybridity to replace the nationalist approach" (36).

Accusations of "essentialism," of "nationalism" and ethnic "purity," or of a "cult of authenticity" (Brydon 98), are thus often found in post-colonial analyses, as part of the cross-cultural argument made, in the name of anti-colonial strategies, against group and national claims. Ironically, given post-colonial claims to political activism and interest in "resistance writing" (Brydon 95), the target of these accusations is sometimes the very minority groups that are championed by post-colonialists but whose resistance strategies are felt to depart from accepted post-colonial tactics. Once again, Brydon:

> While post-colonial theorists embrace hybridity and heterogeneity as the characteristic post-colonial mode, some native writers in Canada resist what they see as a violating appropriation to insist on their ownership of their stories and their exclusive claim to an authenticity that should not be ventriloquised or parodied. . . . Although I can sympathise with such arguments . . . even tactically they prove self-defeating because they depend on a view of cultural authenticity that condemns them to a continued marginality and an eventual death . . . such tactics encourage native peoples to isolate themselves from contemporary life and full citizenhood. (99)

This statement can of course be challenged on the basis of its own positioning, but I would rather draw attention, in terms of my argument here, to the way international, cross-cultural post-colonial ideology (and terminology) reduces the issues raised by the Canadian "appropriation debate" to a binary opposition of "authenticity" and "hybridity." Since post-colonial theory, its "language and politics," and practictioners view "hybridity," "syncreticity" and other manifestations of cultural mixing, as axiomatic of the nature of the post-colonial world, any group efforts that deviate from this "heterogeneity," are to be evaluated as "essentialist," "purist," and "authentic" and condemned accordingly.

Yet surely, as the discussions in ethnic studies indicate, there are many important issues that arise in the area of cultural change and cultural mixing other than the mere opposition of "authenticity" and "hybridity." This is not to deny that cultural mixing is important nor that "hybridity" and "creolization" may have a significant impact on the literary and cultural imagination. But as John Berry's many studies of acculturation options and processes have indicated, there are many other complex choices that in-group and out-group cultural relations pose. For Canadian minority groups, cultural change and cultural mixing ("hybridity") are not things that need to be celebrated simply because they happen or resisted in favour of some static notions of a past ("authenticity"). Rather, they are features of minority life which impinge on a range of core issues: the persistence, rediscovery or affective nature of ethnic identity, the dynamics of generational change, the play between tradition and modernity, the relations between citizenship and group affiliation, the psychology of racism, or (as in Isajiw), the impact of a technological age on both "old" and "new" Olgas.

For some groups, including Canadian Aboriginal peoples, these cultural issues often come down to a question of community survival, in an economic, psychological and even sometimes literal sense. The appropriation debate, returning to Brydon's comments, is thus, at least to my reading of it, not about an attempt to resist "hybridity" in favour of "authenticity" but an attempt, first, to take back control of the cultural agenda from other, more dominant, hands, and secondly, to preserve, develop and nourish a sense of community identity. As Lenore Keeshig-Tobias put it in the premiere issue of *The Magazine to Reestablish the Trickster*, it is time for Native writers to "be our own tricksters," in order to "reclaim the Native voice in literature" (3). Furthermore, as anyone knows who has read or seen the plays of Tomson Highway, viewed the remarkable Indigena exhibit at the Museum of Civilization in 1992 (cf. McMaster and Martin), or encountered the works of many other Native writers and artists, Native writing and art are hardly self-enclosed exercises in "purity" and "authenticity." Cultural mixing has always been a feature of such art, no doubt even before the arrival of Europeans and post-colonialists to this land.

From this perspective, Brydon's celebration of the "white Inuit" and the cross-cultural "contamination" or "hybridity" of Gunnars' *The Prowler* and

Richler's *Solomon Gursky Was Here* can be seen to illustrate, in terms of critical practice, the more general problem post-colonialism has with the local and the national. In the first place, in spite of Gunnars' use of the term "white Inuit" and Richler's Arctic setting, "contaminated" links with Inuit culture are clearly not the primary focus of these two novels. Gunnars does not focus on Inuit experience or culture at all. For her, the term "white Inuit" is a pejorative *Danish* epithet for Icelanders (Section 16). Since Gunnars makes no claim to a knowledge of Inuit culture, her credibility is in no way affected, for example, by the oversight of thinking that "Inuit" (does she mean Inuktitut?) is a language (Section 133). Whether the same should be said for Brydon, however, whose argument centres on the cultural metaphoric use of "Inuit" and who not only cites this mistake without comment (102) but herself repeatedly uses the plural form "Inuit" in the singular, (as in her title "The White Inuit Speaks"), is another matter.

Furthermore, it should be noted, Gunnars' subject in the novel is also not Canada: it is Iceland. If there is "hybridity" in *The Prowler*, therefore, it is between Danish and Icelandic cultures—the "liberation of my father's people from the clutches of my mother's people" (Section 15). So while one might agree with Brydon's point that Gunnars' novel is indeed making "post-modernist devices serve post-colonial ends" (101), it is rather odd for her to choose this Icelandic-oriented novel with barely a reference to Canada in it, and then claim that the narrative strategies within it "derive from the particular circumstances of a Canadian post-coloniality" (101). Gunnars is of course a Canadian writer, and the fact that she chooses, like many other Canadian writers, to write about other countries to which she has experiential and emotional ties, does not make her any less so. But surely if, like Brydon, one wishes to make a claim regarding "the particular circumstances of a Canadian post-coloniality," choosing a work like *The Prowler* instead of the more obvious works by Gunnars which engage her Canadian experience more directly—for example, the *Settlement Poems* or *The Axe's Edge*—requires some explanation. But there is no such discussion in Brydon's article. What this suggests to me is that Brydon is more interested in arguing Gunnars' "hybridity" and "post-coloniality" in general than in contextualizing the national or the local, whether it be Iceland or Canada.

Brydon's analysis of Richler's *Solomon Gursky Was Here* reveals a different aspect of this problem. In her discussion, Brydon once again focuses on the evidence of "hybridity" in the text—the mix of "Jewish" and "Native" customs, the confusion of those seeking "cultural authenticity," and "Richler's celebration of a 'mongrelized' nation" (104). Furthermore, Brydon argues, this "hybridity" is part of a "post-colonial literary strategy" that "clears a space for history's silenced ones to speak" (104), namely, the "effluvium" of British slums, now in Canada, and the male drinkers in "The Caboose and thousands of bars like it" across the country.

Unlike *The Prowler*, then, Richler's novel does provide Brydon with a considerable amount of Canadian material. Further, there is no question that

Richler does create an image of Inuit life and of Jewish-Aboriginal cultural mixing as part of his thematic focus. I would also grant that in this case, "authenticity" of a kind is, as Brydon argues, part of Richler's satiric purpose. Nevertheless, I find a number of difficulties in Brydon's use of Richler.

The first is a corollary to my comments on Gunnars' non-Canadian setting. Since Brydon has not shown how Gunners' overt Icelandic focus "derives" somehow from "the particular circumstances of Canadian post-coloniality," she can hardly substantiate the claim that Richler's narrative "similarities" derive from the same "circumstances" (101). The mere coincidence of Inuit references and the metaphor of the "white Inuit" in themselves cannot make such a case.

Secondly, there is the question of how "post-colonial" Richler's own narrative strategies are. As satirist, Richler is notoriously difficult to pin down when it comes to defining an underlying standard in his works. As critic Victor Ramraj noted some years ago, "Richler himself exhibits a profoundly ambivalent vision of life" (1). Most of his main characters—Duddy, Joshua, Jake, and Moses in this novel—are on a continuing quest, searching, as Richler himself put it almost forty years ago, for "values with which in this time a man can live with honour" ("A Conversation" 38). These questing wandering Jewish non-heroes, I would argue, can hardly be reduced to "Canadian post-coloniality" in Brydon's form, and if they represent Richler's view of the best that can be achieved in these times of a "collapse of absolute values" ("A Conversation" 38), they are also all flawed themselves, each in his own way. In this rather complex Richlerian world, then, it is hardly enough to find evidence of the use of cultural mixing ("hybridity") or of satire on "authenticity," for these are usually part of Richler's larger attack on conventionality, hypocrisy, superficiality and "deadness" of all sorts. For Richler, "authenticity" is certainly bad when it consists of a professor's attempt to characterize (stereotypically) "traditional" Inuit culture (58 ff.). On the other hand, it can also be a positive value, as in his romantically nostalgic portrayal of the cultural group meetings at the Berger home early in the book (12 ff.). Authenticity, it could be argued, is precisely what the so-called poet (L.B. Berger) lacks, when he willingly becomes an "exotic" (19) and sells out to the Gurskys (see 21-22). In similar terms, there does not seem to be a problem, in Richler's view, in a character like Henry Gursky, who is married to a Native woman ("hybridity"!), and is yet at the same time that most "authentic" and traditional of Jews, a Hasid (524). From my perspective, then, Richler's vision of the world and his positive values are more aptly to be located not in the post-colonial contexts that Brydon describes, but in the primary human contexts like friendship, loyalty, freedom, art, and love. Even these, alas for Richler (and us all), are notoriously hard to achieve.

My third point touches on Richler's views on community in general and on Canada in particular. The difficulty with using Richler to illustrate the "particular circumstances of a Canadian post-coloniality" is that he himself has always been a very controversial and ambivalent figure from both a Jewish communal and Canadian perspective. Choosing him as a "spokesperson" (post-colonial or otherwise) on history, community or nation is thus not unproblematic.

When *Solomon Gursky* first came out, I led a discussion on it at an Ottawa synagogue and the participants divided down the middle on things like Richler's "unfair" depiction of A.M. Klein (*i.e.* L.B. Berger), and his representation of Jewish communal issues in the novel (cf. also Richler, "A Conversation" 32-33). Some wondered about Richler's "right" to use Native myths of the raven and others objected to Richler's description of Canada (through the character Callaghan) as "not so much a country as a holding tank filled with the disgruntled progeny of defeated peoples" (398), or of Canadians as "huddled tight to the border, looking into the candy store window, scared by the Americans on one side and the bush on the other" (399).

Objections such as these can of course be addressed, and the way to do so is within the larger narrative framework of the novel's purposes. But Brydon's treatment of Richler and the novel once again does not even address this aspect of Richler's views on communal relations. Brydon is not concerned whether Richler's use of the raven (in part) as "a survivor trickster figure for North American Native mythologies" (Brydon 102) might be viewed as exactly the sort of distortive "appropriation" writing that Keeshig-Tobias laments because she already dismissed such concerns as examples of "cultural authenticity." She has no interest in Richler's depiction of Jewish life or affairs because ethnic minority group concerns are not a post-colonial focus. Nor is she bothered by Richler's satiric depiction of Canadian topics, for, as noted earlier, anti-nationalism is part of post-colonial ideology. With Richler, then, Brydon unproblematically celebrates a new-found Canadian (post-colonial) soul in his depiction of "the survival of working class communal culture," and in a post-colonial "quest for a just society" (104). But if Brydon's post-colonial perspective concurs with Richler in finding Canada's soul in the bar-rooms of the nation, I suspect that many Canadians, myself included, would have some trouble seeing Richler's characters as representative of Canadian working class culture or of "history's silenced ones" (Brydon 104). Nor would it go unchallenged that "Canada's soul" is *not* to be found "in Batoche or the Plains of Abraham or Fort Walsh or Charlottetown or Parliament Hill" (Brydon 103). The fact that, for Brydon, Richler's "effluvium" of the British slums and macho examples of a "working class communal culture" bring a "tough cultural specificity to Canada," but not these specific references to Canadian history, is revealing (and problematic). The former are capable of being generalized as anonymous "local referents" (104) in abstract post-colonial theoretical discourse; the latter would require a more contextualized evaluation of the underlying group relations, social histories and politics that they imply: the Metis struggle in the Riel rebellion, the English-French rivalry in Canada, First Nations-white relations on the frontier, the formation of Canada and its continuing governance.

In sum, post-colonial discussions such as Brydon's (on Gunnars and Rich-ler) illustrate all too well the absence of local, communal or national ethnic dimensions in the analysis of Canadian ethnic minority writing. Writers are instead seen to be serving post-colonial strategies of "hybridity" that "vigor-ously dispute any residual faith in the possibility of cultural authenticity" (104). This approach excludes all consideration of ethnic groups as groups, of problems that communities face in trying to remain communities, or of the rich inter-group social and political history that a national framework implies. It is this post-colonial "language and political analysis" that also allows for the unquestioned shift of an Icelandic term "White Inuit" into a Canadian analy-sis, and for the unproblematic praise of "creolizing" strategies such as the use (appropriation?) of Aboriginal myths of the Raven and of anti-nationalist views of Canada. What has been lost sight of, in spite of claims to the contrary, in this application of post-colonial theory to Canadian "pluri-ethnicity," I would argue, is the perspective of the local, the group and the nation. Under-valuing these factors, particularly in a decentralized country such as Canada, with its complex regional, ethnic, racial and linguistic tensions, would seem to be a serious flaw in post-colonial theories. Their unpositioned application to Canadian ethnic and racial minorities (including minority writing) on issues such as cultural survival, political interaction, and individual and group identity is thus once again not particularly convincing.

The last area I would like to consider here is the perspective of post-colo-nial theory on Canadian multiculturalism, a topic of central concern to eth-nic minority Canadians. The same anti-hegemonic reasoning that has made anti-nationalism a feature of post-colonial theory has also tended to reduce national attempts to accommodate ethnic and racial diversity into hege-monic pacifying strategies. Thus Brydon follows other post-colonial writers in dismissing "the liberal myth of society formed from a plurality of equal differences" (98). Though she does not name this "myth" as "multicultural-ism" until the end of her article (104), it is clear that this is what she has in mind from the outset: "in our care to respect the specificity of particular experiences we run another risk, that of a liberal pluralism which uses the idea of different but equal discourses to prevent the forming of alliances based on a comparative [post-colonial] analysis that can perceive points of connection" (97). The wording here recalls Bhabha's project of a "Third Space" with its aim of replacing cultural diversity with cultural difference, the "anodyne liberal notions of multiculturalism" with an "international culture based . . . on the inscription and articulation of culture's hybridity" ("Commitment" 18, 22). The problem with this "post-colonial" theorizing of pluralism is that once again, it is too generic, too reductive and too un-particular. Though Brydon states that both Richler and Gunnars "write out of positions specifically located in the current debate about multicultural-ism" (104), she never discusses this debate at all. Instead she seems to assume a simple correlation between pluralism, "cultural authenticity" and liberal hegemony.

To reduce pluralism (without historical differentiation) to a hegemonic colonizing practice is, I fear, merely to create another theoretical "master narrative." In practice, at least in Canada, discussions of pluralism and multiculturalism take place on a very complex territory of dispute and contestation— between Quebec and English Canada, between Aboriginals and others, between minorities and majorities, between differing views within minority groupings, between the claims of individuals and groups, and so forth. Far from being a simple and static hegemonic strategy, Canadian pluralism/multiculturalism has been precisely the terrain on which alliances have been formed, racism has been fought, and the shifting needs of Canadian ethnic and racial groups have been argued and developed. This has made Canadian multiculturalism continually contentious from vastly different perspectives (in Quebec, in the Reform country of Calgary, among some minority writers, among some majority leaders), and there is no doubt that there are strong critiques of it to be made. At the same time, it has made Canadian multiculturalism a source of world-wide interest, as the international growth of Canadian studies and the many invitations of Canadian scholars expert in this domain attest. But put in this context, post-colonial dismissals of "liberal pluralism" and unspecified vague hopes of anti-hegemonic "forming of alliances" or of "gathering points of political solidarity" (Bhabha, *Nation* 307) can be seen as not seriously engaging the real problems of inter-ethnic and inter-racial relations in a Canadian national context. As such, once again, it is in ethnic studies, or elsewhere, that these debates do take place and that the "language and political analysis" of these issues relevant to Canadian ethnic minority writing are to be found.

The critiques of post-colonial theory and practice that I have been raising up to this point might give the impression that I consider these approaches irrelevant to Canadian ethnicity and to Canadian ethnic minority writing. But this is not my position. What I have been arguing against here is the view that international post-colonial theory somehow brings with it a ready-made universally applicable "language and political analysis" that can simply be applied to Canadian realities. But terms such as "hybrid" or "creole" not only do not exhaust the issues that surround cultural mixing and cultural change in Canada, they also do not carry the same weight or meaning in Canada as they do in the West Indies, or elsewhere. In a sense, Brydon herself is forced to acknowledge this last point when she focuses her analysis on the "*metaphorical* creolization*" (my emphasis) to be found in Richler and Gunnars. In similar terms, the politics of international comparative post-colonialism arrives in Canada with a baggage of anti-nationalism, anti-liberalism and anti-pluralism that has not been Canadianized. The same can be said about its claims to political activism and anti-hegemonic strategies.

Yet in spite of these caveats, I would argue, the arrival of post-colonial theory (particularly in its multiplicity), like the onset of any new theoretical discourse, does hold some promise for the study of Canadian ethnicity and Canadian ethnic minority writing. There is no doubt, as Hutcheon too acknowledges, that Canada's colonial past, "the machinations of Empire and colony, imperial metropolis and provincial hinterland" (Hutcheon 71) is indeed an important ingredient (though surely not the only ingredient!) in understanding modern Canadian social and cultural diversity. The international focus on colonial and post-colonial experience also offers the possibility (assuming local and group concerns are not forgotten) for a new comparative consideration of Canadian First Nations writers who, as Hutcheon points out, are the most obvious Canadian candidates for post-colonial attention, given their own colonized history. Another strong case can be made for those many minority writers in Canada who trace their origins to other previously colonized lands, bringing with them their own multiple "post-colonial" comparative frameworks. Finally, post-colonialism's transcultural promise can be projected to reach further, when in the course of its encounter with existing Canadian discourses of ethnicity it may lead to new insights regarding other Canadian minority groups and to Canadian national conceptual frameworks as well.

Just as I have argued here that post-colonialists need to "field-test" their theories in the light of Canadian experience, the reverse can also be argued for existing Canadian discourses of ethnicity. Canadian ethnic studies can only gain by being forced to re-examine its current theoretical underpinnings (including its views on cultural change and cultural mixing) in the light of the international and comparative context ("hybridity" and "creolization" in the West Indies, for example) that post-colonialism brings with it, and particularly in the light of the strong literary and cultural perspective embedded in post-colonial theories. (I have argued elsewhere [Padolsky, "Establishing the Two-Way Street"] of the benefits literary theory in general has to offer to ethnic studies.)

In order for these benefits to occur, however, post-colonial critics will need to acknowledge that the post-colonial perspective does not automatically contain a "language and political analysis" fit for Canadian reality and for Canadian ethnic experience. They will have to recognize the error of proceeding into the domain of Canadian ethnicity and race without any serious reference to pre-existing Canadian research on the problematics of these contexts. In order to obtain credibility on issues of Canadian differences (such as ethnicity, multiculturalism, and race relations), they will have to engage the "language and political analyses" developed locally and nationally in Canada over a number of decades, and test their insights in the cauldron of "Canadian history and politics." In sum, if post-colonial theory is to make a contribution to the understanding of ethnic and racial relations in Canada, if it is to engage the issues that Canadian ethnic minority writers embody, if it is to make a significant international comparative contribution to discourses centering on ethnicity and race in the world, it must move beyond its pre-set language to the larger specific issues of Canadian ethnicity, and it must engage the specificity of Canadian national discourses, like Canadian ethnic studies. Not to do so will run the very real risk, as Alice put it at the end of the story, of being dismissed as "nothing but a pack of cards."

WORKS CITED

Adam, Ian, and Helen Tiffin, eds. *Past the Last Post: Theorizing Post-Colonialism and Post-Modernism.* Calgary: U of Calgary P, 1990.

Ashcroft, Bill, Gareth Griffiths and Helen Tiffin. *The Empire Writes Back: Theory and Practice in Post-Colonial Literatures.* London: Routledge, 1989.

Bhabha, Homi K. "The Commitment to Theory." *New Formations* 5 (1988): 5-23.

—, ed. *Nation and Narration.* London: Routledge, 1990.

Brydon, Diana. "The White Inuit Speaks: Contamination as Literary Strategy." Adam and Tiffin 191-203.

Hutcheon, Linda. "'Circling the Downspout of Empire.'" Adam and Tiffin 167-89.

Isajiw, Wsevolod. "Olga in Wonderland: Ethnicity in Technological Society." *Canadian Ethnic Studies* 9.1 (1977): 77-85.

Keeshig-Tobias, Lenore. "Let's Be Our Own Tricksters, Eh." *The Magazine To Re-Establish the Trickster* 1.1 (1988): 2-3.

McClintock, Anne. "The Angel of Progress: Pitfalls of the Term 'Post-Colonialism.'" Williams and Chrisman 291-304.

McMaster, Gerald, and Lee-Ann Martin, eds. *Indigena: Contemporary Native Perspectives.* Vancouver: Douglas & McIntyre, 1992.

Mishra, Vijay, and Bob Hodge. "What is Post(-)colonialism?" Williams and Chrisman 276-90.

Padolsky, Enoch. "Establishing the Two-Way Street: Literary Criticism and Ethnic Studies." *Canadian Ethnic Studies* 22.1 (1990): 22-37.

Ramraj, Victor J. *Mordecai Richler.* Boston: Twayne, 1983.

Richler, Mordecai. "A Conversation with Mordecai Richler." With Nathan Cohen. *Mordecai Richler.* Ed. G. David Sheps. Toronto: Ryerson, 1971. 22-42.

—. *Solomon Gursky Was Here.* Markham: Penguin, 1989.

Said, Edward W. "Traveling Theory." *The World, the Text, and the Critic.* Cambridge: Harvard UP, 1983. 226-47.

Tiffin, Helen. "Post-Colonial Literatures and Counter-Discourse." *Critical Approaches to the New Literatures in English.* Ed. Dieter Riemenschneider. Essen: Verlag Die Blaue Eule, 1989. 32-51.

Williams, Patrick, and Laura Chrisman, eds. *Colonial Discourse and Post-Colonial Theory: A Reader.* New York: Columbia UP, 1994.

20

"How Shall We Read
South Asian Canadian Texts?"*

Arun Mukherjee

A Meeting of Streams: South Asian Canadian Literature (Vassanji, 1985), an anthology of essays that were presented at a 1983 conference on South Asian writing, is the first time one comes across the idea of a grouping of writers defined according to their ethnicity. An earlier volume, entitled *Identifications: Ethnicity and the Writer in Canada* (Balan, 1982), uses terms like "Canadian Hungarian Literature" or "Icelandic Canadian Literature" to describe writings by early immigrants in their mother tongues but does not categorize writing in English in terms of ethnic origins of the writers. *Literatures of Lesser Diffusion* (Pivato, 1990), on the other hand, freely categorizes Canadian authors according to their ethnic or racial origins. Another phenomenon of the nineties is the publication of anthologies like *The Geography of Voice* and *Many-Mouthed Birds* whose criterion of inclusion is the writer's ethnic or racial background.

Thus, ethnicity and race have become important theoretical tools in the analysis and categorization of Canadian literature over the last decade. A theoretical apparatus, recognizable by its vocabulary, has emerged which allows us to speak of Canada's minority writers in terms of categories such as group history, group culture, racial persecution, etc. Insofar as this vocabulary has broken the hold of Canadian literary nationalism, which evaluated writers in terms of their "Canadianness," it has had a beneficial effect. However, the popularization of this vocabulary, or what Foucault would call a "discursive formation," has also lent the reception and analysis of these texts a certain prepackaged quality.

One comes across this vocabulary in reviews of South Asian Canadian writers' works, in journal articles and in course descriptions in university calendars. The following extract from the description of a second-year course entitled "Postcolonial Literature" on offer at a California university provides a good example of the terminology in vogue:

In this course we will address some of the political and theoretical issues raised by such categories of literary study as "the postcolonial." Much of

---

* *Postcolonialism: My Living* (Toronto: TSAR, 1998), 24-40.

the discussion will be grounded in our reading of fiction from the Indian Subcontinent, Africa, the Caribbean and elsewhere. Other issues that will be considered will include: the place of literature in the postcolonial globe, representing the self, mimicry, hybridity, writing in the colonizer's language, the changing foci of second and third generations of postcolonial writers, immigration, subaltern studies, domestic fiction, feminist fiction, national identity, etc.

This course description neatly presses all the right buttons associated with Postcolonial Studies, the usual niche for South Asian Canadian writers. A prefabricated, cookie-cutter theoretical framework not only allots writers from postcolonial countries a place, albeit a marginal one, in the curriculum but also predetermines what will be said about them. Terms such as "mimicry," "hybridity," "writing in the colonizer's language," "immigration," "subaltern studies," "national identity," are tediously familiar and students taking such a course should find producing term papers on the writers included here no more taxing than pulling a tv dinner out of the freezer and zapping it.

The language may differ a bit or the names of writers may vary, but the above course description provides a good snapshot of what postcolonial literature courses look like. Now that most North American universities have their calendars on-line, I got to look at some of these descriptions on the Internet. Here is a course description that was posted by a Canadian university:

Eng 472Y
Representing the Other in Post-Colonial Literature
A study of post-colonial writers who give expression to the voice of the "other": the silenced, the subaltern and the marginalized. The course considers such writers as Keri Hulme, Mudrooroo Narogin, Jack Davis, Suniti Namjoshi, Thomas King, Bessie Head, Salman Rushdie, Rajiva Wijesinha, Lewis Nkosi, Allan Sealy, Satendra Nandan and Rohinton Mistry.

The American and the Canadian course descriptions rely on the same theoretical formulae. The difference, however, is that the Canadian course includes Australian and New Zealand writers whereas the Californian course does not. But, besides that little bit of extra coverage, attributable to Canadian, Australian and New Zealand ties as Commonwealth countries, the basic premise of the two courses is remarkably similar. Both presume that writers from diverse parts of the world can be taught in one course, under the rubric of terms like "mimicry," "hybridity," "the subaltern," "the marginalized," "the other." Both have dispensed with categories that generally apply to literatures of Britain, the United States and European countries: periodization, literary movements, and national or regional groupings.

The key terms mentioned above help place writers flagged as postcolonial in opposition to the canonical, dead white male writers. To repeat a popular phrase, postcolonial writers "write back to the empire." They deconstruct, parody, oppose, and mimic dominant discourses of the centre. In the case of South Asian Canadian writers, this theoretical framework assumes that they continue to give "voice" to the "subaltern"—presumably the people of the countries they emigrated from—even after having come to Canada as immigrants. The egregiousness of this supposition is brought out very well by the following words of Harish Trivedi:

> A primary sense in which much post-colonial writing is not really writing back is that it is hardly resistant or oppositional; it is if anything only too eagerly acquiescent. Another sense in which it cannot be writing back but is rather writing within, or writing from the inside, is the immitigable physical circumstance that, in the case of numerous postcolonial writers of a whole variety of national origins including Indians, the act of writing is actually performed while they are ensconced in the bosom of the centre. Nor were any of the Indian post-colonial writers (unlike several eminent writers for example from Nigeria or Kenya) banished or exiled out of India on grounds of political, racial/ethnic or religious persecution; they have left out of their own free and sweet will. It is misleading therefore to speak, as is often done, of their chosen location in the coercive or oppressive terms of exile or diaspora, when what actually happened was that these writers voted with their feet—to say nothing of their heart and soul—for the many cultural and material attractions of the West. (241-42)

Trivedi's insistence that we take location of the writer into account is helpful while discussing South Asian Canadian writing. First, is the current practice of automatically categorizing it as "postcolonial" correct? Secondly, is it "resistant" or "oppositional"? Thirdly, should one use terms like "exile" or "diaspora" to describe this writing as is so commonly done these days? Fourthly, can writers who have emigrated still be giving voice to the "subaltern"?

These questions, I am afraid, seldom get asked of writers before categorizing them as postcolonial. The course descriptions I discussed above unproblematically group South Asian Canadian writers with other postcolonial writers, all taught and theorized with the help of terms like "resistant," "mimicry," "hybridity," "subaltern," "marginal" and so forth.

While there are many other problems with the postcolonial literature course that crams together writers of diverse cultural and national origins, here I wish to focus on how it accommodates and processes South Asian Canadian writing. Its pedagogical and analytical categories basically render irrelevant the South Asian Canadian aspects of South Asian Canadian writing. For instance, one could pose the following questions to a South Asian Canadian text:

(a) What does it mean to be a South Asian Canadian?
(b) Does a South Asian Canadian writer draw on his or her ethnic origin?
(c) How are South Asian Canadian writers received in Canada?
(d) How are South Asian Canadian writers received in the countries of their origin?

Since South Asians are a racial minority in Canada, the "minority discourse" theory seems promising at first. However, I begin to doubt its usefulness when I find that the term, as employed in Abdul JanMohamed's and David Lloyd's *The Nature and Context of Minority Discourse* stretches to include all the minorities in the west as well as the entire "Third World" (6). We need to be careful that the preoccupations of minorities in North America are not projected back to the countries and cultures from which they trace their origins. When JanMohamed and Lloyd claim that "minority discourse is, in the first instance, the product of damage—damage more or less systematically inflicted on cultures produced as minorities by the dominant culture" (4)— they may be quite right about the experience of racial minorities in the west, but it seems preposterous to think of all the third world literatures as minority literatures or as "products of damage." Nor can I agree that "resistance" and "survival" are the major themes of these literatures, and not two among many.

"Minority discourse," I believe, is riddled with the same problems that I outlined with the postcolonial literature framework. Both theoretical approaches have global intentions and in their universalizing ambition, they fail to take local conditions into account. Or, rather, they universalize on the basis of their own experience. Such a state of affairs comes about because much of publishing and theorizing is concentrated in the hands of a few—the so-called celebrity academics—who set the terms of discourse for others.

At a conference entitled "Interrogating Post-Colonialism," held in Shimla, India, in October 1994, many speakers expressed concern about the hegemonic sweep of academic theorizing originating in "the First World academy," equating it with "a second wave of colonisation" (Trivedi 243-44). Meenakshi Mukherjee's comments on "our professional compulsion to speak the same language and adopt the same frame of discourse that people from our discipline are doing all over the world, in order to belong to an international community" (9), point out the pressures of globalization in the academic arena. Her warning against "making the specific configuration of circumstances in particular regions subservient to a global paradigm" (7) underlines the obverse effects of this globalization.

It is no easy task to stay clear of globally propagated theories that emerge from the centres of dominance. The similarity between the two course descriptions from Canada and the United States, and the similarity of their discourse with that employed by numerous monographs and journal articles, demonstrate the power of "global paradigms." They make it impossible to ask the kind of questions that I asked above. These are questions that relate to the effect of being an immigrant writer in Canada, more specifically, being a South Asian Canadian writer. I would now like to explore those issues.

The South Asian Canadian community is, like all other Canadian communities, except the Aboriginal peoples, a community born out of immigration. Like some other minority Canadian groups, it was and is the target of state and societal racism. Denied entry into Canada until the 1960s because of Canada's racist immigration policies, South Asians began to enter Canada in significant numbers only after the passage of nonracist immigration laws in 1967. Despite being fairly "new," South Asian Canadians have been prolific in their literary output, most certainly because, unlike many other immigrant groups, a significant number of them arrived in Canada equipped with an English education.

As has been pointed out by many commentators, "South Asian" is a bureaucratic term. Covering people who have come to Canada from India, Pakistan, Bangladesh, Nepal, Sri Lanka, and Bhutan (of late, Afghanistan has been added to the list), that is, the geographic region known as the Indian subcontinent, and people from East Africa, Fiji and the Caribbean who trace their ancestry to the Indian subcontinent, this umbrella term might be said to produce a unitary community that is not actually there. Generally, people socialize in their ethnic communities such as Gujarati, Tamil or Punjabi. Or, they congregate as religious groups in temples, gurudwaras, mosques, and churches. Indians and Pakistanis also celebrate their respective independence days by hoisting their flags at the Toronto City Hall, a celebration which does not, of course, appeal equally to all who are given the appellation South Asian.

And yet, it cannot be denied that a South Asian Canadian identity has emerged. It can be encountered in the Little India district of Toronto, patronizing "Indian" grocery, ready-made garment and jewellery stores, "Indian" movie theatres and restaurants, "Indian" tv programmes and in subscribing to newspapers such as *India Abroad* and *India Journal.* However, despite these common patterns of consumption and intermarriages where a "girl" in South Africa may be married off to a "boy" in Delhi—the marriage arranged in Canada—those described as South Asians may often reject the hyphenation altogether or choose another hyphenation. Neil Bissoondath, for example, wishes to be known as a Canadian writer and not a hyphenated Canadian one.

If we needed material proof of South Asian Canadian identity and South Asian Canadian literature, several anthologies have already appeared and several are in the pipeline. Scholarly articles and MA and PhD theses are also in evidence. Thus there is now definitely an object of knowledge called South Asian Canadian Literature that is being interpreted and debated. To the extent that South Asian Canadian writers share certain commonalities such as culture, memory and a repertoire of linguistic signs, they can be seen as producers of an entity called South Asian Canadian Literature that lends itself to analysis.

Here it is interesting to take a backward glance in order to see how the self-evident terms of today came into being. The 1981 Canadian census counted "Indo-Pakistanis," not "South Asians." The Secretary of State, in 1979, invited proposals from researchers "to undertake a study of the writers and writings of any one of the groups (Chinese, Japanese, Vietnamese, Indian, Pakistani, etc.)" (Sugunasiri 5). However, the term had obviously acquired enough cachet by the winter of 1982, when the first issue of *The Toronto South Asian Review* saw the light of day. The first editorial, published in the Summer 1982 issue, is important in view of the fact that the editor, M.G. Vassanji, played a major role in the development of South Asian Canadian literature in his triple role as editor, theorist, and writer. The passage quoted below outlines his vision of the journal's mission:

> *The Toronto South Asian Review* seeks to make accessible to a wider audi-
> ence literature that traces some part of its inheritance and meaning in
> the culture, traditions and history of the Indian subcontinent. It is a
> North American journal and will of necessity reflect perspectives devel-
> oped at least partly here. . . . It is not intended in these pages to set stan-
> dards for what reflects South Asian sensibilities and what does not. Nor
> is it intended for this journal to present a static reflection of the life
> lived in any particular part of the world at any given time period. Peo-
> ple of South Asian origin are found in all corners of the world, speak a
> large number of languages and English dialects, and possess traits from
> many other cultures. Many have passed through two or three continents
> within a few generations and have witnessed enormous historical
> changes. This diversity in backgrounds and experiences will naturally be
> reflected in a dynamic and vital way in the contents of this journal. (1)

It is fascinating that the editorial does not refer to Canada at all. It attrib-utes a transnational identity to South Asians and an examination of the jour-nal's contents shows that it has been publishing the writings of South Asians from many countries. Although the editorial refrains from positing an essen-tialized South Asian sensibility, it does project, albeit very tentatively, a certain shared history, the basis on which people can share a platform.

It is ironic that the journal which was a prime mover in the development of South Asian Canadian literature has now excised the term "South Asian" from its title. It changed its name in 1993 summer to *The Toronto Review of Con-temporary Writing Abroad.* The eight-page editorial in the Spring 1993 issue of the journal muses about the South Asian identity and South Asian Canadian literature and asks the following question: "Is there a South Asian Canadian literature—in terms of a contained, self-referential evolving body of work?" It goes on to answer this question in pessimistic terms:

> I have never sensed any passion behind that label "South Asian"—no political front, not even a loosely defined conscious aesthetic or the probing for one: it seemed to be simply a very convenient and the least discomfiting umbrella to fit under. No controversies, no eloquent voices raised, as happened in the black or Afro-communities. No real anger, but certainly resentment. Docility? Perhaps "South Asians" feel close enough to the mainstream to feel that goal achievable—and so everyone for himself, scrambling to get out of the hole and into the sun of recognition. (6)

Vassanji's diagnosis of South Asian writers' attitudes provides an important corrective to contemporary literary theory's tendency to assume that all minority writers write resistance literature and speak of the collective. Certainly, South Asian Canadian writers do not see themselves as members of a self-identified community, something that happened in the case of Chinese Canadian and Japanese Canadian writers when they got together in 1978 to produce an anthology called *Inalienable Rice*. The introduction to this anthology foregrounds the collective voice of the Chinese- and Japanese-Canadian literary community and the ethnopolitical agenda of their project. The writers of these two communities continue to speak collectively and to each other through their newsletter called *Rice Paper*.

One result of this close relationship among the writers of this group is, as Lien Chao notes in her PhD thesis, the presence in their writing of certain common tropes and themes. Given that these writers maintain such close personal and professional contact, "minority discourse" theory might be quite profitably utilized to study them. However, since South Asian Canadian writers do not participate in such a community, I do not believe that their work displays a shared agenda or a collective consciousness.

It is highly paradoxical that despite the anti-universalist stance taken by contemporary theorists, their unquestioning categorization of racial minority writers in the west and of all writers in the third world as "marginal," "subaltern," "postcolonial," "resistant," etc. ends up producing a new universalism. It seems to me that the application of terms such as "minority discourse," "postcolonial writing," "diaspora writing," "South Asian diaspora," "exile," etc. has provided critics with prefabricated enclosures to put away the racial minority writing after having once taken note of it in the shape of a laudatory review. After that, the theory mill can begin churning and spewing out more categories, more trendy phrases such as "hybridity," "difference," "marginalization," "métissage," etc. The problem is that the pronouncements of these theorists, produced in the specific circumstances of the United States, speak in a universalist vocabulary, never acknowledging their location in a place or time. The following passages from Homi Bhabha's *The Location of Culture* provide a good example of this locationless, timeless style:

> [T]he demography of the new internationalism is the history of post-colonial migration, the narratives of cultural and political diaspora, the major social displacements of peasant and aboriginal communities, the poetics of exile, the grim prose of political and economic refugees. . . .
> What is striking about the "new" internationalism is that the move from the specific to the general, from the material to the metaphoric, is not a smooth passage of transition and transcendence. The "middle passage" of contemporary culture, as with slavery itself, is a process of displacement and disjunction that does not totalize experience. Increasingly, "national" cultures are being produced from the perspective of disenfranchised minorities. (5-6)

> Where, once, the transmission of national traditions was the major theme of a world literature, perhaps we can now suggest that transnational histories of migrants, the colonized, or political refugees—these border and frontier conditions—may be the terrains of world literature. (12)

The ideas expressed in the passages quoted above about the special insights of the "migrant," who is also described as "postcolonial," "hybrid," "marginal," "minority" and "refugee," thus collapsing a diverse range of experiences and life situations, can also be found in the work of other well-known critics such as Abdul JanMohamed and David Lloyd, Edward Said and Françoise Lionnet. They all valorize the deterritorialized, border-crossing sensibility as the possessor of a special kind of truth. Aijaz Ahmad has suggested that such formulations erase "the difference between documents produced within the non-Western countries and those others which were produced by the immigrants at metropolitan locations. With the passage of time, the writings of immigrants were to become greatly privileged and were declared, in some extreme but also very influential formulations, to be the only *authentic* documents of resistance in our time" (91). It is these formulations which are expressed pedagogically in the course descriptions I quoted above where immigrant writers like Rohinton Mistry are grouped with aboriginal and third world writers and said to be giving voice to the silenced, the subaltern and the marginalized.

It is well worth remembering that most South Asian Canadian writers are not "political and economic refugees" or "exiles" or "peasants." M.G. Vassanji came to North America to study at MIT. Himani Bannerji came to University of Toronto as a graduate student. Rohinton Mistry worked at a bank before coming to Canada. They are economic migrants, but their situation should not be equated with refugees. Nor do all of them write about marginalization and resistance. Himani Bannerji's work, definitely, is about resisting racism but not that of Vassanji or Mistry. Vassanji writes about the various migrations of his fictionalized Shamsi community and Mistry about the middle-class Parsis of Bombay. (True, Mistry's new novel, *A Fine Balance*, portrays the marginalized poor of India, but I would not like to think of it as "giving voice to" the marginalized as contemporary theory claims for "postcolonial" and "minority" writers. Also, I don't think that the novel portrays "resistance"; rather, its tone seems to suggest that the poor accept their lot fatalistically.)

Although major literary and cultural critics have valorized immigrant writing, Canadian reviewers and critics do not seem to know what to do with novels like *The Gunny Sack, The Book of Secrets, Such a Long Journey* and *A Fine Balance*. True, Vassanji's *The Book of Secrets* and Mistry's *A Fine Balance* have been honoured by the bestowal of the prestigious Giller prize, yet, their lack of "Canadian content" is noticed. The *Toronto Star*'s book critic Philip Marchand's interview with Mistry is headlined, "Mistry writes home." Marchand reports that "many Canadian readers . . . feel there's something vaguely wrong with Mistry not writing about the country he has lived in for 20 years" (F1, F7). The question of "Canadian content" is often raised about the work of immigrant writers from racial minorities. As Vassanji complains, there is a perception "that a writer matures when he begins to talk of his 'Canadian experience' . . . ." (Introduction 3).

In his ambitious study called *Post-National Arguments: The Politics of the Anglophone-Canadian Novel Since 1967*, Frank Davey attributed only a footnote to Nino Ricci, M.G. Vassanji and Rohinton Mistry, claiming that they did not meet his criteria. Here is how he defines his selection process:

> I have chosen the specific texts of the study, not with the aim of representing any "best" books, or even best-selling books, but of representing instead books that have been important to particular Canadian audiences and have offered some portrayal of Canada as a semiotic field. (7)

Although, to my mind, these criteria can easily accommodate Ricci, Vassanji and Mistry, Davey's appended footnote explains why the above-mentioned writers are not discussed:

> This criterion excludes from direct examination some recent novels of Canadian ethnic communities which are of considerable importance, such as Nino Ricci's *Lives of the Saints*, Moyez Vassanji's *The Gunny Sack*, and Rohinton Mistry's *Such a Long Journey*, novels which contain few if any significations of Canada or of Canadian polity. Their lack of such

significations, however, itself has political implications which contribute to the general suggestions of this study. (7)

If one of the foremost Canadian critics does not know how to make sense of these novels in the Canadian context, it would be futile to expect anything from those who review for newspapers and journals. The usual procedure is to give a plot summary of sorts, comment on things such as characterization, narrative pacing, etc., and then end on some sort of encouraging note. "Canadian" writers, on the other hand, are attributed with the power of giving voice to Canadian experience.

But what I want to ask is, what is the meaning of South Asian Canadian books about "home" if I appropriate Philip Marchand's terminology for a moment? If they do not mean anything to readers like Frank Davey, then whom are they written for? For readers in India?

Given the fact that Penguin India has published Indian editions of M.G. Vassanji, Rohinton Mistry and Arnold Itwaru, it would be very interesting to do a comparative analysis of reader responses to these texts in Canada and India. As I have already suggested, the (white) Canadian response to these texts has been to see them as immigrants writing "home." In Vassanji's opinion, when a writer is categorized as "immigrant," he or she "may seem irrelevant to the ongoing dialectic" (Introduction 3). Not surprisingly, one of the most frequent words I come across in reviews of South Asian Canadian books is the word "exotic."

As to the Indian response, the papers that I heard at the Xth International Canadian Studies conference in Goa, India, spoke of South Asian Canadian writing as "immigrant sensibility," "caught between two worlds," "nostalgic" about India and unable to "become" fully Canadian. This pathologizing of the immigrant, then, is done both by Indian and Canadian readers. Immigrant writing, it seems, is always about longing for homes lost, about the pain of transportation, about adjustment and not about the "ongoing dialectic" of a society.

There is something very smug about this kind of response. I see it as a denial of the possibility that an "immigrant's book" may also have some relevance to readers in India. It seems that "the immigrant's experience" is relevant to no one except "the immigrant." Such a response seems highly inadequate to me in the contemporary world when fifteen million Indian citizens (the number who hold Indian passports) live abroad and have an impact on the lives of those who live in India by sending money home. But that is only one aspect of their impact. It is time for Indian critics to consider the possibility that South Asian Canadian writing may have something valuable to say about Indian life (life as lived in India certainly, if not life of Indians living abroad).

It is worth noticing that neither the Indian nor the Canadian critics use the vocabulary that accords a special insight to the "diasporic" or "exilic" writing, the kind of language one comes across at the high peaks of critical theory.

There is a certain Canadian (white) response that reads Rohinton Mistry's books as evidence of India's backwardness. Philip Marchand of the *Toronto Star* was not the only critic who found Bombay "repulsive":

> The local colour frequently turns repulsive. The Bombay of this novel is a city where sewers are in disrepair, where street food vendors practise doubtful hygiene, and where the wall of Gustad's apartment building . . . is used as a public toilet. The most disgusting, and macabre, imagery involves the Tower of Silence, where Parsis expose the bodies of their dead to the vultures, according to traditional practice. (Review)

Phoebe-Lou Adams of the *Atlantic Monthly* had a similar response:

> Mr Mistry's novel . . . includes such acid comments on Indian politics, metropolitan services, sanitation, and the corruption of Indira Gandhi's government that one can readily see why the author now lives in Toronto.

While such responses show that many readers in the west read the book as evidence of India's "horrors," Indian readers (and many South Asian Canadian readers) were critical of the book for its obsessive descriptions of Bombay's garbage. A visiting professor from India, when asked to respond to *Such a Long Journey*, which was in the news then, just having been nominated for the Booker prize, replied, "Ah, such a long book," and went on to talk about the book's tendency to step down to the gutter. She asked the expatriate writers to explore the beauties of India rather than wallow in the filth. She wanted, she said, a balanced portrayal. Such diametrically opposed responses to the book should give pause to the critics who claim that the "migrant" offers "unique insights" (Lionnet 6). These responses show the power of preconceptions and the readers' tendency to accommodate texts to their own ideological frameworks.

Totally opposed to the responses discussed earlier is that of a South Asian Canadian women's group whose anger at my review, which had been critical of the book's sexist portrayals of women, was reported to me by a friend who was present at the gathering. These women were angry because I had betrayed the community by being negative about one of "our" writers. The tension between Indo-Caribbean and African Caribbean communities around V.S. Naipaul and Neil Bissoondath is a similar case in point. Quite often, the disputants haven't even read the writer in question. However, I am not suggesting that one should not have an opinion before having read the book. What I am pointing out is the phenomenon where the writer becomes either an icon of community pride or a target of community anger.

Second-generation South Asian Canadians have another interesting response to South Asian Canadian writers. A South Asian student of mine is the president of the Rohinton Mistry fan club. He says that the book is important for him because it is located in Bombay, the city of his parents. This response rings a bell with me because I, too, have felt enthralled by books set in Lahore, a city that I have never visited because of partition but that was the home of my parents and grandparents. Young South Asian readers will, then, respond to South Asian Canadian literature in a much more intense way than other Canadians who may find it "confusing" because "it is such a long journey from that world to our own" (McEnteer).

Similar to this student's perspective on Mistry is that of some South Asian students who love reading South Asian Canadian writing because of its representation of South Asian lives as normal. They have suggested to me that finding characters with names like their own in literary texts takes away the pain they have felt because of the way their names were distorted and made fun of by teachers and other authority figures. I suppose entering the world of a South Asian Canadian book is experienced by these youngsters as some kind of affirmation.

For an immigrant from India like myself, the value of South Asian Canadian writing lies in learning about the historic migrations of South Asians during colonial times. Although I spent the first twenty-five years of my life in various academic settings in India, I had never been made aware of the indentured workers who went to the Caribbean, Mauritius, Fiji and Africa. Reading the works of Indo-Caribbean writers like Cyril Dabydeen and Arnold Itwaru and Asian African writer M.G. Vassanji has filled huge gaps in my knowledge of the world. Now that Penguin India has brought out Indian editions of some of these writers' works, Indian readers will have access to a narrative that has been almost forgotten in contemporary India.

It is evident that South Asian Canadian texts evoke multiple responses in Canada and in other parts of the world, responses which call into question theoretical models such as Fredric Jameson's national allegory, postcolonialists' "empire writes back," and minority discourse theorists' "collective subjectivity" (JanMohamed and Lloyd 9). The "resistance" to an antagonist, sometimes defined as "the colonizer" and sometimes "the west," that all these frameworks rely on in their analysis, is far too sweeping and simplistic to serve as an interpretive aid. It has no room, for example, for Vassanji's Indo-Africans who loved the sound of Big Ben or Rohinton Mistry's Parsis who are still not reconciled to the British departure from India. Such revelations, comic as they are, put a crimp in the heroic narratives of Herculean struggles of resistance.

The reality is that the South Asian Canadian community does not have a monolithic perspective, and nor do its writers. And so, while some writers do have a strong political agenda—Himani Bannerji and Krisantha Siri Bhaggiyadatta, for example—others like Neil Bissoondath think literature is apolitical. In his *Selling Illusions: The Cult of Multiculturalism in Canada*, Bissoondath berates antiracist and feminist struggles as reverse racism and reverse sexism. As regards literature, he wishes it to speak only of individuals and not of politics:

> Those who seek to subordinate art, its functions and its freedoms to sexual, racial or religious politics seek nothing less than to impose their own ideological visions on the imaginative expressions of others. (170)

> Literary characters must be true only to themselves and their circumstances. They owe allegiance to neither the writer nor the social group to which they belong. They are, if they truly live, individuals with their own psychology and their own biography, no more and no less representative or symbolic of a group than any live, breathing human being. (181)

Bissoondath's view that literature should be above politics and about individuals, alas, is not unique among South Asian Canadian writers. A recent collection of Urdu stories in translation excludes all Marxist Urdu writers because they failed to explore "what lay beyond the immediate socioeconomic reality." Only a few "independent" writers, according to the editor, "elected to chronicle the events of the elusive and shimmering realms of the individual consciousness" (Memon vi).

Given such a diversity of ideological perspectives among South Asian Canadian writers, I do not see how a "collective consciousness" can be ascribed to them, the criterion so important for minority discourse theorists. Nor can I agree that "marginalization" and "resistance" are the main themes of all South Asian Canadian writers. Insofar as South Asian Canadian writers trace their origins to the Indian subcontinent, their work, if studied together, may yield certain recurring themes and patterns. What I am resisting here is the tendency in contemporary critical theory to categorize these writers a priori as resistant postcolonials, as subalterns and marginals. The fact remains that South Asians are a people divided along class, caste, religious, ideological, and national lines, and, though we seem to communicate with each other without problems in the grocery stores of Little India on Toronto's Gerrard Street, we don't seem to do so anywhere else. To suggest, then, that our writers speak in one voice, the voice of "resistance," or represent the "collective," is to distort the facts.

It is quite ironic that such claims on behalf of "postcolonial" and "minority" writers go unexamined in the era of deconstruction. As readers, we must learn to be as vigilant of the truth claims of these writers' texts as we have of those by "dead white males." Unfortunately, terms like "postcoloniality," "marginality," "subalternity" and "resistance" make it impossible to talk about things such as ideology, mediation and conditions of production and dissemination. These are important questions and productive lines of inquiry would open up if we asked these questions while reading South Asian Canadian texts.

Works Cited

Adams, Phoebe-Lou. Review of *Such a Long Journey. Atlantic Monthly* 267.5 (1991): 124.

Ahmad, Aijaz. *In Theory: Classes, Nations, Literatures.* London: Verso, 1992.

Balan, Jars, ed. *Identifications: Ethnicity and the Writer in Canada.* Edmonton: The Canadian Institute of Ukrainian Studies, 1982.

Bhabha, Homi. *The Location of Culture.* London: Routledge, 1994.

Bissoondath, Neil. *Selling Illusions: The Cult of Multiculturalism in Canada.* Toronto: Penguin, 1994.

Davey, Frank. *Post-National Arguments: The Politics of the Anglophone-Canadian Novel Since 1967.* Toronto: U of Toronto P, 1993.

JanMohamed, Abdul R., and David Lloyd. "Introduction: Toward a Theory of Minority Discourse: What Is to Be Done?" *The Nature and Context of Minority Discourse.* Ed. JanMohamed and Lloyd. New York: Oxford UP, 1990. 1-16.

Lionnet, Françoise. *Postcolonial Representations: Women, Literature, Identity.* Ithaca: Cornell UP, 1995.

Marchand, Philip. "Mistry Writes Home." *Toronto Star* 3 Dec. 1995: F1, F7.

—. Review of *Such a Long Journey. Toronto Star* 4 May 1991: K13.

McEnteer, James. Review of *Such a Long Journey. Calgary Herald* 7 Sept. 1991: D15.

Memon, Muhammad Umar, ed. *Domains of Fear and Desire: Urdu Stories.* Toronto: TSAR, 1992.

Mukherjee, Meenakshi. "Interrogating Post-Colonialism." *Interrogating Post-Colonialism: Theory, Text and Context.* Ed. Harish Trivedi and Mukherjee. Shimla: Indian Institute of Advanced Study, 1996. 3-11.

Pivato, Joseph, ed. *Literatures of Lesser Diffusion.* Edmonton: Research Institute for Comparative Literature, 1990.

Sugunasiri, Suwanda. "The Literature of Canadians of South Asian Origin: An Overview." *The Search for Meaning: The Literature of Canadians of South Asian Origin.* Ed. Sugunasiri. Ottawa: Department of the Secretary of State of Canada, 1988. 5-25.

Trivedi, Harish. "India and Post-Colonial Discourse." *Interrogating Post-Colonialism: Theory, Text and Context.* Ed. Trivedi and Meenakshi Mukherjee. Shimla: Indian Institute of Advanced Study, 1996. 231-47.

Vassanji, M.G. "Editorial." *Toronto South Asian Review* 1.2 (1982): 1.

—. "Editorial." *Toronto South Asian Review* 11.3 (1993): 1-8.

—. Introduction. *A Meeting of Streams: South Asian Canadian Literature.* Ed. Vassanji. Toronto: TSAR, 1985. 1-6.

PART VII
⇉⊢ Negotiating Postcolonialisms ⊣⇇

21

"What Use is Ethnicity to Aboriginal Peoples in Canada?"*

Margery Fee

I want to begin by analysing my own title, a self-reflexive move that I hope is still fashionable, rather than irritating. In doing so I want to try to situate this paper in a larger project: attempting to come to terms with both the discourse of ethnicity/race and one of its most brutal subsets, racist discourse. Both discourses are central to my fields of specialization in literary studies, Canadian literatures and Commonwealth/post-colonial literatures. To talk about the *use* of race/ethnicity is an attempt to talk about it as something that is constructed and once constructed, deployed, by both minority and majority groups, for both liberatory and repressive ends. It exists in some cultures in very static forms and in others in very fluid forms: Canada is one country where these discourses are undergoing rapid modification, sometimes in directions that will lead to greater equality and sometimes not. It is precisely for this reason that it is crucial to try to think and talk about the ways in which ethnicity/race is constructed and deployed, rather than seeing it as simply something we either have or do not have. This is increasingly a world where so-called "mixed relationships" produce children who are nonetheless constrained by the dominant discourse to conform to concepts of racial/ethnic purity and authenticity. Simply to condemn ideas of purity, however, is to risk discounting people's experiences in the world, where their families and their social, geographical, and national locations have written them into positions that they cannot simply abandon even if they wished to. As with gender, it is one thing to talk about it as a construct and another thing to decide to abandon one's gender identity. Nonetheless, like gender, ethnicity/race can be downplayed or spotlighted in particular circumstances; at some moments it is useful to be a woman, at others it is not. Similarly, one's race or ethnicity can be useful at some times and places, and at others is something to be concealed, if at all possible. Obviously, the ability and power to control how one's race/ethnicity is perceived is unevenly distributed in society: power is often, after all, distributed so that one ethnic group is markedly less powerful than another.

Probably my use of the expression "race/ethnicity" has already highlighted

---

* *Canadian Review of Comparative Literature* 22.3-4 (1995): 683-91.

a problem that can only be touched on here. How are these two terms connected? Race is usually seen as a broader category than ethnicity. Ethnicity is usually tied to political, linguistic and cultural markers, rather than to biological and physical ones. Race is often thought to be something that is self-evidently apparent, while ethnicity is usually seen either as optional, or at least as more flexible than race. Racial identity is not usually figured as optional. Citizenship and nationality are often seen as quite optional, particularly in New World nations where the vast majority of the population is descended from immigrants. However, to apply David Theo Goldberg's description of the concept of race in *Racist Culture: Philosophy and the Politics of Meaning* to all these terms is to see them as "fluid, fragile, and more or less vacuous concept[s]" (80-81). Thus to discuss them is necessarily to situate how these terms are used in a particular political and social context.

What follows is an attempt to discuss what use race/ethnicity is to Aboriginal peoples in contemporary Canada in their struggle for equality. Briefly put, I will argue that ethnicity, at least if it is figured at the level of distinctive cultural and linguistic groups, from Haida through Cree to Micmac, is not particularly useful at this point in history. Nor is "race" as it is commonly applied in Canada to the Aboriginal peoples, since the Inuit, Métis and Indian are usually regarded as racially distinct. Rather, most of the breakthroughs that these peoples have had in their dealings with the Canadian state have come through a discourse of citizenship. As Peter Kulchyski notes in "Aboriginal Peoples and Hegemony in Canada," the Canadian government refused for a long time to grant citizenship rights to any Aboriginal people who were not prepared to first give up their Aboriginal rights: "Indians voted with their feet to remain Indians by not applying in significant numbers for enfranchisement" (64). The Trudeau government announced in 1969 that it proposed to move to treat the Aboriginal peoples as ordinary Canadians (they had received the vote in 1959). After over a hundred years of treating them as wards of the state whose rights were a matter for federal bureaucrats to determine, with just the horrifying results that one might expect, the government proposed an about-face that meant that such matters as land claims and other treaty rights were about to be unilaterally abandoned. The Aboriginal reaction was outrage. Widespread demonstrations led to a change in policy (initially called "citizens plus") which recognized these groups as entitled to Canadian citizenship rights and more—to Aboriginal rights also— since essentially the privileges of the immigrant Canadian population were grounded on the wholesale impoverishment of the Aboriginal peoples through the denial of their rights in the past.

Ethnicity, although obviously relevant at many levels, is not useful in political negotiations to a group primarily interested in constructing a pan-Aboriginal nationalism that focuses on what these peoples have in common, rather than on their ethno-linguistic differences. The Aboriginal peoples have based their claims to constitutional equality on their status as sovereign nations, and these claims have been productively hitched to Quebec's nationalist aspirations in recent constitutional negotiations. Ethnicity, unlike nationality, is regarded in the dominant discourse as something deployed by immigrant groups struggling to overcome the marginalization imposed on them by the dominant national culture. In this model, Anglo-Celtic Canadians have no ethnicity. The immigrant's ethnicity is constructed, in part, by the dominant group's confident appropriation of the term Canadian for itself. In English Canada, in most contexts, Canadian is used to mean Anglo-Celtic Canadian, period, although it may extend to suitably assimilated and white Canadians from other ethnic groups. This exclusivity is, indeed, what gave force to the anti-separatist slogan "My Canada includes Quebec."

So there it was—my answer to the self-posed question which forms my title was that for Aboriginal people to deploy race or ethnicity in their writing was a self-defeating tactic. First, it might well undermine political solidarity within the Aboriginal community, and this community is small, widely-spread and ethnically diverse. Second, it would lower rather than raise their status *vis-à-vis* the state and the mainstream public. Third, markers of Aboriginal ethnicity have been subjected to such constant appropriation (literal and symbolic) that to display them for political purposes might well be to expose them to further appropriation, trivialization, and commodification.

Thus, one version of my paper ends right here. But I do not think that the current political situation will remain static: the discourses of "race," ethnicity and nation will continue to be reconfigured. Further, to leave each group in its currently-constructed category assumes these categories make sense. Lee Maracle's story "Yin Chin" is about Aboriginal racism directed against the Chinese: the narrator comments "I have lived in this city in the same neighbourhood as Chinese people for twenty-two years now and do not know a single Chinese person" (66). This isolation is one of the results of reified racial or ethnic categories. Further, to see the struggles of different "minority" groups as separate negotiations with the dominant culture, one on one in every case, strengthens these categories in unproductive ways. As Sneja Gunew puts it, "The dismantling of hegemonic categories is facilitated by the proliferation of difference rather than the setting up of binary oppositions that can merely be reversed, leaving structures of power intact" (1). However, once difference has proliferated, it must not be too severely consolidated, because this weakens the acceptance of a fluid system of issue-related alliances. Divide and conquer, we should never forget, really works.

Most "minority" groups are, like Aboriginal people, faced with racism. But the racism directed at recent immigrants, especially those who are not of European background, usually makes the bland assumption that their languages and cultures must be checked at the door of any mainstream institution (as became obvious in the controversy over allowing Sikh Royal Canadian Mounted Police officers to wear turbans as part of their uniform, rather than the oddly-shaped but symbolically-prized traditional headgear.)[1] Aboriginal peoples are faced with a different attitude to their cultures—all are subject to endless intrusive appropriation. This latter process, which Terry Goldie calls "indigenization," is an attempt by immigrant Canadians to forge an aboriginal link with the land that the Aboriginal peoples in Canada claim for themselves. This move not only short-circuits land claims, it is also a way of avoiding acknowledging how structural racism privileges those defined as "mainstream" Canadian. Thus the "othering" engaged in by Anglo-Canadians takes different forms with respect to Aboriginal and immigrant cultures. But one assumption is common: "they" have race/ethnicity, Anglo-Canadians don't. In *Mapping the Language of Racism*, Margaret Wetherell and Jonathan Potter examine the way that the discourse of "race," based on a Darwinist language of biology, is being supplanted by a superficially less offensive discourse of culture (what I feel could also be called a discourse of ethnicity), based on the idea of culture as heritage. They point out that the discourse of culture sets up a disabling hierarchy that deprivileges New Zealand's indigenous Maori as effectively as did the discourse of race. Maori are believed to have a culture that must be maintained in its traditional authentic form; Pakeha (white New Zealanders) "simply possess society . . . and 'civilization'" (135). If Maori lose their culture "they do not automatically become Pakeha or 'civilized' by default." Instead, they are hollowed out, rootless, and in desperate need of what the authors call, with intentional irony, "heritage therapy." Perhaps needless to say, it is "assumed in this discourse that Pakeha can get by very well without culture" (136).

This system works just as well in Canada, where Anglo-Canadians are seen as without ethnicity, as possessed of a "Canadian" ethnicity (generally depicted as not much different from no ethnicity at all), or as possessing the national high culture, while ethnic minorities are permitted to have broken English, colourful costumes, exotic dances, and unusual food. Their writing, categorized as "ethnic writing," is instantly devalued as both less than national and therefore, less than literature. Derek Walcott's sarcastic depiction of this dichotomy is to note that while the British assume that "blacks can't do Shakespeare," somehow white British citizens are, by contrast, portrayed as all having the classics of British literature at their command. He imagines an unlikely scene in the Brixton riots where "the riot police and the skinheads exchanged quips/you could trace to the Sonnets" (483).

So how can we destabilize these discourses? As Wetherell and Potter point out, when a Pakeha learns Maori, this becomes an add-on benefit: "for the Pakeha, Maori culture can be a rich extra dimension, like having a Constable painting to decorate a wall. Pakeha are free actively to choose this culture, Maori can reject it only at the risk of being found anomic" (134). If I were to learn Haida, say, this could easily become an appropriative or Orientalizing move. Is examining my own Irish, Scottish, English ethnic heritage—or even my own Canadian ancestors—a productive move, or does it also simply add to my privilege, my "cultural capital," my power? One way to read Aboriginal writers in a counter-appropriative way, I feel, is to pay attention to their advice. Several Aboriginal writers have suggested that for immigrant North Americans, coming to terms with one's own ancestors is an improvement over indigenization. Leslie Marmon Silko, a Laguna writer, notes that her elders teach their descendants to remember who they are, while "the Anglo-American attitude for the past two hundred years has been to cast off familial and geographic ties . . . to change identities as easily as changing shoes . . . and to obliterate their white, middle-class ancestry and origins" (213). (Indeed, one might argue that the widespread "rags to riches" myth demands the sacrifice of any original culture that does not match elite norms. Recent immigrants, who are frequently at odds with their original culture either because of political or religious persecution or because of economic inequity, are most susceptible to this myth.) Silko argues that white writers have to come to terms with their own ancestry before they can assume they can come to terms with that of others; to simply slide into a new identity, while enforcing a fixed, authentic identity on the other, is a move that allows Anglo-Americans to avoid accepting that their privilege is based on the oppressive actions of their forebears. Similarly, in a recent interview, Lee Maracle, a Métis, says,

> I think people in this country have to get real. . . . We should be real about who these [Aboriginal] people are and how this country came into being. We should know what its origins are. We should know something, and we don't. And I think it's because people here don't take this being here seriously. I think their parents came here with the idea that they would make their fortune and go home and never went home. But the grandchildren, somehow, and the great-grandchildren, were never given a past to being here. (784)

Maria Campbell, also a Métis, makes the same point about Linda Griffiths, her Scottish-Canadian collaborator on a play about Campbell's life. Campbell says she cannot figure out who Canadians are and Griffiths replies "We all come from somewhere else. People trace their families back to a boat," and Campbell says "Well, if you guys came on a boat from Scotland, then Scotland is your home," but Griffiths points out that Anglo-Celtic Canadians usually know where their ancestors came from, all right, "But ask them about their own bloody grandfather that lived right here and it's, 'He was born, he lived and he died'" (95). Campbell's response is that most Anglo-Canadians came here "broken down and conquered" and continues "As long as you refuse to look at that history, of course you'll be ghosts, because you have no place to come from" (95). Griffiths resists, wanting to move the story to Canadian soil and to try to understand Canadian history and what forces acted to imperialize Canadians here. But despite this disagreement, both do agree that what has happened in Canada has been obliterated, that memories of ethnically-based conflict have been wiped out, and that this obliteration has left its marks on the political attitudes of Canadians of all backgrounds. The assumption of ethnicity may indeed be deployed to add to the privilege of the already-privileged, but it also has the potential to lead to an understanding of how that privilege has been ideologically constructed.

Further, what does it mean to think of myself as white? Leslie Roman concludes in "White is a Color!" that white students must be encouraged to see how they fit into narratives of structural racism without becoming paralysed by guilt or immobilized by defensiveness. Teachers and students, she argues, need "to transform their . . . desire to be included in the narratives of racial oppression as its disadvantaged victims into a willingness to be included in narratives which fully account for the daily ways we (whites) benefit from conferred racial privilege as well as from our complicity in the often invisible institutional and structural workings of racism" (84). This requires that they see themselves, not as without colour, which implies that they are the "hidden norm" against which all other "colours" are measured, but that they acknowledge that they are not without "racial subjectivities, interests and privileges" (71). This is much the tack that Ruth Frankenberg takes in *White Women, Race Matters: The Social Construction of Whiteness* when she points out that "race" is a system that depends as much on the privilege of one "race" (what in contemporary North America is called "white" or "Caucasian") as it does on the underprivileging of other groups, often now termed "visible minorities" or "people of colour." The two last terms imply an invisible majority or people without colour, and this is precisely the implication that she and Roman wish to dispel. As Frankenberg notes, "any system or differentiation shapes those on whom it bestows privilege as well as those it oppresses. White people are 'raced,' just as men are gendered" (1).

Both Roman and Frankenberg situate their focus on race in particular contexts. Roman's paper comes out of classroom experience in Louisiana during the 1990 campaign of David Duke, former Ku Klux Klan and Nazi party member. (Duke called his organization the National Association for the Advancement of White People, appropriating for the 1990s the name of the organization that led the movement for de-segregation, the National Association for the Advancement of Colored People). Frankenberg's work comes out of working in socialist feminist groups in the 1980s where well-meaning white women were trying to grapple with the issue of race in a context where women of colour kept telling them they had got it wrong. In these contexts, the public debate was over how the words race and racism were deployed, over who controlled their meanings. Stuart Hall, writing of much the same period in Britain notes a new relationship between the discourses of race and ethnicity. He comments that "black" as a term was mobilized in post-war Britain to "provide the organizing category for a new politics of resistance, amongst groups and communities with, in fact, very different histories, traditions and ethnic identities" (223). Now, he argues, within the space that this resistance provided in British society, a "new conception of ethnicity" is arising "to set against the embattled, hegemonic conception of 'Englishness' which, under Thatcherism, stabilizes so much of the dominant political and cultural discourses, and which, because it is hegemonic, does not represent itself as ethnicity at all" (227).

Thus, it seems that if race/ethnicity are to become useful conceptual tools for Aboriginal peoples, it will be in a context where race and ethnicity are ascribed to everyone in the society and where they are used as actively changing constructs. Interestingly, the impact of Aboriginal struggle on constitutional negotiations has been to make this aspect of ethnicity obvious. The most recent attempt to produce national consensus, for example, offered greatly enhanced rights to the Métis, recognizing their position that they are a distinctive nation formed mainly of French and Aboriginal cultures and ancestry.

The pan-Aboriginal nationalism that I referred to at the beginning of my paper is, in Canada, largely being constructed by women writers. These writers, including Jeannette Armstrong, Maria Campbell, Beatrice Culleton, Ruby Slipperjack, Annharte Baker, and Lee Maracle, are not simply reproducing a European nationalism. As Jennifer Kelly notes,

> the Native Canadian feminist "nationalism" [these writers] articulate, while like other "nationalisms" in being past-directed (emerging from more than fifty pre-colonial "nations") and comprising an "imagined community" . . . is an effective, multifaceted *strategy* for decolonization—effective because it engages with the crucial issues of gender, racism, sexism, "race," class, because it incorporates heterogeneity within in a "nationalist" community, and, to use Gareth Griffith's words, recognizes "that syncreticity is neither a threat to identity nor a denial of the postcolonial reality." (17)

This revisionist construction of national identity resists the patriarchal structures of both Aboriginal and European culture by straight-forwardly integrating feminist issues into an Aboriginal perspective. Such issues as prostitution, the abduction of children by child "welfare" services, rape, wife or partner battering, and so on, are not downplayed. These are issues that Aboriginal women writers are insisting that all Aboriginal peoples—indeed all Canadians—must deal with before cultural healing can be completed, and perhaps even more significantly, before constitutional changes can be made. Thus the presence of Aboriginal women's groups at the most recent constitutional negotiations, the women's position being that the traditional male-dominated Aboriginal political coalitions should not be allowed to pretend they represented all Aboriginal women. The political energy that fuelled this success in part came out of the political experience that Aboriginal women gained, not just in the struggle for Aboriginal liberation, but also in the context of feminist struggle. Aboriginal women writers are represented in such ground-breaking feminist collections as *Women and Words: The Anthology*, 1984; *Telling It: Women and Language Across Cultures*, 1990; *Language in Her Eye: Writing and Gender*, 1990; and *Returning the Gaze: Essays on Racism, Feminism and Politics*, 1993, and of course, these collections are merely the tip of an iceberg of discussion, interaction and political intervention by women from a variety of different ethnic backgrounds over the past decade. These collections in themselves show the value of transgressive boundary crossing between differences.

Ethnic boundary construction may be common in human interaction, but as Sollors points out "ethnic groups in the United States have relatively little cultural differentiation" and "the cultural *content* of ethnicity . . . is largely interchangeable and rarely historically authenticated" (28). What the boundaries forge is a group that seeks to achieve a collective goal (one that may also be sought by other groups). We may well respect the boundaries without necessarily believing that what they enclose has some sort of authentic essence that determines the membership of all group members either biologically or psychologically. Sollors locates the term *ethnicity* with respect to a discourse of consent (one that figures social relations as freely chosen) or a discourse of descent (one that figures social relations as inescapably marked by descent). *Ethnicity*, for him, is a term that slides between these two positions. I would argue that the more powerful our social group, the more likely we are to believe that our social relations are freely chosen, while the more powerless our social group, the more likely we are to believe, in part because a hard-edged ethnicity is forced on us, that our social relations depend wholly on descent. Thus, I feel that the move away from concepts of ethnic diversity and authenticity to Aboriginal pan-ethnic nationalism is a move towards greater equality for the First Peoples because it allows more freedom from the constraints of a stereotyped category. Similarly, to move towards reinscribing ethnicity on supposedly "ethnicity-free" Anglo-Celtic Canadians is also a positive move, because it forces those who have had the privilege to feel they transcend ethnicity to reconsider their relations with other ethnic groups from a slightly more down-to-earth position. Until the power imbalances in Canada have been reconfigured, both these moves seem useful in asserting the claim of Aboriginal peoples in this country to equality.

These are strategic conclusions, that are intended only to imply that [what] will work for here and for now to achieve a more equitable situation for Aboriginal people can only be achieved by resisting the temptation to map the route to this goal on the basis of generalizations that are not grounded in particular societies and situations at particular points in history. Nor can these generalizations ignore the positions of those subject to exclusion (thus excluding them again). Otherwise we get depressingly common and ironic situations where white people tell people of colour how best they can liberate themselves. (Buyer of the generalizations in this paper beware!)

Notes

1. Baltej Dhillon was the RCMP officer who fought and won the right to wear a turban with his uniform.

WORKS CITED

Frankenberg, Ruth. *White Women, Race Matters: The Social Construction of Whiteness.* Minneapolis: U of Minnesota P, 1993.

Goldberg, David Theo. *Racist Culture: Philosophy and the Politics of Meaning.* Oxford: Blackwell, 1993.

Goldie, Terry. *Fear and Temptation: The Image of the Indigene in Canadian, Australian, and New Zealand Literatures.* Toronto: U of Toronto P, 1989.

Griffiths, Linda, and Maria Campbell. *The Book of Jessica: A Theatrical Transformation.* Toronto: Coach House, 1989.

Gunew, Sneja. "Feminism and the Politics of Irreducible Differences: Multiculturalism/Ethnicity/Race." *Feminism and the Politics of Difference.* Ed. Sneja Gunew and Anna Yeatman. Halifax: Fernwood, 1993. 1-19.

Hall, Stuart. "New Ethnicities." 1989. Partially rpt. *The Post-Colonial Studies Reader.* Ed. Bill Ashcroft, et al. London: Routledge, 1995. 223-27.

Kelly, Jennifer. "Transforming Borders: Gender and Nationalism in Native Canadian Women's Writing." *CHIMO* 28 (1994): 16-18.

Kulchyski, Peter. "Aboriginal Peoples and Hegemony in Canada." *Journal of Canadian Studies* 30.1 (1995): 60-68.

Maracle, Lee. "Yin Chin." *Sojourner's Truth and Other Stories.* Vancouver: Press Gang, 1990. 65-72.

—. "Coming out of the House: Interview with Jennifer Kelly." *ARIEL* 25.1 (1994): 733-88.

Roman, Leslie G. "White is a Color!: White Defensiveness, Postmodernism, and Anti-Racist Pedagogy." *Race, Identity and Representation in Education.* Ed. Cameron McCarthy and Warren Crichlow. New York: Routledge, 1993. 71-88.

Silko, Leslie Marmon. "An Old-Time Indian Attack Conducted in Two Parts: Part One: Imitation 'Indian'; Part Two: Gary Snyder's 'Turtle Island.'" *The Remembered Earth.* Ed. Geary Hobson. Albuquerque: U of New Mexico P, 1980. 211-16.

Sollors, Werner. *Beyond Ethnicity: Consent and Dissent in American Culture.* New York: Oxford UP, 1986.

Walcott, Derek. *Collected Poems, 1948-1984.* New York: Noonday, 1986.

Wetherell, Margaret and Jonathan Potter. *Mapping the Language of Racism: Discourse and the Legitimation of Exploitation.* New York: Columbia UP, 1992.

22

"'A Tough Geography': Towards a Poetics of Black Space(s) in Canada"*[1]

Rinaldo Walcott

We say that a national literature emerges when a community whose collective existence is called into question tries to put together the reasons for its existence. (Glissant 104)

The word must be mastered. But such mastery will be insignificant unless it is an integral part of a resolute collective act—a political act. (Glissant 163)

So we're not going any place, and we're not melting or keeping quiet in Bathurst Subway or on Bathurst Street or on any other street we take over—Eglinton, Vaughan, Marlee. If our style bothers you, deal with it. That's just life happening, that's just us making our way home. (Brand, *Bread* 80-81)

Walking Negro Creek Road

Settler colonies can be characterized by their struggles over race and space. Canada is no exception. The first phase of black demands on the Canadian nation-state must be considered in light of Africadian demands that land grants promised to them be honoured.[2] When some of those grants were indeed honoured, the quality of the land was suitable for little more than housing plots. This originary struggle over space, constituted through a specific and particularized Canadian racial discourse, is what we might call the racial geography of Canada.[3] National historical narratives render these racial geographies invisible, and many people continue to believe that any black presence in Canada is a recent and urban one spawned by black Caribbean, and now continental African, migration.

In 1967 Africville was finally and permanently razed. It continues to exist only in the memories of its former inhabitants and their descendants. Now, the desire to render black peoples and blackness an absented presence in Canada has been made literally and symbolically clear. More recently in

---

* *Black Like Who?: Writing Black Canada* (Toronto: Insomniac, 1997), 35-51.

Ontario, the offensively stupid claim of Holland Township Council, that using the word Negro in the 1990s was uncomfortable, led to that council changing the name of Negro Creek Road to Moggie Road. Renaming the road after George Moggie, a white settler, was yet another paragraph in the continuing and unfolding story of the ways in which Canadian state institutions and official narratives attempt to render blackness outside of those same narratives, and simultaneously attempt to contain blackness through discourses of Canadian benevolence. Thus blackness in Canada is situated on a continuum that runs from the invisible to the hyper-visible.

While contemporary poets, activists, oral documenters and archivists such as George Elliott Clarke, Delvina Bernard, Maxine Tynes, Sylvia Hamilton (who is also a filmmaker), the singer/songwriter Faith Nolan and numerous others, have attempted to counter the writing of black people out of the Canadian nation, the process continues to unfold.[4] It appears that the collecting and documenting of evidence of a black presence that is underway in Nova Scotia is not occurring in Ontario, Quebec, British Columbia and the other provinces. The importance of the Nova Scotian achievement is that it gives us the ability to create a language of blackness in Canada: one that is at once mindful of black migrant cultures, but also recognizes and acknowledges the true genealogy of black existence in Canada.[5]

Canada is a land troubled by race and space, whether we are speaking of First Nations land claims, Quebec nationalism, or the "absented presence" of Canada's others. In 1993 the eruption of what was characterized as a "mini-riot" at a condominium complex on Dixon Road in Etobicoke, involving the Somali community, crystalized the issues of race and space in this nation. Accusations against Somali youths attempted to place their cultural practices firmly outside the nation, even when the accusations were ridiculous. A consequence of the "troubles" was that a move was made to criminalize Somali youth through the use of stringent enforcement of trespass laws. Somalis were made hyper-visible, in an effort to mark and to confine their movements and bodies in space and to a particular place. Nineteen ninety-three signalled the incorporation of the Somali community into the dominant discourses of race and blackness structured by North American white supremacy. That racialized discourse, fostered by and emanating out of slavery, is continually fashioned through an ideology that suggests that black bodies can and must be abused, misused, regulated, disciplined and over-policed. These practices of regulation and discipline occur in the effort to make belonging, as Dionne Brand puts it, "an uneasy place" (*Bread* 67).

Yet black people in North America continue to make both space and place theirs. This, however, is not accomplished by understanding their experiences as isolated and disconnected from other places and spaces. The political identifications of black peoples are crucial and essential to resistance. Making outer-national identifications with other black peoples is important to the kinds of struggles that might be waged within national boundaries. Dionne Brand, by working across different genres (poetry, short stories, oral history, historical and sociological essays, polemical writing, film-making and now the novel), has used her immigrant/citizen status to bring new cartography to the question of race and space in the Canadian context. She redraws and remaps the Canadian urban landscape in order to announce and articulate a black presence that signals defiance, survival and renewal. Brand's work, located in the urban spaces of migrant existences, refigures the actual, literary and figurative landscapes of Canada, and so redraws boundaries of knowing, experience and belonging. But what is characteristically complex about Brand's work is that it offers no orthodoxies on blackness. Instead her Marxist, feminist, lesbian voice and political insights are the bases from which she articulates critiques of patriarchal and essentialist notions of blackness, as well as critiques of racism, patriarchy and class exploitation in Canada.

AFTER THE NOSTALGIA OF IMMIGRANT WRITING

Nostalgia is dead. Dionne Brand's *In Another Place, Not Here*, a complexly woven tale of space, language, identity and place, is uncharacteristic in terms of recent (Caribbean?) black Canadian literature. Brand's refusal to construct a narrative of easy nostalgia that has come to mark much immigrant writing is notable. *In Another Place* puts an end to, or at least signals the demise of such cultural representations and (literary) politics.

Comparatively, Cecil Foster's focus (in his two novels on the ways in which movement, or rather migration, to Canada has affected individuals) is still in large measure concerned with the politics of dislocation constituted via nostalgia for "home." It seems that one of the challenges facing contemporary black Canadian art is to move beyond the discourse of nostalgia for an elsewhere and toward addressing the politics of its present location. Foster's characters, in particular Suzanne in *Sleep On Beloved*, must deal with their inability to put home "behind" them. I am by no means suggesting that one's move to an elsewhere can only be made "successful" by jettisoning the past. Memory often will not allow that anyway. What I am trying to suggest is that "immigrant writing," and in this case "Caribbean (black) immigrant writing," is often shrouded in a nostalgic longing for a past that is neglectful of the politics of the present location. Interestingly, one might read Claire Harris's poetic collections, particularly her recent *Dipped in Shadows*, as another piece in the (re)ordering of black writers' concerns with the cultural politics of "home"—that is, Canada.

But in making these claims, Brand and Harris should be considered with another group of black Canadian writers who have made the question of space one of concern to their artistic endeavours.[6] George Elliott Clarke, Maxine Tynes, Carol Talbot and a number of others have continually emphasized place and space in their work—in particular the places and spaces which, for lack of a better term, I would designate "indigenous black Canadian space." This particular group of "indigenous black Canadians" have not garnered as much attention nationally as they should because their presence—the places and spaces they occupy—makes a lie of too many national myths (or raises too many questions) concerning the Canadian nation-state. Thus, in a perverse way, it is around Canadian blacks of Caribbean descent that definitions of blackness in Canada are clustered. The hyper-visibility of Caribbean blackness makes "indigenous black Canadians" invisible.

With Brand, I want to interrogate and speculate about what the category black Canadian might mean in the context of this historical moment. Brand's last three works concern themselves in no small detail with mapping a black Canadian poetics of space—"a tough geography" (40) as she puts it in *No Language is Neutral*. These efforts are important for the historians and sociologists who have not been able to furnish black Canada with a discourse that recognizes an almost five-hundred-year past, it is up to those of us engaged in other aspects of cultural work to articulate what that means. While I am in no way trying to position literature and its critics as the vanguard of cultural knowing, it appears to me that imaginative works often render much more complex and interesting constructions of our multiple historical experiences than other cultural forms. I think that in the case of black Canada this is particularly so.

George Elliott Clarke, in the important essay "A Primer of African-Canadian Literature," offers a genealogy of African-Canadian literature in which he makes some important claims concerning black writers in Canada. While Clarke is paying attention to the active and political deployment of a constellation of African-Canadian works in an attempt to combat "uninformed commentaries" (7) which reduce black Canadian literature to "West Indian Writers" (7), he also offers an interesting project for internal black dialogues, critiques and conversations. His essay suggests a paradigm for discussing not just black literatures in Canada, but also, I would argue, black cultures. Clarke suggests that "exiles and refugees" (7) are the primary source for black Canadian literature; he writes: "African-Canadian literature has been, from its origins, the work of political exiles and native dissidents" (7). This renders complex and fluid the very constitution of those who might and might not be defined as black Canadian. Clarke's observation holds great promise for formulating a black Canadian discourse conscious of both the locality of national boundaries and the limitations of nation. It is in the context of exiles and refugees that I shall engage a discussion of Brand's *In Another Place*.

Exiles and Refugees

In Another Place, Not Here is the story of two migrant black women, Verlia and Elizete. Verlia's migration is legally accomplished; Elizete's migration is not sanctioned by state authorities. What these two women's stories allow us to see is the ways in which their existence redraws the boundaries of Toronto, Ontario and Canada. Those boundaries are redrawn in the way they resist brutality. Brand uses her characters' experiences to write a text that exists at/on the in-between space; in fact, the very language of the novel occupies the space of the in-between. Brand constructs sentences that bring Canada and Caribbean together in ways that remap both: for example, "She decided to get away from the mall and Gladstone and began to walk the maze of streets trying to get to the sea" (56). Brand's seemingly strange sentences refigure Canada as we know it, implanting the experiences of black peoples, in this case black women, in the very crevices of the nation. Brand's accomplishment is what the black British cultural theorist Paul Gilroy calls "[c]ritical space/time cartography of the diaspora . . . the dynamics of dispersal and local autonomy can be shown alongside the unforseen detours and circuits which mark the new journeys and new arrivals that, in turn, release new political and cultural possibilities" (86).

In Another Place makes demands upon space and place, and they're couched in the demarcations of an in-between. For black Canadians, living the in-between is conditioned by their inside/outside status in the nation-state; whether "indigenous black" or otherwise, in-between-ness in Canada is conditioned by a plethora of national narratives, from the idea of "two founding peoples," to multicultural policies, to immigration policies, to provincial and municipal policing practices, and so on. The impossibility of imagining blackness as Canadian is continually evident even as nation-state policies like multiculturalism seek to signal otherwise. The simultaneity of being here and not being here is, in effect, an in-between position. The prospect of in-between-ness is, however, not only produced by the state: it's also something black folks have chosen through their multiple diasporic and outer-national political identifications. It is in both of the above senses that Elizete and Verlia make demands of the place(s) they find themselves in, whether they're Caribbean or Canadian. Elizete's flight from the Caribbean and Verlia's flight from Sudbury are not entirely differently conditioned: both exist in the in-between. Both women live an outer-national existence characterized by migratory movement and particular political commitments and practices.

In *No Language is Neutral* Brand writes, "walk Bathurst Street until it come like home" (30), insisting and asserting a presence of blackness in Canada, or more bluntly, staking out territory. Her insistence is posed in the context of a national narrative which seeks to render her "the thin/mixture of just come don't exist" (29). The utterance of "just come" is one of the ways in which the life of the in-between is lived out. The idea of "just come" is crucial to the nation-state's construction both of black invisibility and hyper-visibility. Ludicrous excuses like discomfort with the word Negro are used to deny the evidence and existence of an early black historical presence which troubles and worries the national myth of "two founding peoples." Such practices make sense in the context of a sociological discourse of black anti-racism, emanating mainly from Toronto, which has constructed blackness in Canada in ways that ignore or pay only lip service to any black antecedent prior to the 1960s.

The discomfort of Holland Township's Reeve reveals the traces of the ways in which language has been used to denigrate and render black people less than human. Language is only one of the things that is at issue when folks who have been colonized talk back and resist. Remaking language, however, is the way to come to terms with the past in the present, as recent black postcolonial assertions insist. Thus those who marched on Negro Creek Road to retain its name were not just marching so the visible and tangible evidence of the past would not disappear, they were also marching because reclaiming Negro is as important a part of black historical memory and experience as any other artifact or document.

Brand's use of language is essential to her re-ordering of Canadian literary realities because she brings new sounds and tonality to what may be considered Canadian. Her use of language signals the unsettled restlessness of the exile and refugee who must rechart, remap, and regroup so that both self and collectivity are made evident and present. Black diasporic practices of language continually revise and reveal its constructedness, and also its importance in both domination and resistance. The potential of language, to disclose the discredited histories of black peoples, is evident in these practices of revision and reversal. In this sense, reclaiming and insisting upon the name Negro Creek Road is of immense importance. For it is the name, or what the language conveys, that denotes the history of black peoples in the province of Ontario.

STAKING OUT TERRITORY

Dumbfounded I walk as if these sidewalks are a
place I'm visiting. Like a holy ghost I package the
smell of zinnias and lady of the night, I horde the taste
Ignoring
my own money thrown on the counter, the race
conscious landlords and their jim crow flats, oh yes!
here! the work nobody wants to do . . . it's good
work I'm not complaining! but they make it taste bad,
bitter like peas . . .
Our
nostalgia was a lie and the passage on the six hour
flight to ourselves is wide and like another world . . .
(Brand, *No Language* 31-33)

If Negro Creek Road disappears from Ontario and thus Canadian maps, memory and remembering will be the ghost which haunts Holland Township and Canada. Canada's continued forgetfulness concerning slavery here, and the nation-state's attempts to record only Canada's role as a place of sanctuary for escaping African-Americans, is a part of the story of absenting blackness from its history. Erasing all evidence of any other presence (First Nations and black) is crucial if the myth of two founding peoples is to hold the crumbling nation of Canada together in the face of Quebec's impending separation and declaration of nation status.

Many "negro creek roads" exist; they are yet to be found and documented. It is particularly the symbolization of "negro creek roads" that I want to explore because their existence announces the refiguration of the social, political and cultural landscape of Canada. And it is not a barren one. If we want to turn to recent history for a remapping of the Canadian urban landscape, Toronto's Bathurst Street might best stand as a ritualistic locus for migrant Caribbean peoples. The people who live in the in-between, neither here nor elsewhere, redraw and rechart the places/spaces that they occupy.

It is living in an in-between space that Brand, M. Nourbese Philip, Austin Clarke, Cecil Foster, Andrew Moodie and a host of other writers, thinkers, dramatists and choreographers articulate; in doing this they take a political and ethical stance which refuses the boundaries of national discourses. To be black and "at home" in Canada is to both belong and not belong. The Dream Warriors celebrate black diasporic connectedness and passion in their song "Ludi" by calling out and naming black home spaces in Canada and the Caribbean.[7] This naming is a practice of the in-between. For nation-centred discourse can only prohibit black folks from sharing "common feeling," especially when common actions seem to present themselves, time and again, in and across different space/places/nations.

In Brand's collection of essays *Bread Out of Stone*, "Bathurst" stands out as a statement about reconfigured space. When Brand reads the essay, its poetic qualities infuse a black diasporic orality into the polemic and "(re)tune" the sound of Canada. However, "Bathurst" is important for more than its tonal qualities. It chronicles the existence of the vibrant black, mainly Caribbean, community that existed on Bathurst Street in the 1970s. The essay is about space, time, culture and how black peoples' activism refashions Canada. Brand recharts urban identity and populates the literary sphere with black Canadians who recognize that "home is an uneasy place" (67).

"Bathurst" is important for a number of reasons, chief among them being the assertion and insertion of a black presence in Toronto, one that refuses to be silenced, to be made invisible and to exist solely on the margins of North American society. It is the refusal of marginalization in all of Brand's work that transfigures the space/place of domination. Bathurst is the space of self-assertion and political engagement that Verlia seeks:

> She finds a room in a house on a street off Bathurst. She chooses the street because of the barber shops on Bathurst. It is Sunday but she knows that on Monday this is where she will meet the sisters and brothers in the Movement. This is where she will cut her perm and this is where she will begin. (*In Another* 155)

There is an ambivalence in Brand's (re)creation of Verlia's search for, and eventual discovery of, the Movement in Toronto. This ambivalence is the novelist's rendering, in her (re)telling, of the problems of nationalist discourse. It should not be overlooked that Verlia, who grows to become a feminist and lesbian, is always off—Brand does not put Verlia at the centre of nationalist movement. The reasons for this are obvious. Living in a room off Bathurst, where black male spaces—barber shops—dominate, means that Verlia's lived experience must be elsewhere. Brand is not creating a sentimental remembering of the Movement of the 1970s; instead she offers a reassessment of what might have been possible had all aspects of blackness been considered—especially questioning the masculinist tones of the Movement.

In this regard she ushers new tropes into Canadian literature. The importance of black and migrant urban space is revealed as Elizete evades immigration officers, changes names repeatedly to conceal an already invisible existence, and struggles to survive in the context of a hostile land. Verlia, on the other hand, flees Sudbury because it's the site of black suffocation. In effect, the notions of exile and refugee status refigure contemporary Canada as a space where blacks do not belong. In addition, Brand's critique of patriarchal black nationalism brings black internal dialogues to the texture of Canadian cultures.

In Another Place is Brand's lyrical portrayal of the ways in which identity, place, belonging and the politics of self and collectivity are lived out and actualized in language. I want to focus on the remaking of the racialized, gendered and sexualized (literary) landscape of Canada, as another one of the important ways that Brand's novel disrupts Canadian literary practices. Moving beyond the discourse and literary tropes of "roughing it in the bush" and "survival" in a barren landscape (national tropes which deny a First Nations presence), Brand moves through an urban landscape populated with the usual suspects of Canadian migrant cultures. She brings to the Canadian literary landscape the bittersweet taste and metaphor of the tamarind — bittersweet because of its sensuality, its shape, and its hard core or pit.

Staking claim through naming is crucial to the project of redrawing the urban landscape of Canada. Brand names and traverses Toronto in an attempt to make it the "home" of Verlia and Elizete. In doing so she charts many of the home spaces of migrant Caribbean peoples in Canada. *In Another Place* is literally and symbolically a historical and contemporary map/guide to (black) Toronto. Bathurst, St. Clair Avenue, Vaughan Road, Christie, Bloor, Harbord, College Street, Oakwood, Danforth, Regent Park, Avenue Road, Yorkville, Yonge Street, these names exist alongside names of places and spaces in the Caribbean. The Gladstone Hotel, Van Dong Restaurant, Canadian National, factories, rooming houses, barber shops, parks and dance halls (The Paramount), are signifiers which locate place, names that refigure and claim, make one's presence felt. Through Verlia's and Elizete's eyes, voices and experiences we get a different and new cultural, political and economic map of Canada.

Brand's recharting of the Canadian landscape is not in any way romantic. In *No Language is Neutral* she warns that "nostalgia is lie" (32) and in *In Another Place* Elizete's and Verlia's elsewhere, while remembered, is not romantically yearned for. The tales of activism that organize Verlia's life in the novel lead both to her feminist awakening and a critique of black patriarchal nationalism and heteronormative politics. Verlia demands more of black nationalism. Brand, in creating a character who not only challenges white supremacy but also calls into question and challenges the patriarchal and heteronormative politics of black nationalism, is surely redrawing the boundaries of blackness. In fact, she implodes those boundaries.

By mentioning Fanon in the novel, Brand acknowledges his important insight: that to understand black experiences only within the context of singularity (i.e. nation) is to render oneself continually vulnerable to the forces of oppression. Verlia and Elizete attempt to occupy the space between self and collective desires and expressions; this might be called a post-national black lesbian feminist space/place. When Verlia returns to the Caribbean—not in a romantic search for roots (no nostalgia is evident), but rather as an activist—she announces the possibility of change and makes demands on place and space. The latter is the imperative of black diasporic political identifications which seek both to refigure black experiences and to demand justice.

The Space of Pain

The space of pain is what gives teeth to the issues that Brand confronts in *In Another Place*. By this I mean that Brand's insistence on refusing to render the displacements and reconciliations of mothers with daughters as simple and uncomplicated is very important.[8]

> These women, our mothers, a whole generation of them, left us. They went to England or America or Canada or some big city as fast as their wit could get them there because they were women and all they

had to live on was wit since nobody considered them whole people. (230)

Pain is often the trace that binds women together in Brand's work, but in the novel pain is also the necessary evil that must be worked through if reconciliation of any sort is possible. Indeed, she maps a number of pains that occupy the unspoken spaces of blackness in Canada:

> They sent for us, sent for us their daughters, then washed our faces in their self-hatred. Self-hatred they had learned from the white people whose toilets they had cleaned, whose asses they had wiped, whose kitchens they had scrubbed, whose hatred they had swallowed . . . they saw their hands swollen with water, muscular with lifting and pulling, they saw their souls assaulted and irrecoverable, wounded from the insult and the sheer nastiness of white words . . . They made us pay for what they had suffered . . . They did not feel redeemed by it but they themselves had been so twisted from walking in shame that they twisted our bodies to suit their stride. (231)

While Brand as novelist must rethink the context and contours of racist Canada, she also unsentimentally conveys the wretched impact of racism as it is played out in mother/daughter relations. Echoes of Jamaica Kincaid's rendering of daughters' relationships with mothers are evident in her work. The estrangement of daughters from mothers, as Brand writes it, sits at the heart of the question of community, and parallels the question of black nationalist rhetoric and its failures to fully address black multiplicity.

(Re)newals

The *Globe and Mail*'s Joan Thomas suggests that Brand is too angry even when she is at her best. Thomas's back-handed praise of Brand is the kind of stuff of which black erasures in Canadian culture are made. The comparison of Brand's work with Toni Morrison's is simultaneously accurate and troubling, especially when Brand is criticized for not having Morrison's "largeness of spirit" (C20). Fallaciously inferring that there is no anger in Morrison's work denies the ways in which the redemptive and transfigurative moments in her texts are arrived at. What seems behind these readings is a tendency to read black women writers within what we might call "the mammy tradition"—black women, this school of criticism implies, should make all things right or at least smooth everything over.

To arrive at the moment of transfiguration, or to even open up its possibility, the space of anger in black diasporic culture must be explored by black artists, critics and others. And it's just as important for us to question the idea that anger has no place in literature. Thomas's comment, that "memory is full of the sour taste of tamarinds" (C20), is her call for Brand as novelist, and black people generally, to forget a past and present of pain. In recognizing that memory has forgetting as its twin, Brand writes of "[t]he skill of forgetfulness" (*In Another* 13) as something that's learned in the context of the dismissal of women, but important for recognizing how the concerns of those resisting are also dismissed and denied.

Long-time readers of Brand's work have seen her continually redraw and remap the oppressive landscapes of Canada. In short stories like "Blossom, Priestess of Oya, Goddess of winds, storms and waterfalls," "At the Lisbon Plate" and more specifically "Train to Montreal" (all from *Sans Souci and Other Stories*), Brand began the project of rewriting the racialized space of Canada. *In Another Place, Not Here* is a tour de force which recharts this project.

The authorities who sanction the racialized space and place of Canada will continue to have to face and come to terms with the exiles and refugees in their midst. The struggle of diasporic blacks for space in Canada has a long genealogy, and a trajectory that will continue to cause reverberations across all aspects of the national body. I invoke the body, or rather, bodies, here because what is ultimately at stake is the space and place that bodies, both actual and symbolic, occupy in the nation's imagination. Black Canadian literature's unruly bodies will continue to insist upon a space where justice and freedom are possible, and, as Brand puts it, "it doesn't matter that it's Toronto or a country named Canada. Right now that is incidental, and this city and this country will have to fit themselves into her dream" (*In Another* 159).

Notes

1. This essay is an amalgam of ideas which I believe need to be given more attention in approaches to black Canadian literature. In many instances scholars writing on black Canadian literature have been reluctant to address what the literature means for "here" and instead read the works entirely within an outsider discourse. I wish to thank Leslie Sanders for her helpful suggestions.
2. Robin W. Winks, *Blacks in Canada: A History* (Montreal: McGill UP, 1971); George Elliott Clarke, ed., *Fire on the Water: An Anthology of Black Nova Scotian Writing*, Vol. 1 (Porter's Lake, NS: Pottersfield, 1991); Peggy Bristow, et al., *"We're Rooted Here and They Can't Pull Us Up": Essays in African-Canadian Women's History* (Toronto: U of Toronto P, 1994).
3. See Rinaldo Walcott, "Lament for a Nation: The Racial Geography of 'The Oh! Canada Project,'" *Fuse* 19.4 (1996): 15-23.
4. George Elliott Clarke, ed., *Fire on the Water: An Anthology of Black Nova Scotian Writing*, Vol. 2 (Porter's Lake, NS: Pottersfield, 1992).

5. *Fire on the Water*, Vol. 1.
6. George Elliott Clarke, "A Primer of African-Canadian Literature," *Books in Canada* 25.2 (1996): 7-9.
7. The Dream Warriors, *And Now the Legacy Begins* (Scarborough, ON: Island Records, 1991).
8. Foster also tackles the issue of reunification and its not so pleasant side in *Sleep On Beloved*, but I believe that a fundamental difference exists in the way Brand covers this painful territory by extricating it from the realm of the individual to address questions of collective responsibility.

<h2 style="text-align:center">WORKS CITED</h2>

Brand, Dionne. *Bread Out of Stone: Recollections, Sex, Recognitions, Race, Dreaming, Politics.* Toronto: Coach House, 1994.

——. *In Another Place, Not Here.* Toronto: Knopf, 1996.

——. *No Language is Neutral.* Toronto: Coach House, 1990.

Clarke, George Elliott. "A Primer of African-Canadian Literature." *Books in Canada* 25.2 (1996): 7-9.

Gilroy, Paul. *The Black Atlantic: Modernity and Double Consciousness.* Cambridge: Harvard UP, 1993.

Glissant, Edouard. *Caribbean Discourse: Selected Essays.* Trans. J. Michael Dash. Charlottesville: Virginia UP, 1989.

Thomas, Joan. "Poetry Fires Hot Brand Novel." *Globe and Mail* 29 June 1996: C20.

23

"GEOGRAPHY LESSONS: ON BEING AN INSIDER/ OUTSIDER TO THE CANADIAN NATION"*

Himani Bannerji

My first encounter with Canada occurred during my geography lessons as a young girl. There, in an atlas of physical geography, colored green, pink, and yellow, I came across Canada—a place of trees, lakes, wheat fields, ice caps, and an ancient rock formation cut through with glaciers. I don't remember reading anything of the history of this country in my geography book, but somehow there were faint echoes of people and nature blurring into each other—"red Indians," "eskimos," "igloos," "aurora borealis," and "reindeer." From where did these images come if not from my geography book? From literature and scattered visual images perhaps? There were, after all, the books of Fenimore Cooper or Jack London, which irrespective of national boundaries created mythologies of the "North," the "Indian," and wove tales of discovery of the Arctic—of Amundsen and others lost in blizzards on their dog sleds. Eventually, on my fourteenth birthday, I received a book called *The Scalpel and the Sword*, and I decided to be a doctor, like Norman Bethune.

What I am trying to recount is what Canada meant for me—all this jumbled-up information, this fusion of people and nature, my imagination moved by forests and the glow of Arctic ice. Certainly, "Canada" was a mental rather than a historical space. It was an idyllic construction of nature and adventure.

Many years later, the Canada I stepped into was vastly different from the Canada I had constructed in my childhood. When I immigrated to Montreal, I stepped out of my romantic construction of Canada and into a distinctly political-ideological one—one which impressed me as being both negative and aggressive. From the insistence and harshness with which I was asked whether I intended to apply for "landing"—a term I did not understand and that had to be explained—I knew that I was not welcome in this "Canada." I told the officer defiantly that this would never be my country; I had come as a foreign student and would leave upon receiving my degree. That is how it has remained to this day. Had I been received differently, had I been made to feel more "at home," would this be my home, my Canada?

---

* *Dangerous Territories: Struggles for Difference and Equality in Education*, ed. Leslie G. Roman and Linda Eyre (New York: Routledge, 1997), 23-41.

This remains a hypothetical question, since upon "landing" six years later and being labelled an "immigrant," a "visible minority woman," I have remained in limbo. Even after years of being an "immigrant," and upon swearing allegiance to the same Queen of England from whom India had parted, I was not to be a "Canadian." Regardless of my official status as a Canadian citizen, I, like many others, remained an "immigrant." The category "Canadian" clearly applied to people who had two things in common: their white skin and their European North American (not Mexican) background. They did not all speak English. There were two colors in this political atlas— one a beige-brown shading off into black and the other white. These shades did not simply reflect skin colors—they reflected the ideological, political, and cultural assumptions and administrative practices of the Canadian State.

"Canada" then cannot be taken as a given. It is obviously a construction, a set of representations, embodying certain types of political and cultural communities and their operations. These communities were themselves constructed in agreement with certain ideas regarding skin color, history, language (English/French), and other cultural signifiers—all of which may be subsumed under the ideological category "White."[1] A "Canada" constructed on this basis contains certain notions of nation, state formation, and economy. Europeanness as "whiteness"[2] thus translates into "Canada" and provides it with its "imagined community." This is a process that Benedict Anderson speaks of, but he glosses over the divisiveness of class, "race," and ideology— the irreconcilable contradictions at the heart of this community-nation-state project. Furthermore, he does not ask about the type of imagination at work in this project. He does not ask either *whose* imagination is advanced as the national imaginary or what this has to do with organizing practical and ideological exclusions and inclusions within the national space. These questions become concrete if we look at how I was received in Canada. Why was I thus received? Was it just an accident? An isolated instance? What did it have to do with *who* I was—my so-called gender and race? Did this story of mine begin with my arrival, or was I just a tiny episode in a pre-existing historical narrative? Can I or similar "others" imagine a "Canada" and project it as the national imaginary?

So if we problematize the notion of "Canada" through the introjection of the idea of belonging, we are left with the paradox of both belonging and non-belonging simultaneously. As a population, we non-Whites and women (in particular, non-White women) are living in a specific territory. We are part of its economy, subject to its laws, and members of its civil society. Yet we are not part of its self-definition as "Canada" because we are not "Canadians." We are pasted over with labels that give us identities that are extraneous to us. And these labels originate in the ideology of the nation, in the Canadian state apparatus, in the media, in the education system, and in the commonsense world of common parlance. We ourselves use them. They are familiar, naturalized names: visible minorities, immigrants, newcomers, refugees, aliens, illegals, people of color, multicultural communities, and so on. We are sexed into immigrant women, women of color, visible minority women, Black/South Asian/Chinese women, ESL (English as second language) speakers, and many more.[3] The names keep proliferating, as though there were a seething reality, unmanageable and uncontainable in any one name. Concomitant with this mania for the naming of "others" is one for the naming of that which is "Canadian." This "Canadian" core community is defined through the same process that others us. We, with our named and ascribed otherness, face an undifferentiated notion of the "Canadian" as the unwavering beacon of our assimilation.

And what is the function of the many names applied to us? They are categories for organizing the state apparatus, its regulations and policy functions, and for enabling the ideological organization of "relations of ruling."[4] These categories enable the state to extend its governing and administrative jurisdiction into civil society, while, at the same time, incorporating the everyday person into the national project. One might say, then, remembering Althusser, that they are appellations for interpellation.[5] These names are codes for political subjectivities and ideological/pedagogical possibilities, and they have embedded in them both immediate and long-term political effects. They help to construct "Canada" and to place us in certain roles and niches of the nation; and those who are not "Canadians" cannot directly project "Canada." This "Canada's" placement of "others," because it creates feelings of belonging and alienation, not only produces psychological and cultural problems regarding power, but is also integral to the structure of the Canadian polity itself. Its categories of otherness delimit the membership of this nation and this state (Ng 182-96). This situation reveals not only a raced or ethnicized state, but also—more importantly—a crisis in citizenship and a continual attempt to manage this crisis. It tells us that, in the polity of Canadian liberal democracy, there is always already a crisis of gender, race, and class. [. . .]

In the face of my assertion that "Canada," as a national imaginary, is a sexist-racist entity, some will advance a phenomenon known as "multiculturalism."[6] I will be told that, due to this phenomenon, which needs especial scrutiny with regard to citizenship of "others," the whole world looks up to Canada. Although, in practice, multiculturalism has never been effective, it can and does serve as an ideological slogan within a liberal democratic framework. It supplies an administrative device for managing social contradictions and conflicts. This is important since "Canada," as a nationalist project, is perceived to be a homogeneous, solid, and settled entity, though its history constantly belies this.

This is why the language for imagining "Canada" is fraught with such notions as "solitude" and "survival." There is in this national space a legitimation crisis.[7] Other than the dissent and struggle of the indigenous peoples, the raced-gendered "others" who remain a source of dissentience, the national project is deeply riven by the rivalry between Anglophones and Francophones—Canada's "two solitudes."[8] Equally patriarchal and race-inscribed, these two solitudes remain central cultural/political actors, covering over the seething "Indian question," which continually erupts in the form of land claims and demands for self-determination and self-government.[9] A creation of violent and illegal settlers (to whom no one had issued "landing" permits), "Canada" remains an unformed union, its particularist and partisan state formation frequently showing through. Yet a state cannot become liberal and democratic without an element of transcendence.[10] And what, after all, could give Canada the appearance of transcendence as well as "multiculturalism," with its slogan "unity in diversity"? The drive for making an Anglo-North American Canada is partly assuaged by this ideological gesture. "Immigrants," especially "visible minorities," become useful with regard to challenging the substantive claim of more well-entrenched "others" (i.e., the Québecois or indigenous peoples), who cannot be deported to their "home" countries. Nominally and opportunistically introducing those others as entities in the national imaginary, the notion/nation of "Canada" attempts to overcome its legitimation crisis. It is in this way that every social and economic demand can be gutted and reduced to the level of the cultural/symbolic. Ironically, immigrant "others," who serve as categories of exclusion in Canada's nation-making ideology, become an instrument for creating a sphere of transcendence. The state claims to rise above all partisan interests and functions as an arbitrator between different cultural groups. This is the moral high ground, the political instrument with which the state maintains the hegemony of an Anglo-Canada. We might say that it is these oppressed "others" who gave Canada the gift of multiculturalism. In any case, armed with the ideological tool of multiculturalism, Canada manages its crisis in legitimation and citizenship. It offers the Québecois and the First Nations peoples a part in the "national unity," albeit an empty one, while denying them their own governments as separatist enterprises.

Fractured by race, gender, class, and long-standing colonial rivalries, the construction of "Canada" entails two major forms of interconnected crises—that of citizenship and that of the legitimation of a "national" state formation. Differential status in citizenship is paired with a dual state formation, each aspect of which exerts pressures on the other. A White settler colonial state and a liberal democracy, while historically and contingently connected in many cases (such as in Australia, the former South Africa, the United States, the former Rhodesia (Zimbabwe), or Canada) are two separate political projects. They are not genealogically connected in terms of their political ideals and governing structures. This becomes clearer when we look at Britain, which had a vast colonial empire and ruled it autocratically, while developing a liberal democracy inside the country. In liberal democracy, even if it is only in the sphere of polity, the same state structures and legalities govern the entire subject population and show a reliance on the notion of enlightenment. The liberal democratic state, at least at the level of *formal equality*, is the antithesis of a colonial state. But in Canada, as in the case of Australia, for example, certain features of the colonial state coexist with those of a liberal democracy (Watkins). Different laws, with special departments such as the Department of Indian Affairs in Canada, govern the population differently. Indian reserves have laws governing them economically, politically, and socially which are different from the laws governing the rest of Canada. Viewed from the standpoint of indigenous peoples, the state of Canada is based on class, gender, and race, and it continues to administer these reserves as would a colonial state. Even the territorial question is still unsettled, while containment strategies typical of colonial states continue to be in evidence around the administration of reserves. These colonial relations manifest themselves in conflicts around the James Bay Project, Oka, Gustafson Lake, Ipperwash, and so on. Debates on Native self-determination or First Nations self-government further reveal the colonial relations between Canada and its indigenous peoples. According to some scholars, Canada's dual state formation (a liberal democracy with a colonial heart) is matched by a dual economy. Theories of world system and dependency, usually applied to ex-colonized countries, are considered to be applicable to Canada.[11] It is claimed that there is a metropole-peripheral economy within, while the country as a whole displays features of advanced industrial capitalism along with its dependency on foreign, especially U.S., capital.[12] This convoluted state of affairs has given rise to peculiar social formations, whereby colonized nations continue to exist within the "Canadian" nation state. Acknowledged as the First Nations, Native peoples are like the Palestinians, who form a nation without a state and are subject to continual repression. The role that "race" has played in the context of colonization is obvious. Subsequently a dependent but imperialist capital has continued to organize an economy and a society based on "race." It is not surprising that talk of cultural identities in this country quickly veers toward racialization. Not only is "the Indian," so called, a category of "race," but so are other cultural categories used for non-White immigrants tinged with "race."

These colonial relations and representations of "Canada," which run like rich veins throughout its state formation, were overlayered with liberal democratic aspirations in the course of the latter half of the twentieth century. The state faced many contradictions and complexities in this project due to the persistence of the colonial relations and also to the country's own inability to have a bourgeois revolution. Lacking a fully articulated bourgeois class in leadership Canada has in effect a double dependency—on Britain for governmental and certain cultural forms, and on the U.S. for capital as well as for social and political culture.[13] Like all liberal democracies it is not only capitalist, but, as I said, colonial and dependent and autonomously imperialist at the same time. The problems of coherent state formation multiply as a result.

In fact, in the face of Canada's settler colonial origin and the weak development of its capital and capitalist class, the state in Canada has been a direct agent for capitalist development and has performed a substantial role in the accumulation of capital. It has also been the chief agent for procuring labor and creating a labor market, and has assisted in the regulation and exploitation of labor. Canada has depended on imported labor and has organized the labor market along lines of "race" and gender. This was not often an activity undertaken by the accumulating classes but primarily performed by the state, which took over a vast portion of the role of facilitation.[14] The current obedience of the state to NAFTA, or corporate transnational capital, is highly symptomatic of this. "Race" or ethnicity, translated into immigration policy quotas, has actually located different types of labor in different productional recesses.

By locking immigrant workers into zones of menial labor and low wages, the state has brought down the wage structure of the country as a whole. It has actively de-skilled and marginalized Third World immigrants by decertifying them and forcing them into the working class. Long before the present economic crisis, this device had created a reserve army of labor consisting of both males and females. As any study of homeworkers, piece-workers, cleaners of public spaces, or domestics will show, non-White or "immigrant" women occupy the worst position among these marginalized labor groups (Johnson and Johnson). These, then, are the people—straddling the line between surplus exploitation and unemployment—who stand permanently on the threshold of Canadian citizenship. Their paper-thin status is revealed when some family members are deported while others, such as children born in Canada, are allowed to stay. If these are not sufficient reminders of the crises of citizenship faced by non-White "others," one need only remember the Japanese internment.[15]

This situation is guaranteed to produce a double crisis of legitimation, one for the state and one for its citizens. The heart of the matter lies in the fact that a colonial, partisan Anglo-Canada has arrogated to itself the task of constructing "Canada" while being economically dependent on foreign investment capital. This Anglo-Canada has neither moral high ground nor economic solvency to justify its hegemony. The notions of "Canada" and "Canadian" are mocked by gigantic question marks.

During the course of its tortuous formation, Canada has continued to exude irreconcilable contradictions. In following the imperatives of liberal democracy, in being motivated by the ideal of pluralism, and in responding to popular protests against inequality, Canada promulgated both multiculturalism and affirmative action, which both contained dissatisfaction and legitimated existing inequalities. At the same time, through various debates, the state called for sexist and racist responses to all its so-called multiculturalist and equity-oriented proposals. For example, at this moment, the fig leaf of equity and affirmative action has been altogether dropped in Ontario. By constantly calling on and constructing an entity called "Canadians" and pitting it against immigrants, the state has actually stimulated White supremacist attitudes and helped to establish their organizations, as was revealed by a government agent with regard to the Heritage Front.[16] By constantly signifying the White population as "Canadians" and immigrants of color as "others," by constantly stereotyping Third World immigrants as criminals, terrorists, and fundamentalists, the state manages to both manipulate and cancel its alleged dedication to multiculturalism.

A most dangerous state use of racism occurs with regard to its own socioeconomic failures and its inability to cope with the violence inherent within structural adjustment. Since the state and the media jointly portray immigrants from non-White, poor countries as "the problem," it is not surprising that the White population looks at them as the villains of the peace—as "those people who took away our jobs." These immigrants, in turn, look among themselves to find someone to blame for the economic and social disaster they face. Interestingly, this attitude does not apply to eastern Europeans, who are poor but White.

Due to its selective modes of ethnicization, multiculturalism is itself a vehicle for racialization. It establishes Anglo-Canadian culture as the ethnic core culture while "tolerating" and hierarchically arranging others around it as "multiculture." The ethics and aesthetics of "Whiteness," with its colonial imperialist/racist ranking criteria, define and construct the "multi" culture of Canada's others. This reified, mutated product, accomplished through a web of hierarchically arranged stereotypes, can then be both used against "ethnic" communities and commoditized with regard to fashion and current market tastes. Festivals of "ethnic" communities, from the Toronto Caravan to Caribana, provide excellent examples. Such "ethnic" constructs have serious consequences in the perpetuation of violence against women. Frequently, in the name of cultural sensitivity and respect, the state does not address violence against women when it occurs among the multiculturally defined "ethnic" communities. It is rumored that the accused's behavior is a part of "their culture," and that "they" are traditional, fundamentalist, and uncivilized. In this way, an entire population is demonized even though particular men become exempt from indictment. Similarly, Canada's Islamic population has become permanently associated with terrorism and every Arab is seen as a potential terrorist.

One more issue that needs to be stressed with regard to multiculturalism is the fact that it arises at the convergence of a struggle between the state and otherized, especially non-White, subjects. Their demands for justice, for effective anti-racist policies and administration, for the right to a substantive social and cultural life, are overdetermined by the agenda of the state. As long as "multiculturalism" only skims the surface of society, expressing itself as traditional ethics, such as arranged marriages, and ethnic food, clothes, songs, and dances (thus facilitating tourism), it is tolerated by the state and "Canadians" as non-threatening. But if the demands go a little deeper than that (e.g., teaching "other" religions or languages), they produce violent reaction, indicating a deep resentment toward funding "others'" arts and cultures. This can be seen in the Reform Party's stance on immigration and multiculturalism.

The convergence of gender and race oppression in Canada became explicit in the reactions to the New Democratic Party's (NDP) proposal for affirmative action. It was a proposal that extended inclusivity to Canada's women, visible minorities, Aboriginal people, Francophones, and disabled people. The reaction was severe, and it reverberated throughout the entire country— professors and truck drivers displaying the same response. National newspapers advertised the proposal as "Whites need not apply" or "White males need not apply." This is a curious reading, since it completely overlooks the fact that the legislation is in keeping with liberal pluralism, which entails minimal representation. The violent responses also made one realize that the ideologies of race and gender, respectively, are connected. If White women, disabled people, and Francophones are not to be recognized as White, we are left to ask: "What is Whiteness?" The issue of gender is also revealing. If Francophones and disabled people, no matter what their color, are not to be recognized as "males," then what is masculinity? Does speaking French exclude people from being "White males"?

This instance serves to show that "Canada," as a national imaginary, its multiculturalism and its lip service to Quebec's Canadianness notwithstanding, is actually an Anglo-White male idea that blurs the class lines. There is little in the state's notion of multiculturalism that speaks to social justice. More than anything else, multiculturalism preserves the partisan nature of the state by helping to contain pressures exerted by "others" for social justice and equity.

We might, at this point, be asked what legitimized Canada, what provided the basis for its national project, before the arrival of the concept of multiculturalism. What was its justificatory, politically existential discourse? It seems that it was the notion of "survival."[17] The White settler colonial entity devised for itself a threatened identity, whereby the colonizer (erasing colonialism) was faced with the danger of extinction. In the works of Margaret Atwood (*Survival*), such a state of affairs is advanced as a truism, as a fact of "Canada." In Atwood's novel *Surfacing*, for example, a woman discovers her violated- and invaded-self in, or as, an equally violated and invaded wilderness. In spite of her gender and feminism, her race and class allow Atwood to project this particular vision of Canada. But this metaphor of the political psyche of Canada as a threatened femininity/nature obliterates indigenous people, swallowing them up in the myth of an empty wilderness that is to be invaded and populated by White people. In doing this, Atwood follows a literary and artistic tradition already in place, for example, in many of the works of the Group of Seven (Watson). The "Canadian," as the dreamer of the nation, must come to terms with the wilderness in order to find and found "Canada." S/he is White/European. The indigenous peoples are either not there or are one with the primal, non-human forces of nature. The threat to Canada, then, comes not only from south of its border but from within itself—from its denied, unincorporated, alienated nature and its human forms. In reaction to this can the settler, "the Canadian," take an option that Atwood's heroine in *Surfacing*, being a "woman" and pacifist, cannot? Can he, as he is a man, feel justified in killing or conquering that which he cannot comprehend or finally conquer? The "survival" ideological space holds that possibility in suspense. The other threat to Canada comes from without—from its fear of being overrun by, and incorporated into, the United States. This formulation, while anti-American and mildly anti-imperialist, erases Canada's own colonial and imperialist nature and aspirations. And this erasure certainly does not help to create politics or policies that challenge Anglo-White nationalism, with its masculinist inflection, and that call for other ways of imagining and administering Canada.

The possibilities for constructing a radically different Canada emerge only from those who have been "othered" as the insider-outsiders of the nation. It is their standpoints which, oppositionally politicized, can take us beyond the confines of gender and race and enable us to challenge class through a critical and liberating vision. In their lives, politics, and work, the "others" hold the possibility of being able to expose the hollowness of the liberal state and to provide us with an understanding of both the refined and crude constructions of "White power" behind "Canada's" national imaginary. They serve to remind us of the Canada that *could* exist.

Notes

1. On the construction of "Whiteness" as an ideological, political, and socio-historical category, see Allen, Frankenberg, Roediger, Roman, and Ware.
2. On Europeanness as "Whiteness," see Stoler.
3. See Carty and Brand, and Carty.
4. See Dorothy E. Smith for a definition of this term (3, 5-6).
5. For Althusser's concept of interpellation, see Althusser 162-70.
6. On the history of multiculturalism, see Fleras and Elliott.

7. For a discussion of this concept, see Habermas.

8. For details of the French and English conquests of Canada and subsequent contestation between the two colonies, see Ryerson or Morton. Quebec and English Canada have gone through a colonial relationship that, according to Anglophone Canada or Ottawa, has been transformed into a liberal democratic incorporation. A vast portion of Quebec's population have, however, continued to perceive this as a modernized colonial relation.

9. The condition of crisis created by a state that is a White settler colony seeking to become a liberal democracy becomes clear when we look at Tester and Kulchyski, who explore the genocidal consequences of Inuit relocation. There are numerous articles and books on the land claims issue. See, for example, Boldt and Long.

10. On the transcendent nature' of the state as an ideal democratic institution, see Miliband.

11. On world system and dependency theories as readings of the First and Third Worlds in terms of capitalism, imperialism, and dependency, see Wallerstein and Gunder Frank.

12. See Bolaria and Li, chapters 2 and 3. This dynamic is explored in various ways by the Canadian Left nationalist political theorists, such as Teeple. For a marxist critique of the Left nationalist position see Moore and Wells.

13. This dependency is not simply a matter of adopting a British style of government (parliamentary democracy) or an American style of capitalism. Canada was a colony of Britain for a long time, and then, until recently, a dominion. Even now the Crown of England has a significant governmental relationship with the Canadian government. This is evident in the face of the Queen on Canadian currency or swearing allegiance to Her Majesty during citizenship ceremonies or in having to refer to the Crown and the House of Lords in matters of Native land claims. As for Canada's U.S. connection, political theorists of the Canadian Left such as Ian Lumsden, Mel Watkins, and others since the 1960s have drawn attention to a long-standing imperialist presence of U.S. capital in Canada. Canadian publishing, music, film, and cultural production and industry have been increasingly under attack from the U.S. culture industry and export market, and a steady dependency is being cultivated in the popular culture sector. This "Americanization" of Canadian culture has been both noticed and resented by writers such as Margaret Atwood or magazines such as *This Magazine* and *Canadian Dimension*.

14. See Law Union of Ontario, *The Immigrant's Handbook* (Montreal: Black Rose Books, 1981), as well as Canada, *A Report of the Canadian Immigration and Population Study: Immigration Policy Perspective* (Ottawa: Manpower and Immigration, 1974) and *Equality Now: Report of the Special Committee on Visible Minorities* (Ottawa: House of Commons, 1986).

15. See Bolaria and Li, chapter 3.

16. For details on the Heritage Front and other neo-Nazi/White supremacist

groups, see *Hearts of Hate,* a video produced by the National Film Board and aired on the Canadian Broadcasting Corporation in 1995. An exposé carried in the *Toronto Star* in 1994 uncovered evidence that one of the founders of the Heritage Front, Grant Bristow, was a paid agent of the Canadian Security and Information Service (CSIS).

17. Regarding the concept of "survival," see Atwood, *Survival.*

WORKS CITED

Allen, Theodore W. *The Invention of the White Race: Racial Oppression and Social Control.* London: Verso, 1994.

Althusser, Louis. *Lenin and Philosophy, and Other Essays.* Trans. Ben Brewster. London: New Left Books, 1971.

Anderson, Benedict. *Imagined Communities.* London: Verso, 1991.

Atwood, Margaret. *Surfacing.* Toronto: McClelland, 1972.

—. *Survival: A Thematic Guide to Canadian Literature.* Toronto: Anansi, 1972.

Bolaria, B. Singh, and Peter S. Li, eds. *Racial Oppression in Canada.* Toronto: Garamond, 1988.

Boldt, Menno, and J. Anthony Long, eds. (in assoc. with Leroy Little Bear). *The Quest for Justice: Aboriginal Peoples and Aboriginal Rights.* Toronto: U of Toronto P, 1985.

Carty, Linda, ed. *And Still We Rise: Feminist Political Mobilizing in Contemporary Canada.* Toronto: Women's, 1994.

Carty, Linda, and Dionne Brand. "Visible Minority Women: A Creation of the Colonial State." *Returning the Gaze: Essays on Racism, Feminism and Politics.* Ed. Himani Bannerji. Toronto: Sister Vision, 1993.

Fleras, Augie, and Jean Leonard Elliott, eds. *Multiculturalism in Canada: The Challenge of Diversity.* Scarborough: Nelson Canada, 1992.

Frankenberg, Ruth. *White Women, Race Matters: The Social Construction of Whiteness.* Minneapolis: U of Minnesota P, 1993.

Gunder Frank, Andre. *Dependent Accumulation and Underdevelopment.* London: Macmillan, 1978.

Habermas, Jürgen. *Legitimation Crisis.* Boston: Beacon, 1975.

Johnson, Laura Climenko, and Robert E. Johnson. *Seam Allowance: Industrial Home Sewing in Canada.* Toronto: Women's, 1982.

Miliband, Ralph. *The State in Capitalist Society: The Western System of Power.* London: Quartet, 1973.

Moore, Steve, and Debi Wells. *Imperialism and the National Question in Canada.* Toronto: Moore, 1975.

Morton, Desmond. *A Short History of Canada.* Toronto: McClelland, 1994.

Ng, Roxana. "Sexism, Racism, Canadian Nationalism." *Returning the Gaze: Essays on Racism, Feminism and Politics.* Ed. Himani Bannerji. Toronto: Sister Vision, 1993. 182-96.

Roediger, David R. *The Wages of Whiteness: Race and the Making of the American Working Class.* London: Verso, 1993.

Roman, Leslie G. "White is a Color: White Defensiveness, Postmodernism and Antiracist Pedagogy." *Race, Identity, and Representation in Education.* Ed. Cameron McCarthy and Warren Crichlow. New York: Routledge, 1993. 71-88.

Ryerson, Stanley. *The Foundation of Canada.* Toronto: Progress Books, 1960.

Smith, Dorothy E. *The Everyday World as Problematic: A Feminist Sociology.* Toronto: U of Toronto P, 1987.

Stoler, Ann Laura. *Race and the Education of Desire: Foucault's History of Sexuality and the Colonial Order of Things.* Durham: Duke UP, 1995.

Teeple, Gary, ed. *Capitalism and the National Question in Canada.* Toronto: U of Toronto P, 1972.

Tester, Frank James, and Peter Kulchyski. *Tammarniit (Mistakes): Inuit Relocation in the Eastern Arctic.* Vancouver: U of British Columbia P, 1994.

Wallerstein, Immanuel. *Capitalist World Economy.* London: Cambridge UP, 1979.

Ware, Vron. *Beyond the Pale: White Women, Racism, and History.* London: Verso, 1991.

Watkins, Mel, ed. *Dene Nation: The Colony Within.* Toronto: U of Toronto P, 1977.

Watson, Scott. "Race, Wilderness, Territory and the Origins of Modern Canadian Landscape Painting." *Semiotext[e]: Canadas.* Peterborough: Marginal Editions, 1994. 93-104.

24

"Sliding the Scale of Elision: 'Race' Constructs/Cultural Praxis"*

Roy Miki

You are better off not knowing how sausages and laws are made.
—Fortune Cookie

One: It's happening only yesterday and today

"Race" under erasure[1]—not in futurity or in a haloed heritage but in present tenseness—becomes itself a floating signifier, stable only apparently in the conformity of reference. Recent interventions in cultural praxis have dislodged its transparency to make visible its historical and current signs of circulation. Lucius Outlaw, echoing other theorists, calls for the exposure of "race thinking" as "a way of conceptualizing and organizing social worlds composed of persons whose differences allow for arranging them into groups that come to be called 'races'" (61), and he proposes critical work that would "challenge the presumptions sedimented in the 'reference schemata' that, when socially shared, become common sense . . ." (59).[2]

* * *

This, then, is a real story. It happened at Pearson International Airport in Toronto. It is told by Makeda Silvera in "Caribbean Chameleon" (from *Her Head a Village*). "She" is not named. "She" is not the teller of the tale but the narration. "Woman in black polka dot pant suit" (28) returns from a visit to Jamaica. "She" is speech, speaking, spoken, moving in a line, in a line-up, crossing the line from body talk into state discourse.

In the passage through the gauntlet of customs, interrogation is the only form that matters. This border zone tolerates no divergences, no irregularities. Speak in the grid of compliance, "safe" (30), pass through. Speak otherwise, even a miniscule syllable off and the rap trap ties tongue in knots:

"Purpose?" "Vacation, mam." "Where did you stay?" "Kingston, mam." "Did you stay with family?" "No mam, I visit dem, but I stay in a hotel."

---

* *Broken Entries: Race, Subjectivity, Writing* (Toronto: Mercury Press, 1998), 125-59.

Suspicion. "Hotel?" "Yes mam." "Take off your glasses, please." Officer look lady in black polka dot pant suit up and down. (30-31)

Once "she" is gazed as an other, power proceeds to strip "her"—of her rights (though she has, as she *says*, her "'landed papers right here'") and her subject status. The chaoticization of her baggage mimes her own "speaking in tongues," as "Woman in black polka dot pant suit" undergoes linguistic transference into "Black polka dot woman" (31). When a body search is ordered, "she" is pressed into the zone of elision, reduced to mere resistance:

Black polka dot woman don't wait. Tear off shirt. Tear off jacket. Tear off pants. Polka dot woman reach for bra. For drawers. Officer shout for Royal Canadian Mounted Police to take mad woman away. "TAKE HER AWAY. TAKE HER AWAY." Take this wild savage. Monster. Jungle beast. "AWAY. Arrest her for indecent exposure." (32)

The "arrest" brings down the police state, stopping further leakage, further "indecent exposure," through the seams of the event. Ritual banishment then confirms and authorizes the race expectations the "woman in polka dot pant suit" did not, at first, fulfill for the customs officer at the gateway to "Canada." But once "she" is framed by the colonizing discourse of "wild savage," and suitably dehumanized, civilized order (read here "whiteness" as measure) is restored.

The miscodes of elision, then, disperse a semiotics of static and the crisscross of duplicities on the surfaces of race constructs. On the other hand, the power these constructs have to mutate, in the light of exposure, ensures the recirculation of dominant relations. Such odds make the project of antiracism all the more formidable and open to neutralization and containment. The encounter (as in "Caribbean Chameleon") is not unlike the dream landscape suddenly rendered arational by site-specific quicksand, the linguistic body drawn into the collapsing folds of liquid white-out. Where, under erasure, is the line to resist disappearance?

* * *

This, then, is a social construction. This is the narrative as "Neil Bissoondath" who masquerades in the folds of *Saturday Night*—"don't call me ethnic"—saying "i" has transcended race yet speaks as one whose authority derives from his "colour." The resurrected body on the cover identifies "multiculturalism" as an infection that produces "the ethnic deracinated and costumed" (19) who then transforms into the divisive social force embodied in the racialized other. "To be 'racialized,'" says Bissoondath, tying the term to "Miki"—

labelled "Canadian of Japanese descent" by a supposedly beyond race and ethnicity perceiver—"is to have acquired a racial vision of life" (18). The logic of association mimes the state discourse used to justify the internment of persons "of Japanese race" in the 1940s.[3]

"Racialization," as used by Miki, applies to the imposition of race constructs and hierarchies on marked and demarked "groups" whose members come to signify divergence from the normative body inscribed by whiteness. The subject racialized is identified by systemic categories that winnow the body, according privilege to those glossed with dominance and privation to those digressed to subordination.

In reworking the term to re-racialize writers of colour, Bissoondath would have *his* readers believe that racialization is not a social script but an identity formation wilfully assumed—and this willy-nilly recasts the racialized into the racist. Such illogic, through which the victim becomes the victimizer, is a historical model of blame very familiar to those with not-white bodies in Canadian social topographies. But what is finally more telling of the nation's media machine is not Bissoondath's words—it is his own marked body and the privileges it is given for speaking the discourse of whiteness.[4] Long before the *Saturday Night* feature face, Dionne Brand had pinpointed the more pervasive neo-colonial strategy at work: "In producing a Neil Bissoondath to denounce the cultural appropriation critique, the white cultural establishment produces a dark face to dismiss and discredit all the other dark faces and simultaneously to confirm and reinscribe that colonial representation which is essential to racial domination" ("Who?" 19).

* * *

In the title story of Silvera's *Her Head a Village*, the unnamed narrator, a writer, struggles with an essay, "Writing as a Dangerous Profession," while her head is filled with conflicting voices of a "noisy village" all pulling her in contrary directions. The story rejects the autonomous self of western humanism and instead spatializes the narrator's imagination as the site of variable and conflicting subject positions as "Black woman writer" (12). The textual seams she exposes begin to reconfigure a language in which discourses of racialization are revealed as the medium of social and political power. This move acknowledges the limits of representation, while calling for a cultural praxis that can work through the alien-national effects of "racial formation"—a term adopted by Michael Omi and Howard Winant to identify "the process by which social, economic and political [and cultural] forces determine the content and importance of racial categories, and by which they are in turn shaped by racial meanings" (*Racial* 61).

Two: A caveat for this "i"

When the "i" is inscribed in this sentence, what are the signs of race? In an interview with Sneja Gunew in *The Post-Colonial Critic*, Gayatri Spivak says that "the question 'Who should speak?' is less crucial than 'Who will listen?'" (59)—and in that shift displaces the weight already straining the back of the speaker and locates responsibility in those who decode the signs. If the economy of race governs the rules of reception, and if subjects are spoken by discourses even as they speak through them, how do the dynamics of power and the making of identity operate in the contextual field of a text performed, as this one is? Does the signifying body remain the veil of race constructs, or can an interventionist tactic of writing the body enable a transformative act of listening?

Homi Bhabha talks about the encounter with "identity" as a disruption, and when it "occurs at the point at which something exceeds the frame of the image, it eludes the eye, evacuates the self as site of identity and autonomy and—most important—leaves a resistant trace, a stain of the subject, a sign of resistance" (49). The racialized subject in performance enacts such limits and in the effects of dispersal cannot take shelter in the so-called "reasonable" academic model of exchange. In each syntactic turn, even in the vehicular language of information, the racialized seams of social, cultural and political formations produce the "i" as a conditioned pronoun reference. So Chantal Mouffe writes in *The Return of the Political*:

> . . . we are in fact always multiple and contradictory subjects, inhabitants of a diversity of communities (as many, really, as the social relations in which we participate and the subject positions they define), constructed by a variety of discourses, and precariously and temporarily sutured at the intersection of those subject positions. (20-21)

When *this* "i" addresses race elision, in which subject formation (of many "multiple and contradictory") will it be listened to, if such listening occurs in the first place? Media constructions have identified "him" as a "writer of colour," as a member of a group called "Japanese Canadian," as a "Canadian of Japanese ancestry," as an "academic," an "editor," a "cultural activist," even a "trouble-maker." Given space to speak here, in addressing a "you," is this "i" then a given or is this space determined by the proliferation of race signs on the borders of what even now gets told, seen, and heard?

Three: Wither goeth CanCrit?

The institutionalization of CanLit with its twin CanCrit—since the nationalist zealotry of the 1960s—rather than articulating, has left unexamined the cultural conditions conducive to race elision. The "normally" benign rhetoric of "national identity" has worked to cover over the nation-building role of an exclusionary "identity" in the neo-colonial shadows of cultural sovereignty. The ethnocentricity of the quest to possess colonized space, operating through a masking of motive and power, has been disguised in the compulsive will to reify the authority of one's own nation as a sign of liberation. In a critique of this "displaced form of nationalism," Robert Lecker foregrounds the self-serving—that is, insular and unreflexive—production of literary criticism that established, in a period of only twenty years, a canon-forming industry serving as "an expression of national self-consciousness" ("Canonization" 658).

"We do not know why the Canadian canon includes certain texts and excludes others" (659), Lecker argues—but speaking as he does *within* his institutional boundaries, he can only point the finger of blame, not advocate methodological strategies to explode the Anglo-European identity politics that imprints itself through a process of differing at the expense of "its" racialized others. In response to Frank Davey's charge that he has failed to interrogate difference, Lecker admits to his own "split emotion" on the consequences of his "inquiry into value" (the subtitle of his essay) that he promotes.[5] If nationalist CanLit (a "security blanket") is destroyed, the "orthodox fantasy of the peaceable kingdom" ("Critical Response II" 683) will also be destroyed. This "split" in Lecker is less personal than symptomatic of a strategic displacement that simultaneously critiques the institution and protects its territory. Lecker may appear to destabilize boundaries in calling on his colleagues to recognize (citing Louis Montrose) "'the textual construction of critics who are themselves historical subjects'" ("Canonization" 661), but in rationalizing that the "split" in himself "has nothing to do with intellectual validity or sophistication or consistency" ("Critical Response II" 683), he retreats to the already constituted chambers of the institution's cultural authority. In other words, the terminological normalizations that scaffold Lecker's discourse remain intact—in a taken-for-granted position. Terms like "canon," "value," "literary history," "national," and the most telling of all, "Canadian," may allow for gestures towards those "differences" outside, but they function to prevent them from infiltrating the rhetorical borders of the inquiry.[6] What would happen, for example, if the term "Canadian" were dispersed into all the lines of alterity that, in actuality, striate the social body?

The predictable recourse to the unproblematized "we" in the concluding section of Lecker's essay forestalls this question, drawing the discourse into alignment with the originating narrative of cultural sovereignty. CanLit, like the "Canadian" nation, is a formation that cannot be separated from the cultural territorialization of space that accompanies the colonization process. This line of descent echoes D.G. Jones' astounding declaration at the outset of *Butterfly on Rock* that the land is "ours" because "our westward expansion is complete" (3), so that, in national cultural terms, "we" have also "arrived at a point where we recognize . . . that we are the land's" (3). Such an apparently affirmative nativization (the underbelly of nationalism) displaces, while neutralizing, the violent appropriation of First Nations lands and cultures.[7]

The messianic-like declaration of ownership, though, betrays an "ambivalence" (to draw on Homi Bhabha's analysis of "nation" narration) that seeks to be exorcized by assertions of "identity," assertions of "value," assertions that CanLit does indeed exist. The academic labour that went into the three-volume *Literary History of Canada* (1965), with its famous "Conclusion" by Northrop Frye, was less a descriptive task and more the making of a teleological history that narrated CanLit into existence.[8] It is in this context, moreover, that Canadian nationalists (e.g., prominently by Margaret Atwood in *Survival* and Dennis Lee in "Cadence, Country, Silence") adopted the language of victimization to place "Canadian" cultural identity in opposition to its external enemies, American and British imperialisms. This triadic model justified a reductive "Canadianness"—a cultural lineage linked to an essentialized British past—that elided the relations of dominance inside the country, what has been called "internal colonialism."[9] The internal structures of dominance include a racialization process in which non-white subjects in the Canadian state are subordinated as "others" who inhabit a realm of shadows, of chaotic darkness, of "non-persons" (see Crosby 288).[10] If the assumption is that critics, academics, and theorists are social subjects whose actions are necessarily enmeshed with dominant values, then the products of their research and writing must signify in terms of omissions, containments, and displacements.

Even critical work that proposes itself as the cutting edge may be unable to extricate itself from the historical determinants of its institutional setting. One example (of mid-to-late 1980s criticism) is *Future Indicative: Literary Theory and Canadian Literature* (1987), the proceedings of an academic gathering hailed by its editor, John Moss, as "prophetic," the next fold in the "open future" of criticism following the "exhausted condition" of "thematic criticism" (1).[11] The announcement of this radical departure—this movement beyond "thematic"—is nonetheless contained within the familiar walls of the CanLit institution. Despite the fine essays presented by a number of the most accomplished critical theorists in Canada, including essays that address questions of difference,[12] the readers who make their way through the collection find few signs that "Canadian" signifies much more than a diversity of approaches to "Canadian literature," a term that is itself not dismembered. *Future Indicative* may be a welcome relief from the totalizing and homogenizing agenda of nationalist thematic criticism, but critical race consciousness is still parked in the boundary zones both outside and inside the limits of its discourse. When signs of difference and contradiction do appear, the conference context and critical framing—which is to say, the institution of Can-

Crit that governs inclusions and exclusions—neutralize potential disruptions to the projected social and cultural spaces in the texts.

For this reason Moss' praise for the theoretical audacity represented in the collection is misleading, as evident, for instance, in a statement such as the following:

> They have been deconstructing the box in which we have tried to contain our culture; not peering over the garrison walls but walking right through them. Suddenly, people working from a literary base which includes *Wacousta* and Carman along with Wordsworth and Arnold are bringing critical theory from Paris and Oxford and New Haven to bear, from their perspectives in Vancouver or Fredericton or, yes, even Ottawa, on literary experience of their own country. (3)

In the assumption of national maturation, of liberation from colonialism, of an internationalist literary context, and of a cosmopolitanism, the term "Canadian" continues to function as a Derridean transcendental signified, and "flourishing diversity" (1) has more to do with the individual points of view of the speakers than to the cultural condition of Canada. The ambivalences cutting across the institutional history of nation-based criticism are absorbed by a) concluding that "future" work will have to find solutions for exclusions—think here of the racialized "Canadians" who are not represented in the collection; or b) difference is addressed in the attention paid to gender (Godard and Neuman), "the image of the indigene" (Goldie), ethnocentrism (Murray), and ethnicity (Loriggio)—think here of the term race that makes possible "our heritage" (93) as derived from white, patriarchic, Anglo-European, and imperialist/colonialist legacies. For all the implications of change, the critical mapping remains the representation of the national space: there are no writers and critics from First Nations communities and communities of colour in the volume.[13]

Future Indicative, as a textual performance, discloses the power of literary discourse to establish and arbitrate norms, stances, and perspectives in the production of paradigms for framing cultural processes. In the face of contradictions and contestations that threaten to unravel institutional borderlines, establishment discourse can manoeuvre terminology that reinscribes relations of internal dominance. In "'Circling the Downspout of Empire,'" for instance, Linda Hutcheon displaces the immediacy of race issues in contemporary cultural politics by differentiating the "postmodern" from the "postcolonial" in what can be read as a strategic manner:

> The current post-structuralist/postmodern challenges to the coherent, autonomous self or subject have to be put on hold in feminist and postcolonial discourses, for these must work first to assert and affirm a

denied or alienated subjectivity: those radical postmodern challenges are in many ways the luxury of the dominant order, which can afford to challenge what it securely possesses. (70-71)[14]

The critical logic of Hutcheon's statement, while apparently "making sense" of the dividing line between postmodernism and post-colonialism—which is why it sounds the note of clarity—is symptomatic of the pattern in Canadian criticism to establish a binary model that relegates those subject to subordination and alterity to the margin and simultaneously bestows priority and founding status on the centre. In the evolutionary model presented, the "postmodern," as what comes first, becomes an extension of the "dominant order." In a Canadian context this "order" stands in for the Anglo-European (white male) norms that designate certain writers to be "coherent, autonomous" subjects, while those then framed as the excluded "others," i.e., feminists and post-colonials (read here, non-white, immigrant), "must work *first* to assert and affirm a denied or alienated subjectivity" (emphasis added). These poor souls are still struggling with their "alienated subjectivity," so cannot yet enter the "luxury of the dominant order" where the "autonomous self" can be challenged—because the postmodernist has a "self" that is "securely possesse[d]," as securely as the land has been possessed by the nation. By separating the dominant order (postmodernism) from the dominated (post-colonialism), Hutcheon maintains the hierarchic social order that situates the racialized under the sign of those "others" who are still struggling to enter the dominant order (where the postmodernist already resides). This terminology depends on the static and containing model of "centre-margin" (dominant-subordinate) as a means of eliding the instrumental power of racialized assumptions in critical discourse.

Such an effacement, on the other hand, accounts for the very contradiction that exposes the seams of a "beyond" where cultural production is instrumental for those who cannot claim "secure" representation in dominant institutions. [. . .]

FIVE: RE-SITING WRITING THRU RACE

This weekend we've gotten a glimpse, the tip of the iceberg.
—Lillian Allen, Press Conference for "Writing thru Race,"
July 3, 1994, Vancouver

For a brief period, February to May 1994, the traces of race proliferated and came to visibility around a writers' conference when enrollment was limited to "First Nations writers and writers of colour." The speckled bird of media, "Writing thru Race" even infiltrated the House of Commons where, in a posture of white outrage, Reform MP Jan Brown called the conference policy "racist" and demanded the removal of federal loonies. In a posture of response, Minister of Canadian Heritage, Michel Dupuy, announced his *personal* decision—perhaps as himself a cultural activist—to deny support of $22,500 already approved. The event was saved from the dustbin of discarded tropes through a last minute fundraising campaign.[15] In the midst of the verbal spectacle, the institutional silence was systemic. Cultural and literary specialists remained in their garrisons as the "voice" of media isolated writers of colour with the markings of race spectres that spooked the ideological undercurrents of a white Canada. The elision of race in CanLit guaranteed that a conference bringing together writers of colour would be vulturized and canned by the media in the common-sense terms circulating in everyday Canadian life.

The domino effect by which "Writing thru Race" was framed can be tracked to Robert Fulford's appropriation of a report published in the newsletter of the Writers' Union of Canada, to which he had access as a member.[16] But instead of responding to the membership, he capitalized on his privilege by making the report the focus of a *Globe and Mail* column, "George Orwell, Call Your Office" (March 30, 1994), labelling the conference "apartheid" in what he termed the "no-whites rule"—with "rule" a reference to conference policy, not to power, though that may have been intended. The article ignited fellow columnist Michael Valpy. In his "A Nasty Serving of Cultural Apartheid" (April 8, 1994), Valpy transforms Fulford into a cultural hero, as he too echoes "apartheid," then goes one step further to read "Writing thru Race" as the harbinger of a social "cancer" that threatens "Canadian cultural identity." In Valpy's sociopsychic space, there are shades of the demons in the dreams of "white men and women" in colonial BC who were haunted by visions of being "daily over-run by hordes of Chinese laborers" (words of "Amor do Cosmos to the Electors of Victoria District, June 20, 1882," cited by Patricia Roy in *A White Man's Province* [37]). Read here, for Chinese labourers, writers of colour, and the shadows begin to flutter.

After an editorial ("Excluding Whites") in the *Toronto Star*, April 5, condemning the conference for its policy, a critical turn occurred, so notes Sourayan Mookerjea in his reconstruction of media reaction, as "the controversy switched circuits and moved from being something to editorialize about to something to report on" (118).[17] The first report, from Canadian Press, appeared on April 7 (titled "Conference Stirs Controversy" in the *Vancouver Sun*) and functioned to identify—not the purpose and details of the conference—but the media's treatment of the conference as a "controversy." The only story was the "non-whites only policy" (echo of Fulford's "no-whites rule") and the interrogation of funding agencies. In other words, the issue of "white exclusion" took front and centre as the power of whiteness represented by public funders—which included at its apex the Minister of Canadian Heritage—was evoked to threaten writers of colour with retaliation. The naming of the conference as a "controversy," then, established the binary narrative of a conflict: innocent whites excluded on the basis of *their* race versus self-centred writers of colour using "taxpayer" funds to segregate themselves. The assumption, of course, is that the cardboard cut-out of nationhood, the "taxpayer," is white.

On April 16, when Bronwyn Drainie entered the fray with her column, "Controversial Writers' Meeting Is Both Meet and Right," editorials had appeared in the *Globe and Mail*, the *Toronto Star*, and the *Vancouver Sun*, more reports had reinforced the conference as a "controversy," and many letters "for" and "against" had appeared in newspapers. Drainie criticized fellow columnists, Fulford and Valpy, for their "apocalyptic doom and gloom," and pointed to the "all-white-male editorial board" of the *Globe and Mail* in saying she had "no problem, in a democratic society, with groups meeting behind closed doors to share their frustrations and map out their campaigns." Drainie's intervention—supposedly in support of the policy—in effect slotted itself into the narrative terrain that had already been ploughed by the media: the white majority on one side, the "we" which included Drainie; writers of colour as a minority group on the other, the "they" who are feared by whites and who fear whites.

Race had threaded its way through the seams to restabilize the social and cultural model of a white centre with groups of non-whites on the margins whose writers struggle to gain entrance to the centre. The discourse of racial difference, of otherness, had covered over the specificity of the conference itself and the contemporary manifestations of race that had surfaced in reactions to it.[18]

By June, the conference had been so racialized by the media in terms of dominant representations that the "controversy" was ripe enough to be easily plucked for politicization by the moral forces of the white/right, as it was by Jan Brown in the House of Commons.[19] Dupuy's compromised response confirmed the race cover-up that would inevitably lead him to deny funding. Dupuy, as quoted in the press, rationalized that he did not oppose "groups" (read here non-whites homogenized in the media) from meeting together (read here freedom of assembly ensured by the Charter of Rights)—but he did not accept the "principle of discrimination" (read here "no-whites rule"). As the Minister of Canadian Heritage, Dupuy found himself peering down from his seat of power into the border zones of race in this country, and he clearly acted to reproduce the discourse of white rule. Declaring himself opposed to discrimination, he then went ahead and discriminated on the basis of race codes inscribed in the ideology of *his* nation.[20] The historical and contemporary contexts of systemic exclusion, dominance, and white privilege were placed under erasure in the discourse of white moral outrage that substituted for his white body. When the manifestations of his subject position appeared on the front page of the *Vancouver Sun*, the now signified "controversy" had entered the sphere of national news, and by then all the signs of race had been encoded for mass consumption in the headline, "Feds Won't Fund Writers' Workshop That Bars Whites" (Peter O'Neill, June 9, 1994). Indeed, "Writing thru Race" had been read by dominant systems of representation as an event not worthy of public support.[21]

But, of course, another text was written in the seams.

The framing of "Writing thru Race" as having its origins in "white exclusion"—the media plot construction—was the initial act of territorialization that, first, misplaced the specificity of an event that was to address the internalization of racism in writing and, then, re-centred its challenge to mainstream values on the turf of whiteness as the boundary being violated. The conversion of "white" from a norm into an identity-formation made possible the claim, even by those such as Fulford who were supposed to be colour-blind, that "white" is a "colour," an excluded sign, hence the victim of racism. And the guilty perpetrators? Of course, those "writers of colour," the monstrous outgrowth of multicultural policy, whose monolithic aim is to destroy the Anglo-European way of life. It was this demonization of the other that drew a circle around whiteness as the domain of power and concealed the role of the racialization process in maintaining systemic racism.[22]

In this contemporary instance, though, the concealment was only apparent. The disruption of the public sphere and the hyperbolic drive to own "white" as a "colour" exposed the anxieties permeating the white mainstream. Dionne Brand, in her talk at "Writing thru Race," pointed to the "real panic" emanating from the white "intellectual elite" (i.e., Fulford et al): "It now hears other opinions and experiences of the people of colour in the country who challenge its definitions of what the country is and what it looks like. And that panic you can also see in the everyday social life of the country" ("Notes" 13).

That panic lit up the colonized switchboard of normative cultural values that are constituted through the otherization of "non-whites" in its midst. Gayatri Spivak distinguishes between "questions of identity and voice" in cultural struggles, with their risk of collapse into self-defense, and the project of "clearing space . . . to create a perspective" ("Bonding" 278-79). "Writing thru Race" adopted the term "of colour"—problematic though it is *relative* to "whiteness"—to foreground in more provisional ways than state bureaucratic terminology ("racial minority" or "visible minority") the actuality of everyday lives marked by race hierarchies. As an anti-racist tactic, "of colour" was to be a means to construct a space and time—even a transitory institution—to enable the interaction of subject positions, histories, and knowledges that have been conditioned by racialization. "Of colour," then, was to act as a pre-text for the shift in current cultural praxis away from the conflation of ethnicity and race in multicultural ideology.[23] For example, in the identity politics of the 1970s and 1980s, race lines were mapped onto group formations that isolated—and often divided—communities of colour from one another. Ironically, Fulford has a point in arguing that multiculturalism has fostered separate enclaves in which ethnic and race constructs bled into one another. What he fails to question, though, is the complicity that has linked his liberal pluralism to the discourse of multiculturalism. As Scott McFarlane argues in what is, to date, the most thorough analysis of the race politics unleashed by the conference, it is a discourse through which non-whites and First Nations people "are figured outside . . . as, for example, immigrants or non-persons who become 'Canadian' through their relationship to whiteness, as opposed to 'the land'" ("Haunt" 22).

The Multiculturalism Act (1988) can be read as the space of the "other" for the liberalism enshrined in the Charter of Rights and Freedoms. In the inscription of the terms "race" and "racial" as essentialized signs in a national social text, people of colour, or "non-whites," are produced as ethnic and racial identities that differ from the constitutional base. The relativization of culture in what gets called "the cultural and racial diversity of Canadian society" (Canada, *Multiculturalism Act* 13) removes its forms from the political sphere, laying the foundation, as Edward Said writes in *Culture and Imperialism*, for a "radical falsification": "Culture is exonerated of any entanglements with power, representations are considered only as apolitical images to be parsed and construed as so many grammars of exchange, and the divorce of the present from the past is assumed to be complete" (57). The past, then, becomes an apolitical "heritage," a term given official status by the new Department of Canadian Heritage, the space that now subsumes federal multiculturalism and determines which cultural events are to be supported by public funds. Dupuy's actions, in other words, signified the overt political manipulation of the cultural sphere in the interests of state-sanctioned representations of Canadian life.

The divorce of culture from politics in state multiculturalism—a divorce that finds its counterpart in CanCrit—has meant that "Canadian" culture could continue to represent Anglo-European ethnocentricity. It is no wonder, then, that despite multiculturalism as official state policy, dominant literary institutions—for example, English Departments in Canada—bear only faint token effects of its influence. Indeed, as the nesting place for the other, Canadian multiculturalism has proven to be an efficient means of engineering internal inequities in ways that have protected white neo-colonialist cultural representations. It is in this ideological warp that the undoing of multiculturalism is tied directly to the perceived decline of liberal values lamented by Fulford, Michael Valpy, and other malcontents. The two crises, then, are symptomatic of a collapsed cultural system that cannot represent the everyday life of the country.

* * *

The malleability of systemic race constructs poses serious challenges to those who undertake anti-racist work through cultural and literary production. The stabilization of positions through theory, criticism, and pedagogy is always open to complicity and cooptation. Terminology is a shifting field of duplicity and temptation. Subject positions move through contradictions that are often labyrinthine in their effects. Lillian Allen reminds us that "awareness and education," the older eurocentric goals of anti-racist work, are inadequate markers for real change: "There are two significant litmus tests for anti-racism work: meaningful change and critical mass. When does what we do make an actual difference and how much do we need to do to ensure this change?" (50).

The hyperbolic reaction to "Writing thru Race," along with the deathly silence from academia, would suggest that the cultural transformation necessary to render obsolete the technologies of race remains in the future tense. Under erasure, race has to be continually brought to visibility as a construct that never stands still, or if it does stand still, then its nets will continue to snare the body. Cultural praxis—in this "meantime" that becomes "our" historical condition—becomes itself a performance of the political which opens what Homi Bhabha calls "a space of translation: a place of hybridity, figuratively speaking, where the construction of a political object that is new, *neither the one nor the other*, properly alienates our political expectations, and changes, as it must, the very forms of our recognition of the moment of politics" (25). More than ever, textual production becomes a survival tactic in the construction of the imaginary that enacts the actual in our lives. "It is in the realm of imaginary writing that relationships other than those authoritatively prescribed come to be" (Arteaga 33). Dionne Brand said as much at the conference when she advised writers "to guard against only writing about our encounter with 'whiteness,' or exoticizing our experiences for 'white consumption'" ("Notes" 15). The more productive necessity, at this moment, is to "write the interiority of our real lives in detail, in minutiae" (15). That much, at least, "Writing thru Race" brought to crisis.

Listen, then, for a moment to Jam. Ismail, a poet whose cultural praxis generates the text of a theoretical engagement that looks to future possibilities, future cultural formations. Listen as her imagined figure, "young ban yen," puns a way through exploding race constructs in a flurry of sound, syntax, and intellect:

> ratio
> quality

young ban yen had been thought
    italian in kathmandu, filipina in hong
kong, eurasian in kyoto, japanese in anchorage, dismal in
london england, hindu in edmonton, generic oriental in
calgary, western canadian in ottawa, anglophone in
montreal, metis in jasper, eskimo at hudson's bay

department store, vietnamese in chinatown, tibetan in vancouver, commie at the u.s. border.

on the whole very asian. (128)

Notes

I would like to thank Kirsten Emiko McAllister, Scott Toguri McFarlane, and Charmaine Perkins for sharing many of the race issues that are part of this paper. I have been encouraged by their comments, friendship, and scholarship.

1. "Race," in quotations, is understood throughout this essay [. . .] as a construct, but to avoid typographical clutter I have removed the quotations and ask the reader to imagine them present in every use of the term. The phrase "under erasure," borrowed from Jacques Derrida, is here extended to evoke race signs beneath the surface of erasure—in what perhaps can be understood as the realm of the negative.
2. Aside from such collections as *Anatomy of Racism* (ed. David Theo Goldberg), *The Bounds of Race* (ed. Dominick LaCapra), *"Race," Writing and Difference* (ed. Henry Louis Gates, Jr.), and *Race Identity and Representation in Education* (ed. Cameron McCarthy and Warren Crichlow), the rethinking of race is evident in numerous publications. Significant for this essay are Homi Bhabha's *The Location of Culture*, Trinh T. Minh-ha's *When the Moon Waxes Red*, Edward Said's *Culture and Imperialism*, and Gayatri Spivak's *The Post-Colonial Critic* and *Outside in the Teaching Machine*. Work on race theory in relation to cultural production in Canada has lagged, but important publications include Marlene Nourbese Philip's *Frontiers*, *Returning the Gaze*, edited by Himani Bannerji, and articles in *Fuse, Border/Lines, Harbour, West Coast Line, Parallélogramme*, and *Fireweed*.
3. Bissoondath perhaps takes the term "racialization" from a report on the "Writing thru Race" conference, "A Mid-Stream Report," by Roy Miki, which was published in the *Newsletter of the Writers' Union of Canada*; or he is drawing from Robert Fulford's attack on the conference based on the same report; see his "George Orwell, Call Your Office," *Globe and Mail* March 30, 1994.
4. It is not surprising that Robert Fulford, in a follow-up column to his attack on the "Writing thru Race" conference, endorses Bissoondath as the legitimate voice in the condemnation of multiculturalism. "I share Bissoondath's view that, in racial matters, Canada is plunging blindly down the wrong road, heading toward a place we don't want to be. The Vancouver conference is worth debating because it's a minor symptom of a major problem" ("Down the Garden Path of Multiculturalism," *Globe and Mail* June 9, 1994).
5. Robert Lecker's essay, which was published in *Critical Inquiry* and likely intended for an American academic readership, is critiqued by Frank Davey in the same

issue. Lecker's response to Davey is also included. I agree with Davey that Lecker's model of "CanLit" is too homogenous and bounded, given the heterogeneity of the cultural field, and given too the contestations within "Canadian" literature and criticism ("Critical Response I" 680-81).

6. In what reads as a follow-up to the issues raised in "The Canonization of Canadian Literature," Lecker, in "Privacy, Publicity, and the Discourse of Canadian Criticism," historicizes what he calls the "privatization" of CanCrit that led to the formation of a professional group of specialists who have lost contact with the public realm. Again, however, Lecker situates himself as operating only within the confines of that "privatization" and makes no attempt to address the actual cultural conflicts that have erupted all across Canada in the past decade. The divorce of the academic sphere from contemporary cultural praxis, particularly that of minority writers and artists, has brought into focus a conspiracy of silence that implicates mainstream CanCrit in a neocolonialist perspective. The situation, fortunately, is not as monolithic as it once was, as more critics and theorists deconstruct the institution both from within and without. The most vital critiques in recent years have come from racialized writers and artists, for instance, Dionne Brand, Marlene Nourbese Philip, Ashok Mathur, Himani Bannerji, Richard Fung, and Marie Annharte Baker, whose works necessarily position themselves in the midst of struggle and contestation.

7. First Nations writers have spoken against the appropriation of "Indian" identity and culture, often provoking emotional defenses by white mainstream writers who claim immunity on the basis of western liberal notions of freedom. But as Richard Fung argues in "Working through Cultural Appropriation," "The critique of cultural appropriation is . . . first and foremost a strategy to redress historically established inequities by raising questions about who controls and benefits from cultural resources" (18). Lenore Keeshig-Tobias, among a number of First Nations writers, has written compellingly on the devastating effects of cultural appropriation from First Nations positioning; see, for instance, her "Stop Stealing Native Stories"; see also Jeannette Armstrong's "The Disempowerment of First North American Native Peoples and Empowerment through Their Writing"; Loretta Todd's "Notes on Appropriation"; Lee Maracle's "The 'Post-Colonial' Imagination"; Richard Hill's "One Part Per Million: White Appropriation and Native Voices"; Marie Annharte Baker's "Dis Mischief: Give It Back Before I Remember I Gave It Away"; and Janisse Browning's "Self-Determination and Cultural Appropriation."

8. I am thinking here of Said's comment that "the ruling elites of Europe felt the clear need to project their power backward in time, giving it a history and legitimacy that only tradition and longevity could impart" (*Culture* 16). In the Canadian colonial narrative, the lands conquered are projected as embodying monstrous amoral forces that the administrative, military, and cultural power of "civilization" had to tame and control. "Survival," then, became the term to displace the estrangement of the European humanist colonizer, transferring his

own emptiness onto the body of a founding metaphor, "the land." Read in this light, George Grant's description of colonization as the "meeting of the alien and yet conquerable land with English-speaking Protestants" (*Technology* 19) shares the anxiety of exposure that underlies the colonialist obsession to take possession of "the land."

9. The phrase, used by Julia Emberley in *Thresholds of Difference*, comes from Paul Tennant; see Emberley for a discussion of its application to First Nations issues.

10. Crosby says that the federal government through the Indian Act not only produced the homogenizing legal term "Indian" which divided First Nations people into "status Indians" (those on reserves under the jurisdiction of the Department of Indian Affairs) and "non-status" (those not on reserves), but also identified "Indians" as "non-persons." As a result, "The laws pertaining to the many nations contained within the large geographical area now called Canada address an imaginary singular Indian" (288).

11. This publication collects the papers and talks presented at a conference held at the University of Ottawa, April 25 to 27, 1986.

12. Barbara Godard, for instance, raises a concern for writing by "minorities"— "women, natives and immigrants" (44)—and she comments that "reading deconstructively in Canada is ultimately a political practice" (46). Francesco Loriggio inserts the material existence of "ethnic" texts into what has been, for him, the homogenous space of mainstream literature. Heather Murray critiques the totalizing discourse of nationalist thematic criticism, its determination to construct coherence by subordinating difference to sameness, and proposes discourse analysis to read for "contradiction" in the "discursive organization of Canadian literature and literary study" (80). Murray admits to "residual essentialism and considerable ethnocentrism" in her own work—but looks to a new theorization that would assist in a cultural understanding of "who is included and who excluded, who speaks and who is spoken for" (81). Terry Goldie endorses a semiotic approach for his interest in "the image of the indigene," a construct in the texts of "Canadian" imperialism and colonialism that projects the doubled "fear and temptation" of the "native" in Canada. The methodology, for him, enables the possibility of contributing to the liberation of First Nations people and may even be "an agent of native sovereignty" (92).

These gestures of bumping against the walls of CanCrit, while directed toward the future, nevertheless subscribe to a progressivist model of already institutionalized authority. The intent to expand boundaries retains the stability of a nationalist centre—"Canadian" remains unproblematized—which, in turn, allows for a recognition of differences not accounted for in previous critical methods (primarily thematic criticism), but without actually shifting its power base.

13. I acknowledge that my own critique could be seen as itself reductive because the conference itself was not intended to address the problems of race that are the focus of my attention. Nevertheless, the identification of obvious absences, such as the absence of critics and writers of colour, points to a more systemic

absence in CanCrit. The race silence, then, may serve as a means of maintaining unity in diversity, a liberal ideal that would certainly have been challenged through the insertion of race issues into the conference.

14. The term "post-colonial" is variously defined depending on the contexts of its use and purpose. For a critique of Linda Hutcheon's containment of the post-colonial in Canada, which comments on her "'Circling the Downspout of Empire'" and its companion essay, "'The Canadian Mosaic: A Melting Pot on Ice,'" both in *Splitting Images*, see Diana Brydon's "The White Inuit Speaks." See also the essays collected in *Colonial Discourse and Post-Colonial Theory* (ed. Williams and Chrisman) for analyses of the critical contexts through which the term has been represented.

15. For reports on the conference from the perspective of participants, see the articles by Gerry Shikatani, Monika Kin Gagnon and Scott Toguri McFarlane, Cecil Foster, Cyril Dabydeen, and Afua Cooper.

16. In his column, "George Orwell, Call Your Office," Robert Fulford focused on my progress report, "A Mid-Stream Report," to the Writers' Union of Canada, as the Chair of their Racial Minority Writers' Committee; the committee was given the responsibility for establishing a Conference Committee in Vancouver, which was to include many non-union writers of colour, to organize "Writing thru Race."

17. Mookerjea's essay was first presented as a paper at the conference.

18. In 1992, when the Racial Minority Writers' Committee was organizing the first gathering of First Nations writers and writers of colour, "The Appropriate Voice," held in Ontario in May 1992, the issue of cultural appropriation—with all the accompanying signs of race—flared up in the media and stirred up defensive, and often hyperbolic, responses from self-identified "white" writers. Prominent writer Timothy Findley, for instance, trivialized the issue by saying, "if I want to write in the voice of the tea cozy sitting in front of me, believe me, I'm not going to ask for its permission" (qtd. in Hurst "Can(not!) lit," *Toronto Star*, April 11, 1992, and cited by Fung in "Working through Cultural Appropriation").

19. Then Calgary MP Jan Brown, for instance, condemned the conference as "racist" and was instrumental in having the federal funds withdrawn, but later when donations came in, she said she supported it as an initiative of private citizens. "It seems," as Scott McFarlane writes in his account of the politics surrounding the conference, "she doesn't mind 'racist' conferences as long as they are privately funded" ("Haunt" 30). Special thanks to Ashok Mathur for keeping track of Brown's political machinations and for sending this news from Calgary.

20. When Dupuy wrote to the Writers' Union, a long time after the event, he said he supported the Writers' Union anti-racism work but he did not support the conference because he is against all forms of "discrimination." What precisely did he mean by "discrimination"? Was he not "discriminating" when he judged that the conference did not deserve the funds that had been approved by his office?

Dupuy's intellectual collapse elicited vocal opposition. In the weeks following his decision, many writers, artists and cultural workers, artist-run associations, cultural and labour organizations rallied to save the conference. They wrote letters and donated badly needed funds. In the wave of support were two petitions urging Minister Dupuy to reinstate the grant. The participants of a Japanese Canadian conference on the arts in Toronto pointed to the way the conference had been misrepresented: "Media constructions of the conference have avoided contextualizing the event and have served to further the views of mainstream gatekeepers and arbiters of 'Canadian culture.' Their rush to denounce the conference reveals the high stakes involved in any discussion about 'race' and racialization that challenges the *exclusive* power, authority and entitlement of white Anglo English Canada to control the processes used to define literature in this country." Delegates at the "Crossing Frontiers" conference in Ottawa—a conference sponsored by the Department of Canadian Heritage!—referred to principles of human rights affirmed by the United Nations and the Canadian Charter of Rights when they declared that "the Writing thru Race conference is a significant historic event moving forward the long standing debates on race, representation, cultural voice and racism for the *entire* writing and publication community of Canada."

21. As for the conference itself, in one brief weekend—including Canada Day—at the Coast Hotel in the heart of Vancouver's West End, 180 First Nations writers and writers of colour from all across the country came together in what was the largest gathering of its kind. Energy levels were high, and the air of the conference site was abuzz with rich helpings of language spillage. Total immersion was the only workable strategy—a full weekend, day and night, of talk, talk, and more talk, punctuated by spontaneous sessions all over the hotel and in scattered restaurants in the neighbourhood. Conversations expanded long into the night, during walks along the beach and in the more cramped space of the conference hospitality suite.

The atmosphere was carnivalesque—initially dazzling with all the writers commingling—yet there were currents of urgency and purpose: in a country as vast as ours, with writers spread out far and wide, the conference had taken on massive weight for having to pack so much into so little time. It was a mere weekend, after all.

The program included concurrent panel talks, small group writing workshops, plenaries, and evening literary events. There were numerous thought-provoking sessions—on First Nations storytelling, the politics of editing anthologies and magazines, writing from a position of "mixed race," the positioning of "mother tongue" for writers working in so-called non-official languages, the use of literary and cultural theory, strategies for accessing mainstream cultural institutions and granting agencies, and storytelling for children. The highlight had to be the evening readings open to the public. On Thursday, Friday, and Saturday, some 400 listeners each night were captivated by a collage of stories, styles, genres, performances, and voices by over forty writers attending the conference. Saturday night featured tributes to two senior writers who had died that year, Roy Kiyooka and Sam Selvon.

The Sunday morning plenary session concluding the conference began with a resolution addressed to Minister Dupuy. In a motion passed unanimously the delegates asked him to recognize that his decision not to support the conference was "ill-considered and precipitous" and urged him to "actively fund and support initiatives such as the Writing thru Race Conference, toward the total elimination of racism in Canada." Then followed a discussion of recommendations that would help resolve the cultural constraints facing First Nations writers and writers of colour. In the limited time available, many were offered, prominent among them:

—lobby to get copyright protection for oral storytellers, particularly from First Nations communities, whose stories have been appropriated by non-native writers and then published as a written text

—work to ensure equal access to government grants for writers who do not write in either of the two "official" languages

—establish regular national festivals of readings, performances, and events that celebrate achievements of First Nations writers and writers of colour

—form coalitions in local communities to continue the work begun at the conference

—approach a cross-section of Canadian cultural and literary magazines to request space to feature First Nations writers and writers of colour

—create a newsletter to disseminate information of new publications and forthcoming events relevant to anti-racism work in the literary arts

—set up a mentor system by which established First Nations writers and writers of colour can provide assistance to younger writers

—organize a national conference, similar to "Writing thru Race," every three years

—develop marketing strategies to distribute books in First Nations communities and communities of colour

—foster closer ties by bringing in First Nations writers and writers of colour to local literary events

—produce a national database of First Nations writers and writers of colour

—establish an editorial advisory committee to seek out ten manuscripts per year from First Nations writers and writers of colour, and approach ten publishers to publish them with the assistance of committee members

22. The one exception was a mild piece in the Saturday book section of the *Vancouver Sun*, by Marke Andrews, "Racism Charges Color a Conference on Race."

For the record, only one newspaper editorial looked upon the public hysteria over "Writing thru Race" as a positive sign for contemporary writing. The *Vancouver Sun*, in "Victim-Writers Meeting the Stuff of Great Art," defended government funding for the event: "If anything, the conference . . . strengthens the writers' case that they deserve public support, since they are demonstrably performing their proper task of wrestling with new and hazardous ideas and then writing the rest of us about their experiences."

23. Up until recently, "race" has stood in for "non-white," though it has now become common to hear, in the untheorized corridors of social formations, the term appropriated by those positioned as normative to construct "white = race." "Colour," a term often used for "race," has been adopted by those marked by racialization, not to identify, but to acknowledge the wider nets of "race" formation in Canada. Kwame Dawes, for instance, defends the use of "people of colour" to articulate the shared "experience of oppression and disenfranchisement at the hands of white society" (7), and he uses "First Nations people" to foreground "the relevant and pressing nature of oppression and abuse that is distinctly and undeniably Canadian—that of its relationship with the First Nations of this geographical area" (7). Such terminology, which Dawes admits is an "artificial construct" (7), serves a specific purpose of mobilization and coalition-building at a specific moment in the cultural struggle against racism.

WORKS CITED

Allen, Lillian. "Transforming the Cultural Fortress: Setting the Agenda for Anti-Racism Work in Culture." *Parallélogramme* 19.3 (1993-94): 48-59.

Andrews, Marke. "Racism Charges Color a Conference on Race." *Vancouver Sun* 11 June 1994.

Armstrong, Jeannette. "The Disempowerment of First North American Native Peoples and Empowerment through Their Writing." *An Anthology of Canadian Native Literature in English.* Ed. Daniel David Moses and Terry Goldie. Toronto: Oxford UP, 1992. 207-11.

Arteaga, Alfred. "An Other Tongue." *An Other Tongue: Nation and Ethnicity in the Linguistic Borderlands.* Ed. Arteaga. Durham: Duke UP, 1994. 9-33.

Baker, Marie Annharte. "Dis Mischief: Give It Back Before I Remember I Gave It Away." *Colour. An Issue.* Ed. Roy Miki and Fred Wah. *West Coast Line* 28.1-2 Nos.13-14 (1994): 204-13.

Bannerji, Himani, ed. *Returning the Gaze: Essays on Racism, Feminism and Politics.* Toronto: Sister Vision, 1993.

Bhabha, Homi K. *The Location of Culture.* London: Routledge, 1994.

Bissoondath, Neil. "I am Canadian." *Saturday Night* (1994): 11-12, 16-20, 22.

Brand, Dionne. "Notes to Structuring the Text and the Craft of Writing." *Front* 6.1 (1994): 12-15.

——. "Who Can Speak for Whom?" *Brick* 46 (1993): 13-20.

Browning, Janisse. "Self-Determination and Cultural Appropriation." *Fuse* 15.4 (1992): 31-35.

Brydon, Diana. "The White Inuit Speaks: Contamination as Literary Strategy." *Past the Last Post: Theorizing Post-Colonialism and Post-Modernism.* New York: Harvester Wheatsheaf, 1991. 191-203.

Canada, Multiculturalism and Citizenship. *The Canadian Multiculturalism Act: A Guide for Canadians.* Ottawa: Communications Branch, 1990.

"Conference Stirs Controversy." *Vancouver Sun* 7 Apr. 1994.

Cooper, Afua. "Opinion: Writing thru Race." *Possibilities* 1.3 (1994): 5-6.

Crosby, Marcia. "Construction of the Imaginary Indian." *Vancouver Anthology: The Institutional Politics of Art.* Ed. Stan Douglas. Vancouver: Talonbooks, 1991. 267-91.

Dabydeen, Cyril. "Celebrating Difference." *Books in Canada* 23.6 (1994): 23-25.

Davey, Frank. "Critical Response I: Canadian Canons." *Critical Inquiry* 16 (1990): 672-81.

Dawes, Kwame. "Re-Appropriating Cultural Appropriation." *Fuse* 16.5-6 (1993): 7-15.

Drainie, Bronwyn. "Controversial Writers' Meeting Is Both Meet and Right." *Globe and Mail* 16 Apr. 1994.

Emberley, Julia V. *Thresholds of Difference: Feminist Critique, Native Women's Writings, Postcolonial Theory.* Toronto: U of Toronto P, 1993.

"Excluding Whites." Editorial. *Toronto Star* 5 Apr. 1994.

Foster, Cecil. "An Infusion of Colour." *Quill and Quire* Sept. 1994: 12.

Fulford, Robert. "Down the Garden Path of Multiculturalism." *Globe and Mail* 9 June 1994.

——. "George Orwell, Call Your Office." *Globe and Mail* 30 Mar. 1994.

Fung, Richard. "Working through Cultural Appropriation." *Fuse* 16.5-6 (1993): 16-24.

Gagnon, Monika Kin. "Writing thru Race in Vancouver: Landmarks and Land-mines." *Front* 6.1 (1994): 6-8.

Gates, Henry Louis, Jr., ed. *"Race," Writing, and Difference.* Chicago: U of Chicago P, 1986.

Godard, Barbara. "Structuralism/Post-Structuralism: Language, Reality and Canadian Literature." Moss 25-51.

Goldberg, David Theo, ed. *Anatomy of Racism.* Minneapolis: U of Minnesota P, 1990.

Goldie, Terry. "Signs of the Themes: The Value of a Politically Grounded Semiotics." Moss 85-93.

Grant, George. *Technology and Empire: Perspectives on North America.* Toronto: Anansi, 1969.

Hill, Richard. "One Part Per Million: White Appropriation and Native Voices." *Fuse* 15.3 (1992): 12-22.

Hutcheon, Linda. *Splitting Images: Contemporary Canadian Ironies.* Toronto: Oxford UP, 1991.

Ismail, Jam. "From *Sacred Texts.*" *Many-Mouthed Birds: Contemporary Writing by Chinese Canadians.* Ed. Bennett Lee and Jim Wong-Chu. Vancouver: Douglas & McIntyre, 1991. 124-35.

Jones, D.G. *Butterfly on Rock: A Study of Themes and Images in Canadian Literature.* Toronto: U of Toronto P, 1970.

Keeshig-Tobias, Lenore. "Stop Stealing Native Stories." *Globe and Mail* 26 Jan. 1990: A7.

LaCapra, Dominick. *The Bounds of Race: Perspectives on Hegemony and Resistance.* Ed. LaCapra. Ithaca: Cornell UP, 1991.

Lecker, Robert. "The Canonization of Canadian Literature: An Inquiry into Value." *Critical Inquiry* 16 (1990): 656-71.

——. "Critical Response II: Response to Frank Davey." *Critical Inquiry* 16 (1990): 682-89.

——. "Privacy, Publicity, and the Discourse of Canadian Criticism." *Essays on Canadian Writing* 51-52 (1993-94): 32-82.

Loriggio, Francesco. "The Question of the Corpus: Ethnicity and Canadian Literature." Moss 53-68.

Maracle, Lee. "The 'Post-Colonial' Imagination." *Fuse* 16.1 (1992): 12-15.

McCarthy, Cameron, and Warren Crichlow, eds. *Race, Identity, and Representation in Education.* New York: Routledge, 1993.

McFarlane, Scott Toguri. "The Haunt of Race: Canada's Multiculturalism Act, the Politics of Incorporation, and Writing thru Race." *Fuse* 18.3 (1995): 18-31.

Miki, Roy. "Writing thru 'Race': A Midstream Report." *The Writers' Union of Canada Newsletter* 21.8 (1994): 1-2, 13-14.

Mookerjea, Sourayan. "Some Special Times and Remarkable Spaces of Reading and Writing thru 'Race.'" *West Coast Line* 28.3 No.15 (1994-95): 117-29.

Moss, John, ed. *Future Indicative: Literary Theory and Canadian Literature.* Ottawa: U of Ottawa P, 1987.

Mouffe, Chantal. *The Return of the Political.* London: Verso, 1993.

Murray, Heather. "Reading for Contradiction in the Literature of Colonial Space." Moss 71-84.

Omi, Michael, and Howard Winant. *Racial Formation in the United States: From the 1960s to the 1980s.* New York: Routledge, 1986.

O'Neill, Peter. "Feds Won't Fund Writer's Workshop That Bars Whites." *Vancouver Sun* 9 June 1994.

Outlaw, Lucius. "Toward a Critical Theory of 'Race.'" *Anatomy of Racism.* Ed. David Theo Goldberg. Minneapolis: U of Minnesota P, 1990. 58-82.

Philip, Marlene Nourbese. *Frontiers: Essays and Writings on Racism and Culture.* Toronto: Mercury, 1992.

Roy, Patricia. *A White Man's Province: British Columbia Politicians and Chinese and Japanese Immigrants, 1858-1914.* Vancouver: U of British Columbia P, 1989.

Said, Edward W. *Culture and Imperialism.* New York: Vintage, 1993.

Shikatani, Gerry. "Writing thru Race a Step Toward Shaping a Vision." *Globe and Mail* 9 July 1994.

Silvera, Makeda. *Her Head a Village.* Vancouver: Press Gang, 1994.

Spivak, Gayatri Chakravorty. "Bonding in Difference: Gayatri Spivak Speaks." *An Other Tongue: Nation and Ethnicity in the Linguistic Borderlands.* Ed. Alfred Arteaga. 273-85.

—. *Outside in the Teaching Machine.* New York: Routledge, 1993.

—. *The Post-Colonial Critic: Interviews, Strategies, Dialogues.* Ed. Sarah Harasym. New York: Routledge, 1990.

Todd, Loretta. "Notes on Appropriation." *Parallélogramme* 16.1 (1990): 24-33.

Trinh T. Minh-ha. *When the Moon Waxes Red: Representation, Gender and Cultural Politics.* New York: Routledge, 1991.

Valpy, Michael. "A Nasty Serving of Cultural Apartheid." *Globe and Mail* 8 Apr. 1994.

"Victim-Writers Meeting the Stuff of Great Art." Editorial. *Vancouver Sun* 9 Apr. 1994.

Williams, Patrick, and Laura Chrisman, eds. *Colonial Discourse and Post-Colonial Theory: A Reader.* New York: Columbia UP, 1994.

25

"To Essentialize or Not To Essentialize: Is This the Question?"*

Sherene Razack

How do we negotiate an intellectually charged space for experience in a way that is not totalizing and essentializing—a space that acknowledges the constructedness of and the differences within our lived experiences while at the same time attending to the inclining, rather than declining, significance of race, class, culture, and gender?

Ann duCille, "The Occult of True Black Womanhood: Critical Demeanor and Black Feminist Studies"

Essentialism, Trina Grillo writes,

> is the notion that there is a single woman's, or Black person's, or any other group's experience that can be described independently from other aspects of the person—that there is an "essence" to that experience. An essentialist outlook assumes that the experience of being a member of the group under discussion is a stable one, one with a clear meaning, a meaning constant through time, space, and different historical, social, political, and personal contexts. (19)

Throughout these essays [*Looking White People in the Eye*], I have explored the limitations of an essentialist understanding of women's experiences by focusing on *how* a woman's race, class, sexuality, and physical or mental condition combine in historically specific ways to produce her, and the responses to her, in classrooms and courtrooms. For example, in the preceding chapter, in exploring how a white, middle-class woman with a developmental disability was perceived in a sexual assault trial taking place in a North American city in the 1990s, it became clear that a series of assumptions about the meaning of her gender, race, class, and disability operated simultaneously to obscure the violence in her life. She was not considered to have suffered from the violence to the same extent as would another woman of her race and class who did not have a developmental disability. Disability did not simply combine

---

* Conclusion, *Looking White People in the Eye: Gender, Race, and Culture in Courtrooms and Classrooms* (Toronto: U of Toronto P, 1998), 157-70.

with gender, race, and class, as bricks piled one on top of the other. Rather, the social response to mental disability *in a woman*, a response that would surely have been different if the woman in question had been Black, or poor, or both, included assumptions about her capacity to know she was being violated, ideas about men's right to women's bodies, and in particular, white men's right to violate with impunity.

The point of anti-essentialism—the complex tracing of the social narratives that script how women experience their gender and how others respond to it—is to determine how to identify and interrupt those assumptions and practices that deny women their human rights. Put another way, the point of anti-essentialism is antisubordination. The tracing of these multiple systems of domination as they come together at one site for different kinds of women helps us to evaluate feminist law reform strategies. For example, rape shield laws restricting the introduction of prior sexual history may work well for many women but can work against women with developmental disabilities, because these laws make it difficult to introduce the social histories of violence that mark the women's lives. Without these social histories of violence—the way, for instance, that a woman with developmental disabilities often has a long history of being sexually abused and assaulted by men around her—it is difficult to make sense of her behaviour and the behaviour of others to her. We cannot begin to evaluate how laws work for women, or don't work, without understanding that gender comes into existence through race, class, sexuality, and physical or mental capacity.

In identifying the multiple narratives that script women's lives, we come to see that women are socially constituted in different and unequal relation to one another. It is not only that some women are considered to be worth more than other women, but that the status of one woman depends on the subordinate status of another woman in many complex ways. To take just one example, a middle-class woman gains her respectability, hence her value, from a number of sources, among them the social status she gains from not cleaning her own house, and not engaging in paid work to clean the houses of others. These sources of her status are not merely in representation, that is, in how she is likely to be perceived. They are also material. The houses of the middle class are cleaned by working-class women, and more often than not by Black women and women of colour. Here the material and ideological arrangements of patriarchy, class exploitation, and white supremacy combine in uneven ways to structure relations among women. While these oppressive systems do not come together in ways that ensure that socially advantaged women can successfully press their claims in court (there are still powerful narratives that work against them), belonging to the dominant race, class or culture does alter the forms of marginalization women encounter in the justice system.

Given the many ways in which women are implicated in one another's lives, anti-essentialism as a methodology takes us well beyond a politics of inclusion. That is, we can no longer devise political strategies that start with something we might call women's experience, on to which we would then graft the special strategies that would apply to women with disabilities, women of colour, or lesbians. To do so is to install a norm that privileges one group of women at the expense of others. A more fruitful approach is to ascertain how, at specific sites, patriarchy, white supremacy, and capitalism interlock to structure women differently and unequally. When we pursue these shifting hierarchical relations, we can begin to recognize how we are *implicated* in the subordination of other women. Our strategies for change then have less to do with being inclusive than they have do with being accountable.

What would a politics of accountability look like? Clearly it begins with anti-essentialism and the recognition that there is no one stable core we can call woman's experience. Equally important, it is a politics guided by a search for the ways in which we are complicitous in the subordination of others. A feminist politics of accountability cannot proceed on the assumption that as women we are uninvolved in the subordination of others. If we take as our point of departure that systems of domination interlock and sustain one another, we can begin to identify those moments when we are dominant and those when we are subordinate. Our implication in various systems of domination means that there are several ways in which we can perform ourselves as dominant at the same time that we understand ourselves to be engaging in liberatory politics. For example, Western middle-class women benefit from those economic and political processes that produce immigrant and refugee women from the South. When we engage in political action, for example efforts to use international law to protect women from male violence, we cannot understand the context in which this violence takes place without examining how our own positions of middle-class respectability help to sustain and produce such violence. In the search for appropriate strategies, we will need to examine those systems which benefit us, as well as those which subordinate us. As Western women we perform ourselves as dominant when we engage in a politics of saving other women. Instead of seeking to save women we consider less fortunate than ourselves, we might begin to organize against the racism that structures migration and flight, and that continues to structure the lives of women fleeing to the North.

Obviously, such political projects cannot get underway if we do not *recognize* our own habits of dominance and our complicity in systems of domination. A goal of this book [*Looking White People in the Eye*] has been to develop our capacity to engage in this kind of re-visioning through a critical appraisal of the social construction of gender, race and class. The anti-essentialism that is the thrust of much of what I have argued enjoyed considerable popularity in many academic circles over the past five years. Of late, however, it has become increasingly clear that the honeymoon is over and the critics of anti-essentialism, who are by no means a unified group, have begun to assert themselves. In this last chapter, I want to explore some of the criticisms directed at anti-essentialist approaches and reiterate my conclusion that feminist politics must pursue the charting of hierarchical relations among women if we are to change the world.

Criticisms of anti-essentialist approaches have come from feminists and others. Some concerns have taken the form of a general condemnation of anti-essentialists who rely on postmodernism. There is also a more specific charge from within feminism that an anti-essentialist approach is politically ineffective and slides too easily into a disparagement of white women. As these criticisms suggest, the salient question is, "To essentialize or not to essentialize?" I want to suggest here that this question must be asked alongside of another: How does essentialism or anti-essentialism contribute to anti-subordination?

Anti-essentialists who rely on postmodernism have been criticized for the apparent contradiction between seeing identity as socially constructed in multiple ways and maintaining, nonetheless, that there are identifiably oppressed groups; that there is, as Fanon wrote, "a fact of Blackness" (220). Keenan Malik, for instance, articulates the gist of this concern when he argues that a postmodern understanding of difference can lead to the position that all identities have equal validity. One could not, therefore, make an objective assessment that specific groups of people are oppressed by others. Like many others who fear that anti-essentialism leaves us hopelessly stuck in a relativist position, Malik suggests that we have to return to "real social and economic mechanisms." In his words, we "require a standard of significance to distinguish between real or significant facts and irrelevant ones" although such a standard has to be historically specific (13). This standard must enable us to name inequality, for example, as a by-product of capitalism, and enable us to chart the specific groups that are oppressed under capitalism.

In this book, while I have relied on postmodern theories for understanding the construction of subjectivity, I tried to keep a modernist eye on domination. Who is dominating whom is not a question I reply to with the answer that we are all constituted as simultaneously dominant and subordinate. While we *are* all simultaneously dominant and subordinate, and have varying degrees of privilege and penalty, this insight is not the most relevant when we are seeking to end specific hierarchies at specific sites. For example, when we confront the whiteness of the academy and note that an overwhelming majority of professors are white, we cannot change this situation by responding that white professors also belong to subordinate groups— some are women, some are disabled, some are lesbians. Such a response amounts to a statement that race does not matter, an outright denial of the impact of white supremacy on the lives of people of colour.

Thus, my own pursuit of anti-essentialism has often required the kind of historically specific standard to which Malik refers, even though I do not understand postmodernism to be as dangerously relativist as he does. Throughout this work, I have talked about dominant and subordinate groups as though they exist, and I have named patriarchy, white supremacy and capitalism as three systems that interlock to structure women, differently, in subordinate positions. I have therefore operated under the assumption that to have white skin is to have privilege, for example, but noted repeatedly that the significance of this privilege could only be ascertained when we considered how privileges combine with penalties in specific situations to produce hierarchies of women. The work I have presented here is mainly a tracing of the production of these hierarchies, utilizing postmodern tools about the constitution of subjectivity, in order to determine how we might disrupt these systems of subordination. [. . .]

The way we talk currently about differences is most assuredly socially produced and specific to our historical moment, but that moment continues to be one in which white supremacy is alive and well and deeply influencing how subordinate groups talk about their difference and the way in which they are heard. We still cannot speak out loud about the complexities of racial identities without risking that the oppressive contours of racism will be denied. How do we distinguish a denial of racism from the argument that we cannot speak of social construction and facts of oppression in the same breath?

Critics of what are variously called "the problem of difference," identity politics, ethnic particularism, or race essentialism have argued that we need to return to a concept of the universal, although most of those making this argument acknowledge that the old image of the Enlightenment's universal man, rational, and autonomous, has to be refashioned.[1] For Naomi Shor, a well-known white academic, the problem of difference today is that, in the move away from universalism, we have turned to a particularism that is dangerous, narrow, and exclusive. Her complaint, like most of this kind, focuses on racial differences. Simply put, the complaint is that in our bid to move beyond universalism and gender essentialism (two slightly different ideas for some),[2] we have come to a dreadful and dangerous place of race essentialism and regressive ethnic enclaves. In a sobering paragraph, in which the name Auschwitz invokes the genocide of European Jewry, Shor writes:

> If Auschwitz dealt the Enlightenment ideal of universalism—a notion rejected by fascism—a death blow, what may pass for the repetition of Auschwitz, the ongoing ethnic cleansing in Bosnia Herzegovina, has if not revived universalism, then called into question the celebration of particularisms, at least in their regressive ethnic form. (28)

Significantly, it is only in a footnote attached to the end of this quote, that Shor completes the progression of signs that begins with Auschwitz (where

Nazis clearly did not believe in a universal humanity), moves to Bosnia, and ends, cryptically, with a footnote that references a point made by Cornel West, a Black scholar who writes that the new cultural politics of difference is about trashing the monolithic and the homogeneous in the name of diversity and multiplicity. Since West warns of ethnic chauvinism at the same time as he decries a faceless universalism (34), and is clearly in favour of the new cultural politics of difference, it is unclear whether Shor means to indicate that he endorses her position. Certainly, many Black scholars share her concerns about the dangers of particularism, but they also note, usually in the same sentence, the persistence of racism and the need to counter its destructive effects.[3] Patricia Hill Collins, responding to a reviewer's criticism that her book *Black Feminist Thought* is built on the notion of a unitary or essential Black subject, noted that she deliberately decided not to focus on diversity among Black women. To do so, she countered, would have made them disappear as subjects, a tendency that is all too prevalent in a racist society (qtd. Balos and Fellows 65).

It can be argued that when white feminists essentialized gender, they were making a similarly strategic move. Strategic essentialism, however, is less of a defence at sites where it is employed by dominant groups in order to exclude subordinate groups, for example, when white women employ essentialism in order to privilege their own experience of gender. Collins's essentializing also could not be justified if it were to be applied at a site where power and access are granted to Black subjects who most closely fit the standard she sets for Blackness. For example, she could not rely on a unitary Black subject in an all-Black organization where the interests of Black lesbians were being disregarded.

Recognizing differences and multiplicities cannot be automatically conflated with a terrible celebration of particularisms or a self-serving essentialism. I doubt that Shor would say that all articulations of difference lead to Bosnia, but the risk is clearly present and it is a risk that makes most of our hearts skip a beat. If paying attention to race can take us to Auschwitz and Bosnia, let us stamp out the evil before it is full-grown. I can read such passages no other way in spite of the author's numerous distractions, philosophical detours, and earnest declarations of being really and truly in favour of diversity. This is a different kind of critique than the one made by women of colour to white women that a homogeneous description of women's oppression re-centres white women and leaves racism unexamined. Shor's critique speaks to something more terrible than a maintenance of the status quo. It is addressed to us "ethnics" who would speak of our differences in so essentialist a fashion, or perhaps, who would speak of our differences at all. In this way, as Ann duCille has noted of the response to Black women scholars, legitimate complaints about oppression and attempts to resist are dismissed as anti-intellectual identity politics (606). That this is the case in as refined a criticism as

Shor's is evident in her vague references to the misery caused by identity politics (29), to "all we have lost" as a result of it (41) (begging the question, Who has lost what?), and to the good old days of 1970s feminism.

Along with bell hooks, I am suspicious of those who warn of the dangers of identity politics, race essentialism, or ethnic particularism without paying attention to the specific relations of domination and subordination in any one context, and without contextualizing the responses subordinate groups make to domination, thus distinguishing acts of resistance from acts of domination (hooks 83). As hooks suggests in her assessment of Diana Fuss's exploration of the misuses of essentialism by minority students in the classroom, critiques of identity politics may be "the new, chic way to silence students from marginal groups" (83).

In a white-dominated classroom or courtroom, those who talk about their differences are likely to be heard as essentialist, while those who listen to the talk about differences get to sit in judgment. In such a scenario, those who judge have a better chance of appearing calm, confident, all knowing, and in control, while the natives, pleading their case, can only be described as restless.[4] Without taking into account the context of persistent and destructive racism, it is possible to equate Black women's desire to set up a counter-canon of Black women's writings with the universalizing of Enlightenment thinkers who did not think Black people could have access to their notion of the universal. Similarly, only in failing to keep the realities of white supremacy front and centre could one see, as Christina Crosby does, in Audre Lorde's "fact of difference," a similarity to the willingness of Charlotte Bronte's white heroines so eager to make themselves into universal subjects.[5]

We can and we must transcend these positions and we must do so by talking about how we are implicated in the "particularisms," which I will put in quotation marks. I am not suggesting that articulations of difference by subordinate groups remain beyond critique, but that those making this critique closely examine their own subject positions. Who is describing and assessing the realities of whom, how do we hear these descriptions and what relations do they secure? Shor declares that her goal is a revised universal that "would include all those who wish to be included, and that would above all afford them the opportunity to speak universal while not relinquishing their difference(s)" (41). This goal is unreachable because our differences are precisely what cannot be acknowledged without confronting the fact of domination. What has prevailed in the views I have so far been discussing is that dominant groups have been arguing from a point of subordination, a position of innocence and non-implication in systems of oppression. It is white women who are really disparaged, these scholars argue; and it is they who are the outsiders in the academy today.

As I noted in my introduction, the point of theorizing differences among women is not for the sake of inclusion but for the sake of antisubordination.

There is little chance of disturbing relations of domination unless we consider how these structure our subject positions. What most distinguishes the critics discussed in this chapter is their inattention to these relations, an inattention that has led to a denial of the continuing effects of white supremacy (for example, the erroneous view that women of colour now have most of the jobs in the academy and get all the grants), claims of mutuality between vastly different contexts (Auschwitz, Bosnia, and attempts to establish a counter-canon of Black women's writings), and an arrogance of subject position that does not ask about the sources of the yearning for the good old days of lost sisterhood and the rush to critique how women of colour essentialize differences but not how white women do. What all of these features secure is innocence, a determined non-involvement in the social relations being analyzed.

Before we can determine how far we can go, either in essentializing or not essentializing, we need to examine how we explain to ourselves the social hierarchies that surround us. We need to ask: Where am I in this picture? Am I positioning myself as the saviour of less fortunate peoples? as the progressive one? as more subordinated? as innocent? These are moves of superiority and we need to reach beyond them. I return here to my notion of a politics of accountability as opposed to a politics of inclusion. Accountability begins with tracing relations of privilege and penalty. It cannot proceed unless we examine our complicity. Only then can we ask questions about how we are understanding differences and for what purpose.

Notes

1. Shor cites several prominent thinkers who argue this way, including several French feminists, Cornel West, Seyla Benhabib, Nancy Miller, and others. Although I cannot do so here in depth, I argue that there is a qualitative difference in the way many scholars of colour call for a revised universalism and the way some white feminists interpret this goal. The latter often indirectly mean a universal and unraced woman, as the writings of French feminists and of Shor herself indicate, when paying attention to race is considered essentialism or ethnic chauvinism.

2. Shor makes the distinction between universalism and essentialism an important point in her article, giving the example of Simone de Beauvoir, who believed in a universal human nature but knew that men had defined this in such a way that women had no access to it. For Shor, de Beauvoir knew that all women did not share a common feminine nature and she was extremely hostile to the idea of an eternal feminine. She was not therefore a gender essentialist (see "French Feminism" 24). As much as this distinction is valid in de Beauvoir, Shor describes "certain communities of feminist theorists," namely those who wanted to build a counter-canon of Black women's writing as making universalizing

moves (25). She also notes that the reason for returning to universalism is that in giving it up, feminists of the 1970s gave up commonality and political clout. Here, it seems to me that the distinction between universalism and essentialism has collapsed in her work.

3. See Stuart Hall, "New Ethnicities" 252; Gilroy, *The Black Atlantic* 32; West, "The New Cultural Politics" 29; Grillo, "Anti-Essentialism" 24.

4. No better explication of whose voices are heard as native exists than Trinh T. Minh-ha's *Woman, Native, Other: Writing Postcoloniality and Feminism* (Bloomington: Indiana UP, 1989).

5. Crosby begins and ends her article with the example of Lucy Snowe, Bronte's heroine in *Villette*, who gains access to the male universal by remaking her self.

WORKS CITED

Balos, Beverley, and Mary Louise Fellows. *Law and Violence Against Women: Cases and Materials on Systems of Oppression.* Durham: Carolina Academic Press, 1994.

Crosby, Christina. "Dealing with Differences." *Feminists Theorize the Political.* Ed. Judith Butler and Joan Scott. New York: Routledge, 1992. 130-43.

duCille, Ann. "The Occult of True Black Womanhood: Critical Demeanor and Black Feminist Studies." *Signs: Journal of Women in Culture and Society* 19.3 (1994): 591-628.

Fanon, Frantz. "The Fact of Blackness." *"Race," Culture and Difference.* Ed. James Donald and Ali Rattansi. London: Open University Press, 1992. 220-40.

Gilroy, Paul. *The Black Atlantic.* Cambridge: Harvard UP, 1993.

Grillo, Trina. "Anti-Essentialism and Intersectionality: Tools to Dismantle the Master's House." *Berkeley Women's Law Journal* 10.1 (1995): 16-30.

Hall, Stuart. "The New Ethnicities." *"Race," Culture and Difference.* Ed. James Donald and Ali Rattansi. London: Open University Press, 1992. 252-59.

hooks, bell. *Teaching to Transgress.* New York: Routledge, 1994.

Lorde, Audre. *Sister Outsider.* New York: Crossing, 1984.

Malik, Keenan. "Universalism and Difference? Race and the Postmodernists." *Race and Class* 37.3 (1996): 1-18.

Shor, Naomi. "French Feminism Is a Universalism." *Differences* 7.1 (1995): 15-42.

West, Cornel. "The New Cultural Politics of Difference." *Out There: Marginalization and Contemporary Culture.* Ed. Russell Ferguson, Martha Gever, Trinh Minh-ha, and Cornel West. New York and Boston: New Museum of Contemporary Art and MIT Press, 1990. 19-36.

PART VIII
⚌ Postcolonial Pedagogies ⚌

26

"TRANSVESTIC SITES:
POSTCOLONIALISM, PEDAGOGY, AND POLITICS" *

Richard Cavell

"Beyond" signifies spatial distance, marks progress, promises the future; but our intimations of exceeding the barrier or boundary—the very act of going beyond—are unknowable, unrepresentable, without a return to the "present" which, in the process of repetition, becomes disjunct and displaced. The imaginary of spatial distance—to live somehow beyond the border of our times—throws into relief the temporal, social differences that interrupt our collusive sense of cultural contemporaneity. The present can no longer be simply envisaged as a break or a bonding with the past and the future, no longer a synchronic presence: our proximate self-presence, our public image, comes to be revealed for its discontinuities, its inequalities, its minorities.

Homi Bhabha, The Location of Culture

1.

In the spring of 1993, I taught a graduate seminar at the University of British Columbia called "Cultural Transvestism and Postcolonial Discourse." By the phrase "cultural transvestism" I sought to indicate the borderline tendencies of postcolonialism—its hybridity—as well as to provide a base from which to argue the intersections and complications of gender, race, class, and colonialism. My agenda in the seminar was to facilitate the demonstration of "postcolonialism" as a theoretical position that could bring together texts normally not considered in conjunction with one another in the academy and, in so doing, to provide a forum for critiquing such texts, the academic constraints that keep them separate, and "postcolonialism" itself (which, I felt, was rapidly becoming commodified as a core set of specific texts). While crossdressing was the focus of the seminar, I hoped to examine other forms of crossing as well. In addition to canonical postcolonial texts such as Coetzee's *Foe*, Naipaul's *The Mimic Men*, Findley's *Not Wanted on the Voyage*, Rushdie's *Shame*, and Hulme's *The Bone People*, I also introduced texts

---

* *Dangerous Territories: Struggles for Difference and Equality in Education*, ed. Leslie G. Roman and Linda Eyre (New York: Routledge, 1997), 99-112.

designed to trouble essentialized readings of postcolonialism *as canonized*—texts such as Aquin's *Blackout*, Burroughs's *Tarzan of the Apes*, Cliff's *No Telephone to Heaven*, Furphy's *Such is Life*, Grenville's *Joan Makes History*, Hwang's *M. Butterfly*, Lawrence's *Seven Pillars of Wisdom*, Moodie's *Roughing It in the Bush*, Stowe's *Uncle Tom's Cabin*, and Kureishi's "With Your Tongue Down My Throat." The seminar was designed interactively, partly to emphasize that its production was a collective responsibility and partly to displace the notion that "postcolonialism" was a specific "content." I presented as many texts to the students as I could think of, they added yet others, then we decided collectively which texts would be studied and in what order. (Much of this was done informally, during the term preceding the seminar.) The results of this process were instructive: Coetzee got in, but Findley did not; Hulme but not Furphy; Kureishi but not Naipaul; Cliff but not Stowe; and Hwang but not T.E. Lawrence. It appeared that a certain disciplinary imperative was operating here, whereby issues of race were not to be complicated by issues of class, and according to which the category of the "postcolonial" was to be associated with texts that had been produced "outside" of Europe (with Kureishi being an interesting exception) in the second half of the twentieth century. This "historical bias" might not seem at all odd, given that postcolonialism is supposed to have arisen after the end of the great European empires. But it was precisely this historical linearity I wanted to question, both because it did not take neocolonialism into account and because it is insensitive to the complexities of resistance—a resistance that often exists coterminously with colonization itself.

After we had decided on a rough order of readings (first "theory," then "texts"—another problematical binary indicative of the instrumentalization, and thus marginalization, of theory), we remained dissatisfied with the exclusion of so many texts as well as with the implied teleology of the reading list. So we created two additional lists ("Supplements" and "Further Readings") that allowed us to juxtapose texts according to what might be called a *spatial* historicism (e.g., Butler/Kureishi/Wittig; Benetton Ads/hooks/Fanon), and which had the additional value of undermining the utilitarian theory/fiction binary and the linear relationship attendant upon it (first you do theory, then you apply it). The "lack" of direction within this spatialized syllabus enabled me to dislocate myself further as instructor.

The seminar ended up being "large" (around 25 participants in a department in which 10 to 12 is the norm), with auditors, drop-ins, and guest lecturers; we held it not in the assigned seminar room but on the top floor of the Graduate Student Centre. Weekly journals replaced individual seminar presentations (what I refer to as the "Queen-for-a-Day" phenomenon), and I made it clear from the outset that I saw my role as facilitator rather than as Source-Of-Knowledge. Grades were based on journals and a project, which did not have to be text-based. (One student produced a photographically-based work, thereby raising important issues of evaluation, through which the student read *my* role in the academy.) Upon completion of all work for the seminar, I met with each student individually in order to discuss the bases on which I had arrived at his or her grade. Given my insistence on the indeterminacy of the seminar as *site of production*, most of these meetings took place off campus.

The student evaluations were instructive. The use of journals was favored, as were the consultative processes at the beginning and end of the seminar (though subsequently a few students expressed reservations about meeting off campus and about my discussing the grading process with them). The use of discussion groups was seen as a viable response to the size of the seminar, though it was also seen as leading, at times, to a lack of focus. One student was challenged "intellectually and politically." Another felt the course was "too tightly scheduled" and had a "too extensive reading list." Instructors sometimes see these apparent contradictions as cancelling each other out (and I have certainly reacted in this way), thereby indirectly reaffirming their authority; however, these contradictions can also be read as asserting that the seminar occupies not a unified space but a number of transvestic sites that are *produced* by and through the agendas of those who participate in it, including the instructor. In these terms, the subject of the seminar (if there could be said to be only one) could be seen to coincide with the performance of its pedagogy.

2.

By their very location in the academy, fields such as women's studies are grounded in definitions of difference, difference that attempts to resist incorporation and appropriation by providing space for historically silenced peoples to construct knowledge.

Chandra Talpade Mohanty, "On Race and Voice"

This coincidence of the seminar's subject with the way in which it was taught has both disciplinary and pedagogical implications. As a teacher of what has come to be known as "postcolonial literature," I have often found myself confronted with having to decide whether the term "postcolonial" refers to a coherent body of texts or to a mode of reading texts. The distinction has farreaching implications. If "postcolonial" refers to a body of texts, this, on the one hand, allows for the valorization of a number of texts (all of which have in common that they were produced "after" colonialism) that are now excluded from the canon, while, on the other hand, such a list runs the risk of becoming canonical in its own way. If "postcolonial" refers to a way of reading, however, it appears to lose its specificity and perhaps even its historicity, becoming merely another formalism. Both of these positions embody historical attitudes, the one reified, the other process-oriented. What I sought to argue (largely through my style of pedagogy) was a third position—a position involving theorizing non-linear modes of history and a processual notion of location. My argument was that the act of reading "postcolonially" is double, in that it responds both to the historical context of the work and to the moment of localized, materialized reading, such that through our readings we locate *ourselves* in a series of discontinuous histories. For the seminar, that process of reading was inevitably defined by—and therefore involved a critique of—the academy and our places in it.

The crucial point to be noted here is that location is a significant aspect of pedagogical practice, "explicitly articulating epistemological and ontological concerns," as Elspeth Probyn has suggested (184). Yet, as Probyn goes on to argue, "location" has become, through its constant invocation, an increasingly abstract term, less a counter discourse to universalism than another version of it. This is not, however, to suggest that notions of the local should be abandoned; rather (Probyn continues), the local should be redefined as "a fragmented set of possibilities that can be articulated into a momentary politics of time and place" (187). The point to be underlined in this formulation is that space/place/location are *produced* and, therefore, inflected by their historical moment and social context. How we locate ourselves within practices of knowledge, then, is related to how we produce space (see also Cavell, "Theorizing Canadian Space").

The implications for pedagogy are significant. If what is being taught is a particular attitude towards a text, a particular way of reading, then content gives way to theory, to the text re-presented as process. Reading as pedagogy becomes a locating in (spatial) history as opposed to the deciphering of a timeless meaning. This position has the advantage of encouraging postcolonial readings of ur-canonical texts as well as of not restricting the postcolonial to the written text—a restriction that severely diminishes its force. As Bogumil Jewsiewicki and V.Y. Mudimbe write in a recent issue of *Transition*, "new forms of representation—such as rap, music videos, etc., whose structures are more polyphonic than linear, and that spatialize more than they historicize the experiences of the world—are generally left totally out of the [postcolonial] debate" (47). Their comments also signal the danger that the "postcolonial," if allowed to define a specific set of texts, could become dehistoricized and thereby inhibited from critiquing contemporary, technology-based society, what Arjun Appadurai has called the "mediascape" of "fundamental disjunctures between economy, culture and politics" (6).

Perhaps the most limiting aspect of seeing "postcolonial" as designating a certain sort of text is the elision of the question of the production of textuality, thus making of "postcolonialism" merely a reified historical category, like "Renaissance." This tendency is clearly evident in the recent special issue of *PMLA* (1995) on postcolonialism, in which over half the articles are interpretations of texts. The implication is that these texts are stable and that it is possible to arrive at the hard core of their meaning through a series of hermeneutic procedures. One of the lessons of postcoloniality, however, is that texts are not simply "there" to be read; rather, they are actively produced "here" according to locational determinants. Thus, texts are constantly shifting sites of production and reception, as Jean Rhys demonstrates so tellingly in *Wide Sargasso Sea*'s rewriting of *Jane Eyre*. Rather than being commodified as the latest model of "litcrit," postcolonialism can become politically transformative at the moment it begins to juxtapose the imperial production of texts with the decolonizing process of critically re-reading them. What this double reading recognizes is that the history of the production of knowledge is inevitably associated with the "other" (most clearly in the case of anthropology). Postcolonialism seeks to dislocate this nexus, turning the light of inquiry back onto the *production* of otherness. And, if "postcolonialism" is a product of the academy (which it is), then it is also a site of resistance to the academy precisely through its ability to foreground the moment of the production of knowledge and, thereby, to highlight the inflectedness of knowing. A comment Juliet Mitchell makes in *Psychoanalysis and Feminism* has, thus, a degree of paradigmatic veracity: "I am interested not in what Freud did, but in what we can get from him, a political rather than an academic exploration" (xx). In the view that I have been developing here, this would constitute a postcolonial reading of Freud, demonstrating, in the process, sites of confluence among histories of colonization, psychoanalysis, and gendering (as emblematically foregrounded in the African icons of Freud's consulting room).

If "postcolonial" is conceived of not as a content but as a way of reading, a pedagogy whose anti-colonialism is focused upon cultural objects and one of whose major and most productive sites is the university, then content-oriented curricula, which are the major sites of canon production (including postcolonial canons), would be resisted. As Rajeswari Mohan states:

> The important question in these pedagogic deliberations is not what texts to teach but how to teach them, and in the nineties this may be the question that frames the multicultural enterprise in general. Already, multiculturalism exerts pressure on existing disciplinary configurations and their various legitimating narratives as newly authorized knowledges challenge the content as well as the methodologies of disciplinary enquiry. (385)

To read texts in juxtaposition both to other texts and other histories (including those defining the moment of reading) is to work towards that "new and overwhelming space which annihilates time and imperial purpose," of which Ashcroft, Griffiths, and Tiffin (34) speak in *The Empire Writes Back*. Implicit in such readings is the realization that the history of empires is double—that it is made up both of colonization and of resistance, and that the relationship between the two is one not of succession but of co-determination. Such readings, as Jewsiewicki and Mudimbe remark, are "probably the only way to subvert the recurring metaphor of paternal authority so central to the postcolonial world" (49). They go on to note that when the central activity of postcolonialist critiques becomes not the content of the texts but their juxtaposition (which acknowledges the historical moment of reading) postcolonial cultures will be opened to a post-Freudian analysis (50).

3.

Let us attempt to read the possibility of our unwilling or unwitting perpetration of a "new orientalism" as the inscription of an "overall strategy." . . . If we keep the possibility of such inscriptions in mind, we might read differently the specific examples of the working of "local forces," close to home.

Gayatri Spivak, *Outside in the Teaching Machine*

A number of the pedagogical implications of the "cultural transvestism" seminar are addressed in *Pedagogy: The Question of Impersonation*, the first being that teaching is itself a form of transvestism, whether it express itself as the "im-personation" about which Jane Gallop writes in her introduction (1) or the "racial drag" of which Indira Karamcheti speaks (143). Clearly, these writers mean to signal not only the theatrical element that has long been acknowledged as a component of teaching but also, as the title of the collection indicates, the displacement of the person/al and the attendant paradox that the "personal in pedagogy acts not unlike the personal on talk shows, a performance that nonetheless functions as real" (Gallop 17). The implication of this assertion is that the ungrounded subject can have political agency in a way not allowed for by a "generic ethnicity" (see Simon 93). Thus, Gregory Jay writes: "To pose cultural identity in the form of a question . . . already introduces an element of agency, freedom, or voluntarism that strict essentialists or determinists reject" (120).

As Jay suggests, the question of agency provides a crucial line of demarcation between essentialist and performative notions of identity. This question also identifies one of the major "discontents" of postcolonialism, which is that it has (or appears to have) no agency outside the academy, that it is just another disciplinary practice. This discontent, however, has its source in an "inside/outside" binary that acts to contain and reify the possibilities of agency. It is useful to examine, from this position, the controversies surrounding "political correctness," which can be seen as a construction designed to contain a discourse—let us call it "postcolonial theory"—which is posited as spreading from "inside" the academy into the "real" world "outside," while at the same time "those proposing reform are depicted as outsiders whose agenda will only subvert an essentially good system" (Scott 113). Witness the volume *Debating P.C.: The Controversy over Political Correctness on College Campuses* (Berman), the title of which belies itself: its essays by no means all emerge from the "campus," thereby demonstrating that the debate around political correctness (PC) refuses to stay "inside" the academy and that the book (like the notion of PC) is itself an act of containment. As Fredric Jameson remarks in an essay on cultural studies, "At a time . . . when the Right has begun to develop its own cultural politics, focused on the reconquest of the academic institutions, and particularly of the foundations and the universities themselves, it does not seem wise to go on thinking of academic politics, and the politics of intellectuals, as a particularly 'academic' matter" (17). And Gauri Viswanathan has shown that this connection between colony and college need not be thought of as "merely" ideological; as she has recently demonstrated, Yale University "has deep, abiding roots in the mercantile activities and imperial politics of England's East India House" (1). The occlusion of these linkages is directly related to the devaluation of the role of the public intellectual in the United States and (perhaps even more so) in Canada. To write regularly in the popular press is quite common among my colleagues in Europe, but to do so in Canada is to risk not being considered a serious academic, so rigidly are town and gown constructed as separate places.

The university, however, occupies a transvestic site; it is both "inside" and "outside" its sociocultural emplacement, both "public" and "private." And what emerges from *After Political Correctness* (Newfield and Strickland) is an awareness that the political positions of Left and Right (between which the PC debate has oscillated) have themselves become displaced. While "the Left . . . reads [the 1970s] as a narrative of its own decline" (13), the Right continues to splinter (cf. Diamond 26-27). No longer are Right and Left, Liberal and Conservative, the verities they were (in the Canadian context) for George Parkin Grant when he was writing *Technology and Empire* and *Lament for a Nation.* The homogenous constituencies that allowed Grant to produce such works no longer exist (if, in fact, they ever did). Today the categories of Left and Right, Liberal and Conservative, appear to have rhetorical value precisely as ways of *eliding* differences of race, class, gender, and orientation. And if master narratives of the political are no longer possible, the same can be said for the *grands récits* of culture.

This becomes startlingly clear when one examines a non-mainstream political/cultural movement such as Gay Rights, as does Andrew Sullivan in *Virtually Normal: An Argument about Homosexuality.* While the topic of the book might immediately position its author as left of center, he is in fact the neoconservative editor of *The New Republic.* Yet Sullivan rejects positions put forward on homosexuality by both "The Conservatives" *and* "The Liberals" as well as by "The Prohibitionists" and "The Liberationists," stating that "there are as many politics of homosexuality as there are words for it" (19). "Moreover," he continues, "these terms are not mutually exclusive" (20); in fact, "by 'conservative' I mean rather a variety of liberal" (95). Sullivan's own "Politics of Homosexuality" (ch. 5) seeks to "reconcile the best arguments of liberals and conservatives, and find a way to marry the two" (169-70; the metaphor is significant). He proposes to do this by affirming "a simple and limited principle: that all *public* (as opposed to private) discrimination against homosexuals be ended and that every right and responsibility that heterosexuals enjoy as public citizens be extended to those who grow up and find themselves emotionally different" (171). As in the debate over political correctness, the public/private binary asserts itself here as a strategy of containment, given that, as Foucault argues in *The History of Sexuality*, it is the State which constructs the category of homosexual. In fact, the struggle for Gay Rights has shown the extent to which the State operates what Deniz Kandiyoti calls a "gender agenda" (patria as patriarchy) through which "a sphere marked out as 'private' at one stage of nation-building may reappear with the full trappings of the 'public' at another, their boundaries being fluid and subject to redefinition" (431). Ironically, what undoes Sullivan's argument is his unwillingness to disengage from traditional categories of political thought, even though he spends much of his book pointing out their inadequacies with regard to the issue of homosexuality. Thus the most concrete political proposal he can make at the conclusion of his study is that homosexuals have "equal access to the military and marriage" (173).

If Sullivan is correct in stating that "Western society is in the middle of a tense and often fevered attempt to find its own way on the matter [of homosexuality]" (18), then this suggests that political issues are being engendered in terms traditional politics cannot adequately address. Paul Gilroy has suggested that this is because the

old industrial order has begun to decompose and social and political collectivities based away from the workplace have become as vocal, militant and politically significant as the residues of the workers' movement. . . . These new movements are part of a new phase of class conflict so far removed from the class struggles of the industrial era that the vocabulary of class analysis created during that period must itself be dispensed with, or at least ruthlessly modernized. (225)

Gilroy goes on to note that these changes have resulted in a renewed emphasis on the body, and this observation may be linked to Kandiyoti's contention that to question gender is to question one of the foundational bases of political expression.

All of this renders highly problematical Susan Faludi's notion of "backlash," which, increasingly, has come to define the reactionary rhetoric of the 1990s. Yet, when Left and Right have become destabilized into New Left and New Right, when "Conservative" is sometimes defined as "Liberal," of what value are Faludi's essentialist assumptions? And who are the "American Women" referred to in her subtitle (*The Undeclared War Against American Women*), given that "lesbian" is not in her index but "housewives" is? These questions are rhetorical, of course, but it is precisely in political rhetoric as disseminated through the media that Faludi seeks to locate the backlash phenomenon:

> The press first introduced the backlash to a national audience—and made it palatable. Journalism replaced the "pro-family" diatribes of fundamentalist preachers with sympathetic and even progressive-sounding rhetoric. . . . The press didn't set out with this, or any other, intention; like any large institution, its movements aren't premeditated or programmatic, just grossly susceptible to the prevailing political currents. Even so, the press, carried by tides it rarely fathomed, acted as a force that swept the general public, powerfully shaping the way people would think and talk about the feminist legacy and the ailments it supposedly inflicted on women. (77)

While the terms of this argument are naive, Faludi nevertheless identifies the importance of the media in the production of "backlash" rhetoric. The effect of this "mediatization" is to "discursify" political issues, thereby dislocating them from any presumed origin and placing them within discourse itself. In this way, political issues can no longer claim authoritative sites of discourse, as in "who speaks for the Left" (or "for the Right"), but must engage in strategies of (re-) appropriation. As Paul Gilroy writes, these strategies seek "the transformation of new modes of subordination located outside the immediate processes of production and consequently require the reappropriation of space, time, and of relationships between individuals in their day to day lives" (225).

Appadurai places this struggle in the larger context of "the new global cultural economy [which] has to be seen as a complex, overlapping, disjunctive order, which cannot any longer be understood in terms of existing center-periphery models (even those which might account for multiple centers and peripheries)" (6). "Economy," Appadurai notes (as does Gilroy), can no longer be defined solely in terms of capital; rather, it is comprised of ethnoscapes, mediascapes, technoscapes, finanscapes, and ideoscapes—where "-scape" points to "fluid, irregular shapes" (6-7).

> These terms with the common suffix -scape also indicate that these are
> not objectively given relations which look the same from every angle of
> vision, but rather that they are deeply perspectival constructs, inflected
> by the historical, linguistic and political situatedness of different sorts of
> actors: nation-states, multinationals, diasporic communities, as well as
> sub-national groupings and movements (whether religious, political or
> economic), and even intimate face-to-face groups, such as villages,
> neighborhoods and families. (7)

And if this decentering suggests that "backlash" cannot be seen as a univocal phenomenon of a unified "Right," it also suggests that a transformative politics of the "Left" can no longer presume to speak for all women, all gays, all persons of color, and so on.

The notion of "category crisis," which Marjorie Garber develops in *Vested Interests: Cross-Dressing and Cultural Anxiety,* is useful here. Arguing that category crisis is "not the exception but the ground of culture itself" (16), Garber defines the term as "a borderline that becomes permeable, that permits of border crossings from one (apparently distinct) category to another." Thus, "a transvestite figure, or a transvestite mode, will always function as a sign of overdetermination—a mechanism of displacement from one blurred boundary to another" (16) as well as "*a space of possibility structuring and confounding culture*" (17; emphasis in original). It is this power of displacement that makes notions of the transvestic especially productive in theorizing race, class, gender, and sexual orientation, for it complicates such categories through a constant shifting of figure and ground (where race, for example, is now figure to the ground of gender, now ground to the figure of class, and so on).

Yet what I am arguing here might, once again, appear to beg the question of agency: if one of the major signs of postmodernity, of the simulacral, is the "discursification" of the political, does this not appear to deprive the political of any forum other than the discursive? One way this question can be addressed is by placing it in the context of what Peter Dickinson (and others) have called the discursive representation of Acquired Immune Deficiency Syndrome (AIDS). Dickinson notes that AIDS has occasioned "a whole new industry of discursive inquiry" (219) that tends to make abstract the very real suffering of individuals. Yet it would be a mistake, he continues, to devalorize this discursive aspect of AIDS, for, "as Foucault reminds us, discourse is itself an *event,* an event, moreover, that involves not only the text or utterance but also their position within a given social space" (221). To this formulation of discursification I would add the concept of linguistic performativity (which underlies much of Judith Butler's theorizing of gender)—quite simply, the concept that words *do* things, that they are both abstract *and* located. As Butler writes in *Bodies That Matter,* "if the power of discourse to produce that which it names is linked with the question of performativity, then the performative is one domain in which power acts *as* discourse" (225). This *materiality* of signification returns us to the question of academic agency so often invoked by postcolonial critique and serves to remind us of the interestedness of language; as Fanon puts it at the beginning of *Black Skin, White Masks,* "I ascribe a basic importance to the phenomenon of language" (17). Homi Bhabha develops this notion in *The Location of Culture:*

> "What is to be done" must acknowledge the force of writing, its metaphoricity and its rhetorical discourse, as a productive matrix which defines the social and makes it available as an objective of and for, action. Textuality is not simply a second-order ideological expression or a verbal symptom of a pre-given political subject. . . . The political subject—as indeed the subject of politics—is a discursive event. (23)

Discourse, as a polyvocal site of translation, of what I have elsewhere called "liminal incommensurability" (Cavell, "'Same Difference'" 3), constantly militates against universalism and essentialism. It is, in fact, precisely such an argument for difference *within* the heavily politicized term "equality" that animates Catherine MacKinnon's *Only Words.* This book argues in the strongest possible way for the importance of discursivity in the political arena: "Social inequality is substantially created and enforced—that is, *done*—through words and images. Social hierarchy cannot and does not exist without being embodied in meanings and expressed in communications" (MacKinnon 13). In her discussion of the "law of equality," MacKinnon cites the Supreme Court of Canada's definition of the Charter of Rights and Freedoms' notion of equality as one that is "more substantive than formal, directed toward changing unequal social relations rather than monitoring their equal positioning before the law" (98). In contrast, the United States defines inequality

> as distinction, as differentiation, indifferent to whether dominant or subordinated groups are hurt or helped. . . . The positive spin of the Canadian interpretation holds the law to promoting equality, projecting the law into a more equal future, rather than remaining rigidly neutral in ways that either reinforce existing social inequality or prohibit chang-

ing it, as the American constitutional perspective has increasingly done in recent years. (98)

MacKinnon manages what Sullivan does not, namely, to dislocate the central term of her argument; whereas Sullivan wishes, finally, to reassert the "normal" as univocal and hegemonic, MacKinnon argues that "equal" occupies more than one site—that it is not a universal given but a condition towards which society must work.

A good deal of the efficacy of MacKinnon's argument emerges from her refusal to consider the concepts she is dealing with apart from their contextual implications, so that "principle [is] defined in terms of specific experiences, the particularity of history, substantively rather than abstractly" (109). In her insistence on the confluence of experience *and* history, MacKinnon identifies a postcolonialist pedagogy which asks that we locate ourselves in difference.

4.

I address you from your place [*place*] in order to say to you that I have no place [*place*], since I am like those who make their trade out of resemblance—the poets, the imitators, and the sophists, the genus of those who have no place. You alone have place and can say both the place and the nonplace in truth, and that is why I am going to give you back the floor. In truth, give it to you or leave it to you. To give back, to leave, or to give the floor to the other amounts to saying: you have (a) place, have (a) place, come.

Jacques Derrida, "*Khōra*"

Acknowledgments

I am grateful to Leslie Roman for comments on an early draft of this paper and to Peter Dickinson for his advice and insights throughout.

Works Cited

Appadurai, Arjun. "Disjuncture and Difference in the Global Cultural Economy." *Public Culture* 2.2 (1990): 1-24.

Ashcroft, Bill, Gareth Griffiths, and Helen Tiffin. *The Empire Writes Back: Theory and Practice in Post-Colonial Literatures*. New York: Routledge, 1989.

Berman, Paul, ed. *Debating P.C.: The Controversy Over Political Correctness on College Campuses*. New York: Dell, 1992.

Bhabha, Homi. *The Location of Culture*. London: Routledge, 1994.

Butler, Judith. *Bodies That Matter: On the Discursive Limits of "Sex."* London: Routledge, 1993.

Cavell, Richard. "Theorising Canadian Space: Postcolonial Articulations." *Canada: Theoretical Discourse/Discours théoriques.* Ed. Terry Goldie, Carmen Lambert, and Rowland Lorimer. Montréal: Association for Canadian Studies, 1994. 75-104.

——. "'Same Difference': On the Hegemony of 'Language' and 'Literature' in Comparative Studies." *Canadian Review of Comparative Literature* 23.1 (1996): 1-8.

Diamond, S. "Managing the Anti-PC Industry." Newfield and Strickland 23-37.

Dickinson, Peter. "'Go-Go Dancing on the Brink of the Apocalypse': Representing AIDS—An Essay in Seven Epigraphs." *Postmodern Apocalypse: Theory and Cultural Practice at the End.* Ed. Richard Dellamora. Philadelphia: U of Pennsylvania P, 1995. 219-40.

Faludi, Susan. *Backlash: The Undeclared War Against American Women.* New York: Doubleday, 1991.

Fanon, Frantz. *Black Skin, White Masks.* New York: Grove Weidenfeld, 1967.

Foucault, Michel. *The History of Sexuality: Vol. 1: An Introduction.* Trans. Robert Hurley. New York: Vintage, 1990.

Gallop, Jane. "Im-Personation: A Reading in the Guise of an Introduction." Gallop 1-18.

——. *Pedagogy: The Question of Impersonation.* Ed. Gallop. Bloomington: Indiana UP, 1995.

Garber, Marjorie. *Vested Interests: Cross-Dressing and Cultural Anxiety.* New York: Routledge, 1992.

Gilroy, Paul. *There Ain't No Black in the Union Jack.* London: Hutchinson, 1987.

Jameson, Fredric. "On 'Cultural Studies.'" *Social Text* 34 (1993): 17-52.

Jay, Gregory. "Taking Multiculturalism Personally: Ethnos and Ethos in the Classroom." Gallop 117-28.

Jewsiewicki, Bogumil, and V.Y. Mudimbe. "For Said." *Transition* 63 (1994): 34-50.

Kandiyoti, Deniz. "Identity and its Discontents: Women and the Nation." *Millenium* 20.3 (1991): 429-43.

Karamcheti, Indira. "Caliban in the Classroom." Gallop 138-46.

MacKinnon, Catherine. *Only Words.* Cambridge: Harvard UP, 1993.

Mitchell, Juliet. *Psychoanalysis and Feminism.* London: Allen Lane, 1974.

Mohan, Rajeswari. "Multiculturalism in the Nineties: Pitfalls and Possibilities." Newfield and Strickland 372-88.

Newfield, Christopher, and Ronald Strickland. *After Political Correctness: The Humanities and Society in the 1990s.* Boulder: Westview, 1995.

——. "Introduction: Going Public." Newfield and Strickland 1-20.

PMLA 110.1 (1995). Spec. issue on postcolonialism.

Probyn, Elspeth. "Travels in the Postmodern: Making Sense of the Local." *Feminism/Postmodernism.* Ed. Linda J. Nicholson. New York: Routledge, 1990. 176-89.

Scott, J.W. "The Campaign Against Political Correctness: What's Really at Stake." Newfield and Strickland 111-27.

Simon, R. "Face to Face with Alterity: Postmodern Jewish Identity and the Eros of Pedagogy." Gallop 90-105.

Sullivan, Andrew. *Virtually Normal: An Argument About Homosexuality.* New York: Knopf, 1995.

Viswanathan, Gauri. "Yale College and the Culture of British Imperialism." *Yale Journal of Criticism* 7.1 (1994): 1-30.

27

"Critical Correspondences:
The Diasporic Critic's (Self-)Location"*

Smaro Kamboureli

There is no document of civilization which is not at the same time a document of barbarism. And just as such a document is not free of barbarism, barbarism taints also the manner in which it was transmitted from one owner to another.

Walter Benjamin (256)

Would that the gods could make all exile a birth, all dismissal childbirth.

Michel Serres (89)

"[D]iasporic consciousness" is perhaps not so much a historical accident as it is an intellectual reality—the reality of being intellectual.

Rey Chow (15)

I

This book [*Scandalous Bodies*] could be seen as the other of the manifesto on ethnicity that I wanted to write but never did. I realized this one day in the mid-nineties when I reread Robert Kroetsch's "I Wanted to Write a Manifesto." It was not what he says in that essay that put things into perspective for me; rather, it was the Möbius effect of his title that offered momentary relief from the critical impasse I had reached: a "political paralysis," an "inability to make difficult critical choices" (Roman 73), and, along with that, a reluctance to commit myself to the fixity of words on the page. This was the time of the presumed certainties of political correctness, the "politics of blame" (Said, "Intellectuals" 45)[1] and vociferous advocacies, but also a period of global upheavals.

Like other Canadians at that time, I felt the excitement of social and cultural changes, yet was also discomfited by the pressures of the struggles over the politics of location and agency on the home front and, globally, those over ethnocentrism. I experienced the various events and debates of those

---

* *Scandalous Bodies: Diasporic Literature in English Canada* (Toronto: Oxford UP, 2000), 1-26.

years as if they belonged to a "revolutionary moment," yet I also felt suffocated by the tendency of the sides involved to reduce them to "brutal simplicities and truncated correspondences" (Hall, "For Allon White" 288). As a teacher and an immigrant who was trying to write a study I had come to call my "ethnic project," I tried to achieve a meaningful balance between experience and political analysis. It was not easy; in fact, I found it to be virtually impossible.

I felt that my study was in search of a different author. It kept changing direction, resisting the narrative threads I was intent on following, moving in and out of Canada and its literature, conflating various temporalities—and thus revealing my historical imagination to be *other* than what I thought it was. I soon began to show signs of personal and academic weariness, the effects of the seemingly tangible gap that separates academic discourse from social reality, government and institutional policies from practice, the intricacies of academic argument from the heat and pressures of personal emotions and engagement.

I was caught in the web of what Immanuel Wallerstein calls the "very passionate political debates [that] hinge around" the names of difference:

> Are there Palestinians? Who is a Jew? Are Macedonians Bulgarians? Are Berbers Arabs? What is the correct label: Negro, Afro-American, Black (capitalized), black (uncapitalized)? People shoot each other every day over the question of labels. And yet, the very people who do so tend to deny that the issue is complex or puzzling or indeed anything but self-evident. (Wallerstein 71)

The "people" Wallerstein talks about, I realized, are not the only culprits in this denial of complexity, a denial that speaks of the incommensurability of identity. Even when we bear "labels" different from theirs, we all move among them; we are them by virtue of contiguity, if not consanguinity. This realization made all the more painfully ironic the recognition—a commonplace, indeed—that people's warfare, be it cultural or military, continues despite the fact that colonialism, nationalism, diaspora, race, and ethnicity have already been analyzed rigorously, often with the cool precision that is afforded the cadavers of the past.

As academics, we have learned to tread gingerly on these paths of history. Indeed, those "labelled," and others like them, are no longer the *objects* of our studies; they are the *subjects* of their own discourse—at least that is what many of us academics argue. But who are we? Whose interests do we represent beyond our own academic interests? Who do we write for, and why? Is it only the colonial subject that practises mimicry? And, for that matter, what is the range of states of being and mind that colonialism covers? Does self-location, that most frequently recurring and debated issue today, suffice to immunize academic discourse against the perils of representation (speaking for or about others), against the politics of the institutions that we are complicit with—however strong our avowed desire to change them? What cultural and political dynamics does the theatre of the classroom dramatize? How do we as individuals negotiate our political stance vis-à-vis the history both of ideas and of the institutions in whose contexts we teach? In other words, how do we position ourselves in relation to representation? More to the point, how do I, as an academic, as someone who teaches Canadian literature—and does so with an accent, as I am sometimes reminded by peers and students alike—fit within these debates?

I sought answers to these questions, questions that relate in a tangible way to the theories and practices of colonialism, nationalism, diaspora, and racism. I immersed myself in narratives and histories that were significant and relevant to my "ethnic project," but that spoke as well to my own life-narrative as a Canadian citizen who is also a member of the Greek diaspora. I saw the global state of affairs in general, Canadian culture in particular, and my personal condition as part of the same continuum. This was a matter not of synchronicity, but rather of the "kind of disjunctive temporality" that Bhabha talks about, a double recognition of "causality" as what "displace[s] the present" and what "make[s] it disjunctive" (*Location* 177). At the same time I wanted to affirm, in the light of threats to Canadian post-secondary education in general and the backlash against the humanities in particular, that my academic and pedagogical interests were not at odds with myself as reader, with my responsibilities as a Canadian citizen, with the "accountability" that the Canadian state demands of academics today—as if we had so far been either irrelevant to or irresponsible towards the production of our culture.

As I went about learning and unlearning, so my "ethnic project" kept being written and unwritten continuously. I could not reconcile in a single study the two imperatives I had come to think of as my guiding principles: first, to locate my "ethnic project" within pedagogy—pedagogy in the sense both of my own teaching practices in the classroom, and of the subtle and not so subtle ways in which the desire-machine of the state socializes us; second, to negotiate the contingencies that inform an academic's task. This was not just a matter of finding the right shape and scope for my project; it was, above all, a matter of the difficulty I encountered in negotiating, let alone incorporating into my study, what both personal experience and theoretical insight compelled me to confront.[2]

As theorists and critics of postcolonial and ethnic writing we have devised ingenious and eloquent tropes by which to account for such rifts: irony, inherent contradictions, distanciation, autobiography, reflexivity, ambivalence, filiation and affiliation, hybridity. All these figures pay tribute to our deliberate attempts to problematize our academic and writerly conditions, to position ourselves in the midst of our academic communities and in between the communities we write about. Still, I couldn't help recognizing the psycho-medical metaphors of, say, Tom Nairn's and Homi Bhabha's theories—the pathology of the body national, the neurosis of the state—as collapsing into their literal references. Illness was no longer a metaphor; the situation they were describing was actually diseased. Reading "the social body as a process" (Burroughs and Ehrenreich 3) was no longer a matter of figurative speech. As Mary Douglas says, "The human body communicates information for and from the social system in which it is a part" (83). I began to see the material signs of my body—including my whiteness (the whiteness of a southern European) and my accent—as stress signs symptomatic of the condition of the social body I was trying to understand. I had become a medium of representation. I was reminded at that stage of what Judith Butler says about bodies: that their "materiality [must] be rethought as the effect of power, as power's most productive effect" (2). The physical symptoms of my frustration, then, were signs of what was wrong with the social body I was trying to understand—and, closer to home, of what was wrong with me.

"Practices of representation," Stuart Hall says, "always implicate the positions from which we speak or write—the positions of *enunciation*" ("Cultural Identity" 222). Acknowledging from the start the four most frequently cited factors determining one's subjectivity—gender, race, class, and diaspora—could provide me with an "imaginary coherence" (Hall, "Cultural Identity" 224): they would locate me unequivocally in a position that would be characterized as ambivalent, at best. Although my race and class would put me close to the "centre" of things, there could be no doubt that, when combined with my gender and diasporic experience, they would also modify that "centrality," would sway my position towards a certain "marginality." I could frame myself within these categories only if I assumed them to be stable and coherent, internally unvaried. But they are not. That "[i]dentity is not as transparent or unproblematic as we think," that it is a "production" (Hall, "Cultural Identity" 222), has become a commonplace of many discussions of identity and ethnicity today.

At the same time, however, the insistence on positioning ourselves has assumed the force of a political imperative: only by doing so can we give our arguments credibility, only by labelling ourselves will we locate ourselves securely within history. But constructing our books as mirrors of ourselves does not do away with the persistent question of representation. The logic of self-location, it seems to me, is no less fraught with problems than the positions of alleged neutrality and liberalism are.

Positioning myself in these terms and ways did not promise to frame my study productively. If anything, it promised instead to reveal my complicity with the kind of "ethnic absolutism" (Gilroy)—once a Greek, always a Greek; once an immigrant, always an immigrant—that I have always found to be reductive. Self-fashioned authenticity can easily become a straitjacket that is not that different, either ideologically or structurally, from the social attitudes that make diasporic subjects Other to their host societies.

As Asha Varadharajan writes:

> The reflection on subject positions has become unavoidable for the sympathetic Western critic who chooses to engage with the other without presumption or patronage. The danger of this timely recognition of a perhaps inescapable ethnocentrism is that it could be turned easily enough into an excuse for inaction. This conscientious refusal to speak for those whom the discourse of Empire designates as other would become a way of absolving oneself of the responsibility for the brutality of history. Since the Western critic is inevitably implicated in the history of colonization, any intervention on behalf of the other, it could be argued, will be contaminated by that history and therefore futile. The process of self-scrutiny would then translate itself into consolation for the wrongs of the past and into paralysis in the present. (xvi)

Varadharajan proceeds to show that the "native informant is equally subjected to these problems" (xvii). And, in the case of a diasporic critic like myself, these problems are further amplified by the hybridity of my position.

The pressure I felt to position myself, instead of resolving my tensions, kept pointing to various layers of my subjectivity, revealing my identity to be unsettled, continuously disrupted, determined by different alliances on different occasions. Was this a symptom of the incommensurability of identity? Or was it a sign of my co-optation, a symptom of fickleness (capricious or not) in my politics? Whether this pressure was the result of intellectual demands originating within Western theory or of specific calls from my Canadian peers, at conferences and other social gatherings, to position myself, it took on the appearance of disciplinary action. The more I failed to see the salience of giving credibility to my critical discourse by locating myself in precise (and presumably authentic) terms, the more frustrated I felt because of the social and academic pressures to do so. For the location I was expected to inhabit seemed to suggest, on the one hand, a reification of the categories of race and ethnicity and, on the other, a withdrawal from the arena of *critical* debates that were themselves generally regarded not as discursive practices but as absolute stances.

The disciplinary, hence totalizing, intent that informs the gestures of self-location might be seen as an instance of restricted economy, a closed system of relations that articulates events in regulated ways while remaining unaware of the effects of its control.[3] Moreover, that intent points to a desire to avoid or eliminate or—at the very least—control the presumed infection of one's subjectivity by that of another. Were subjectivities unalloyed, unequivocal entities, such preventive gestures would be necessary. But if subjectivity is, as

I believe it to be, irresolute, the product of filiation together with the frequently mutilating practices of nationalist warfare and coercive assimilation, then reflexivity, as Varadharajan argues, "reveals itself as an inadequate comprehension of the functioning of ideology." In this instance, reflexivity "assumes that there are no chinks in the armor of the system and fails to recognize that the processes of both colonization and decolonization were and will remain incomplete" (Varadharajan xviii). Thus the implicit narrative in the politics of self-location—that we can only speak for ourselves—often leads to what Linda Alcoff calls a "'retreat' response" (17). This ranges from strategic silence, or self-inflicted silence, to other forms of retreat that renounce advocacy and hence relinquish the intention to bring about change.

In trying to understand the intricacies of the politics of self-location, I felt trapped within Vico's view of human history as a cycle of repetition—and without the optimism of his vision. There is no human history without repetition, Vico tells us in *The New Science*. But as Said writes:

> if we question the neatness of a cycle imposed by Vico on the huge variety of human history—then we are forced to confront precisely what the cycle itself circumvents, the *predicament of infinite variety and infinite senselessness*. Take history as a reported dramatic sequence of dialectical stages, enacted and fabricated by an inconsistent but persistent humanity, Vico seems to be saying, and you will equally avoid the despair of seeing history as gratuitous occurrence as well as the boredom of seeing history as realizing a foreordained blueprint. (*World* 113; my emphasis)

I wanted to write a manifesto that would circumvent that "predicament"; to act on my desire to begin *in media res*, in the liminal space I inhabit in the present, while turning my back on the past of the critical tradition, resisting "the subservience that always accompan[ies] the classic pedagogical procedures of forging links, referring back to prior premises or arguments, justifying one's own trajectory, method, system" (Derrida, *Ear* 3).

That was how I came to want to write a manifesto that would free me from the legacy of master narratives, that would release me into the future of history, while dangling from the trembling wings of the *angelus novus*—Walter Benjamin's angel of history.[4] I wanted to shatter the mirrors of repetition. At the very least, I wanted my repetition to make a *critical* difference, to interrupt, however briefly, the cycle of repetition. "[R]epetition is useful as a way of showing that history and actuality are all about human persistence, and not about divine originality" (Said, *World* 113).

As Benjamin says, "To articulate the past historically does not mean to recognize it 'the way it really was' (Ranke). It means to seize hold of a memory as it flashes up at a moment of danger" (255). I knew that this moment of danger is always located in the present. That was why I did not want to be held hostage by the past, the past as archive but also as the lived, and living, present. For I could not reconcile the disturbing realities of, say, the breakdown of Yugoslavia, or the Canadian soldiers' behaviour in Somalia, or the reactions to the Writing Thru Race conference, with the realism of the media's representation of those events. Behind those representations lurked the spectre of history as repetition. Nor could I always find an easy and unambiguous position for myself in the debates that took place in the early 1990s.

Without necessarily believing in an evolutionary vision of history, I began to despair at the thought that the old adage about history repeating itself might be, after all, the one and only true instance of determinism. I failed to see any "forces troubling the continuity" (Said, *World* 119) that repeated history. I had not realized at the time that the problem lies not in the dichotomies of "academy vs reality," or "theory vs practice," but in the slippages that occur between the constructed categories of the real and realism as they facilitate and/or impede the traffic of critical discourse from one category to the other. And so I toyed with the idea of writing a manifesto as a way of moving beyond my position of retreat.

A manifesto is supposed to rise above history. It is intended to take us beyond the cultural predicament of historical repetition, to defy determinism. Its historical value is posthumous, for a manifesto wants to be judged by the future it announces. The method behind the promises it makes is not supposed to be simply additive. Its rhetoric, its pledge to deliver something new, speaks of radical breaks. It didn't take me long to realize that, if my manifesto were to have any efficacy, it would reside in the manifesto's promise to redeem me/us from the spectre of historical catastrophes. The manifesto has, in other words, a messianic message.

Still, I reminded myself, I have always found messiahs to be as dangerous as they are seductive. Their power and seductiveness reside in their absolutist vision. They have the power of a sign that is at once eschatological and apocalyptic, of the past and of the future. Redemption is always the antecedent of catastrophe. A manifesto, then, cannot help being accountable to the past. The past, as Benjamin so acutely says, "carries with it a temporal index by which it is referred to redemption" (254).

I am thankful that my messianism was only ephemeral. I could not turn my back on the temporality of our present moment, on the disjunctiveness of the space we inhabit. Nor could I remain suspended from the wings of the angel of history. In no time I would be swept away by the violence of the storm that holds the *angelus novus* suspended between past and future. For the angel of history, Benjamin says, has his face

> turned toward the past. Where we perceive a chain of events, he sees one single catastrophe which keeps piling wreckage upon wreckage and hurls it in front of his feet. The angel would like to stay, awaken the

356 Postcolonial Pedagogies

dead, and make whole what has been smashed. But a storm is blowing from Paradise; it has got caught in his wings with such violence that the angel can no longer close them. This storm irresistibly propels him into the future to which his back is turned, while the pile of debris before him grows skyward. This storm is what we call progress. (257-58)

The angel's position was too precarious for a mere human, and an academic at that, to mimic. The *angelus novus* is, after all, the "guardian angel of the critics of nationalism" (Bhabha[5]); Tom Nairn, Benedict Anderson, Anne McClintock—to mention just a few—all look in his direction. The *angelus novus* is the allegorical figure epitomizing the contingencies that determine the relationships between communities and individuals. He hovers, as Bhabha so aptly puts it, over "anxious nations & nervous states." We live in the shadow of his open wings. We may empathize with his predicament, to the extent that our fallen condition allows us to do so, but we live in the midst of the debris that he only gazes upon from afar.

II

If it was the image of the *angelus novus* that made me acknowledge defeat, the image of a different kind of angel helped me overcome my critical impasse. It was one of the angels in Wim Wenders' film *Wings of Desire* (1987),[6] those angels who gather together in the soft silence inside the walls of Berlin's public library as dark falls, whose presumed freedom is limited by their inability to intervene substantially in the affairs of humans.

These library scenes are among my favourites in *Wings of Desire*. But only on seeing the film for the third time did I hear one of the anonymous humans in the library reading a passage that refers to Paul Klee's *Angelus Novus*, a painting owned by Benjamin, and to Benjamin's flight to Paris. Since I did not know German, it was only the names that caught my attention.[7] Until then, the fluttering wings of Benjamin's *angelus novus* had struck me as the image of an entropic movement; but upon rereading "Theses on the Philosophy of History," the essay in which he talks about the *angelus novus*, I remembered that Benjamin also says that "the 'state of emergency' in which we live is not the exception but the rule," and that it is "our task to bring about a real state of emergency" if we are to "improve our position" in political struggles such as the ones against fascism (257) or racism.

Although in *Wings of Desire* this "state of emergency" is highly aestheticized, it is what haunts the angels about the past and the present, and as a result about the future. The film's action takes place in Berlin before the collapse of the Wall. Unlike the Berliners who live on either side of the Wall, the angels effortlessly cross that borderline. But both East and West Berlin were equally ravaged by the Second World War. German nationalism, political ideologies, and the fragmented life-narratives of most of the humans for whom the angels show concern are all part of the film's address to the questions that emerge from the lived and living histories enacted by its angelic and human characters alike. Above all, the film dramatizes the politics of diaspora without pitting substantive political judgement against non-committal cosmopolitanism, individuals against communities, narcissistic authenticities against cultural pluralism. *Wings of Desire* visualizes what we cannot see, but it does not yield to the seductive illusion of transparency. It is the crisis of (total) knowledge, a resistance to the fetishization of origins, that motivates one of its angels to become an immigrant. [. . .]

V

The confrontation with history in *Wings of Desire,* the film's prescient mode, its ambivalence concerning strategies of representation, its complex positioning of diasporic subjects—all these made my viewing of it an enabling experience. It became, literally, a heuristic strategy that facilitated my attempts to deal with multiculturalism in Canada. The film became relevant to my "ethnic project" not as an allegory, a parable of the many issues involved in a study of minority subjectivities and the construction of ethnicity, but as a complex text that gave me both the distance and the proximity I needed to read Canadian multiculturalism. Its simultaneous depiction of reality and realism, its problematizing of visuality and the remembering of history, helped me to realize the importance of including in this study more than one set of articulations, of avoiding a unifying theme, a single thesis.

VI

What determines the role of the diasporic critic? How does she move inside the cultural and political syntax of the communities in which she participates? And what is her intellectual task?

Given her hybridity, the diasporic critic might function as a "native informant" on two fronts. As a diasporic subject, she might easily claim the "authenticity" of her ethnicity. She would thus speak with a degree of authority on what constitutes otherness as a double sign: a sign of (her) minoritization as well as a sign of (her) difference articulated in positivistic terms. As a Canadian subject, she might claim a different kind of authenticity, one encompassing the presumed cohesiveness of the dominant position. She could then use this authenticity strategically in order to critique the dominant system from within or, possibly, to embrace it with irony, even complicity.

However, both configurations of the diasporic critic as "native informant" imply ideological contradictions. "[S]potlighting," as Chow says, "the speaker's own sense of alterity and political righteousness" does not automatically "turn powerlessness into 'truth'" (13, 12). By positing herself as ethnic, the diasporic critic practises "self-dramatization," what Chow calls "tak[ing] the route of self-subalternization, which has increasingly become the assured means to authority and power" (13). Conversely, were the diasporic critic to relinquish her claim to ethnicity by adopting a seemingly neutral position, she would have little choice but to resort to a kind of liberal pluralism or relativism— and thus face further entanglement with the forces that demand she assume a stable position. In either case, the diasporic critic would suffer detrimental effects from the very act of self-location. Aligning herself with one *or* the other position, she would perform her declared identity while forgetting the incommensurability of history.

As Trent Schroyer says in his foreword to Adorno's *The Jargon of Authenticity*, "Dialectically conceived 'subjectivity' is historically formed and yet not reducible to historical determinations" (xii). There are always elements that are unassimilable, that extend beyond the binary structure within which the diasporic critic has traditionally situated herself. Thus the pressure to take a position becomes a form of intellectual swindling, of giving in to the "jargon of authenticity" that Adorno calls "a professional illness" (18). The authenticities of each position are complicitous with each other. As Adorno suggests, the jargon of self-location aspires to erase the distance between the two positions by representing the critics either as "sharers in higher culture" or as "individuals with an essence of their own" (18). The two positions are "mediated through each other in frightful ways. And since they are synthetically prepared, that which is mediated has become the caricature of what is natural" (19).

Predictably, we can understand the diasporic critic as a Janus-faced figure. She is at once Canadian and ethnic. But this doubleness does not necessarily present her with a choice that will resolve the either/or condition of her hybridity. Like the Janus-faced figure[8] that Bhabha uses to talk about linguistic ambivalence and national discourses, the diasporic critic's twinned figure is characterized by "prodigious doubling" ("Introduction" 3). There is no symmetry between the particularities of the diasporic critic's background and her present condition, no way (and for that matter no reason) to reduce once and for all the complexity that informs either position. As her ethnic background cannot be reduced to a stable and essentially "true" past, so her national identity as Canadian resists simplification. Ethnicity is not a condition that she possesses naturally; nor is her ethnic identity fixed and stable in her birthplace or in relation to her ancestral origins. Her ethnicity is determined as much by her intellectual and life trajectories as by the Canadian state's and Canadian society's construction of the national imaginary and multiculturalism. Were the diasporic critic to speak from the dominant perspective, adopting a Canadian point of view (assuming, for a moment, that

"Canadian" is to be exclusively construed as a sign of dominance), she would at once announce her right to do so and run the risk of eliding the particularity of her diasporic perspective. The objective is neither to construct an opposition nor to effect a balance between these positions; instead, it is to produce a space where her hybridity is articulated in a manner that does not cancel out any of its particularities.

These particularities, however oppositional they may seem, are related through contextualities and historical contingencies. They are the constituent elements of the *mise en scène* of diasporic subjectivity, a scene that is constantly under revision in a *mise en abîme* fashion. Indeed, these elements apostrophize each other in the way Derrida suggests when he defines apostrophe as "A genre and a tone. The word—apostrophizes—speaks of the words addressed to the singular one, a live interpellation (the man of discourse or writing interrupts the continuous development of the sequence, abruptly turns toward someone, that is, something, addresses himself to you), but the word also speaks of the address to be detoured" (Derrida, *Post Card* 4). Such detours are essential if I am to remain vigilant with regard to both the diasporic critic's "shuttling self" (Spivak, "Marginality" 63) and the historical modalities that inform hybridity.

In the same way that hybridity must be understood not only as the distinguishing characteristic of diasporic subjects but also as a constituent element of the culture they inhabit, so apostrophe as gesture and modality addresses the diasporic critic but is also that critic's address to her culture. It is a gesture that speaks against cultural relativism—that is, against the anthropological view of culture as an organic and cohesive whole. It is also a gesture that should point, given current global developments, towards a radically revised concept of nationalism. We may live in a postcolonial era, as many insist, but globalism and certain kinds of transnationalism may well prove to be more than a political and economic phase—possibly even the antecedents of new colonialisms. If it is part of the diasporic critic's task to foreground hybridity, she should also be vigilant against constructing that hybridity as a "closet idealism" that may "reduce the complex givenness of material reality to its symbolic dimensions" (Cheah 302).[9] Thus an acknowledgement of hybridity does not signal a resolution of the politics and historical materiality of diaspora. It must be accompanied by the will to question the metanarratives of development and progress that assent to hybridity. Lest I be misunderstood, let me say that I am not arguing against development in the sense of efforts to, for example, improve the conditions of ethnic labourers or women immigrants, or programs addressing systemic discrimination. Rather, I am talking about the need to continue questioning the "enlightened" reason in whose name a society, usually mobilized by the juridico-political agendas of the state, sets a course towards the future as a means of salvaging itself from history. As prosperity does not guarantee happiness, so progress does not necessarily transform history. As Rudolph Vierhaus puts it, "The suspicion is that progress brings with it immeasurable dangers and that a stage has been reached wherein the social costs have outstripped the gains" (332). Given this state of affairs, what is the responsibility of the diasporic critic?

VII

If the problems of colonialism, nationalism, and multiculturalism have been "forcefully articulated and thought out," as Michel de Certeau says, why "the violence, the tensions, and ultimately the failure? Simply because history does not obey the speech that challenges it" (63).

Simply. The lucidity with which de Certeau exposes the artlessness of the beast that history is, and the teasing gap between discourse and action, was another thing that made me aware of the rift that has shaped my project. This is the rift that exists between my desire to write—"a desire . . . that is ceaseless, varied, and highly unnatural and abstract, since 'to write' is a function never exhausted by the completion of a piece of writing" (Said, *World* 131)— and my desire to see this writing *translated* into a certain kind of efficacy. And I have remained conscious, throughout the process of this study, of yet another rift, one that acknowledges the contradictions between my original desire to see my writing, potentially, as translation and my belief in writing as just one more discursive practice among many.

If in expressing these contradictions I appear to shy away from the intellectual task at hand, if this discussion strikes some readers as too coy, I would point to Spivak's comments in her essay "Responsibility" (1994). "[O]ne way of being responsible to the thinking of responsibility," she writes, is "that whatever is formalizable remains in a sort of intermediary stage. . . . Full formalization itself must be seen not as impossible but as an experience of the impossible, or a figure for the impossible, which may be to say the 'same thing'" (22). It is through this spirit of responsibility that we can appreciate what is constructive about the irreducibly ambivalent condition of the diasporic critic. Spivak is very persuasive when she observes that "(the thinking of) responsibility is also (a thinking of) contamination" (23), that a "'responsible' thought describes 'responsibility' . . . as attending to the call of that irreducible fact" (26).

There are two ways in which I understand "that irreducible fact." Being responsible does not mean feigning disinterestedness in the name of academic objectivity—a pretence that Spivak, among others, rightly sees as "an unacknowledged partisanship to a sort of universalist humanism" (20); nor does being responsible entail the obligation (this, too, part of the humanist legacy) of furnishing solutions to problems, of putting into action a progressivist vision—that is, measuring our success as critics by the efficacy of our conclusions or the alternative visions we offer. This is not merely a case of the "end" testifying to the validity of the "means," but rather of the "end" being beyond our horizon of understanding. Envisaging a progressivist "end" to today's cultural and social malaise may sound like a worthwhile and heroic project. Nevertheless, it is the kind of project that, I believe, attempts to transgress the coercion of historical paradigms, to exit from history instead of employing history against itself; it forfeits the reality of contamination and the perils implicit in emancipatory discourses. As Radhakrishnan writes:

> In our attempts to change the subject on the basis of what we hold to be good and desirable, and moral and politically correct, we cannot afford to forget how this very blueprint or telos that we are acting upon could be potentially wrong and repressive, even barbaric. For example, did humanity always know that racism is wrong and sexism abhorrent, that colonialism and imperialism are illegitimate and unconscionable bodies of knowledge, that homophobia and normative heterosexuality are unacceptable? Briefly, did we always know that our norms have a flip side that is objectionable? Is not the very moment of the emancipatory critique the expression of a contradiction? (20)

Practising responsibility in the name of progress leads to teleological narratives; this is definitely not the answer to questions about self-location, diasporic identities, and accountability. While responsibility is, in part, a response to urgency, to the states of emergency that Benjamin talks about, being responsible does not promise a smooth transition from the position of witness to that of activist.

Instead, being responsible, in my understanding, means negotiating our position in relation both to the knowledge we have and to the knowledge we lack. It means practising "negative pedagogy," "inhabiting . . . that space where knowledge becomes the obstacle to knowing" (Johnson, "Teaching Ignorance" 166, 182). Responsibility, then, entails the recognition that what we know may already be contaminated by what we do not know, and vice versa. Thus knowledge is no longer conceived as an object that is already valorized and therefore worthy of remaining in circulation. Rather, negative pedagogy redefines the object of knowledge as nothing other than the process leading towards ignorance. If we are responsible enough to admit that knowledge is at once what fills in gaps and itself creates gaps, what both "enlightens" and destroys, then knowledge produces ignorance; negative pedagogy is thus the exact opposite of what we may call positive pedagogy, that is, teaching as a teleological narrative.

This is what Barbara Johnson, Shoshana Felman, Barbara Freedman, Robert Con Davies, Rey Chow, Gayatri Spivak, and R. Radhakrishnan, among others, argue in their different, and often contradictory, ways. Although not all of these arguments have emerged within a diasporic context, negative pedagogy is relevant to a multicultural society because it may enable us to begin to address history and the historicity of our present moment *responsibly*—without, that is, maintaining the illusion of innocence or non-complicity. Whether we call this mode of being and learning negative pedagogy or "oppositional pedagogy" (Freire, Con Davies) or "teaching terminable or interminable" (Felman), or "learned ignorance" (Freedman), or "deconstructive," "critical," and "radical pedagogy" (Radhakrishnan),[10] there are some recurring elements in the way responsibility materializes in this kind of practice.

Negative pedagogy thematizes not only the object of knowledge, but also the method of learning and unlearning inherited truths. It is thus self-reflexive with regard to its methods as well as the positions of teacher and student. In fact, the purpose of its self-reflexiveness is to disturb the binary relation, and the accompanying hierarchical model, of pedagogue and student. Since one of the objectives of this method of learning is to radically question knowledge and its modes of production, the teacher can no longer occupy an axiological position: teacher and student alike become learners.

"Learner" does away with *and*, a paradoxical word signalling at once conjunction and separation, the two conditions that conventionally mark the teacher/student dyad, whose dynamics are structurally not all that different from those of the centre/margin dialectic. In its traditional usage in education and sociology, "learner" suggests the democratization of teaching, yet it retains the stamp of elaborate and careful attempts to measure success and failure, to quantify pedagogical results. In these contexts learners are regarded, more often than not, as receptacles of knowledge-as-product; they are to be taught through devices tailored to serve knowledge, which, although not always axiomatically conceived, is carefully packaged as a "terminable" object with transparent value and truth.

The learner I have in mind, though, is not to be considered as part of a "teaching machine" (Spivak), territorialized and therefore controlled through the desire-machine of the state (Deleuze and Guattari); this learner is not a construction of the rampant empiricism that operates through various guises of benevolence. Rather, negative pedagogy creates the conditions for a learner defined not only as someone who desires to learn, but also as someone who learns how to desire. This kind of desiring is intransitive.

The primary task of this learner is to decode the guises in which knowledge is made manifest. Thus he is firmly situated within history, including the history of pedagogy as a teaching practice and as the body of disciplinary methods employed by the state apparatus. As Radhakrishnan remarks, this learner's "'subject position' in history precludes the possibility of generating ex nihilo a pedagogical method identical with her desire" (111-12). What this means for learners is that they don't simply learn knowledge as a specifically designated object: they also learn how knowledge is produced, perceiving the power relations usually concealed behind the force of knowledge. This pedagogy, then, deals with a different kind of knowledge, the kind that traces the relationship of knowledge to ideology, and vice versa. Not merely the job of the diasporic critic, practising responsibility through this pedagogical perspective is a task that all members of a given community, especially those in academe, must begin to come to terms with.

Notes

1. Said attributes the "politics of blame" to postcolonial critics, but the theoretical and political context in which he uses the term is similar to the one in question here.

2. Sara Suleri views the different discourses and fields of practice that pit "the 'academy'" against the 'real world'" as "a simplistic binarism," a "most tedious dichotomy" (756). Despite the vexing questions raised by this opposition, dismissing this binarism as tedious does nothing to address either its lived reality or the factors that have constructed the academy-vs-reality dichotomy in the first place. See "Woman Skin Deep: Feminism and the Postcolonial Condition," *Critical Inquiry* 18 (1992): 756-69.

3. On the concepts of restricted and general economy, see Georges Bataille, *Inner Experience*, trans. Leslie Anne Boldt (Albany: State U of New York P, 1988) and "The Notion of Expenditure" in *Visions of Excess: Selected Writings 1927-1939*, ed. and with an introduction by Allan Stoekl, trans. Allan Stoekl, with Carl R. Lovitt and Donald M. Leslie, Jr (Minneapolis: U of Minnesota P, 1985), 116-29.

4. Benjamin bought Paul Klee's watercolour *Angelus Novus* in Munich in the spring of 1921; see Momme Brodersen, *Walter Benjamin: A Biography*, trans. Malcolm R. Green and Ingrida Ligers, ed. Martina Dervis (London: Verso, 1996), 120. See also Benjamin's essay "Theses on the Philosophy of History" (1969).

5. This quotation, as well as the next one from Bhabha, is from his essay "Anxious Nations, Nervous States," published in Joan Copjec, ed., *Supposing the Subject* (London: Verso, 1994); my citation is from the manuscript version of the essay that Bhabha read at the University of Victoria in 1994. Parts of this essay are also included in Bhabha, "Are You a Man or a Mouse?" published in Maurice Berger, Brian Wallis, and Simon Watson, eds., *Constructing Masculinity* (New York: Routledge, 1995).

6. The film's title in German is *Der Himmel über Berlin* ("The Sky over Berlin"). Its script was co-written by Wenders and the Austrian writer Peter Handke. The two had collaborated before in the film *Falsche Bewegung*, translated into English as *Wrong Move* (1974). The lead roles in *Wings of Desire* are played by Bruno Ganz (Damiel) and Otto Sander (Cassiel); Marion is played by Solveig Dommartin; Homer is Curt Bois, "an actor who worked with Max Reinhardt and Bertolt Brecht and fled Nazi Germany in 1933" (Paneth 2); Peter Falk plays Peter Falk—with a difference. The cinematographer is Henri Alekan, who was the

cinematographer for Jean Cocteau's 1946 *Beauty and the Beast. Wings of Desire* won numerous awards, including Best Director at Cannes.

7. Since then I have come across an essay on *Wings of Desire* by Roger Cook, who also refers to Benjamin's inscription in the film; Cook's main argument centres on the film's relation to history.

8. See my discussion of the Janus-faced figure in the chapter on Grove in *Scandalous Bodies* 53-57.

9. My point here about the need to negotiate diasporic subjectivity and nationalism, as well as the need to be cautious about globalism, certainly requires elaboration, but this is not the place for it. On the various aspects of diasporic and cosmopolitan identities, and their relation to different manifestations of global development, see the recent collection of essays edited by Pheng Cheah and Bruce Robbins, *Cosmopolitics: Thinking and Feeling Beyond the Nation* (Minneapolis: U of Minnesota P, 1998).

10. It is not my intention here to collapse the complex differences among these theorists and teachers, but rather to draw attention to what I perceive as their common concern, the need to question the means in which we disseminate knowledge and the kind of knowledge taught. See Paulo Freire, *Pedagogy of the Oppressed* (New York: Continuum, 1995), and Robert Con Davies, "A Manifesto for Oppositional Pedagogy: Freire, Bourdieu, Merod, and Graff," in Bruce Henricksen and Thaïs E. Morgan, eds., *Reorientations: Critical Theories and Pedagogies* (Urbana: U of Illinois P, 1990). References to the other critics can be found in the works cited.

Works Cited

Adorno, Theodor W. *The Jargon of Authenticity*. Trans. Knut Tarnowski and Frederic Will. Fwd. Trent Schroyer. Evanston: Northwestern UP, 1973.

Alcoff, Linda. "The Problem of Speaking for Others." *Cultural Critique* (1991-1992): 5-32.

Benjamin, Walter. *Illuminations*. Ed. Hannah Arendt. Trans. Harry Zohn. New York: Schocken, 1969.

Bhabha, Homi K. "Introduction: Narrating the Nation." *Nation and Narration*. Ed. Bhabha. London: Routledge, 1990. 1-7.

—. *The Location of Culture*. London: Routledge, 1994.

Burroughs, Catherine B., and Jeffrey David Ehrenreich. "Introduction: Reading the Social Body." *Reading the Social Body*. Ed. Burroughs and Ehrenreich. Iowa City: U of Iowa P, 1993. 1-14.

Butler, Judith. *Bodies that Matter: On the Discursive Limit of "Sex."* New York: Routledge, 1993.

Cheah, Pheng. "Given Culture: Rethinking Cosmopolitan Freedom in Transnationalism." *Cosmopolitics: Thinking and Feeling Beyond the Nation*. Ed. Cheah and Bruce Robbins. Minneapolis: U of Minnesota P, 1998. 290-328.

Chow, Rey. *Writing Diaspora: Tactics of Intervention in Contemporary Cultural Studies.* Bloomington: Indiana UP, 1993.

Cook, Roger. "Angels, Fiction and History in Berlin: Wim Wenders' *Wings of Desire*." *Germanic Review* 56.1 (1991): 34-47.

de Certeau, Michel. *Heterologies: Discourse on the Other.* Trans. Brian Massumi. Foreword Wlad Godzich. Minneapolis: U of Minnesota P, 1986.

Deleuze, Gilles, and Félix Guattari. *Anti-Oedipus: Capitalism and Schizophrenia.* Preface Michel Foucault. Trans. Robert Hurley, Mark Seem, and Helen R. Lane. Minneapolis: U of Minnesota P, 1983.

Derrida, Jacques. *The Ear of the Other: Otobiography, Transference, Translation. Texts and Discussions with Jacques Derrida.* Trans. Peggy Kamuf. ("Otobiographies" trans. Avital Ronell). Ed. Christie V. McDonald. New York: Schocken, 1985.

—. *The Post Card: From Socrates to Freud and Beyond.* Trans. Alan Bass. Chicago: U of Chicago P, 1987.

Douglas, Mary. *Implicit Meanings: Essays in Anthropology.* London: Routledge, 1975.

Felman, Shoshana. *The Literary Speech Act: Don Juan with J.L. Austin, or Seduction in Two Languages.* Trans. Catherine Porter. Ithaca: Cornell UP, 1983.

—. "Psychoanalysis and Education: Teaching Terminable and Interminable." *Yale French Studies* 63 (1982): 21-44.

Freedman, Barbara. "Pedagogy, Psychoanalysis, Theatre: Interrogating the Scene of Learning." *Shakespeare Quarterly* 41.2 (1990): 174-86.

Gilroy, Paul. *Small Acts: Thoughts on the Politics of Black Cultures.* London: Serpent's Tail, 1993.

Hall, Stuart. "Cultural Identity and Diaspora." *Identity: Community, Culture, Difference.* Ed. Jonathan Rutherford. London: Lawrence and Wishart, 1990. 222-37.

—. "For Allon White: Metaphors of Transformation." *Stuart Hall: Critical Dialogues in Cultural Studies.* Ed. David Morley and Kuan-Hsing Chen. London: Routledge, 1996. 287-305.

Johnson, Barbara. "Taking Fidelity Philosophically." *Difference in Translation.* Ed. Joseph F. Graham. Ithaca: Cornell UP, 1985. 142-48.

—. "Teaching Ignorance: *L'Ecole des Femmes*." *Yale French Studies* 63 (1982): 165-82.

Kroetsch, Robert. "I Wanted to Write a Manifesto." *A Likely Story: The Writing Life.* Red Deer: Red Deer College P, 1995. 41-64.

Paneth, Ira. "Wim and His Wings." An Interview with Wim Wenders. *Film Quarterly* 42.1 (1988): 2-8.

Radhakrishnan, R. *Diasporic Mediations: Between Home and Location.* Minneapolis: U of Minnesota P, 1996.

Roman, Leslie G. "White is a Color! White Defensiveness, Postmodernism, and Anti-Racist Pedagogy." *Race, Identity and Representation in Education.* Ed. Cameron McCarthy and Warren Crichlow. New York: Routledge, 1993. 71-88.

Said, Edward. "Intellectuals in the Post-Colonial World." *Salmagundi* 70-71 (1986): 44-81.

—. *The World, the Text and the Critic.* Cambridge: Harvard UP, 1983.

Serres, Michel. *The Parasite.* Trans. Lawrence R. Schehr. Baltimore: Johns Hopkins UP, 1982.

Spivak, Gayatri Chakravorty. "Marginality in the Teaching Machine." *Outside in the Teaching Machine.* Ed. Spivak. New York: Routledge, 1993. 53-76.

—. "Responsibility." *Boundary 2* 21.3 (1994): 19-64.

Varadharajan, Asha. *Exotic Parodies: Subjectivity in Adorno, Said and Spivak.* Minneapolis: U of Minnesota P, 1995.

Vierhaus, Rudolph. "Progress: Ideas, Skepticism, and Critique—The Heritage of the Enlightenment." *What Is Enlightenment? Eighteenth-Century Answers and Twentieth-Century Questions.* Ed. James Schmidt. Los Angeles: U of California P, 1996. 330-41.

Wallerstein, Immanuel. "The Construction of Peoplehood: Racism, Nationalism, Ethnicity." *Race, Nation, Class: Ambiguous Identities.* Ed. Etienne Balibar and Wallerstein. London: Verso, 1991. 71-85.

Wenders, Wim. *Wings of Desire.* Script by Wenders and Peter Handke, 1987.

28

"Always Indigenize!: The Radical Humanities in the Postcolonial Canadian University"*

Len Findlay

The word itself, "research," is probably one of the dirtiest words in the indigenous world's vocabulary.

> Linda Smith, *Decolonizing Methodologies: Research and Indigenous Peoples*

I'm not human. I'm an Indian.

> Alphonsine, three-year-old daughter of Judge Mary Ellen Turpel-Lafond, as told by her mother.

This essay is in four parts. The first part deals with the form and force of the exhortation, "always Indigenize!" The second part offers no single solution to the struggle for justice inside and outside universities but instead suggests the doublet, "vision and conspiracy," as a way of taking advantage of millennial dependencies in governments and elite institutions while recognizing that such dependencies exist within neo-paternalistic structures designed to be perceived as ethical and inclusive while practising an oppressive and contradictory politics of difference. The third part argues for the radical humanities as a crucial piece of the decolonizing puzzle and offers an example of the kind of critique that non-Indigenous scholars should undertake as one element in their contribution to the Indigenization process. And finally, I turn more particularly to the discipline of English within the grand narrative of English as a world language, a narrative constantly and uncontrollably interrupted and abducted by both native and non-native speakers in familiar as well as exotic settings. Here I argue for a more concertedly activist disciplinarity which will have at its centre new alliances between English literary studies and Indigenous studies. This argument, like the exhortation always to Indigenize, gestures towards rather than guarantees a particular future. In transforming each other through new rapprochements and *articulations* that both express and connect in strategically contingent ways (Hall 141), academic English and Indigenous studies can help transform the institutions that

---

* *ARIEL* 31.1-2 (2000): 307-26.

house them and the publics which fund them, but only if "we" work together to make that happen.

I. ALWAYS INDIGENIZE!

In the (human) beginning was the Indigene. This hypothesis is a necessary but inscrutable pretext for the historical and current distribution of our species in diverse groupings across the globe. With oral and written histories of a recoverable past have come difference and conflict, competing versions of residency, conquest, settlement, entitlement, and the limited circulation and decidedly mixed benefits of Indigenous status. It seems fair to say that all communities live as, or in relation to, Indigenes. And so there seems a general warrant for supplementing Fredric Jameson's famous exhortation, "Always historicize" (9), with *always Indigenize.* In so Indigenizing, however, we should bear in mind James Chandler's recent demonstration of how unclear and general Jameson's urging to historicize is and how divergently it has been interpreted by literary scholars (Chandler 51ff.). And we should also clarify at the outset who the "we" in question are and how they stand in relation to Indigenousness and its increasingly explicit protocols of self-determination and self-representation.

The employment of the English language to express a sentiment like "always Indigenize!" that may have important consequences for Indigenous peoples, in Canada and elsewhere, is neither innocent nor "merely" practical. But the dangers of Anglocentric presumption are perhaps offset somewhat by the form this exhortation takes, specifying no particular addressee, definition, or outcome, but instead promoting participation in an activity whose nature and consequences will depend on who is listening and how they understand and act upon what they hear or read. It can be understood as an allusive command to include Indigenous issues within the broader and more "developed" project of Western marxism. It can be understood as academic vanguardism playing variations on its own dearest illusions about what it can make happen. Or it can be heard, as I intend it to be heard, as a strategically indeterminate provocation to thought and action on the grounds that there is no *hors-Indigène,* no geopolitical or psychic setting, no real or imagined *terra nullius* free from the satisfactions and unsettlements of Indigenous (pre)occupation. The necessity and difficulty of Indigenizing is therefore no global shell game involving entities and essences that come and go according to sleight of hand or mind or cartographic ruse but an overdetermined play of forces and processes that produce particular determinate moments subjected in their turn to contestation and change. Indigenizing today is undertaken in face of the realities and dangers of "aggravated inequality" (Martin), the fact that development's twin continues to be underdevelopment, and the reality that the emergence of a so-called new economy has so far altered little the only too predictable global distribution of poison and prosperity.

Having drawn in a general way on deconstruction for some of my comments so far on Indigenizing, let me now turn to an Indigenous authority to frame what follows more firmly and prescriptively. The Maori educational theorist, Linda Tuhiwai Smith, has just published a powerful book, *Decolonizing Methodologies: Research and Indigenous Peoples*, which provides what Terry Goldie, for example, lacked (and mourned) in his analysis of the reified and commodified Indigene within white-settler semiotic economies (4, 13, 19). Smith's work deserves to inspire other Indigenous scholars and to direct the efforts of non-Indigenous colleagues. She defines Indigenization variously as demystification (16), recentring (10, 39), "researching back" (7), "*re*writing and *re*righting" (149), as multilevel and counterhegemonic (20, 189), and as "inevitably political" and connected to "broader politics and strategic goals" (178, 189). Smith identifies Indigenizing with the processes of "decolonization, healing, transformation, and mobilization" (116) and with "Twenty-Five Indigenous Projects" (142ff). There is clearly much work to be done, and to be done according to an Indigenous division of labour which simultaneously employs and critiques the division of labour's Euro-imperial and now transnational corporate agenda. This double strategy of working with and against, defining by connection and by difference, suggests that, despite Linda Smith's approving citation (19) of Audre Lorde, some of the master's most important tools—like the domestic and international division of labour—can be used "to dismantle the master's house," though not if they are the only tools used and if they remain within dominant patterns of ownership of the means of production.

II. VISION AND CONSPIRACY

Canadian universities have made some progress in the last two decades in moderating their traditional Eurocentrism. That Eurocentrism has for more than a century been underpinned by two related fictions which, in their most extreme forms, are captured in the doctrines of *terra nullius* (*empty land*) and *scientific objectivity* (Smith 53). The legal, religious, political, and cultural armatures of colonization constantly circulated the notion that Canada was an *empty land*—empty, that is to say, in the sense of being largely uninhabited, or empty of any social organization capable of meeting European standards for the fully "human" (Henderson et al.; Smith 26). At the same time, European colonization came to depend on an ever more ascendant science and technology to ensure the profitability of its civilizing mission. Commercial society extended its domains and enhanced its profit margins in part by using science and technology to reinforce stereotypes of Canada's First Nations as hostile to or incapable of participating in modernity and hence ripe for assimilation or elimination. This stark picture of greed and genocide needs to be modified in light of the treaties signed between (often competing) colonizing powers and the First Nations, but much of the modification to date has attempted to reconceal, minimize, sanitize, or even justify colonial practices radically at variance with Canada's professed sense of itself, domestically and internationally.

The consequence of academic complicity with colonialism has been a massive and persistent deficit in the national understanding of the rights of Indigenous peoples and the value and potential relevance of Indigenous knowledge to economic prosperity and social justice in Canada. The Canadian academy continues to face a formidable challenge in self-education and public education in this area. The academy must therefore begin anew to decolonize its traditional presumptions, curricula, faculty complement and student body, and research and teaching practices, and do so more radically and more rapidly than hitherto.

But where do we begin (again)? How do we proceed? Who are the "we" in question, and why? And how can scholars best record and most effectively share the most successful decolonizing practices across disciplines, institutions, regions? One might decide to start where one might presume progress most likely, "enlightenment" most assured—namely, in the humanities. And such a presumption could find support in the massive outpouring across the world recently of creative and scholarly work dealing with or claiming to exemplify one or another version of the postcolonial (see, for example, Spivak; Prakash; Ahmad; Williams and Chrisman; Rahnema and Bawtree; and Willinsky). Yet Canadian universities, despite (or because of) their crucial role in producing and responding to social change, have not themselves featured very prominently as an object of anticolonial or actively decolonizing inquiry (compared, for instance, with the case of India in, say, Symonds, Viswanathan, and Majeed). Alas, more often than not Canadian universities have been seen (and seen themselves to be) sites of feuding about so-called political correctness (Keefer), feuding which coexists as a distraction or embarrassment beside a wide range of traditional disciplinary activities which are assumed or asserted to be "objective." Canadian universities remain complicitous with residually colonial and defiantly neocolonial policies and practices that continue to produce Indigenous academic "homelessness" (Monture-Angus) and that define what counts as knowledge and who will benefit from its acquisition and exercise, while the beneficiaries and casualties of colonialism stay much the same as they have always been.

Of course, colonialism has a particular history within and across all disciplines, old and new, and it is not only theology and law and genetics that need to hang their heads when invited to return the increasingly emboldened gaze of Canada's First Nations, and Inuit and Metis peoples who are currently "looking white people in the eye" (Razack). Professedly objective methods have brought many benefits to Canada, but only at a price—a price that has been paid disproportionately by so-called surplus populations standing inconveniently in the way of "progress" and "development." The claim to objectivity, whether made in published form or from a podium, habitually depends on formulations and explorations of research questions that play down or attempt to suspend sociopolitical determinants without ever fully or permanently erasing evidence of their agency. Elite institutions are still much too implicated in inappropriate presumptions and practices which in effect replay colonial encounters in the names of excellence, integration, moderni- ty, and so on (as part of a more general threat to difference posed by the "University of Excellence" [Readings 21ff.; Findlay "Runes"]). The persis- tence of this reality, despite abundant good will and public commitments by universities to Indigenous issues, recalls a similar discrepancy between the institutions' professed enthusiasm for interdisciplinarity and the zealously and narrowly disciplinary nature of most of their teaching and research. These related discrepancies suggest an analogous solution in Indigenously led, strategic interdisciplinarity, which draws on the fluid, permeable, holistic features of Indigenous knowledge to suspend or renegotiate academic terri- toriality (and the property regimes that underpin it [Battiste and Henderson, *Protecting*]). We may still in general be far short of a *post-paternalistic* research and teaching agenda centred in and productively addressing the concerns of Indigenous peoples and the conceptual and practical deficits and disfigure- ments in the residually colonial or aggressively biotechnologizing, neocolo- nial Canadian academy. However, Linda Smith offers very constructive as well as sobering advice for the development of new academic and more broadly social formations involving "non-indigenous activists and intellectuals" while "centr[ing] a politics of indigenous identity and indigenous cultural action" (39).

Following Smith's advice, we may be able to produce and reproduce the conditions of possibility of innovative, nonappropriative, ethical cross-cultur- al research, postcolonial institutional ethnographies, and a more just under- standing and achievement of the strategic as such. But what counts as strate- gy here, as strategic research and teaching in particular, and how does it connect to postcolonial notions like "strategic essentialism" as understood and practised by Gayatri Spivak, Sherene Razack, and others? What might strategic interdisciplinarity look like in the future? Such questions seem to me straightforward in the context of Indigenization, because essentialism is "the galvanizing idiom of insurgency but the lethal accomplice of hegemony" (Findlay, "Retailing" 503), and not fully allowable when the Indigenizing is being undertaken by the non-Indigenous academic collaborator rather than the insurgent Indigene. Outsider essentializing of Indigenous history and cul- tural practices must be respectfully strategic rather than presumptuously exotic, and driven by the need to benefit Indigenous people according to their rights, needs, and aspirations. Non-Indigenous learning which crosses disciplines and cultures but remains unidirectional cannot avoid reinscribing diffusionist colonialism and the only too predictable classification of polymaths and primitives, masters and servants.

There is no single remedy for the problems of colonialism, neocolonialism, and the prematurely postcolonial. The (re)doubling remedies I propose deliberately eschew singularity by attempting to be always constructive as well as deconstructive, addressing both a deficiency and an oppressive reality. By invoking *vision* as the first term in my doublet here, I point to the fact that millennial federalism in Canada is conceptually challenged, woefully lacking in vision (as well as literal and metaphorical millennial fireworks!), the proliferation of institutional and official "vision statements" notwithstanding. Indigenizing vision can be of enormous benefit to all people, as will be more evident once Marie Battiste's new collection of essays is published [see Battiste's introduction to this collection, reprinted in this volume]. Whether one is thinking of new pedagogies or sustainability, or institutional internationalization, or other topical issues, Indigenous knowledge can be an invaluable resource, if only in the first instance on its own terms. As we seek new national imaginaries in the new millennium, while federal budgetary surpluses melt away in the reactive restitution of things as they (arguably) were, publicly funded institutions will be looked to for inspiration, guidance—in sum for *content* for new information networks and a freshly skeletal cyber-state. Universities, meanwhile, will be doomed to recycle the neo-imperialist platitudes of *Star Trek* as *their* vision, unless they act on their obscured dependency on Indigenous vision and knowledge. Such vision honours the Other of Eurocentric, instrumental reason while exposing the latter's arbitrariness and connections to injustice. Such vision is available in the traditional teachings of Indigenous peoples, though no longer as part of the larcenous practice of "trading the Other" (Smith 89); it is available also in colonial forms of hybridization and resistance such as the ledger drawings readable by non-Indigenous scholars (Findlay, "Interdisciplining"); and it is perhaps most compellingly available as mobilization and critique in such strategic Indigenizing of Canadian identity as Sharilyn Calliou's "Peacekeeping Actions at Home: A Medicine Wheel Model for a Peacekeeping Pedagogy" or the strategic traditionalism of J.Y. Henderson's "Postcolonial Ghost Dancing."

In contrast to vision, *conspiracy* may seem to pose problems associated with aversion rather than narrowly instrumental understanding. Conspiracy may seem like the wrong term for facilitating new solidarities and coalitions across the Indigenous/non-Indigenous line. Indeed, it may seem to concede too much in a self-incriminating way. However, I prefer it to a more positive term like *concert* from which Victor J. Ramraj elicits such power in his recent collection of *World Writing in English*. Ramraj convenes and skilfully plays up commonality while respecting difference and promoting imagination as one of politics' invaluable Others. In contrast to Ramraj's emphases in what is an evenhanded but not at all a wishy-washy introductory anthology, I am more concertedly political in aiming to mobilize difference as dissonance and dissent against the dominant ideology which so often presents itself as social and other forms of *harmony*—whether in readings of Ulysses' great speech on social degree in *Troilus and Cressida* (Findlay, "Valuing" 7ff) or Sir William Jones's export to Bengal of the idea of "the great *orchestra* of the nation" (qtd. in Findlay, "Liberty" 10).

Another reason for preferring conspiracy to concert may lie in the latter's source in Ramraj's epigraph from Geoffrey Hartman, whom I will take to task in the next section of this essay. More important, however, I wish to rehabilitate conspiracy as a valuable term for articulating resistance by aligning its Indigenization with the so-called "Pontiac Conspiracy" of which Francis Parkman wrote so revealingly and influentially in 1851, a conspiracy explicitly and prominently linked to the deeply problematic notion of "the Conquest of Canada." In the Preface to the sixth (1870) edition of this his first historical work, Parkman reaffirms its value as a portrait of "forest life and the Indian character" within which the use of smallpox and rum as official means of pacifying Indigenous peoples is thought "sufficiently startling" (345). From the outset, however, Parkman worked from the conviction that he was writing of "the American forest and the American Indian at the period when both received their *final* doom" (347; emphasis added). And he was writing in a tradition that had already firmly racialized conspiracy in the so-called "New York Conspiracy" or "Negro Plot" of 1741-42 (Horsmanden), a tradition that has received a "fresh lease on life" in the US today in the prejudging and demonizing of marginal groups thought to threaten dominant American interests at home and abroad (see Jameson, *Geopolitical* xvii, 9ff.).

In endeavouring to rehabilitate conspiracy as a necessary strategic step on the way from the Indigenous margin toward the academic centre, I wish to invoke especially the history of Pontiac even while running the risk of new, conspiratorial knowledge-coalitions being mistaken for the work of the Michigan Militia and their ilk. What I am proposing is not conspiracy marked by silence, secrecy, violence, and hate, but linked instead to vigorous self-representation and to a very public process of envisioning, and then achieving, a thoroughly Indigenized future for all citizens. Indigenous insurgency may be driven to, but not necessarily driven by, conspiracy. Official academic channels remain inadequate and zealously self-sustaining in the name of tradition, academic freedom, and institutional autonomy (see essays by Battiste and Findlay in Bidwell). How otherwise can one account for the meagre and overwhelmingly cultural rather than scientific presence of Indigenous scholars and Indigenous knowledge in Canadian universities, still, today (MacIvor)? But a self-identified conspiracy might remind Indigenizers and others of a rhetoric and politics of dismissal which both deplored and denied the possibility of Indigenous leadership and solidarity in Parkman's version of Pontiac's case—there was little to be expected yet much to be feared from the "radical peculiarity of Indigenous language[s]" and the paradoxically fierce individualism of "an all-believing race" (359, 371). Parkman's contradictions proliferate as Pontiac's power is attributed to the "hero-worship" recently popularized by Thomas Carlyle but also to the essentially uncontrollable members of "one of these savage democracies" (360-61). The latter description of Indigenous polities was intended as a self-destructive oxymoron giving way to spasmodic forms of social cohesion: positively cast as "alliances" when connected to the colonial French or English, but negatively cast as plot and political seizure among "the great mass of Indians" (489) when a modestly legitimating European connection was absent. Parkman aggravates the ambivalence of the Harvard scholar towards his less educated fellow Euro-Americans while projecting it into political analysis of "savage democracies." There, instead of revolution by virtue of the general will, he could find only conspiracy in the course of which "the Indians concealed their designs within the dissimulations of their race" (487).

Such "dissimulation" is part of a larger problematic of representation which elicits from Parkman an imperious intervention concentrating in one place many of the terms and tactics still used in some quarters of the academy and society today:

> Of the Indian character, much has been written foolishly, and credulously believed. By the rhapsodies of poets, the cant of sentimentalists, and the extravagance of some who should have known better, a counterfeit image has been tricked out, which might seek in vain for its likeness through every corner of the habitable earth; an image bearing no more resemblance to its original, than the monarch of the tragedy and the hero of the epic poem bear to their living prototypes in the palace and the camp. The shadows of his wilderness home, and the darker mantle of his own inscrutable reserve, have made the Indian warrior a wonder and a mystery. Yet to the eye of rational observation there is nothing unintelligible in him. He is full, it is true, of contradiction. He deems himself the centre of greatness and renown; his pride is proof against the fiercest torments of fire and steel; and yet the same man would beg for a dram of whiskey, or pick up a crust of bread thrown to him like a dog, from the tent door of the traveller. At one moment, he is wary and cautious to the verge of cowardice; at the next, he abandons himself to a very insanity of recklessness; and the habitual self-restraint which throws an impenetrable veil over emotion is joined to the unbridled passions of a madman or a beast. (386)

AMERICAN HISTORY is self-consciously speaking here. *The Conspiracy of Pontiac* was dedicated to Parkman's teacher and the first Harvard professor of modern history "Jared Sparks, LL.D, President of Harvard University . . . as a testimonial of high personal regard, and a tribute of respect for his distinguished services to American history." The modern and the American converge to execute narrative interruption of chilling confidence and evil omen. The passage moves from the "counterfeit" as emotional, imaginative, and irresponsible to "rational observation" and complete intelligibility. Parkman proceeds according to a visual schema that panoptically commands "every corner of the habitable earth" *and* arterioscopically invades the innermost recesses of the living Indigene. Tragic and epic mimesis are no longer up to the task, especially in a new republic where any actual monarch will always turn out by definition to be worse than his or her dramatic image, and where only the historical fiction of Fenimore Cooper comes close to sharing history's epic vocation to define the heroic anew. Human inconsistency is read harshly so as to distract the reader from the displacement onto the Indigene of precisely those contradictions on which colonialism depends in order to function. Educated reason offers the Indigene a "home" in insanity, animality, or inferiority; while the attribution to him of "inscrutable reserve" ironically anticipates the only too scrutable reserves to which native Americans would soon be confined and also the impending treatment of the inscrutable oriental immigrant. It is in face of just such selective reading and monodisciplinary imperiousness as Parkman exemplifies that we urgently need a transdisciplinary, oppositional politics of reading which embraces conspiracy in order to redefine it, while looking to Indigenous vision to help meet Canada's substantial discursive, ethical, and social deficits.

III. The Radical Humanities

In conjunction with an emergent, counter-hegemonic Indigenous humanities which alone will be able fully to expose injustice while remaining partially, deliberately unreadable to the dominant Other (Menchu ctd. by Spivak 245), there needs to be a radicalizing of the Eurocentric humanities from within. What this requires is not an abandonment of traditional humanist competencies (and Parkmanian deficiencies), but their Indigenizing employment otherwise to redefine the human (see Smith 26; Findlay, "Valuing"), as may become clearer from the following, only too recent example.

In 1998-99, Emory University inaugurated a lecture series with a talk by the distinguished comparativist and deconstructionist, Geoffrey Hartman of Yale University. Hartman's theme was *AESTHETICIDE: or, Has Literary Study Grown Old?* Multiple copies of the published version of this talk have been widely disseminated at no charge to Humanities Centres and Institutes across North America and across the world. Emory clearly thinks its new series has got off to a good start, and there is institutional pride as well as generosity behind the free dissemination of Hartman's lecture and in the covering letter. One of the many remarkable features of this lecture is how it combines radical textualism and cultural conservatism. This combination is used to convey concerns about a decline in academic standards in the shift from Comparative Literature to Cultural Studies and about the "politicization" that the latter apparently brings with it. According to Hartman these developments are two of the "many reasons for the recession of literary criticism and a diminishment in its standards and quality" (2). He attempts to discredit this recession further by connecting it to the early-modern relocation of liberty in western Europe, and its subsequent "translation" to the "universities of the New (now not so new) World [which now may be] weakening in their will to teach and transmit the Western heritage" (3).

Hartman deals with diversity as academically unmanageable excess and "demographic upheaval" in three main moves: reaffirming deep rather than superficial learning, returning to sacred hermeneutics and the canons it authorizes, and rediscovering the Western tradition as sufficiently rich and complex to warrant continued educational concentration in a world where no one can or should seek to know all that qualifies as art and culture. Hartman's argument turns on a reading of the following passage from Tacitus's *Agricola* which he cites selectively and paraphrases tendentiously:

> The winter which followed was spent in the prosecution of sound measures. In order that a population scattered and uncivilized [*dispersi ac rudes*], and proportionately ready for war, might be habituated by comfort [*voluptates*] to peace and quiet, [Agricola] would exhort individuals, assist communities, to erect temples, market-places, houses: he praised the energetic, rebuked the indolent, and the rivalry for his compliments took the place of coercion. Moreover, he began to train the sons of the chieftains in a liberal education [*liberalibus artibus erudire*], and to give a preference to the native talents [*ingenia*] of the Briton as against the trained abilities [*studii*] of the Gaul. As a result, the nation which used to reject the Latin language began to aspire to rhetoric [*eloquentia concupiscerent*]: further, the wearing of our dress became a distinction and the toga came into fashion, and little by little [*paulatimque*] the Britons went astray into alluring vices [*delenimenta vitiorum*]: to the promenade, the bath, the well-appointed dinner table. The simple natives [*apud imperitos*] gave the name of "culture" [*humanitas*] to this factor of their slavery [*servitutis*]. (Tacitus 21)

Hartman sees this passage as "anticipat[ing Cultural Studies'] skepticism" about "the link between liberty and the art of the past" and "remind[ing] us of what postcolonial literary and political critics have been saying: the colonizers use culture to weaken the resolve of the colonized, to prevent them finding their own genius and resources" (2-3). This is in every sense a powerfully *partial* reading, a telling example of patronizingly weak Indigenizing and depoliticizing deconstruction.

Hartman uses humanist learning to imply that the Western canon already knows what its critics (in this case he cites Fanon) are eager to tell it. But that prior knowledge exists within a commitment originating in the ancient world to the "idea of a sacred succession, or of a canonical order of works, guiding both scholarly and artistic tradition" (3). While sloppily renaming Agricola Agrippa in his discussion of Tacitus's account of his father-in-law, Hartman seizes on the Loeb translation of *humanitas* as "culture" to underscore the prescience of an ancient text and to confirm his personal awareness that particular translations of "humanity" have been exposed at the racist heart of modern colonialism and boldly brandished by postcolonial culturalism. But it is not enough simply to register the fact of "humanity's" portentousness; it has to be read as rigorously as Hartman reads Wordsworth or Nietzsche. And such a reading might be introduced as a reflection on the lesson that Agricola learned from his predecessors, namely, that "little was accomplished by force if injustice followed" (Tacitus 19). The problematic of pacification (see also Findlay, "Liberty" 15) and the unhealthy undertow of "sound measures" (*saluberrimus consiliis*) begin to disclose desire, stress, contradictions, circularities. The presence or absence of "civilization" turns unhelpfully on the same root in *rudes/erudire*, but is clarified by connection to urbanization, education, and language acquisition. Agricola's civilizing mission depends (as does my counter-civilizing mission) on an exhortation (*hortari privatim*) and is confirmed by an act of naming (*vocabatur*), that is to say, by rhetorical details which ought to have been grist to Hartman's deconstructionist mill. However, he passes them over in favour of the lexical reduction of *humanitas* to "culture," and his later preference of *studium* to *ingenia* (5).

Hartman recognizes the loaded nature of a liberal arts education in the context of colonization, but he fails to comment on the irony of translating *erudire* as "training" when later in the same sentence training is associated with the Gauls rather than the Britons. This irony points to the substantial biases of the English translation, biases evident also in the interpolated description of the Britons as a "nation." The contribution of cultural presumption and projection to hegemony are scarcely acknowledged, never mind adequately translated. The process here is composite, involving contamination as well as education, going "astray" as well as going straight, while Indigenous deficiency and error keep pace with civilizing activities and policies. Eloquence seems possible only in Latin, and only as an object of desire for Britons who are learning Latin as a second language. The Roman vices that some subject Britons *do* readily master leads them to a humiliating sociolinguistic catachresis—taking as emblems of *humanitas* sartorial self-display, sensual hygiene, and gluttony in a proto-decadent care of the self. Tacitus keeps them in their inferior place, yet the enslaved Britons are both right and wrong in naming a set of overdetermined practices *humanitas*. These signifers of "distinction" (*honour*) draw on political and material surpluses unjustifiable and unsustainable over time. They represent Roman superiority and also the empire's "final doom." What Tacitus both welcomes and worries about as acculturation will both perpetuate the empire and create the conditions for its dissolution from within. Motivated and partial appropriation of the past in the present, as is done by Tacitus the historian, his Loeb translators, by Hartman, and by me, is ideological as well as intellectual work, and it is unnecessary and dangerously "humane" to pretend otherwise in the name of scholarly standards that too often appeal to the best and the brightest in order to privilege the best-off and the whitest.

Such humanistic resistance to Hartman's reinscription of Eurocentric privileges—and problematic outcomes like an apolitical academy, reluctantly inclusive canon and curriculum, and self-renewing but exclusive civil society—needs to be effective and influential. Otherwise, Tacitus and his heirs (like Parkman who admiringly cites the *Germania* [495]) will never be made to yield an adequate measure of anti-colonial truth, nor will scholarship fully demonstrate "the power to transform history into justice" (Smith 34). So, the capacity for careful reading and the knowledge of dead languages must coexist alongside anticolonial resolve, if "real" rigour and scholarly distinction are not to confine themselves even more obsessively to "the" Western tradition. The new, radical (and hence Indigenizing) humanities need to retain as well as supplement and redeploy the benefits of a "classical" education.

IV. ENGLISHES AND OTHERS

I want to conclude by arguing against "English" as imperious singularity and academic accomplice of the current hegemony, and by urging a new beginning for Englishes as the redrawing of the academic map and redistribution of cultural legitimacy and territoriality under Indigenous educational leadership. This I take to be an explicitly interested as well as interesting endeavour, an energizing departure from the colonial practice of Kantian and Arnoldian disinterestedness. Englishes ought to be a source of good instrumentality, by which I mean in part traditional disciplinarity but also a set of interdisciplinary and multidisciplinary connections that define more by (politicized) commonality than by difference, and that defetishize expertise and writing, at least so far as to re-empower generalists and the work of going public and "going native" alongside publishing in academic journals and with academic presses. I mean also a set of activities self-defined and widely recognized as forms of useful knowledge—useful today and tomorrow as enhanced communicative and interpretative skills, and invaluable over a lifetime of engaged and critical citizenship and development of new solidarities.

Engaged and critical citizenship should start inside universities but not stop there or prove separable from the rest of life. The critical citzenry that looks to the political and cultural history of English as a world language and "family" of literatures must see or be taught to see in this living archive, and in its old and new technological modalities and mediations, the endlessly artful masking of "the violence of production" (Caygill 389), the endlessly adroit yet oppressive management of the meanings of class, race, and gender, the endless silencing and mockery imposed or undertaken in the name of humane ideals and moral universals. The meaning of literary knowledge resides primarily not in the elitist interactions of guardians with their own underclass and with student consumers under the aegis of excellence and standards; it resides in the social relations of production and reproduction of the linguistic and the literary. Focus on the latter version of productivity can lead, and quickly, to the transformation of pedagogy, curriculum, merit, status, that bourgeois individualism that claims originality for itself, and that capitalist value forms at the heart of everything we currently do, or fail to do, or are prevented or prohibited from doing. It can and should also involve the radical, Indigenizing redefinition of what is meant by "culture" from all quarters of the Canadian academy, and perhaps especially from the radical humanities.

The nature and value of academic disciplines are determined by economic and social forces. (The President of SSHRCC, for example, identifies three such current, powerfully determinative forces: the "revolution" in *communications*, the processes known as *globalization*, and the turn to a *knowledge-based economy*. Dr. Renaud recommends to his constituents that they busy themselves *adapting creatively* to this reality. This may well result in *bad creativity*.) The precise effects of such determination of the academic agenda can and should be demonstrated, and the task of doing so is important scholarly as well as administrative work, but such demonstration can never be complete or unequivocal. Disciplinarity remains a site for the staging of invidious, oppressive, or productive difference, but also, alas, disciplinarity remains a set of determinations and symptoms of unexamined privilege or indifference or fear. The humanities are in particular danger, perhaps (as Marc Renaud suggests) most of all in English-speaking countries. Certainly they are in danger all across Canada. The current beleaguerment of the humanities is in part the consequence of "external" misunderstanding and hostility elsewhere in the university and in society at large. Much of this misunderstanding and hostility can be captured by the expression, *bad instrumentality*. However, the current beleaguerment is also the result of what happens—or fails to happen— "inside" the humanities. Many of the problems internal to the humanities can be captured in the notion of *anti-instrumentality* or *knowledge-for-its-own-sake*.

The past, present, and future of English literary studies in particular is intimately connected to the legacy of nineteenth-century philology as a Euro-imperial tool (Olender), and to the related fate of "the" English language:

English as a world language but not necessarily as a compliantly technocratic, multinational corporate instrument and/or conduit for cultural dumping or defoliation. Any quasi-imperial formation, including cultural formations like a *lingua franca* and the canon it sustains and is sustained by, acquires "impurity" while extending its authority or penetration across differences of class, race, gender, nationality. Such "impurity" *will* be the locus of intensified oppression, but also the focus of resistance and critique such as that offered by the Terra Lingua group of scholar-activists who work for the preservation and promotion of Indigenous languages across the world. The end of English-in-the-singular—understood as a project for the extension of hegemony combined with the ever more zealous policing of purity and maintaining of "proper standards"—is long overdue and too long delayed by the passing of the Anglo-imperial torch from Britain to the US. A new goal for Englishes is an enhanced capacity for analytical and imaginative critique of the current (Amerocentric, neocolonial, capitalist) hegemony. In making this end explicit and effective, English(es) will not be politicizing the university but simply endeavouring to change its tacit but well established politics. And in taking their lead from a new generation of Indigenous theorists and activists, Englishes and their critical promoters can contribute in highly practical ways to economic and social justice for all—for as long as the sun shines, the curriculum flows, and the text of treaties between the Crown and Canada's First Nations is not reduced to the rhetoric of entreaty.

Works Cited

Ahmad, Aijaz. *In Theory: Classes, Nations, Literatures.* London: Verso, 1992.

Battiste, Marie, ed. *Reclaiming Indigenous Voice and Vision.* Vancouver: U of British Columbia P, 2000.

—, and J.Y. Henderson. *Protecting Indigenous Knowledge.* Saskatoon: Purich, 2000.

—, and Jean Barman, eds. *First Nations Education in Canada: The Circle Unfolds.* Vancouver: U of British Columbia P, 1995.

Bidwell, Paul, and L.M. Findlay, eds. *Pursuing Academic Freedom: "Free and Fearless"?* Saskatoon: Purich, 2001.

Calliou, Sharilyn. "Peacekeeping Actions at Home: A Medicine Wheel Model for a Peacekeeping Pedagogy." Battiste and Barman 47-72.

Caygill, Howard. *Art of Judgement.* Oxford: Blackwell, 1989.

Chandler, James. *England in 1819: The Politics of Literary Culture and the Case of Romantic Historicism.* Chicago: U of Chicago P, 1998.

Findlay, L.M. "'[T]hat liberty of writing': Incontinent Ordinance in 'Oriental' Jones." *Romantic Circles Praxis Series,* 2000. Forthcoming special issue on "Containing British India."

—. "Valuing Culture, Interdisciplining the Economic." *Aldritch Interdisciplinary*

Lecture and Conference for Graduate Students. St. John's: Memorial U of Newfoundland P, 1998. 3-22.

——. "Interdisciplining Canada: ''Cause Breaking Up is Hard to Do.'" *Essays on Canadian Writing* 65 (1998): 1-15.

——. "Runes of Marx and *The University in Ruins.*" *University of Toronto Quarterly* 66
(1997): 677-90.

——. "Retailing Petits Recits or Retooling for Revolution? Cultural Studies and the
Knowledge Industries in Canada." *University of Toronto Quarterly* 64 (1995): 493-505.

Goldie, Terry. *Fear and Temptation: The Image of the Indigene in Canadian, Australian,
and New Zealand Literatures.* Kingston: McGill-Queen's UP, 1989.

Hall, Stuart. "On Postmodernism and Articulation: An Interview with Stuart Hall."
Ed. Lawrence Grossberg. *Stuart Hall: Critical Dialogues in Cultural Studies.* Ed. David
Morley and Kuan-Hsing Chen. London: Routledge, 1996. 131-50.

Hartman, Geoffrey H. *Aestheticide: or, Has Literary Study Grown Old?* Atlanta: Emory
Humanities Lectures, 1998.

Henderson, J.Y., Marjorie Benson, and Isobel M. Findlay. *Aboriginal Tenure and the
Constitution of Canada.* Toronto: Carswell, 2000.

Henderson, J.Y. "Postcolonial Ghost Dancing: Diagnosing European Colonialism."
Battiste, *Reclaiming* 57-76.

Horsmanden, Daniel. *The New York Conspiracy, or a History of the Negro Plot, with the
Journal of the Proceedings against the Conspirators at New-York in the Years 1741-2.* 1744.
New York: Negro UP, 1969.

Jameson, Fredric. *The Geopolitical Aesthetic: Cinema and Space in the World System.*
Bloomington: Indiana UP, 1992.

——. *The Political Unconscious: Narrative as a Socially Symbolic Act.* Ithaca: Cornell UP,
1981.

Keefer, Michael. *Lunar Perspectives: Field Notes from the Culture Wars.* Concord, ON:
Anansi, 1996.

MacIvor, Madeleine. "Redefining Science Education for Aboriginal Students." Battiste and Barman 73-98.

Majeed, Javed. *Ungoverned Imaginings.* Oxford: Clarendon, 1992.

Martin, Paul. "Education and the Public Good." Unpublished Address, Breakfast on
the Campus, University of Ottawa, 1998.

Monture-Angus, Patricia. "On Being Homeless: One Aboriginal Woman's 'Conquest'
of Canadian Universities." *Critical Race Theory Conference Proceedings.* Ed. Frank
Valdez, Jerome Culp, and Angela Harris. New Haven: Yale UP, forthcoming.

Olender, Maurice. *The Languages of Paradise: Race, Religion, and Philology in the Nineteenth Century.* Trans. Arthur Goldhammer. Cambridge: Harvard UP, 1992.

Parkman, Francis. *The Oregon Trail [and] the Conspiracy of Pontiac.* Ed. William R. Taylor. New York: Viking, 1991.

Prakash, Gyan, ed. *After Colonialism: Imperial Histories and Postcolonial Displacements.*
Princeton: Princeton UP, 1995.

Rahnema, Majid, and Victoria Bawtree, eds. *The Post-Development Reader*. London: Zed Books, 1997.

Ramraj, Victor J., ed. and intro. *Concert of Voices: An Anthology of World Writing in English*. Peterborough: Broadview, 1995.

Razack, Sherene H. *Looking White People in the Eye: Gender, Race, and Culture in the Courtrooms and Classrooms*. Toronto: U of Toronto P, 1998.

Readings, Bill. *The University in Ruins*. Cambridge: Harvard UP, 1996.

Renaud, Marc. *Universities for Tomorrow: From the Ivory Tower to the Market Square*. Annual Sorokin Lecture. Saskatoon: U of Saskatchewan P, 1999.

Smith, Linda. *Decolonizing Methodologies: Research and Indigenous Peoples*. London: Zed Books, 1999.

Spivak, Gayatri Chakravorty. *A Critique of Postcolonial Reason: Toward a History of the Vanishing Present*. Cambridge: Harvard UP, 1999.

Symonds, Richard. *Oxford and Empire: The Last Lost Cause?* Oxford: Clarendon, 1986.

Tacitus. *Agricola*. Trans. M. Hutton. Rev. R.M. Ogilvie. Cambridge: Harvard UP, 1970.

Turpel-Lafond, Mary Ellen. "The Challenge of Building Indigenous Education." Dialogue on Indigenous Education in the Americas. Saskatoon: Wanuskewin Heritage Park, 1999. Unpublished Keynote Address.

Viswanathan, Gauri. *Masks of Conquest: Literary Study and British Rule in India*. New York: Columbia UP, 1989.

Williams, Patrick, and Laura Chrisman, eds. *Colonial Discourse and Post-Colonial Theory*. New York: Columbia UP, 1994.

Willinsky, John. *Learning to Divide the World: Education at Empire's End*. Minneapolis: U of Minnesota P, 1999.